Eastern Africa Series

DISRUPTING TERRITORIES

Eastern Africa Series

Women's Land Rights & Privatization in Eastern Africa
BIRGIT ENGLERT & ELIZABETH DALEY (EDS)

War & the Politics of Identity in Ethiopia KJETIL TRONVOLL

Moving People in Ethiopia
ALULA PANKHURST & FRANÇOIS PIGUET (EDS)

Living Terraces in Ethiopia ELIZABETH E. WATSON

Eritrea GAIM KIBREAB

Borders & Borderlands as Resources in the Horn of Africa
DEREJE FEYISSA & MARKUS VIRGIL HOEHNE (EDS)

After the Comprehensive Peace Agreement in Sudan
ELKE GRAWERT (ED.)

Land, Governance, Conflict & the Nuba of Sudan
GUMA KUNDA KOMEY

Ethiopia JOHN MARKAKIS

Resurrecting Cannibals HEIKE BEHREND

Pastoralism & Politics in Northern Kenya & Southern Ethiopia
GŰNTHER SCHLEE & ABDULLAHI A. SHONGOLO

Islam & Ethnicity in Northern Kenya & Southern Ethiopia
GŰNTHER SCHLEE with ABDULLAHI A. SHONGOLO

Foundations of an African Civilisation DAVID W. PHILLIPSON

Regional Integration, Identity & Citizenship in the Greater Horn of Africa
KIDANE MENGISTEAB & REDIE BEREKETEAB (EDS)

Dealing with Government in South Sudan CHERRY LEONARDI

The Quest for Socialist Utopia BAHRU ZEWDE

Disrupting Territories
JÖRG GERTEL, RICHARD ROTTENBURG & SANDRA CALKINS (EDS)

*The African Garrison State**
KJETIL TRONVOLL & DANIEL R. MEKONNEN

*The State of Post-conflict Reconstruction**
NASEEM BADIEY

*Gender, Home & Identity: The Nuer Repatriation to South Sudan**
KATARZYNA GRABSKA

**forthcoming*

Disrupting Territories

Land, Commodification & Conflict in Sudan

JÖRG GERTEL,
RICHARD ROTTENBURG
& SANDRA CALKINS (EDS)

JAMES CURREY

James Currey
an imprint of Boydell & Brewer Ltd
PO Box 9, Woodbridge, Suffolk IP12 3DF (GB)
www.jamescurrey.com

and of

Boydell & Brewer Inc.
668 Mt Hope Avenue, Rochester, NY 14620–2731 (US)
www.boydellandbrewer.com

First published 2014

British Library Cataloguing in Publication Data

A catalogue record for this book is available from the British Library

ISBN 978-1-84701-054-4 (James Currey Cloth)

This publication is printed on acid-free paper

Typeset in 10/12pt Cordale
by CPI Typesetting

Contents

List of Maps & Tables

Maps

Tables

Notes on Contributors

Musa Abdul-Jalil is an Associate Professor of Social Anthropology at the University of Khartoum. He obtained his Ph.D. from the University of Edinburgh in1980. His research deals with ethnicity, identity, migration, local level politics, legal anthropology and customary land tenure, with an ethnographic emphasis on Darfur.

Sandra Calkins worked on this book while she was a research associate at the Collaborative Research Center 'Difference and Integration' at the Universities of Halle and Leipzig, Germany – the context in which this book was prepared. She is now a research fellow at the Max Planck Institute for Social Anthropology (Halle) and a member of the LOST Group at the University of Halle.

Barbara Casciarri holds a Ph.D. in Ethnology and Social Anthropology of the EHESS (Ecole des Hautes Etudes en Sciences Sociales), Paris. Her researches focus on dynamics of political and economic change among pastoral groups. She carried out fieldwork in Sudan (1989–1997; 2006 until today) and in south-eastern Morocco (2000–05). She is Associate Professor at the University of Paris 8 at Saint-Denis, Paris, France.

Jörg Gertel holds a Ph.D. in Geography from Freiburg University, and is Professor for Economic Geography at Leipzig University. Among his more recent books are *Pastoral Morocco: Globalizing Scapes of Mobility and Insecurity* (2007, Reichert, co-edited with I. Breuer); *Globalizing Food Crises – Cairo* (2010, transcript, in German); *Economic Spaces of Pastoral Production and Commodity Systems. Markets and Livelihoods* (2011 Ashgate, co-edited with R. Le Heron); and *Seasonal Workers in Mediterranean Agriculture: The Social Costs of Eating Fresh* (2014, Routledge, co-edited with S. R. Sippel).

Enrico Ille holds a Ph.D. in Social Anthropology from the University of Halle and is Assistant Professor at Ahfad University in Omdurman. His Ph.D. thesis discusses attempts of development projects to change organizational practices in post-war South Kordofan. His present research interests are food sovereignty and resource distribution regimes in northern Sudan.

Guma Kunda Komey was Assistant Professor of Human Geography at University of Juba, and is currently Associate Professor at University of Bahri, Khartoum, Sudan and Associate Senior Research Fellow, Max Planck Institute of Social Anthropology, Halle. He is author of *Land, Governance, Conflict and the Nuba of Sudan* (2010, James Currey).

Janka Linke studied Sinology, Oriental Studies and Anthropology (M.A.) at the University of Leipzig, Germany. Currently she is a Research Assistant and Ph.D. candidate at the DFG (German Research Foundation)-funded Collaborative Research Center 'Difference and Integration' (SFB 586) at the University of Leipzig.

Elhadi Ibrahim Osman received his Ph.D. in Social Anthropology from the University of Khartoum in 2008 for his research on pastoral Fulbe. He is an Assistant Professor at the Faculty of Agriculture, University of Sennar, Sudan and has conducted several consultancies on pastoralists' integration into irrigation projects in central and eastern Sudan (2009–2012).

Sara Pantuliano is the Head of the Humanitarian Policy Group at the Overseas Development Institute (ODI), London. Prior to that she led the United Nations Development Programme (UNDP) Sudan's Peace Building Unit, acted as a resource person and an observer at the Intergovernmental Authority on Development (IGAD) Sudan peace process and managed a high-profile post-conflict response in the Nuba Mountains. She holds a Ph.D. in Politics and has lectured at the University of Dar es Salaam. Sara has written extensively on Sudan and is the Managing Editor of *Disasters Journal.*

Richard Rottenburg holds a chair in Anthropology at the University of Halle, Germany. His research focuses on the anthropology of law, organization, science and technology (LOST). He has written and edited books on economic anthropology, networks of formal organizations, the transcultural production of objectivity, biomedicine and society, and on theorizing post-neoliberal governance.

Günther Schlee is director of the 'Integration and Conflict' Department at the Max Planck Institute for Social Anthropology at Halle/Saale, Germany. His book publications include *Identities on the Move: Clanship and Pastoralism in Northern Kenya* (International African Institute, 1989), *How Enemies are Made* (Berghahn, 2008), *Pastoralism and Politics* and *Islam and Ethnicity* with Abdullahi Shongolo (both James Currey, 2012).

Siddig Umbadda holds a Ph.D. in Economics from the University of London. He is currently Research Co-coordinator at Mamoun Beheiry Center for Economic and Social Studies and Research in Africa, Khartoum. Previously, he was head of the Department of Economics, University of Khartoum, and Principal Economist with the African Development Bank, Abidjan, Côte d'Ivoire.

Acknowledgements

We thank all contributors to this volume for their hard work and patience in researching, writing and rewriting their chapters until publication.

This publication was prepared in a specific institutional context, namely the Collaborative Research Center 586 'Difference and Integration' at the Universities of Halle-Wittenberg and Leipzig. This multidisciplinary research programme was financed by the German Research Foundation (2001–2012). Two projects in the programme's last phase (2008–12) dealt with Sudan, one headed by Jörg Gertel, the other headed by Richard Rottenburg. This volume is a result of their fruitful collaboration. Without the generous financial support from the German Research Foundation this volume and the results presented in it would not have materialized.

Richard Rottenburg and Sandra Calkins would also like to thank their 'Sudan Reference Group' in Khartoum, but especially Atta Al-Battahani and Musa Adam Abdul-Jalil, for their tremendous intellectual and administrative support over the years. Jörg Gertel also wishes to thank the research team funded by the Australian Research Council (ARC) in Brisbane, Trondheim and Leipzig ('The New Farm Owners: Finance Companies and the Restructuring of Australian and Global Agriculture') for their ongoing and stimulating engagement with agri-food questions.

We thank Lea Bauer for preparing the maps and Erena Le Heron for her thoughtful language editing. Further thanks are due to Jaqueline Mitchell, Lynn Taylor and Douglas Johnson at James Currey. We thank two anonymous reviewers for their insightful comments. Remaining errors are our responsibility.

The Editors

List of Abbreviations & Glossary

Abbala (Ar.)	collective noun derived from *'ibl* (Ar. camel) for Arabic-speaking camel herders
Amir (Ar.)	tribal leader between omda (or sheikh) and nazir
Baggara	(Ar.) collective noun derived from *baqara* (Ar. cow) for Arabic-speaking cattle herders
CNPC	China National Petroleum Company
CPA	Comprehensive Peace Agreement
DUP	Democratic Unionist Party
ECOS	European Coalition on Oil in Sudan
ESPA	Eastern Sudan Peace Agreement
Feddan (Ar.)	measurement unit for land: one feddan equals 0.42 hectares (1.038 acres)
GRAS	Geological Research Authority of the Sudan
JEM	Justice and Equality Movement
Khor (Ar.)	seasonal water course
MFC	Mechanized Farming Corporation
MOA	Ministry of Agriculture
MOI	Ministry of Investment
Native Administration	system of indirect rule through local headmen, established under British colonial rule
Nazarah (Ar.)	territory of a Native Administration
Nazir (Ar.)	head of a Native Administration
NCP	National Congress Party
NDA	National Democratic Alliance
NIF	National Islamic Front
NGOs	Non-Governmental Organizations
Omda (Ar.)	paramount sheikh
Omodia (Ar.)	customary 'tribal' land administered by an omda
SAF	Sudan Armed Forces
SPLM/A	Sudan People's Liberation Movement/Army
ULA	Unregistered Land Act
UNEP	United Nations Environmental Programme
WB	World Bank

Notes on Transliteration

For the transliteration of Arabic words we have adopted a pragmatic approach which will not fully satisfy the Arabist but is more friendly to a wider readership. We take the transliteration guide of the *International Journal of Middle Eastern Studies* as orientation (IJMES, http://web.gc.cuny.edu/ijmes, accessed 28 October 2013). This is a modification of the transliteration system of the *Encyclopaedia of Islam* (Bearman, P., Bianquis, T., Bosworth, C. E., van Donzel, E. & Heinrichs, W. P., eds. Leiden: Brill and online). Accordingly, to enable an easy reading, diacritical marks and italics are only used on technical terms and not on personal, group or place names. For example, dār as a technical term bears the diacritical mark but does not in the place name Darfur. Words in the Webster's *Collegiate Dictionary*, such as jihad or sheikh, are not considered technical terms. We have decided to desist from transliterating technical terms that are frequently used in the text and that are commonly known to readers of literature on Sudan: we refer to cattle herders as Baggara (instead of *baqqāra*), camel herders as Abbala (*'abbāla*), Janjawid (instead of *ǧanǧawīd*) and do not fully transliterate the administrative terms introduced by the British (nazir/nazarah instead of *nāẓir/naẓāra*, omda/omodia instead of *ᶜumda/ᶜumudīya*) – except for *dār* and *ḥākūra*, which are central terms for our argument pertaining to land rights. However, for the sake of simplicity and readability, we often use 'false' Anglicized plurals, such as *dār*s, instead of the proper Arabic plurals, such as *diyār* or *dūr*; to mark this we do not italicize the English plural -s. Accepted English spelling for names and places is applied or relevant people's preferences (at times, this is the authors' preference when multiple acceptable renderings are in use), and when there are no common or preferred English spellings *ᶜayn* and hamza are added. In view of various Arabic dialects in Sudan, we have decided to use technical terms sparingly and cite only the standard Arabic transliteration of technical terms, which corresponds to the written form of words (*qabīla* instead of colloquial Sudanese *gabīla*). When an essential technical term is not found in a dictionary or when citing non-Arabic terms (e.g. Fulani, TuBedawiye), we follow authors' suggestions.

1

Disrupting Territories: Commodification and its Consequences

JÖRG GERTEL, SANDRA CALKINS
& RICHARD ROTTENBURG

On 9 July 2011, the world looked on as many Sudanese, hopeful and delirious with joy, danced in the streets of Juba celebrating the independence of the Republic of South Sudan. The day's cheerful festivities stood out in a region that is regularly reported on in terms of dejection and gloominess. The drawing of international borders separating South Sudan from Sudan is the most dramatic of territorial reorganizations in the region. It has strong repercussions for people, but especially for those living in the immediate border regions. Uncertainty prevails as both Sudans look into the future.

The initially hopeful expectations have already been marred by renewed armed conflicts and warfare – between and within the two states. Many of these conflicts relate to struggles over the rights to land and its effective control: borders are being contested, territorial claims are being challenged, territorially-bound resources and the entitlements to agricultural land are being disputed. *Disrupting Territories* reveals the antagonistic configurations that put pressure on Sudanese communities, Land is immobile: for millions of people in Sudan, it serves as a reference for the formation of identity and constitutes their most important means of livelihood. But drought, hunger and armed conflicts have displaced millions of people from their land. In combination with the establishment of resource-extracting economies – namely, the new dynamics of land grab, the search for gold, oil and other minerals – this contributes to what we call 'disrupting territories': the dissolution of the fundamental relationships between man and land, related to the process of commodification.

Against the backdrop of critical moments, such as the foundation of two new states, the recent political upheaval in North Africa as well as the global financial and food crises, we investigate the incremental and deeply penetrating structural transformations in the interconnections between society and territory. We focus on the relationship between man, land, and human security. *Disrupting Territories* juxtaposes place-based livelihood systems and articulations of attachment with the commodification and privatization of land. This conversation does not limit itself to describing the territorial impacts of global capital on Sudanese localities or modes of earning a living. Rather, it seeks to disentangle some of the complex assemblages of land, identity, and human security, which have been historically precipitated in various institutions that people experience, perpetuate, negotiate and contest. Such assemblages are constituted by the practices of very diverse actors – from local land users, farmers and pastoralists to legislators and officers at the state and national levels, to international enterprises, agencies and banks. Aside from the physical landscape, their actions are also intertwined with a hodgepodge of entities and technologies, such as livestock, arms or infrastructural elements (roads, electrical power grids, wells, pipelines), legal documents and classifications (ethnic groups, tribes) to name but a few. This book seeks to explore the processes and mechanisms of territorial disruptions related to the conversion of collectively-held land under customary law into private property – a historical process that regained current timeliness and accelerated in the past decades with the financialization of exchange relations (Epstein 2005, Burch & Lawrence 2009, Krippner 2011), the internationalization of agribusiness (Woertz 2011, Borras et al. 2013, Sassen 2013) and the spread of neoliberal governance (cf. Harvey 2005, Gibson-Graham 2006, Peck & Theodore 2012).

FRAMINGS

Even before the recent division, Sudan's present territorial shape was comparatively young and was largely determined through violent encounters. The physical confrontation between the British Empire and people of what was to become the Sudan – the coalition of northern tribes forming the Mahdiyya alliance[1] – was violent and brutal. On 2 September 1898, during the battle of Karari, just north of Omdurman, around 16,000 Mahdists were wounded and 11,000 lost their lives on a single day, fighting machine guns and artillery shells, while the condominium forces of the British and Egyptian armies counted only 48 dead and 382 wounded soldiers (Gertel 1993: 82). This outcome reflected the force and direction of changes to come. It took a further 18 years to integrate Darfur into the Anglo-Egyptian Sudan (1916) and continuous border work was required for 'Sudan in the making'. More recently in 1989, during Operation Lifeline Sudan, a temporary corridor was created and the government relinquished its sovereign rights over a contested territory for one month (cf. Johnson 1994). In 2011, the borders of 'Sudan' were again renegotiated and temporarily fixed when the contested borderline between south and north hardened. We hence have to note that sovereignty and territorial interventions are limited to discrete points in time and space. They neither encompass the complete surface of Sudan's state territory or of delimited parcels, nor do they unfold continuously or uninterrupted. Rather they are non-contiguous, creating temporal and territorial disruptions.

The emergence and reproduction of disrupting territories in Sudan is largely shaped by three trajectories: state institutions that are unable to work for the welfare of all Sudanese and to arbitrate between divergent views; recurrent emergencies of drought, hunger, war and connected

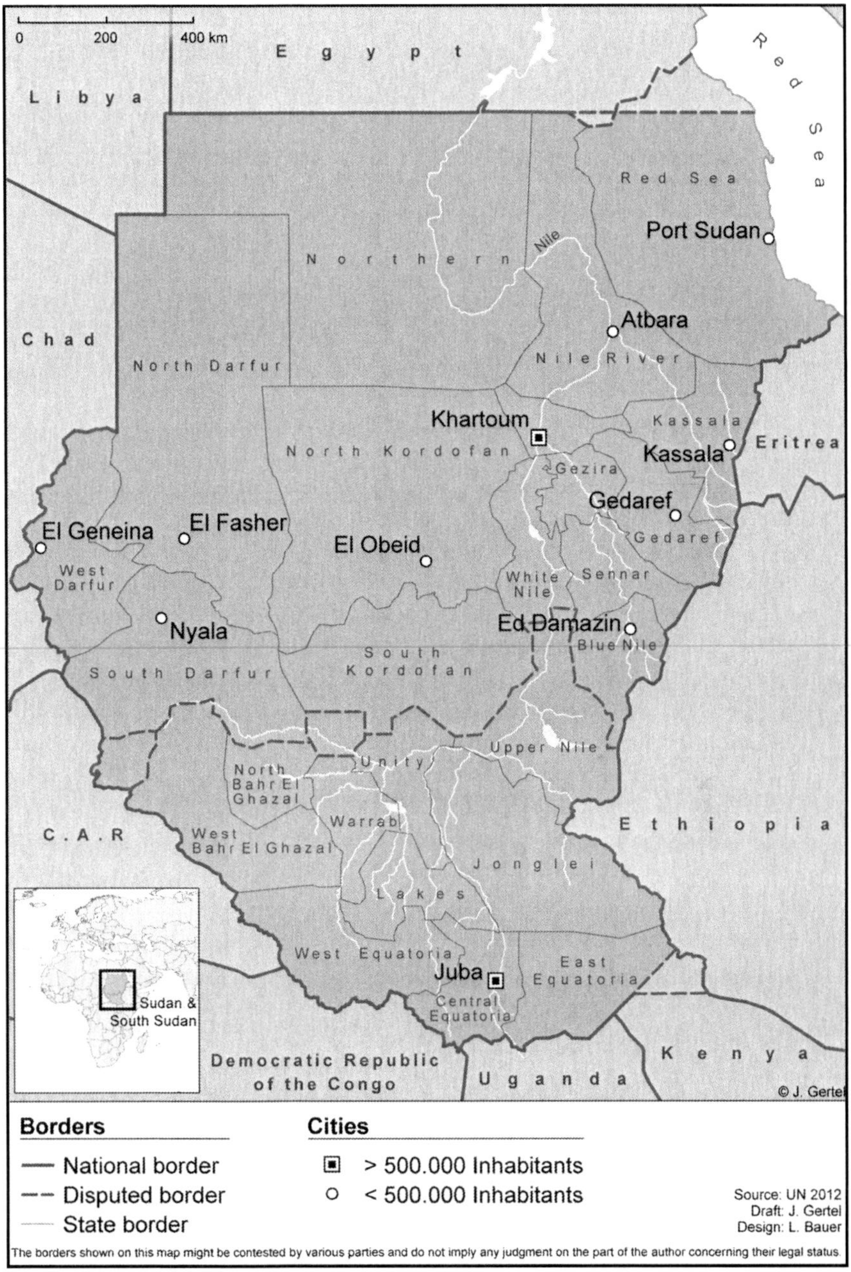

Map 1.1 Sudan and South Sudan in 2012

mobilities; and high modernist dreams of development through foreign mega-projects and technology transfers in energy and agriculture.

Sudan is seldom absent from scholarly debates on weak, failing, fragile or dysfunctional states (cf. Debiel & Klein 2002; Rotberg 2003, 2004; Schlichte 2005).[2] We argue that such characterizations are related to pervasive institutional failures. In post-colonial Sudan the chance was missed to build state institutions that could service the entire country and all of its populace regardless of ethnic, racial and religious affiliations, and that could arbitrate between competing and often conflicting interests in a peaceful manner (Rottenburg 2008: VIII, IX). A dire consequence is the recurrence of violent conflicts. Civil wars between north and south shook the country 1955–1972 and 1983–2005, and since the 1980s and 1990s between the Government of Sudan and other armed groups in South Kordofan, Blue Nile State, Eastern Sudan and Darfur (Johnson 2003). In 2011 war escalated again in South Kordofan, Blue Nile State and Darfur – as many had anticipated – due to unresolved political grievances (Komey 2010, Rottenburg et al. 2011). We contend that the separation of South Sudan is the most outstanding evidence of these failures.

However, the birth of a new nation state or rather two new countries – Sudan and South Sudan – was historically already prepared through separate administrative arrangements by means of which the Anglo-Egyptian Condominium (1898–1955) governed the northern and southern areas (Howell 1973: 163, 164). The process of nation building after independence in 1956 was highly problematic as it replaced British colonial rule with an internal colonialism: the hegemonic rule of northern riverine Arabs over the rest of the vast country, which produced internal peripheries in the south, east and west (Sharkey 2008: 28). This failed integration of large populations, paired with the coercive processes of Sudanization and then from the 1980s on Islamization and Arabization, led up to multiple armed conflicts and civil wars (Sharkey 2008: 28, 29, Johnson 2003). These multiple and relentless conflicts for power bespeak the political disorder in the contested state.

But doesn't talk of state failure in Africa too unproblematically assume a Euro-centric perspective, wherein Western (European) capitalist states are assumed as 'normal' while other forms of statehood are labelled as deviant? Certainly, across the African continent a wide array of forms of statehood have emerged, stabilized, and transformed themselves – some like Botswana even very successful and allegedly even more 'democratic' than European democracies, as Jean and John Comaroff (2012a) propose. We thus contend that the concrete forms, discourses and practices through which 'the state' as a travelling model becomes visible, entrenched and is held accountable are necessarily empirical questions. Already an early contribution to Sudanese ethnography points to a blind spot in debates on state failure by showing how order can be conceived of coming into being in stateless polities (Evans-Pritchard 1940).

A further important work on African politics is Bayart's *The Politics of the Belly*, which is a pledge to desist from exoticizing African states

(1989/2010: 268, 269). Bayart (and other authors) move away from relativistic stances which imply that African statehood defies comparison or can only be classified as pathological in terms of failure, weakness or dysfunctionality. Taking dichotomies such as state/society for granted which may work elsewhere is short-sighted in African countries, argues Bayart, where private and public are enmeshed. This understanding also resonates in Joel Migdal's call for a 'state-in-society perspective' (Migdal 1994). A related observation was made by Fatton (1992). He likewise argues that dominant classes in Africa use the state to gain political power through public office while enriching themselves privately. A result is the 'predatory' state, in which its employees plunder coffers and do not provide any benefits for populations, apart from small favoured constituencies. History, however, remains important. Mahmoud Mamdani (1996) highlights how elements of colonial rule endure – often forming African subjects, rather than citizens. The technologies of colonial rule are seen as responsible for a fragmentation of population and the constitution of the tribe as a main political and administrative unit, leading to a situation of unequal rights to land between 'natives' and 'settlers' (Mamdani 2009: 145–170). He thus emphasizes that new territorial orders have arisen from colonial rule, but these are not the only territorial orders with which this volume is concerned.

Rather, taking a cue from Sassen (2006), we seek to overcome a state-centric perspective. Sassen identifies three transhistorical elements – territory, authority, and rights (TAR) – and examines how they are assembled into different historical formations. She conceptualizes 'post-national' entities that unbundle and re-bundle nations as assemblages of actors, practices, sovereignties and other social relations under globalization. Such spatio-temporary assemblages have to be considered to make sense of the dispersed, decentred, and fragmented powers constituting 'the state'. The changing political and economic alliances seeking to exploit Sudan's resources exemplify the shifting and fluid topological spaces of governance (Allen & Cochrane 2010). National state institutions are still important, but they operate in a multi-scalar institutional hierarchy (cf. Brenner 2004).

We are particularly interested in exploring the entanglements between Sudanese institutions on various scales, from local grazing agreements to national land laws, and globally moving ideas – such as privatization and commodification. The volume critically addresses the spaces generated by such entanglements. Three points are crucial:

(1) The 'national' Sudanese territory is far from stable or fixed. Rather, it is contested and has been since its early colonial demarcations. Analyses have to be attentive to the making and unmaking of boundaries and therewith properties that are part of complex processes of institutionalization.

(2) Sudan has always been a resource reservoir for invading powers: from ancient pharaonic invasions seeking for gold, Arab invaders' quest for gold, ivory and slaves (Ḥasan 1973/2005: 56), to more recent extractive economies under colonial Anglo-Egyptian rule, various 'Western'

states and most recently Asian countries in energy and mining (Large & Patey 2011). This supports Sassen's point of the un/rebundling of nation states. Authority in Sudan seems to be decentred, it is dispersed, shifting from government to governance and fragmenting into different cores and institutional settings, fostering spatial expressions that we understand as 'disrupting territories'. Historical continuities and the changing sites and sources of authority are investigated in the coming chapters.

(3) Ultimately, rights and particularly rights to land are of crucial importance. They refer to entitlements and frame the capabilities of doing certain things while forbidding others.[3] Different chapters analyse what shaped the successive legal transformations of land rights in Sudan. But a reference to the legality of rights alone disregards everyday experiences and moral understandings, particularly of rural people. Claims to land and their respective references in Sudan are often connected to other ideas of justice, such as the need for local populations to receive benefits from wealth on 'their land'. How claims to land are made, justified, and challenged thus are important issues in grasping what disrupting territories encompass in Sudan.

Four historical processes – largely exceeding, but nevertheless impacting Sudan – are crucial to capture changing TARs, and particularly to understand the ongoing privatization and state-centred regulation of land: the enclosure of the commons, colonial land appropriation, more recent neoliberal privatization projects, and the vulnerabilities of financial capitalism.

The first historical process to which we refer is the so-called enclosure of the commons in England and Wales, which ended collective rights to use pastures and to farm in open fields (Giordano 2003). Under enclosure, formerly collective land was fenced-in and deeded or entitled to one or more owners. This erosion of common land rights occurred during the sixteenth century. This coincides with the cartographic revolution, based on innovative technologies of measurement and of controlling land property. By 1700 only one quarter of the commons of England and Wales were still open for common use (Blomley 2003). This promoted the commercialization of the British agricultural sector. Land markets came into being, enabling the augmentation of productive output per land unit, but also leading to new societal inequalities. By losing their access to the commons, small farmers became impoverished, whereas a small new group of rich landowners emerged, thereby also gaining greater political power (cf. Wallerstein 1974). These processes of transforming and privatizing the commons never stopped and are still ongoing.

Second, we draw attention to the impacts of European colonial rule which, often by means of brute force, drew completely novel borders in Africa and Asia. Territorial boundaries were imposed, separating local societies, creating new political (national) units and fundamentally transforming existent land tenure systems. The British Empire alone colonized and imprinted more than a quarter of the world with its spatial conceptions and political visions, constituting the largest transformation of landscapes under colonial rule (Christopher 1988). 'Traditional' land rights henceforth figure as leftovers and are pushed aside by (newly emerging 'independent') national and state claims to land, leading to many present-day conflicts.

Third, against the backdrop of the international debt crisis and enforced by neoliberal globalization, the pressure to privatize land and property rights has increased globally since the 1980s (Harvey 2005, Turner & Wiber 2009). Structural adjustment programmes and other austerity measures forced post-colonial governments to open their economies to the foreign interests of companies, banks and private investors, turning African countries into 'radical testing grounds for neoliberal policies' (Hilgers 2012: 83, Van der Walle 2001). These privatization processes are also unwinding in post-socialist countries. Producer cooperatives and people's communes were dissolved, herds redistributed to local populations, like in China (Tibet) or Mongolia, and new private rights to pastures were allocated and contracted (Gertel & Le Heron 2011).

Fourth, since 2007/8 the consequences of finance capitalism are unfolding, whereby land increasingly becomes an object of speculation (McMichael 2013). The international food crisis (2007/8) was largely triggered by speculation on futures in commodity markets and the increasing conversion of agricultural land into zones for biofuel production, resulting in artificially high food prices, and subsequently resulted in protests in over 30 countries (Holt-Giménez & Patel 2009, Matondi et al. 2011). From 2007 to 2008 an additional 100 million people were classified as food-insecure; since then the mark of one billion hungry people was crossed (Gertel 2010). In 2011/12, as in 2008, many countries imposed a ban on food exports, especially staples, in order to buffer high food prices on the world market. In view of rising financial uncertainties and food insecurity, the search for agricultural land for investment accelerated. Allen et al. (2012) stress a shift of power centres from the actors who until recently dominated the global food system and food supply chains – such as the grain export nations (USA, Canada, Argentine, Australia) and transnational corporations like Cargill, Monsanto, Wal-Mart – to sovereign wealth funds from the Arabian Gulf and Asian states. The latter are the key protagonists of the new investments in African land and water resources. 'Land grabbing', the purchase and the long-term lease of agricultural land in foreign countries, has developed a new dynamic. Financially wealthy but land-poor countries, like Saudi Arabia, Japan and the United Arab Emirates, are interested in growing their food abroad (cf. McMichael 2013). In early 2013, Landportal.info counted 924 international deals since 2000, amounting to an estimated 49 million hectares. Thirty-five per cent of these are said to be located in Africa (cf. also landmatrix.org, farmlandgrab.org; see Umbadda in Chapter 2).

The unwinding of these historical processes indicates a tendency towards privatization of collectively used resources. But this in itself does not explain why Sudanese governments have been open to accommodate foreign investors. What are the logics governing governmental planning? We would suggest that not only the interest of filling their own coffers but also master narratives of civilization, development, modernization and globalization have been shaping the visions of Sudan's ruling elites. The hydro-dam projects figured as 'new modernist temples' signifying progress and development at the turn of the century, and today again, are imbued with the same modernist visions in connection with the recent Sudanese Agricultural Revival Programme (Verhoeven 2011, 2012). The idea that agricultural export production is the only attainable scenario to develop Sudan's rural potential – at times represented as being indispensable for the progress of the entire country – dates back to the inception of the Gezira Scheme under Anglo-Egyptian rule (Barnett 1977) and was revived in the framework of the so-called breadbasket strategies of the 1970s (Tetzlaff & Wohlmuth 1980). The breadbasket strategy can be read as a precursor to the present-day rush for Sudan's agricultural land. The plan was to turn Sudan into a food exporting country by initiating capital-intensive agricultural production, financed by investors from the Gulf States. According to textbook assumptions of modernization theory, this should have led to trickle-down effects, stimulating growth in other economic sectors. But these grand developmental schemes failed. Nonetheless, the vision for an agriculture-based development of Sudan resurfaced after the economic collapse when South Sudan seceded and took most of the oil resources with it, perhaps driven – as Verhoeven (2012: 146) suggests – by alleged success stories of countries like Brazil.

Parallel to and articulated with these discourses, a combination of nearly relentless war, drought, hunger and displacements had disastrous consequences in Sudan over the last decades: millions lost their lives, were internally displaced or became refugees in third countries. Insights from political ecology literature present valuable contributions to reflect on the causes and effects of multiple emergencies in Sudan.[4] Early political ecology approaches from the 1980s emphasize three points: land degradation is not a natural event but of social origin; poverty causes peasants and nomadic people to overuse and even destroy their environment in attempts to delay their own collapse; instead of mono-causal theories one must accept plural perceptions, definitions and rationalities in order to comprehend resource management strategies (Blakie & Brookfield 1987). Although acknowledging a certain environmental framing that enables pastoral production, rain-fed farming, and irrigated cultivation along the Nile and its tributaries, we – corresponding to political ecology analyses[5] – do not intend to endorse environmental determinism. Instead we draw attention to the dynamic, creative and ever-shifting engagement of people with their material environments. Especially in view of the ongoing civil wars in Sudan, we refrain from purely 'environmentalist' explanations of crisis and instead point to the role of dysfunctional (state) institutions, land appropriations for mechanized farming schemes, the spread of small arms and shifting political alliances as further causes of conflict (Komey 2012, Johnson 2003, Abdul-Jalil this volume Chapter 5).

A second approach investigates mobility as a key characteristic of modernity (Urry 2000, 2007). This is of particular relevance for Sudan, as on the one hand nomadic people and their mobile livelihood systems constitute an important part of society, surviving for centuries on 'meagre resources' (Manger et al. 1996), while on the other hand modern communications technology, such as mobile phones, fosters new forms of connectivity and enables the territorial extension of interactions (Giddens 1990, Castells 2004). Movements of people, animals, capital, goods and information entail benefits, but there are also damages associated with mobility, namely increasing insecurity. Since the 1980s millions of internally displaced people in Sudan, experiencing dramatic changes and ruptures in their livelihoods, have been heading to urban centres and relief organizations – often only to be further marginalized in other ways. The Greater Khartoum area accommodated almost two million displaced people in the 1980s, constituting a multi-ethnic urban society that embodied the 'murkiness' of war frontiers (Maliqalim Simone 1994: 117). Some managed to set up successful businesses in urban centres. Some, labelled as enemies, were deported. Others had to live in urban despair and still others, at critical moments in the Gulf War in the 1990s, served as 'human shields', protecting dams and other infrastructure from anticipated air strikes (Gertel 1993, Assal 2003). Hence, through these precarious mobilities rural-urban divides were reproduced alongside urban segregation, both materializing as disrupting territories (see Casciarri in Chapter 10).

SPACE, LAND AND TERRITORY

To disentangle these complexities, by means of more theoretical reflections, we introduce, define and position the most important concepts within this volume: namely space, land and territory, and their relations to claims, technology, property and violence. Space is considered to be the superordinate category. It may encompass land and territory, but need not relate to geo-referential positions at all. In the past decades, a broad theoretical debate has re-emerged on space. We follow Massey (1999, 2005) in conceiving of space as an action-oriented category. Accordingly, space is delineated by the outcome of interrelations, by the existence of multiplicity, i.e. as a sphere of possibility that is continuously transformed. Space is always under construction, it is never completed (Massey 1999, 2005: 9). Land, in contrast, is there. It is physically tangible and immobile, but it can be transformed. However, land is more than the mere surface. It is three-dimensionally extensible, and includes soil and subterranean resources. The notion of territory again encompasses more than land and is different from space. It emerges from claims to land. These claims – political as they are – entail three aspects: technologies, control and violence (Blomley 2003). Elden (2010: 801) notes that the concept of territory 'can be understood as a political technology' and, more precisely, 'as a calculative category that is dependent on the existence of a range of techniques'.[6] We suggest a number of points we believe to be relevant to our argument.

First, notions of land are contested. We have to ask: is land always (only) physically tangible, experienced by bodily encounters with soil, its texture and smell, or does it also exist as an imagined entity, something fictional, reproduced by narrations, or both? Different ontologies make land subject to measurements and abstract mathematical calculations or handle it as an innumerable and incommensurable entity, given its singularity. Only when land is intimately associated with the 'modern' conception of territory does it become mathematically calculable, three-dimensionally extensible and based on geometric co-ordinates (Casey 1997). Thereby territory figures as the abstract grid in maps that is imposed over locations and contributes (among many other factors) to the making of land property. The production of property is hence intricately intertwined with technologies of measurement, cartographic illustration and registration in centralized cadastres (Elden 2005). These technologies establish equivalences (categories, classifications, standards, etc.) by turning land into a measurable, calculable and classifiable form, represented by numbers and maps (November et al. 2010).

Second, property and land property are not static, pre-given entities, but depend upon continuous activities. These enactments centre on communicative claims against others (Rose 1994), but property is also enacted in more material and corporal ways. Bodies, technologies and things must be enrolled and mobilized into organized and disciplined practices (Delaney 2001, cf. Callon 1986). When we talk about land and property we are also engaging some deeply moral questions about social orders. Embodied and narrated references to land offer a dense and pungent set of social symbols, stories and meanings (Blomley 2003). The formation of ethnic or national identities is, in part, a meditation of the meanings and significance of belonging to a certain land, an appropriated place, and that not only in African societies (cf. Zenker 2011, Geschiere 2009). Therefore rights to land are closely connected to belonging to certain communities; however, belonging is contested, negotiated and made (Kuba & Lentz 2006). Property is about the human relationships with regard to things (Moore 1998: 33). Property contains a bundle of rights: to access and use resources, to exclude others, to be compensated if infringed (see Table 1.1). Hence, property is a most central social institution, confirming patterns of behaviour. In providing a normative orientation for social practices, it orders the world and allows the categorizing and ranking of spaces and people according to their relationships to things (cf. Boltanski & Thévenot 2006).

Third, the separation of land from its social references and its transformation into numbers (length, width, price, etc.) is a fundamental prerequisite of its commodification (Castree 2003). In order to convert land into a commodity, the rights to land must be delimited by identifiable and reproducible borders, and these must remain stable without overlapping territories. Nomadic land use contrasts with this capitalistic conception of land, as it depends on territorially flexible and temporary borders (cf. Gertel & Le Heron 2011). The multiplicity of property regimes, when new elements are imposed on 'old' patterns, leads to collisions

Table 1.1 Land Rights and Conflicts

Land rights	State property	Private property	Leasehold	Community possession	Customary right
Bundle of rights					
right of access	X	X	X	X	(X)
right to exclude	X	X	X	X	(X)
right to use	X	X	X	X	(X)
right to transfer claims	X	X	(X)	X	( )
right for compensation	–	X	(X)	(X)	( )
Context of **legitimation**	Government (International law & global public)	**State (1)**	Owner (2)	Community (3)	User groups (4)
Layers of legitimation & **conflict**		**(1)**	**(1)**(2)	**(1)**(2)(3)	**(1)**(2)(3)(4)
X = existent; (X) = partly existent; ( ) = non-existent					Draft: J. Gertel 2011

Note: The categories of land rights depicted above are neither comprehensive, nor is the inherent complexity and the relational character of claims captured. The same applies to the rights displayed. Such preliminary classifications of land rights are nevertheless useful to distinguish between state property, private property, leasehold, community possessions and customary rights. The respective categories implicate different bundles of rights, such as the right of access or to cross the land, the right to exclude others, the right to use or to extract resources, the right to transfer claims or the right for compensation in case of dispossession. These rights are asymmetrically distributed, shaping different land categories. Moreover, discrete bundles of rights are embedded in different frames of legitimation. Today nation states are often still seen as being central to property regimes, exercising sovereign power over national territory, superimposing and subordinating older and weaker bundles of rights encoded as private property, leasehold or customary rights. Correspondingly the frames of legitimation might be complex: private property is legitimized by the state, leasehold refers to both, the owner and the state, while community possessions are additionally accountable to the community. Conflicts over land are hence subject to different layers of legitimation.

of state ownership, communal land claims, leasehold or customary usage and private property – a situation in which 'what is' and 'what counts' is unclear and often generates conflicts. These conflicts again are about the justice of social orders, about the gap between 'what is' and 'what ought to be' in view of claims made to different legitimating rationalities, such as state or customary law (Gertel 2011: 9, Boltanski 2011).

Fourth, governments are key actors in the ongoing negotiation of territorial orders, since they enforce the property laws that transnational capitalism builds upon, administer a country's territorial sovereignty rights and are in charge of contracting its land, minerals and oil (Scott 1998, Sassen 2006, Wacquant 2012). However, the state is more than a 'bordered power container' (Giddens 1981: 5–6) and one has to be aware of the 'territorial trap' (Agnew 1994: 53), contrary to actual history, of restricting state action to a prescribed territory – a fixed unit of sovereign space and container for 'its' societies. Nevertheless, contractual legality that the national government can confer upon transnational firms has become a most significant property of sovereignty, often outweighing the control over national territories and states' legitimate monopoly on violence (Ferguson 2006: 207, Rottenburg 2009a: 429). This leads to an increasing disjunction between extractive and productive enclaves of transnational capital investment and the surrounding socio-political developments (Watts 2004: 61). Local people are losing out – not only as returns from national resources do not turn into their benefits, but also as the control over local resources is under assault. For example, government-backed militias wreaked havoc on and displaced local populations from their homes to clear the area for oil exploration (Linke this volume Chapter 4).

Fifth, processes of commodification and privatization do not work in agreement with the way small-farming and pastoralist communities conceive and make 'their' territories. The underlying conceptions of land in rural Sudan starkly contrast with the measurability of clearly delimited parcels and holdings. These tensions are not negotiated but rather collective systems of land ownership are increasingly superimposed and displaced by force through private property rights (Gertel 2011: 9, Komey this volume Chapter 6).

Sixth, results of the marginalization of rural populations are recurrent outbreaks of violent conflicts. While at a first glance many conflicts in Sudan seem to be caused by antagonisms between ethnic groups or the competition for scarce land and water resources, we argue that responsibility should also be placed upon (state) institutions that fail to mediate between diverging interests and moral claims (Rottenburg 2009a: 429, Rottenburg 2008). It is perhaps, as Hilgers (2012: 89) surmises, that 'beneath its apparent apology of freedom, neoliberalism produces a specific state that reinforces control and coercion'. In the following, we disentangle some of the specificities of the commodification of land rights in Sudan.

LAND AND ITS COMMODIFICATION IN SUDAN: AN OVERVIEW

This volume concentrates on how the commodification of customary land rights and their increasing privatization play out in Sudan. The empirical case studies reflect on globally unwinding processes and connect these insights with debates on property and commodification under recent neoliberal governance. Perhaps, as some recent scholarship has suggested, it is in countries like Sudan, the undersides, the uncertain and deregulated margins of neoliberal capitalist expansion, that the effects of these processes are felt first (Comaroff & Comaroff 2012b). Hence, while investigating the specificities of the Sudanese case, we explicitly seek to move beyond the parochialism that at times is encountered in Sudan studies.

In the past years, grey literature on land has burgeoned: consultancy papers, reports, briefing papers from various international organizations, think-tanks, policy groups and independent consultants dealing with land and land rights in Sudan abound (e.g. Mosley 2012, see also www.grain.org, www.landgrab.org). Some offer precious insights or pieces of analysis and add onto an impressive body of literature on land rights in Sudan. Academic scholarship of land rights in Sudan has resulted in a number of in-depth studies of specific regions of Sudan, such as Darfur (Flint & de Waal 2008, Manger 2008), South Kordofan (Komey 2010) or Eastern Sudan (Miller 2005). Two publications are devoted to developments in Sudan as a whole: first, a special issue of *Nomadic Peoples* entitled *Pastoralists under Pressure in Present-Day Sudan*, edited by Barbara Casciarri and Abdel Ghaffar Ahmed (2009), highlighted various challenges that one occupational group, namely nomadic pastoralists, encounter in claiming and securing access to land. Second, Gaim Kibreab's study on *State Intervention and the Environment in Sudan, 1889–1989* (2002), examines communal land rights systems in Sudan and traces their erosion through different historical phases.

Kibreab seeks to debunk the widespread 'tragedy of the commons' type of argument, according to which collective ownership of resources necessarily leads to their exploitation (Hardin 1968, Ostrom 1990). To do so, he discusses the institution of *dār* rights, which in northern Sudan have been known already since the early sixteenth century. A *dār* implies a commonly recognized link between a certain territory and a group of people, leading to a conceptualization of *dār* rights as exclusive tribal property and an entitlement for members of the respective group to exploit various collectively-owned resources, farm and pasture land, water, timber, etc. The *dār* institution is conceived as a communal resource management system, enabling an effective, prudent, and sustainable organization of resource use. It entailed the landowning tribal group's right to exclude other groups from their land or to demand the payment of tributes. This institution had strong effects on latecomers and strangers, who could not claim a *dār* and thus had to forge agreements or risk conflicts with *dār* owners. Pastoral *dārs* were somewhat less territorially circumscribed than those of farming groups, due to the seasonality of resources and the constant negotiations required. Furthermore, conflicts between groups indicate that the boundaries of *dār* were constantly renegotiated, especially in view of the absence of a central force intervening in tribal affairs (Kibreab 2002: 444).

Dār rights were consolidated under Turko-Egyptian and later British rule, where they did not interfere with interests in cash crop cultivation and infrastructural projects. Under British rule the *dār* institution was later integrated as a cornerstone of Native Administration. Kibreab argues that Native Administration, imposed by the British, was only so successful because it strengthened the customary communal systems of resource management and connected mechanisms of arbitration and reconciliation. Codifying the established customary system in an encompassing legal framework, the demarcation of pastures and farming zones and the regulation of seasonal migrations overall mitigated conflicts and reduced the colonizers' administrative costs to maintain law and order (Kibreab 2002: 34–36, 43, 449–450).

Miller (2005) and Mamdani (2009), in contrast, emphasize how a formerly flexible kinship-based organization was rendered rigid through the colonial formalization of structures of authority and the reconfiguration of 'tribal' entities, and how in this period differences were drawn between natives with native land (*dār*) and a political representation and non-natives without land, leading to a delineation of zones for herding and farming (Miller 2005: 13, 14, 26). For Kibreab, however, not change but the continuities define the colonial period and especially the British introduction of Native Administration: based on historical evidence of various grazing agreements, he argues, it recognized and consolidated the enduring communal land rights institution – the *dār* system.

There is scholarly consensus on the dramatic effects of post-colonial nationalization policies, which 'through a single act abrogated rights that had been in existence for several centuries' (Kibreab 2002: 456). This especially refers to the Unregistered Land Act of 1970 and the related abolition of Native Administration. The declaration of communally owned land as government land, its distribution to wealthy farmers, and the conversion of formerly group-specific territories (*dār*) into open access regimes, spawned agricultural encroachment upon rain-fed and herding land, overgrazing, competition for land and the eruption of farmer-herder conflicts (Kibreab 2002, Miller 2005, Schlee forthcoming). These reforms enabled the development of a mechanized farming sector in Sudan aimed at large-scale production and food export. The recurrent breadbasket strategies symbolize this export-driven developmental vision (O'Brien 1986). Yet, these policies had profound effects upon the relationship between ordinary people and their land, resulting in famines, poverty and often violent conflicts (cf. de Waal 1989, 1997, Duffield 1990, Elnur 2009).

For instance, the situation of the Humr branch of the Missiriyya illustrates the effects of such developments. Today they are squeezed between an embattled oil-rich region, Abyei, and agricultural encroachments on their northern grazing areas. Here, conflicts erupted with sedentary farmers who at times contested the pastoralists' access to water sources, corridors or pastures, fearing damage to their crops from trespassing herds (Braukämper 1992: 73). Furthermore, due to the mobilization of Missiriyya as government militias in raiding Ngok Dinka, their passage to southern pastures across the border to southern Sudan is insecure (Salih 1993: 17, Calkins & Komey 2011). This case demonstrates the pressures exerted on rural populations and how the loss of access to land is seemingly inextricably paired with conflicts in Sudan (cf. Johnson 2007, 2010, 2011).

It was this predictable eruption of conflicts over land and water along with the inability to settle them after the abolition of communal resource management systems in the early 1970s that again led to federal reforms and the gradual return of Native Administration since the late 1980s. Miller (2005: 15–17) draws attention to a paradoxical development to which some of the authors in this volume refer: the re-introduction of Native Administration served as a means to regulate resource conflicts, but also to strengthen ethnic divides, often described as part of governmental divide and rule strategies. Furthermore, it increased the range of manoeuvre for various formerly landless and excluded groups, who with the administrative reorganization have often managed to enter different governmental bodies and to enforce a reappraisal of their situations. Already Cunnison had pointed out an important argumentative resource of nomadic pastoralists in accessing land: 'In Humr theory there are no individual or sectional rights, within Dar Humr, to grazing land and surface water "because the land belongs to the Government"' (Cunnison 1966: 27). Beck (1988: 170) describes a similar practice among Kawahla as regards their southern pastures, where they were not considered as the landowners. This tendency to deduce group rights to land, a *dār*, from governmental ownership of resources received a recent upswing and is a justification of a new territorial/administrative model in different regions of Sudan – what some have called 'ethnic administrative units'. These are built upon an inherent contradiction: new and mushrooming local administrative units are overtly based on citizenship, yet at the same time they foster the subdivision of both land and political power along ethnic identifications. This contradictory development is mainly due to the attempts by groups without customary claims to land (e.g. settlers, camel herders) to gain an ethnically exclusive access to agricultural and settlement land, further adding to the fragmentation of rural territories (see Abdul-Jalil in Chapter 5, Komey in Chapter 6, Calkins in Chapter 8). These recent dynamics of land appropriation from below underscore that the effects of commodification under neoliberal regimes are not unidirectional and inevitable, but rather that 'neoliberalisation is a signifier for an always contradictory process, and for an evolving/rolling programme of restructuring' (Peck & Theodore 2012: 379).

Related to these everyday negotiations of land access, the contributions in this volume also explain how people increasingly make sense of their territories and identities as being inextricably linked. Conflicts for land are therefore also struggles for identity and belonging (Pantuliano in Chapter 7). Overall, the importance of land to conflicts in Sudan that appear to be ethnically motivated has been underlined by recent scholarship (Flint & de Waal 2008, Komey 2010). For instance, Guma Kunda Komey's (2010) *Land, Governance, Conflict & the Nuba of Sudan* provides a thorough analysis of the conflicts in the Nuba Mountains. Komey shows how successive governments have systematically excluded Nuba populations from their land and how this has marginalized them. He argues that explanatory models which highlight competing occupational and/or ethnic identifications or resource scarcity fall short of explaining conflicts in the Nuba Mountains. Rather discriminatory land laws and the failure to manage land disputes are central to the crises in the region. With Komey's example from the Nuba Mountains, we suggest that land has been and is a crucial point of contestation in all of Sudan that merits close examination.[7]

PROPERTY AND CONFLICT

As a consequence of the long history of colonization, post-colonial politics of capture and its current – perhaps neo-colonial – successions, land in Sudan is increasingly conceived and also practically registered as property of legal persons. The scale of this privatization process appears new, although the introduction of capitalist principles has been unfolding for a long time. The mechanisms through which subsistence economies buffered themselves against capital penetration were an established theme in Sudan ethnography. Drawing on a case study from Darfur, Fredrik Barth proposed that circulation in an economic system is ordered into spheres of exchange which are protected by institutional barriers. For example, he identified an exchange of beer and labour as a sphere that could not be combined with monetary exchanges. But more importantly, land was the inalienable right of descent groups, not individuals (Barth 1967: 152). Similarly, Rottenburg (1991) showed that the flow of money from towns to the Nuba Mountains did not fundamentally change social organization among Lemwareng or provoke a broad differentiation in accumulation. Access to land and labour power remained unsalable and firmly in communal hands, ruling out the emergence of marked inequalities (Rottenburg 1991: 89–92). But these mechanisms have meanwhile been disrupted by relentless wars.

Property has become almost synonymous with private property, where the owner is identifiable by a formal title, rather than holding other types of claims, like belonging to a community with autochthonous roots to the land as the most important alternative in rural Sudan. Empowered by the neoliberal vision of governance, this narrow notion of private property travels as a depoliticized technology of market regulation and suppresses the availability of other options as delineated by Amartya Sen in his book *The Idea of Justice* (Sen 2009: 42). Often the capitalist way is expressly viewed as the only natural way of doing things, as it allegedly denotes social standing, responsibility and self-control in the most fair and rational way that is best for all (Blomley 2003, 2005, Gibson-Graham 2006, 2008). But, while the owner enjoys all rights – the right to exclude others, to use the property as he wishes and to transfer and sell it – he is hardly held responsible for the communal well-being that was formerly related to the land.

We suggest examining private property as a travelling technology (Rottenburg 2009b): On the one hand, private property depends on state law and means of law enforcement, and thereby force and violence play an integral role. On the other hand, through the connected means of enforcement it promotes the alienation of resident communities from 'their' land and its assigned responsibilities (i.e. caring for people). While a root cause of conflicts consists in the particularly narrow capitalist concept of property, this becomes a serious problem in the Sudan because the institutions linking private property with the responsibility towards the community through taxation and democratic representation are not in place. Hence, private property becomes disconnected from the other institutions that make it work elsewhere. Thus, ultimately the privatization of land rights constitutes the corner stone for the fragmentation of land and of spaces of social reproduction. In view of this, it is our primary goal to identify the processes through which land is being converted and privately appropriated in Sudan as well as to draw attention to the consequences of these processes, which for instance in the case of oil exploitation led to a governmental and thus legal but nonetheless utterly brutal and illegitimate depopulation of land. This volume, however, also points out another peculiarity of private property in Sudan, especially when vast concessions are allotted to investors: whereas rights to land are privatized, this does not in all cases mean that investors actually control the land or that the government polices the concessions (cf. Calkins & Ille in Chapter 3). Above we noted that territorial disruptions are point- and time-specific. Similarly, the enforcement of property as travelling technology is ambiguous and likewise is contingent upon interests, places and temporal conjunctures.

The trajectories of the 2007/8 food and financial crises and the dramatic food price hikes in 2010/11 have accelerated the privatization of land appropriations in Sudan (Babiker 2011, Deng 2011, Calkins 2012, Mosley 2012). But the transnational appropriation of land is not only driven by the desire to engage in farming and often export production, but rather investors may also use the rights to farmland as a security for loans or for speculation (Umbadda in Chapter 2). Sudan certainly has been one of the most interesting destination countries for such transnational business ventures, not only in agriculture, but also in the classical extractive industries, such as mining for gold and other minerals (Calkins & Ille in Chapter 3) and oil (Linke in Chapter 4). Resource grab in this sense is – as we argue – a forceful, large-scale, and violent extension of capitalist property regimes, which carries the technology of private property at its centre.

However, there are some indications that populations in this part of the world are increasingly resisting such violent processes which disenfranchize them from their essential means of production. The recent popular uprisings in the Middle East and North Africa that led to the ousting of Ben Ali in Tunisia and Mubarak in Egypt as well as the fall of Gaddafi in Libya provided not only resources for the justification of rebellion but also figured as models for the projection of a life free of oppression, fear and tyranny for the many marginalized communities. The sense of justice articulated in these protests often emphasized the will of the people to free themselves from exploitation through totalitarian regimes. Central grievances for which the Government of Sudan is held responsible are the lack of access to resources and the inability to live a life free of fear and want. Certainly the Arab uprisings have added pressure on the Government of Sudan, and the continued brutal crackdowns on protesters in Sudan attest to this as does the new impetus that the opposition movements in Sudan gained.

INTRODUCTION TO CHAPTERS

Disrupting Territories extends and goes beyond the reviewed literature in several ways: it contributes primarily to the ongoing debate about land rights and their commodification with new insights from Sudan. Most chapters in this volume are based on long-term ethnographic research between 2006 and 2011, and in some cases on many years of engagement in different regions of Sudan. To capture the relationships between people, land, its commodification and conflicts, the book is structured into two main parts: the first section focuses on the spatial impacts of resource extracting economies in Sudan, i.e. foreign agricultural land acquisitions, Chinese investments in oil production, and competition between artisanal and industrial gold mining. The second section assembles detailed ethnographic case studies, which from a bottom-up perspective highlight how rural people experience 'their' land and engage in the construction of territories vis-à-vis the latest wave of massive privatization and commercialization of land rights. The concern for the disrupting relationships between people and land is articulated in nine chapters. Siddig Umbadda discusses recent 'Agricultural Investment through Land Grabbing in Sudan'. He traces different phases of land appropriation and the volume of 'grabbed' land, linking this to technologies of governance, such as land acts and development plans since colonial times. National governments, Umbadda argues, largely continued the course of 'development' instigated by the British, opening the land to agricultural investments often from abroad. In view of the enormous scope of recent land deals, Umbadda highlights a crucial contradiction: the government, while continuously contracting land rights to receive loans and foreign direct investment, is unable to guarantee the enforcement of contracts on the ground. This is corroborated by the low implementation rate of projects. He suggests that the Government of Sudan may be pursuing short-term extractive rather than development policies.

A similar general point concerning the commodification of land rights in Sudan is made by Sandra Calkins and Enrico Ille. In 'Territories of Gold Mining: International Investments and Artisanal Extraction in Sudan', they focus on the burgeoning gold mining sector in Sudan and its spatial trajectories. In the past years vast areas were allocated to mainly foreign private enterprises for gold mining. Ille and Calkins show how these contracts have ignored rural populations, alienating them from their land, while concomitantly informal gold mining has turned into a new source of income for thousands of small-scale actors. Based on a case study from north-eastern Sudan, they indicate various unresolved tensions between artisanal and industrial mining that lay claim to the same territories. Their account highlights the discrepancy between official mining contracts with investors and the pragmatic negotiations on the ground that artisanal miners forge with whoever effectively controls the territory, resisting their prohibition. Calkins and Ille argue that the government, instead of defusing such tensions, works rather as a passage point in channelling transnational investment flows into Sudanese territories, collecting fees in exchange for an access to Sudan's natural resources.

Janka Linke takes a closer look at one type of investment in Sudan – Chinese companies – and analyses their rationalities. In the chapter 'Oil, Water, Agriculture: Chinese Impact on Sudanese Land Use', Linke complements micro-scale ethnographic studies of specific processes in certain localities by offering insights on Chinese engagements across Sudan and their public relations from a macro perspective. Examining the examples of Chinese investments in the oil sector, infrastructural projects and Sudanese agriculture, the chapter traces the emergence of China as Sudan's main business partner, implementing 'its pragmatic politics'. Linke reviews three types of Chinese literature – official documents, scientific articles and corporate news to understand how Chinese go about, and make sense of, their activities in Sudan. She shows how Chinese talk of Sudanese land as 'vast', 'full of natural resources', 'fertile' and of 'great potential' largely ignore that this land is inhabited and serves as a means of livelihood for local populations. She shows that reflexive tools are lacking. Thus, the ability to learn from failures and to reckon with the social costs of implementing large-scale projects has not matured.

Linking recent conflicts in Darfur to a historically discriminatory land rights situation, Musa Abdul-Jalil follows nomadic-sedentary relations in Darfur from early times until today asking how they have come to be interpreted predominantly as dichotomous and conflictual. In the chapter 'Nomad-Sedentary Relations in the Context of Dynamic Land Rights in Darfur,' he traces how, from a situation in which flexible complementary relationships between different occupational groups prevailed and where land access was organized communally, land titles were introduced: the private *ḥākūra* for Islamic scholars and merchants, and the administrative *ḥākūra*, creating a difference between groups with a landholding and those without. This laid the basis for the colonial prescription of a situation in which there are 'tribes with and without tribal land (*dār*)'. In the 1970s a series of land acts converted unregistered lands into state property to facilitate the expansion of mechanized farming schemes. This legal reform had far-reaching consequences: it provided landless groups with a new argument to back their claims, namely citizenship as opposed to ethnic identification. But Abdul-Jalil stresses that complexities in Darfur cannot be reduced to the matter of the legality of land rights, rather that different contradictory land tenure systems coexist, which, along with the failing mechanisms of governance and other international, ecological and demographic factors, strongly shape how claims to land are made and are being contested.

Guma Kunda Komey's chapter 'Sedentary-Nomadic Relations in a Shared Territory: Post-conflict Dynamics in the Nuba Mountains, Sudan' has a sad timeliness, as it focuses on the dynamic relations between nomadic Arabs of the Baggara and the sedentary Nuba in South Kordofan – an area which returned to war in June 2011 and fighting was ongoing in 2013. Komey explores the transformation of local discourses and practices of social and political belonging and attachments of these two groups in the region since the early 1980s, during the civil war, and until today. The main focus is on autochthonous identity politics – the claim of indigeneity to an ancestral homeland – which creates strong emotional ties to issues of land ownership and usage rights. To illustrate how long-standing historical relations of conflict and cooperation between sedentary Nuba and nomadic Arab people of South Kordofan were reconfigured through the civil war, Komey relates the struggle, following the Comprehensive Peace Agreement, of the people of Keiga Tummero to regain their farmland, occupied by Arabs from the north. Claims of autochthony and their contention by other groups and the state in a situation of competition for resources and violent suppression led to multiplied lines of conflict.

Claims of land and identity are inextricably intertwined. This is the starting point for Sara Pantuliano. In her chapter 'Entangled Land and Identity', Pantuliano discusses how Beja define 'Beja-ness' and which markers they use in support of their identity claims. She argues that the discussion about whether the Beni Amer figure as part of the Beja is fundamentally political, tied to the general situation of marginalization and underdevelopment in Eastern Sudan and the need to protect Beja land and identity – in view of new encroachments on land. She reveals how the ethnic category 'Beja' was adjusted to accommodate the Beni Amer and forge a joint political platform between Hadendowa and Beni Amer. She relates such political processes to the loss of land and the breakdown of 'traditional' institutions, in which land and identity were intimately entangled.

'Gaining Access to Land' focuses on land appropriations from below. Sandra Calkins discusses how pastoral Rashaida, classified as landless newcomers, gained access to settlement land in Kassala. Calkins juxtaposes peoples' land relations in two regions – the Lower Atbara area and Kassala, focusing on the entanglements between regional economic opportunities, political mobilization and the modes in which belonging is articulated. Furthermore, drawing upon Thévenot's idea of 'investment in forms' (1984), she theorizes the jump in scale from individual to collective (ethnic) land negotiations. She argues that processes of social stratification, which resulted in the formation of an elite in Kassala, were fundamental to a successful 'investment in form', the translation of specific land-related grievances into a concern of the ethnic group. This mobilized many Rashaida to join an armed insurgency. Calkins shows how political leaders legitimized their claims to land in the political sphere by reference to the principle of citizenship, given that as immigrant pastoralists Rashaida are unable to argue by means of autochthony.

In a vivid chronological account Elhadi Osman and Günther Schlee describe the development of a land conflict between two groups leading up to its violent escalation in 2009, a year of drought. The chapter 'Hausa and Fulbe on the Blue Nile: Land Conflicts between Farmers and Herders' focuses on skirmishes between Hausa farmers from Rigeiba town and a group of Fulbe, the Farig Malakal, in the vicinity of the Roseiris dam reservoir, south of Damazin. Osman and Schlee associate the genesis of the conflict with the socio-economic, environmental and territorial transformations at the local, the state and the national levels, elaborating how other groups are incorporated into the conflict. They argue that interpretations that view resource competition as the prime trigger of conflict are too short-sighted, though acknowledging conflicting interests with regard to resource use at a local level. Attention is rather placed upon diverging interests on higher political levels, amongst them the promotion of mechanized agriculture and total negligence of pastoralists' interests in the Blue Nile State. Furthermore, they point out the increasing privatization of land and vegetation and the processes that lead to a resource contraction and the breakdown of complementary relationships.

In the final chapter 'A Central Marginality: the Invisibilization of Urban Pastoralists in Khartoum State', Barbara Casciarri addresses the relationship between land and identity along a rural-urban divide, particularly concerning the rapid urbanization around Greater Khartoum. She sheds light upon an often ignored periphery at the centre, namely pastoralists living in the capital region of Sudan. These were either integrated by sedentarization or through the centre's gradual encroachment upon the surrounding rural territories, but still are politically and economically disadvantaged. The oxymoron of the 'central marginality' throws up the question of ethnic spaces in urban surroundings. It denotes that pastoralists' localization within the centre is connected to an unrecognized marginality, but that this marginality is not absolute as they may constitute an important political constituency and may be used for economic gains. Based on an ethnographic study of pastoral groups originating in Eastern Sudan today living in Khartoum State, Casciarri gives insights into the various configurations of pastoralists in the setting of a town that is encroaching upon rural territories, questioning the modes and reasons for pastoralists' lack of visibility and the specificity of their urban situation. She applies the centre/periphery paradigm, inspired by dependency theory for describing North/South relations, which is frequently invoked to interpret uneven development in Sudan. Focusing on the asymmetries in political power and access to economic resources – among them land – she argues that this paradigm allows the reading of relations within the centre, whereby urban pastoralists figure as the 'inner periphery'.

Disrupting Territories deals with the consequences of commodification in Sudan. It starts from the observation that the conversion of collective land into private property has accelerated in Sudan with the internationalization of agribusiness and the rise of neoliberal governance. The chapters problematize the dissolution of fundamental relationships between man and land, dealing with land and claims to land on various scales and with reference to different legal sources. We suggested that private property is a globally circulating model, based on Western spatial conceptions, that is travelling to different places in the sway of neoliberal reforms, streamlining land tenure and crowding out other forms of land resource management, often to the detriment of rural populations.

This volume contributes to scholarship that seeks to overcome a culturally relativist tendency in social studies of Sudan, which are grounded on an assumed Sudanese exceptionalism and result in theoretical parochialism (cf. Sharkey et al. forthcoming). Most chapters theorize from empirical observations and offer sophisticated, nuanced arguments that allow qualifying as to how local communities in Sudan experience processes of urbanization, marketization, conflict and state-building. The effects of these processes are far from uniform; within Sudan and elsewhere people experience a great diversity of consequences and respond in a multitude of ways – from accommodation to outright opposition. A strong historical dimension to many chapters strengthens the analysis offered, allowing the reader to get a better sense of shifting dynamics of land rights, not just across space, but also through time. The situation at hand and how people interpret it strongly affects what they consider as options and how they respond to changing entitlements to land.

This volume also goes beyond recent publications on foreign land acquisitions in Sudan, such as reports, memorandums of understanding, letters of intent, newspaper information or website announcements, which tend to reduce the phenomena to numbers (size, price, etc.) in economic projections and on maps. This volume offers first-hand insights from long-term empirical research in Sudan. Several contributions focus on the claims to land made by small farmers and pastoralists, how they bundle their claims to have a broader impact and the moral understandings upon which they ground them. Individuals and groups who 'cannot speak' (Spivak 1988), such as nomadic people and subsistence peasants who are often not heard in official reports and media releases, are given a voice in this collection.

At the same time, we endorse a project of reflexive science, acknowledging that there is no view from nowhere. All knowledge is situated, positioned, partial and selective (see Haraway 1991). For scholars, this implies acknowledging the theoretical concepts that always guide perception and choices, especially concerning assumptions about the ontological reality of what is out there and how it can be observed and known. We hope that this attempt at producing knowledge that is contextualized and situated, mostly through long-term ethnographic fieldwork, will contribute to challenging coercive, top-down knowledge that is announced, stated and proclaimed as true, official and authentic, while marginalizing other understandings.

ACKNOWLEDGEMENTS

We would like to acknowledge the critical comments of Peter Woodward and Harry Verhoeven in developing the argument of the chapter. Jörg Gertel gratefully acknowledges the funding by the Australian Research Council (ARC): 'The New Farm Owners. Finance Companies and the Restructuring of Australian and Global Agriculture' (Discovery Grant DP 110102299, 2011–2014).

REFERENCES

Agnew, J. 1994. 'The Territorial Trap: The Geographical Assumptions of International Relations Theory'. *Review of International Political Economy* 1(1), 53–80.

Allen, J., Keulertz, M., Sojamo, S., Warner, J. (eds) 2012. *Handbook of Land and Water Grabs in Africa: Foreign Direct Investment and Food and Water Security.* London and New York: Routledge.

Allen, J., Cochrane, A. 2010. 'Assemblages of State Power: Topological Shifts in the Organization of Government and Politics'. *Antipode* 42 (5), 1071–1089.

Assal, M. A. 2003. 'A Discipline Asserting its Identity and Place: Displacement, Aid and Anthropology in Sudan'. In Ahmed, A. G. M. (ed.), *Anthropology in Sudan: Reflections by a Sudanese Anthropologist.* Utrecht: International Books, 95–127.

Babiker, M. 2011. 'Mobile Pastoralism and Land Grabbing in Sudan: Impacts and Responses'. Paper presented at the International Conference on the Future of Pastoralism in Africa, March 2011. Organized by Future Agricultures Consortium, University of Sussex, and Feinstein International Center, Tufts University.

Barnett, T. 1977. *The Gezira Scheme. An Illusion of Development.* London: Frank Cass.

Barth, F. 1967. 'Economic spheres in Darfur'. In Firth, R. (ed.), *Themes in Economic Anthropology*. London: Tavistock, 149–174.

Bayart, J.-F. 1989/2010. *The State in Africa: The Politics of the Belly*. Cambridge and Malden: Polity Press.

Beck, K. 1988. *Die Kawāhla von Kordofan: ökologische und ökonomische Strategien Arabischer Nomaden in Sudan*. Stuttgart: Franz Steiner.

Bijker, W., Hughes, T., Pinch, T. 1987. *The Social Construction of Technological Systems: New Directions in the Sociology and History of Technology*. Cambridge MA: MIT Press.

Blakie, P., Brookfield, H. (eds) 1987. *Land Degradation and Society*. London: Methuen.

Blomley, N. 2003. 'Law, Property, and the Geography of Violence: The Frontier, the Survey, and the Grid'. *Annals of the Association of American Geographers* 93 (1), 121–141.

Blomley, N. 2005. 'Remember Property?' *Progress in Human Geography* 29 (2), 125–127.

Boltanski, L., Thévenot, L. 2006. *On Justification: Economies of Worth*. Princeton NJ: Princeton University Press.

Boltanski, L. 2011. *On Critique: A Sociology of Emancipation*. Cambridge and Malden MA: Polity Press.

Borras, S. M., Franco, J. C., Wang, C. 2013. 'The Challenge of Global Governance of Land Grabbing: Changing International Agricultural Context and Competing Political Views and Strategies'. *Globalization* 10 (1), 161–179.

Braukämper, U. 1992. *Migration und Ethnischer Wandel: Untersuchungen aus der Östlichen Sudanzone*. Stuttgart: Franz Steiner.

Brenner, N. 2004. *New State Spaces: Urban Governance and the Rescaling of Statehood*. Oxford: Oxford University Press.

Buck, S. J. 1998. *The Global Commons: An Introduction*. Washington DC: Island Press.

Burch, D., Lawrence, G. 2009. 'Towards a Third Food Regime: Behind the Transformation'. *Agriculture and Human Values* 26 (4), 267–279.

Burr, J. M., Collins, R. O. 1995. *Requiem for the Sudan: War, Drought & Disaster Relief on the Nile*. Boulder CO: Westview Press.

Calkins, S., Komey, G. K. 2011. 'Umkämpfte Weiden: Landzugang und Überleben im Sudan.' *Geographische Rundschau* 63 (7–8), 28–35.

Calkins, S. 2012. 'Agricultural Encroachment in Wadi Mukabrab Area: Policies of Recompense, Differentiation and "Tribal" Belonging'. In Kleinitz, C., Näser, C. (eds), *"Nihna nâs al-bahar – We are the People of the River." Ethnographic Research in the Fourth Nile Cataract Region, Sudan*. Meroitica 26. Wiesbaden: Harassowitz, 229–251.

Callon, M. 1986. 'Some Elements of a Sociology of Translation: Domestication of the Scallops and the Fishermen of St. Brieuc Bay'. In Law, J. (ed.), *Power, Action and Belief: A New Sociology of Knowledge?* London: Routledge, 196–233.

Casciarri, B., Ahmed, A. G. 2009. 'Pastoralists under Pressure in Present-Day Sudan.' Special Issue of *Nomadic Peoples* 13 (1).

Casey, E. S. 1997. *The Fate of Place: A Philosophical History*. Berkeley CA: University of California Press.

Castells, M. (ed.) 2004. *The Network Society: A Cross-Cultural Perspective*. Cheltenham: Edward Elgar.

Castree, N. 2003. 'Commodifying What Nature?' *Progress in Human Geography* 27 (3), 273–297.

Christopher, A. J. 1988. *The British Empire at its Zenith*. London & New York: Croom Helm

Comaroff, J., Comaroff, J. L. 2012a. 'Figuring Democracy: An Anthropological Take on African Political Modernities'. In *Theory from the South: Or, how Euro-America is Evolving Toward Africa*. Boulder CO and London: Paradigm Publishers, 109–131.

Comaroff, J., Comaroff, J. 2012b. *Theory from the South: Or, how Euro-America is Evolving Toward Africa*. Boulder CO and London: Paradigm Publishers.

Cunnison, I. 1966. *Baggara Arabs: Power and the Lineage in a Sudanese Nomad Tribe*. Oxford: Clarendon Press.

Debiel, T., Klein, A. (eds) 2002. *Fragile Peace: State Failure, Violence and Development in Crisis Regions*. London: Zed Books.

Delaney, D. 2001. 'Making Nature/Marking Humans: Law as a Site of (Cultural) Production'. *Annals of the Association of American Geographers* 91 (3), 487–503.

Deng, D. 2011. *The New Frontier: A Baseline Survey for Large-scale Land-based Investments in South Sudan*. Oslo: Norwegian People's Aid.

de Waal, A. 1989. *Famine that Kills: Darfur, Sudan, 1984–1985*. Oxford: Oxford University Press.

de Waal, A. 1997. *Famine Crimes: Politics & the Disaster Relief Industry in Africa*. African Issues. Oxford: James Currey.

Duffield, M. 1990 'Absolute Distress: Structural Causes of Hunger in Sudan'. *Middle East Report* 166, 4–11.

Elden, S. 2005. 'Missing the Point: Globalization, Deterritorialization and the Space of the World'. *Transactions of the Institute of British Geographers*. New Series 30 (1), 8–19.

Elden, S. 2010. 'Land, Terrain, Territory'. *Progress in Human Geography* 34 (6), 799–817.

Elnur, I. 2009. *Contested Sudan: The Political Economy of War and Reconstruction*. Abingdon: Routledge.

Epstein, G. 2005. 'Introduction: Financialization and the World Economy'. In

Epstein, G. (ed.), *Financialization and the World Economy*. Cheltenham: Edward Elgar, 3–16.
Escobar, A. 1995. *Encountering Development: The Making and Unmaking of the Third World*. Princeton NJ: Princeton University Press.
Evans-Pritchard, E. E. 1940/1969. *The Nuer: A Description of the Modes of Livelihood and Political Institutions of a Nilotic People*. Oxford and New York: Oxford University Press.
Fatton, R. 1992. *Predatory Rule: State and Civil Society in Africa*. Boulder CO: Lynne Rienner.
Ferguson, J. 2006. 'Governing Extraction: New Spatializations of Order and Disorder in Neoliberal Africa'. In Ferguson, J., *Global Shadows: Africa in the Neoliberal World Order*. Durham NC: Duke University Press, 194–210.
Fischer, M., Schmelzle, B. (eds) 2009. *Building Peace in the Absence of States: Challenging the Discourse on State Failure*. Berlin: Berghof Research Center.
Flint, J., de Waal, A. 2008. *Darfur. A Short History of a Long War*. London and others: Zed Books.
Foucault, M. 1988. 'The Political Technology of the Individuals'. In Martin, L. H., Gutman, H., Hutton, P. (eds), *Technologies of the Self*. Amherst MA: University of Massachusetts Press, 145–162.
Freidberg, S. 2009. *Fresh: A Perishable History*. Cambridge MA and London: The Belknap Press of Harvard University Press.
Gertel, J. 1993. *Krisenherd Khartoum: Geschichte und Struktur der Wohnraumproblematik in der Sudanesischen Hauptstadt*. Saarbrücken: Breitenbach.
Gertel, J. 2010. *Globalisierte Nahrungskrisen: Bruchzone Kairo*. Bielefeld: Transcript.
Gertel, J. 2011. 'Konflikte um Weideland: Zwischen Aneignung und Enteignung'. *Geographische Rundschau* 63 (7–8), 4–11.
Gertel, J., Le Heron, R. (eds) 2011. *Economic Spaces of Pastoral Production and Commodity Systems: Markets and Livelihoods*. Farnham and Burlington VT: Ashgate.
Geschiere, P. 2009. *The Perils of Belonging: Autochthony, Citizenship, and Exclusion in Africa and Europe*. Chicago IL: University of Chicago Press.
Gibson-Graham, J. K. 2006. *The End of Capitalism (As We Knew It): A Feminist Critique of Political Economy*. Minneapolis MN and London: University of Minnesota Press.
Gibson-Graham. J. K. 2008. 'Diverse Economies: Performative Practices for "Other Worlds"'. *Progress in Human Geography* 32 (5), 613–632.
Giddens, A. 1981. *A Contemporary Critique of Historical Materialism. Volume 1: Power Property and the State*. London: Macmillan.
Giddens, A. 1990. *The Consequences of Modernity*. Stanford CA: Stanford University Press.
Giordano, M. 2003. 'The Geography of the Commons: The Role of Scale and Space'. *Annals of the Associations of American Geographers* 93 (2), 365–375.
Hagmann, T., Hoehne, M. 2009. 'Failures of the State Failure Debate: Evidence from Somali Territories'. *Journal of International Development* 21(1), 42–57.
Haraway, D.1991. 'Situated Knowledges: The Science Question in Feminism and the Privilege of Partial Perspective". In *Simians, Cyborgs and Women: The Reinvention of Nature*. New York and London: Routledge, 183–202.
Hardin, G. 1968. 'The Tragedy of the Commons'. *Science* 162 (3859), 1243–1248.
Harvey, D. 2005. *A Brief History of Neoliberalism*. New York: Oxford University Press.

Hasan, Y. F. 1973/2005. *The Arabs and the Sudan: From the Seventh to the Early Sixteenth Century*. Khartoum: SUDATeK.

Heynen, N., McCarthy, J., Prudham, S., Robbins, P. (eds) 2007. *Neoliberal Environments: False Promises and Unnatural Consequences*. London: Routledge.

Hilgers, M. 2012. 'The Historicity of the Neoliberal State'. *Social Anthropology* 20 (1), 80–94.

Holt, P. M., Daly, M. W. 2000. *A History of Sudan: From the Coming of Islam to the Present Day*. 5th edition. Harlow: Pearson.

Holt-Giménez, E., Patel, R. (eds) 2009. *Food Rebellions! Crises and the Hunger for Justice*. Cape Town and others: Pambazuka Press.

Howell, J. 1973. 'Politics in the Southern Sudan'. *African Affairs* 72 (287), 163–178.

Ibrahim, F. N. 1984. *Ecological Imbalance in the Republic of the Sudan: With Reference to Desertification in Darfur*. Bayreuth: Druckhaus Bayreuth.

Ille, E., Calkins, S., Rottenburg, R. (forthcoming). 'Introduction: Emergence and Contestation of Orders in the Sudans.' In Ille, E., Calkins, S., Rottenburg, R. (eds), *Emerging Orders in the Sudans*. Bamenda: Langaa.

Johnson, D. H. 1994. 'Deconstruction and Reconstruction in the Economy of Southern Sudan'. In Harir, S., Tvedt, T. (eds), *Short-cut to Decay. The Case of the Sudan*. Uppsala: The Scandinavian Institute of African Studies, 125–142.

Johnson, D. H. 2003. *The Root Causes of Sudan's Civil Wars*. Oxford: James Currey.

Johnson, D. H. 2007. 'Why Abyei Matters. The Breaking Point of Sudan's Peace Agreement?' *African Affairs* 107 (426), 1–19.

Johnson, D. H. 2010. *When Boundaries Become Borders. The Impact of Boundary-Making in Southern Sudan's Frontier Zones*. London and Nairobi: The Rift Valley Institute.

Johnson, D. H. 2011. 'Abyei: Sudan's West Bank'. The Enough Project. 4 April 2011. <www.enoughproject.org/files/abyei_west_bank.pdf>, retrieved 20-05-2012.

Keen, D. 1994. *The Benefits of Famine. A Political Economy of Famine & Relief in Southwestern Sudan, 1983–89*. Oxford: James Currey.

Kerven, C. (ed.) 2003. *Prospects for Pastoralism in Kazakstan and Turkmenistan: From State Farms to Private Flocks*. London and New York: Routledge Curzon.

Kibreab, G. 2002. *State Intervention and the Environment in Sudan, 1889–1989: The Demise of Communal Resource Management*. New York and Lampeter: Edwin Mellen Press.

Komey, G. K. 2010. *Land, Governance, Conflict & the Nuba of Sudan*. Woodbridge: James Currey.

Komey, G. K. 2012. 'Climate Change and Recurring Conflicts: An Interplay Between Nature and Humans'. *New Routes* 17 (2), 34–37.

Krippner, G. 2011. *Capitalizing on Crisis: the Political Origins of the Rise of Finance*. Cambridge, MA and London: Harvard University Press.

Kuba, R, Lentz, C. (eds) 2006. *Land and the Politics of Belonging in West Africa*. Leiden and Boston: Brill.

Large, D., Patey, L. A. (eds) 2011. *Sudan Looks East. China, India & the Politics of Asian Alternatives*. Woodbridge: James Currey,

Latour, B. (trans. Porter C.) 1993. *We Have Never Been Modern*. Cambridge MA: Harvard University Press.

Mamdani, M. 1996. *Citizen and Subject: Contemporary Africa and the Legacy of Late Colonialism*. Princeton NJ: Princeton University Press.

Mamdani, M. 2009. *Saviors and Survivors. Darfur, Politics, and the War on Terror*. New York, London, etc.: Doubleday.

Manger, L., Abd el Ati, H., Harir, S., Krzywinski, K., Veetas, O. (eds) 1996. *Survival on Meagre Resources. Hadendowa Pastoralism in the Red Sea Hills*. Uppsala: Nordiska Afrikainstitutet.

Manger, L. 2008. 'Land, Territoriality and Ethnic Identities in the Nuba Mountains'. In Rottenburg, R. (ed.), *Nomadic-Sedentary Relations and Failing State Institutions in Darfur and Kordofan (Sudan)*. Mitteilungen des SFB "Differenz und Integration" 12. Orientwissenschaftliche Hefte 26/2008, Martin-Luther-Universität Halle-Wittenberg, 71–99.

Massey, D. B. 1999. 'Power Geometries and the Politics of Space-Time' (Hettner Lecture 1998). Heidelberg: Department of Geography, Heidelberg University.

Massey, D. B. 2005. *For Space*. London: Sage.

Matondi, P. B., Havnevik, K., Beyene, A. (eds) 2011. *Biofuels, Land Grabbing and Food Security in Africa*. London: Zed Books.

McMichael, P. 2013. 'Land Grabbing as Security Mercantilism in International Relations'. *Globalizations* 10 (1), 47–64.

Migdal, J. 1994. 'State in Society: An Approach to Struggles for Domination'. In Migdal, J. S., Kohli, A., Shue, V. (eds), *State Power and Social Forces: Domination and Transformation in the Third World*. Cambridge and New York: Cambridge University Press, 7–34.

Miller, C. 2005. 'Power, Land and Ethnicity in the Kassala-Gedaref States: An Introduction'. In Miller, C. (ed.), *Land, Ethnicity and Political Legitimacy in Eastern Sudan*. Cairo: CEDEJ, 3–58.

Moore, S. F. 1998. 'Changing African Land Tenure: Reflections on the Incapacities of the State'. *European Journal of Development Research* 10 (2), 33–49.

Mosley, Jason 2012. 'Peace, Bread and Land: Agricultural Investments in Ethiopia and the Sudans'. Chatham House briefing paper 2012/01.

November, V., Camacho-Hübner, E., Latour, B. 2010. 'Entering a Risky Territory: Space in the Age of Digital Navigation'. Environment and Planning D: Society and Space 28 (4), 581–599.

O'Brien, Jay 1986. 'Toward a Reconstitution of Ethnicity: Capitalist Expansion and Cultural Dynamics in Sudan'. *American Anthropologist* 88 (4), 898–907.

Ostrom, E. 1990. *Governing the Commons: The Evolution of Institutions for Collective Action*. Cambridge: Cambridge University Press.

Pantuliano, Sara (ed.) 2009. *Uncharted Territory: Land, Conflict and Humanitarian Action*. Rugby: Practical Action.

Peck, J., Theodore, N. 2012. 'Reanimating Neoliberalism: Process Geographies of Neoliberalism'. *Social Anthropology* 20 (2), 177–185.

Peet, R., Watts, M. J. (eds) 1996. *Liberation Ecologies*. London: Routledge.

Peet, R., Robbins, P., Watts, M. J. (eds) 2011. *Global Political Ecology*. Abingdon: Routledge.

Rose, C. M. 1994. *Property and Persuasion: Essays on the History, Theory, and Rhetoric of Ownership*. Boulder CO: Westview Press.

Rotberg, R. I. (ed.) 2003. *When States Fail: Causes and Consequences*. Princeton NJ: Princeton University Press.

Rotberg, R. I. 2004. 'Strengthening Governance: Ranking States Would Help'. *Washington Quarterly* 28 (1), 71–81.

Rottenburg, R. 1991. *Ndemwareng: Wirtschaft und gesellschaft in den Morobergen*. München: Trickster.

Rottenburg, R. 2008. 'Introduction'. In Rottenburg, R. (ed.), *Nomadic-Sedentary Relations and Failing State Institutions in Darfur and Kordofan (Sudan)*. Mitteilungen des SFB "Differenz und Integration" 12, *Orientwissenschaftliche Hefte* 26/2008, Martin-Luther-Universität Halle-Wittenberg, VII-IX.

Rottenburg, R. 2009a. 'Social and Public Experiments and New Figurations of Science and Politics in Postcolonial Africa'. *Postcolonial Studies* 12 (4), 423–440.

Rottenburg, R. (Trans. Brown, A., Lampert, T.) 2009b. *Far-Fetched Facts: A Parable of Development Aid*. Cambridge MA: MIT Press.

Rottenburg, R., Komey, G. K., Ille, E. 2011. 'The Genesis of Recurring Wars in Sudan: Rethinking the Violent Conflicts in the Nuba Mountains / South Kordofan'. Working Paper, University of Halle, October 2011. Halle.

Salih, M. A. 1993. 'Pastoralists and the War in Southern Sudan: The Ngok Dinka/ Humr Conflict in South Kordofan'. In Markakis, J. (ed.), *Conflict and the Decline of Pastoralism in the Horn of Africa*. Basingstoke: Macmillan, 17–29.

Sassen, S. 2006. *Territory, Authority, Rights: From Medieval to Global Assemblages*. Princeton NJ: Princeton University Press.

Sassen, S. 2013. 'Land Grabs Today: Feeding the Disassembling of National Territory'. *Globalizations* 10 (1), 25–46.

Schlee, G. (forthcoming). 'Competing forms of land use and incompatible identifications of who is to benefit from policies in the South of the North: Pastoralists, agro-industry and farmers in the Blue Nile region.' In Ille, E., Calkins, S., Rottenburg, R. (eds), *Emerging Orders in the Sudans*. Bamenda: Langaa.

Schlichte, K. (ed.) 2005. *The Dynamics of States: The Formation and Crises of State Domination*. Aldershot and Burlington VT: Ashgate.

Scott, J. C. 1998. *Seeing Like a State: How Certain Schemes to Improve the Human Condition Have Failed*. New Haven CT and London: Yale University Press.

Sen, A. 2009. *The Idea of Justice*. Cambridge MA: Harvard University Press.

Sharkey, H. J. 2008. 'Arab Identity and Ideology in Sudan: The Politics of Language, Ethnicity, and Race'. *African Affairs* 107 (426), 21–43.

Sharkey, H., Vezzadini, E., Seri-Hersch, I. (forthcoming). Draft introduction to a journal special issue on 'Rethinking Sudan Studies after the Independence of the South'.

Simone, A. M. 1994. *In Whose Image? Political Islam and Urban Practices in Sudan*. Chicago IL: University of Chicago Press.

Shiva, V. 1997. *Biopiracy. The Plunder of Nature and Knowledge*. Cambridge MA: South End Press.

Tetzlaff, R., Wohlmuth, K. (eds) 1980. *Der Sudan: Probleme und Perspektiven der Entwicklung eines weltmarktabhängigen Agrarstaates*. Frankfurt: Metzner.

Spivak, G. C. 1988 'Can the Subaltern Speak?' In Nelson, C., Grossberg, L. (eds), *Marxism and the Interpretation of Culture*. Urbana IL: University of Illinois Press.

Thévenot, L. 1984. 'Rules and Implements: Investment in Forms'. *Social Science Information* 23 (1), 1–45.

Turner, B., Wiber, M. 2009. 'Paradoxical Conjunctions: Rural Property and Access to Rural Resources in a Transnational Environment'. *Anthropologica* 51 (1), 3–14.

United Nations (UN). 2012. 'Sudan' and 'South Sudan'. <www.un.org / depts / Cartographic / english / htmain.htm>, retrieved 25-06-2013.

United Nations Environment Programme (UNEP) 2007. 'Sudan: Post-conflict Environmental Assessment'. Khartoum, Sudan.

Urry, J. 2000. *Sociology Beyond Societies: Mobilities for the Twenty-First Century*. London: Routledge.

Urry, J. 2007. *Mobilities*. Cambridge: Polity Press.

Van der Walle, N. 2001. *African Economies and the Politics of Permanent Crisis, 1979–1999*. Cambridge and New York: Cambridge University Press.

Verhoeven, H. 2011. '"Dams are Development": China, The Al-Ingaz Regime & the Political Economy of the Sudanese Nile'. In Large, D., Patey, L. A. (eds), *Sudan Looks East: China, India & the Politics of Asian Alternatives*. Woodbridge: James Currey, 120–138.

Verhoeven, H. 2012. 'Sudan and its Agricultural Revival: A Regional Breadbasket at Last or Another Mirage in the Desert?' In Allan, J., Keulertz, M., Sojamo, S., Warner, J. (eds), *Handbook of Land and Water Grabs in Africa: Foreign Direct Investment and Food and Water Security*. London and New York: Routledge, 132–166.

Wacquant, L. 2012. 'Three Steps to a Historical Anthropology of Actually Existing Neoliberalism'. *Social Anthropology* 20 (1), 66–79.

Wade, R. H. 2003. 'What Strategies are Viable for Developing Countries Today? The World Trade Organization and the Shrinking of "Development Space"'. *Review of International Political Economy* 10 (4), 621–644.

Wallerstein, I. 1974. *The Modern World System. Capitalist Agriculture and the Origins of the European World Economy in the Sixteenth Century*. New York: Academic Press.

Watts, M. J. 1994. 'Development II: The Privatization of Everything?' *Progress in Human Geography* 18 (3), 371–384.

Watts, M. J. 2004. 'Resource Curse? Governmentality, Oil and Power in the Niger Delta, Nigeria'. *Geopolitics* 9 (1), 50–80.

Woertz, E. 2011. 'Arab Food, Water, and the Big Landgrab that Wasn't'. *Brown Journal of World Affairs* 18 (1), 119–132.

Zenker, O. 2011. 'Autochthony, Ethnicity, Indigeneity and Nationalism: Time-Honouring and State-Oriented Modes of Rooting Individual-Territory-Group Triads in a Globalizing World'. *Critique of Anthropology* 31 (1), 63–81.

ENDNOTES

1. The use of the term 'tribe' does not suggest that we believe in a stable, clearly delineated unit based on agnatic descent that exists 'out there'. Anthropological scholarship has long indicated that tribes or ethnic groups are based on ascriptive practices, which people use to identify and to draw boundaries between self and others. Tribe merely figures as an English equivalent to the vernacular Arabic *qabīla*, which denotes a level of social organization among rural people. For more on the Mahdiya, see Holt & Daly (2000: 73–99).

2. The failed states index in 2013 placed Sudan at rank three of 178 countries, only Somalia and Congo score worse (http://ffp.statesindex.org). For a critical debate of the state failure, see Hagmann and Hoehne (2009) or Fischer and Schmelzle (2009).

3. Sassen notes that 'old capabilities are critical in the constituting of the new order, but that does not mean that their valence is the same', and says that when capabilities 'jump tracks, they are in part constitutive and at the same time can veil the switch' (Sassen 2006: 8).

4. At times the situation in Sudan has been characterized, for example, in terms of 'ecological imbalance' (Ibrahim 1984), 'decade of despair' (Burr & Collins 1995), 'famine that kills' (de Waal 1989), 'inadequacy of relief' (Keen 1994) and 'economy of war' (Elnur 2009) to name but a few positions.

5. From early debates within political ecology, 'liberation ecology' (Peet & Watts 1996) emerged, focusing on the development discourse (Escobar 1995, Rottenburg 2009b) and juxtaposing local knowledge, resistance and environmental movements within an accelerating neoliberal policy. Now, the transfer of power from states to markets unleashed deregulation and 'the privatisation of everything' (Watts 1994) was in question. Since, a bundle of topics relating to the articulations between nature and society and focusing on property rights have been discussed, such as the new enclosures and the destruction of the (global) commons (Buck 1998, Heynen et al. 2007), the role of WTO empowered TRIPs (trade related intellectual property rights) and of biopiracy in disenfranchising peasants and poor nations (Shiva 1997, Wade 2003), and also the impact of transgenes, cyborgs and technoscience as exclusive corporate knowledge systems (Haraway 1991), and lately of buyer-driven audit economies that are responsible for realigning producer-consumer relations within the global political ecology (cf. Peet et al. 2011).

6. Following Bijker et al. (1987), technology is understood in a broad way, encompassing, for instance, small tools and devices, like hammers or mobile phones, techniques and reproducible procedures, such as herding practices or ways of extracting gold, and complex infrastructures, such as telecommunication systems. Whereas Bijker et al. focus strongly on material 'hard' technologies, we apply a broader understanding of technologies, including in a Foucaultian reading methods of governance, such as laws or classifications, technologies of representation and 'technologies of the self' (see Rottenburg 2009b, Foucault 1988).

7. This argument concerning the importance of land rights to conflicts was also made in the volume *Uncharted Territory: Land, Conflict and Humanitarian Action*, edited by Sara Pantuliano (2009). The volume assembles case studies from different parts of the world, allowing a comparative perspective on countries like Sudan, Angola and Colombia, and addresses specifically the practical challenges of humanitarian responses in dealing with intricate land questions in conflict settings.

2

Agricultural Investment through Land Grabbing in Sudan

SIDDIG UMBADDA

This chapter traces different phases of land appropriation in Sudan and highlights the enormous amount of land that has been reallocated since colonial times (1898–1956). Furthermore, it discusses the legal instruments used for this 'land grab' and the rationale explicitly put forward for such actions. Despite the strategy of developing the agricultural sector to spearhead the country's overall development, outcomes have been modest and, as I will suggest, the rural poor shouldered its costs disproportionately. National governments, nonetheless, pursuing development but also eager to satisfy their own need for foreign currency, have continued to foster large-scale investments in mechanized agriculture, irrespective of the risks associated with foreign investment in agriculture. This chapter will suggest that the current government (since 1989) has been unable to protect investors' rights and to enforce contracts on the ground, as is evidenced by the low implementation rate of projects. Therefore, it is proposed that it is pursuing extractive rather than developmental policies. The government's dire need for resources to finance the on-going civil war, and the greed of some of its top officials may have blinded it from seeing the necessity of addressing some major challenges, such as good governance, which are impairing both the success of foreign investment and rural populations' livelihood opportunities.

BACKGROUND: GLOBAL PRICE HIKES, CRISES AND THE NEW DEMAND FOR LAND

Several colluding factors have led to the phenomenon often referred to as global land grabbing. I will here concentrate on three intertwined drivers of this new dynamic in commercial demand – rising fuel prices, speculation on agricultural commodities futures, and the recent food crisis (2006–08) (Anseeuw et al. 2012b). First, in the early 2000s, oil prices rose sharply, boosting the global development of alternative energy sources. For instance, US President George Bush offered huge financial incentives to farmers in the Midwest to turn their maize into biofuel (ethanol). Simultaneously, the European Union (EU) encouraged companies in its member states to find land for the production of biofuel. It is estimated that this type of investment constituted 75 per cent of new agricultural investments of EU companies abroad (Palmer 2010). Second, in the financial crisis of 2007/8 big businesses and corporate managers sought new opportunities to make profits; managers of huge private equity funds at that time managed more than 2.5 trillion dollars (Merian Research & CRBM 2010: 3). Based on predictions of increased future pressures on food and energy (Anseeuw et al. 2012b: viii) and encouraged by already sharp rises in both fuel and food grain prices, they turned to investment in and speculation on agricultural commodities and energy crops. Thus, international financial capital became another major driver in the current process of commoditization of land. Third, between 2006 and 2008 food prices skyrocketed: the prices for major food items rose by 78 per cent, whereas the prices of some crops and vegetable oils more than doubled (FAO 2009). A number of grain exporting countries responded to these dramatic price hikes by banning food exports. Suddenly, many rich countries, like the Gulf States, became aware that their large foreign exchange reserves were not in themselves a guarantee of food security. Furthermore, densely populated countries, like China, India and South Korea, also started to outsource food production to feed their growing populations. Consequently, many countries and private companies started the search for suitable land to grow food and other crops for biofuel production. These explorations focused mainly on Latin America and Africa, in particular countries with abundant land and water resources, such as Sudan.

In Sudan, the stripping of rural populations of their land dates back to colonial times (1898–1956). The driving forces of these land appropriations, however, have differed over time. Thus, while the colonial administration confiscated land to serve British interests, Sudanese national governments justified expropriating rural populations of their land overtly by reference to development plans for the good of the country. More recently, the need for foreign currency and alternative income sources, following the loss of oil revenues to South Sudan, certainly combines with the above-mentioned global dynamics, leading to a new wave of large-scale commercialization of land rights in Sudan. Rural people are adversely affected by these foreign investments and are struggling for recognition of communal rights to land.

In the following sections, I will discuss legal instruments for the appropriation of land in the colonial and national governments, a historical overview of the amount of land expropriated from communal land owners and the groups that have been affected most severely, the performance of the agricultural sub-sectors that expanded on the new commercial farms, the capacity of Sudan Government to seize opportunities with few risks, and finally some concluding remarks.

APPROPRIATING LAND: CUSTOMARY RIGHTS AND LEGISLATION

The conversion of communally-owned land into government property began immediately after the British re-conquered Sudan in 1898. The new administration used the so-called 'right of discovery' as a principle to maximize the benefits of the colonial centre at the cost of the colonized. According to Alden Wily (2010:8) it is 'a founding principle of European feudal tenure whereby the sovereign claimed not only political jurisdiction but also rooted ownership of land within the territory. It must be remembered that civilization was not the real goal of colonized occupation; the raison d'être for staging colonial wars was to exploit the resources of the occupied territory.

Land was confiscated, but this step was institutionalized and legitimized by legislation. A number of ordinances and legal acts were issued by the colonial administration. The first of these ordinances, the Titles to Land Ordinance,[1] was drawn up in early 1899. With this the administration started to register land on the banks of the River Nile. Importantly, only the riverine land that was continuously cultivated was registered as privately owned land, excluding rain-fed and pasture areas which were largely under communal ownership. Significantly, the ordinance classified communally held land as government land. An important consequence of this was that the customary usufruct rights associated with communal ownership were not recognized as legal entitlements to land and could therefore be withdrawn by the government. A number of ordinances and declarations then followed,[2] all of which were tailored to satisfy government needs to acquire additional land. The most important of these acts are (Egemi 2006, WB 2010):

- The 1920 Declaration on the Gash: this transferred land rights to the fertile Tokar and Gash Delta in Eastern Sudan to the colonial government to facilitate cotton growing.[3]
- The Land Settlement and Registration Act of 1925: this supplemented the Titles to Land Ordinance. It recognized communal land ownership as the de facto ownership in its ability to set principles for land usage, but only within the framework of government ownership. Thus it did not reduce the vulnerability of communal rights to withdrawal by government.[4]
- The Gezira Land Ordinance (1921) (repealed by the Gezira Land Act of 1927): this set the basic principles for land acquisition, which, according to Gordon (1986), endure to this day. This ordinance endowed the government with the right to expropriate communal land (notwithstanding that it made provisions for compensation of land owners). The rights to land in the Gezira, between the White and Blue Niles in central Sudan, were first settled and registered. Land was then compulsorily rented from its registered owners, at the on-going rate of fallow land, which was very low (MacMichael 1954: 198) and then acquired by government,[5] paving the way for the British company, Sudan Plantation Syndicate, which received the concession to grow cotton in the Gezira.
- The Land Acquisition Ordinance (1930) gave the government the right to expropriate tribal land that is required permanently or temporarily for public use, but only after adequate compensation based

> on the 'actual use of land', which again excludes usufruct rights, based on intermittent use, which is the norm. Moreover, a so-called expropriation officer or a committee of arbitration decides upon compensation without consultation with users.[6]

Equipped with these instruments, the colonial administrators dispossessed rural communities of more than half a million hectares of communally owned land and made them available to other users, often foreign investors.[7] However, the colonial system, overall, recognized by law, tribal or communal land (Bell 1930: 1, Bolton 1954: 188), and had in place a strict policy of compensation in kind (land) or cash (irrespective of its fairness) (Bolton 1954: 193, MacMichael 1954: 198, Komey 2010a: 350, 351).

After Sudan gained its independence in 1956, the practice of land expropriation continued. National governments, in line with their economic development plans, passed legislation to appropriate land for agricultural investment. This time the goal was quick economic development spearheaded by investment in the agricultural sector. This was then an acceptable theory of development advanced by both academics and international financial institutions. It rests on the necessity to develop the sector which produces commodities in which the country has comparative advantage. Nearly all less-developed countries believed that was the only way to catch up with advanced nations, given their lack of capital and technology, and low educational attainment.

In 1970 the Nimeiri regime (1969–85) issued the Unregistered Land Act (ULA). The act placed all land that is not privately registered under the government's control and denied the legitimacy of customary property rights. The ULA converted into government land 99 per cent of the Sudanese territory, then 596.6 million feddans, 250.6 million hectares or 619.3 million acres (1 feddan equals 0.42 ha and 1.038 acres) (Gordon 1986). The ULA further enabled the government to evict customary owners by force, if necessary. With this legal reform, customary owners were suddenly converted into tenants or squatters on what they considered their own land. In addition, public interest was not clearly defined and thus the criteria of confiscation also remained unclear. The ULA, given its strong bias against communal land owners, was far worse in its territorial consequences than colonial legislation. Unlike the various colonial Land Ordinances, it included unregistered but 'occupied' land, enabling the government to appropriate land from individuals and communities without compensation (Komey 2010b: 66, 67).

The Law of Criminal Trespass of 1974 and the Sudan Penal Code of 1974 were two additional instruments that restricted pastoralists' and small farmers' access rights to schemes, even when they were demarcated upon 'their' land. Crossing the demarcation would be considered a criminal trespass.[8]

In 1984, with the Islamization of the Nimeiri regime, another act came into effect, the Civil Transaction Act (CTA), which replaced the ULA but maintained and strengthened its prescriptions on land ownership.

It further stipulated that while 'land belongs to God' the state is responsible for its usage and control (Gordon 1986). This act also conferred the right to grant private persons usufruct rights upon the central and regional authorities. The last privilege, however, was reversed with an amendment of the Regional Government Act of 1985, which restricted this right to the central government alone (Gordon 1986: 173). This resulted in widespread confusion regarding which authority can grant land rights, a confusion that continues today. Many people no longer saw any 'relationship between formal legislation on land rights and what [was] actually taking place on the ground'.[9]

The CTA was amended in 1990. The amendment invalidated customary titles to land. Furthermore, it decreed the closure of court cases dealing with land, in which the government's decisions on allocation were questioned (Egemi 2006, MOA 2009).[10] Then in November 2011, in a move to protect foreign investors, Sudanese national newspapers reported that the presidential adviser for investment announced that government had decreed fundamental amendments to the 1999 investment act, including a provision to prohibit nationals from taking foreign investors to court.[11]

The Comprehensive Peace Agreement (CPA) of 2005, which ended the long civil war in Sudan, stipulated that a National Land Commission (NLC) be established. The provision was later included (Article 187) in the Interim National Constitution (INC) that followed. The main function of the NLC, an independent body, would be to arbitrate between conflicting parties in claims over land and also to review current laws governing land (El Tahir 2006). The act constituting the NLC was passed by the legislative bodies, but the commission is yet to be established. Therefore, it appears that it is not a priority, because the ULA and its successor the CTA are widely opposed by land owners on the ground, and government may not be interested in boosting that opposition by an independent body, which may propose major amendments to those laws.[12]

The legislation on land tenure in Sudan has severely affected rural populations. A common feature of the different acts passed over the years, especially since 1970, has been the discrimination against communal land owners, mainly small farmers and pastoralists. Legislation has consistently paid little or no respect to communal land rights, an attitude that is also displayed by government officials. In fact, government officials today (mid-2012) still advertise the availability of millions of feddans of land for agricultural investment, treating it as an uninhabited, unused and unclaimed resource.[13]

HISTORY AND EXTENT OF LAND DISPOSSESSIONS

Sudan has a vast amount of arable land. The figure of 200 million feddans (207.6 million acres or 84 million hectares) appears in many historical and more recent estimations, but only 20 per cent of this is said to be under cultivation. Sudan lost an estimated 28 million hectares

(69.2 million acres) of arable land to South Sudan in 2011, thus the figure was adjusted to 56 million hectares (138.4 million acres). Two types of agriculture have expanded in Sudan's history of land appropriation, irrigated farming, and semi-mechanized rain-fed farming – generally referred to as mechanized farming (MF). These two agricultural technologies constitute commercial agriculture in Sudan and are qualified as 'modern'. The expansion of these technologies was a predicament for hundreds of thousands of rural poor, mainly small farmers and pastoralists, who have lost their land over the years (IFAD 2008, 2010).

Irrigated farming, started vigorously with the Gezira Scheme in the 1920s and 1930s (0.45 million ha, 1.1 million acres), which later expanded, through its extension of Managil, Rahad, and New Halfa projects, to 0.84 million ha (2.08 million acres) in the 1970s. In addition, further land grabbing took place with the establishment of sugar schemes in the 1970s – Elginaid, Asalaya, West Sennar, Kenana, and lately the White Nile Sugar (2002–12). All in all, the area under irrigated agriculture is said to amount to nearly 1.8 million ha or 4.4 million acres (MOA 2008).

Mechanized farming, on the other hand, was first introduced in the 1940s in the central clay plains of Sudan, mainly in the Gedaref area. It was meant to secure the sorghum supply, the main staple food, for the British army fighting the Italians at the borders to Ethiopia towards the end of the Second World War. The area under semi-mechanized farming quickly expanded from 1,550 hectares (3830 acres) in 1948 to 0.84 million hectares (2.08 million acres) in the early 1970s, and to 7.3 million ha (18 million acres) in 2001 (Egemi 2006, El Karouri 2010).[14] A much higher figure (13.3 million ha or 32.9 million acres in 2003) was reported by an ex-director of the Mechanized Farming Corporation (MFC), a government body that has overseen the sector since 1968 (Seirab 2007: 28).[15] The most recent estimate by the Sudan Farmers Union gives a lower figure for 2011 – namely 10.1 million hectares (25 million acres).[16] Albeit these are merely estimates, if we take the more conservative figure from 2011, this still would be an increase of 1,200 per cent compared to 1970/71.

Areas under mechanized farming expanded rapidly from Gedaref, to Kassala, Blue Nile, Sennar, Upper Nile, White Nile and South Kordofan states. Later this kind of cultivation was even started in North Kordofan, a poor savannah area with a very fragile environment, suitable only for traditional shifting cultivation and camel herding. This rapid proliferation entailed both legal leasehold agreements with investors and unplanned (illegal) encroachments on grazing land, but other factors also had a bearing on this development. According to Seirab (2007), after the MFC was dissolved in 1992, its responsibilities were taken over by the General Authority of Investment (GAI), a newly established but influential body, politically connected to the then new Bashir Government (1989–present). The GAI then granted millions of feddans, including in marginal and unsuitable areas, to investors with varying sincerity toward engaging in farming. The areas allocated in the few years of the

GAI were more than the MFC planned and demarcated from its founding in 1968 until its dissolution in 1992 (Seirab 2008:70–71).

Successive national governments after independence (1956) viewed mechanized farming as a main driving force of agricultural development. The progressive expansion of irrigated and semi-mechanized rain-fed farming was therefore largely state driven. The Ten Year Development Plan (1960/61–70/71) proposed to increase the land under semi-mechanized cultivation by around 1.2 million hectares annually. In turn, the Six Year Plan (1977/78–82/83) directed 88 per cent of investment in agriculture to the 'modern' sector. The Food Investment Strategy of 1977 and the Arab Fund's Basic Programme for Agricultural Development (1976–85) also targeted development through 'modern' agriculture. The latter conceived of Sudan as the breadbasket of the Arab countries and envisaged quadrupling the irrigated and semi-mechanized rain-fed areas under cultivation by the end of the period (ILO 1987). Subsequent development plans and programmes to this very day continue to promote mechanized farming.

Agricultural development plans during the 1980s were supported financially by such international institutions and organizations as the World Bank (WB) ($1.5 billion), the African Development Bank ($350 million) and the Islamic Development Bank ($162 million), among others. For instance, nearly half of the WB loans ($744 million) were used to finance projects in the agricultural sector. The WB loans financed expansions of nearly the entire irrigated sub-sector and 1.68 million hectares of mechanized farming projects in five states (Elzubeir 2009: 113–114). Only the International Labour Organization (ILO), observing the social and environmental costs of MF, recommended that its expansion should be stopped (ILO 1987: 67).

The state-owned Agricultural Bank of Sudan also strongly supported mechanized farming by providing credit to investors below the market rates. Furthermore, investors were granted land at a nominal rent and were allowed to import agricultural machinery at subsidized foreign exchange rates. These initiatives turned mechanized farming into a highly lucrative business and led not only to the mushrooming of new schemes, but also to illegal appropriation of land by influential domestic investors. UNEP (2002) reports that in Gedaref area almost 66 per cent of the 2.6 million hectares under semi-mechanized farming in 1997 were not demarcated (i.e. illegal). In Habila, South Kordofan in 1985 the ratio was 45 per cent (UNEP 2002: 6). Another source indicates that 54 per cent of the total area under mechanized farming in Sudan in 2003 is said to have been illegally appropriated (Seirab 2007: 28). The United Nations Environment Programme (UNEP) notes that 'mechanized farming in Sudan has in effect degenerated into a crude form of extensive shifting cultivation with a tractor, exploiting land to exhaustion' (UNEP 2007: 167).

It should be noted that not all land was appropriated for foreign investors. Most MF schemes were developed by domestic investors. A WB Report found that 78 per cent of the 3.97 million hectares allocated to 132 projects approved during the period 2004–08, were allotted to

Table 2.1 Recent International Land Grabbing in Sudan, 2011

Country	Area (ha)	Location	Type of contract	Period
Syria	30,000	Unknown	Gov-to-gov	50 year lease
China	100,000	Gezira Scheme	Private investors	Unknown
South Korea	700,000	Unknown	Unknown	Unknown
UAE	400,000	Unknown	Unknown	Unknown
Egypt	400,000	Unknown	Unknown	Unknown
Saudi Arabia	60,000	Nile State	Private (Al-Rajh Group)	40 year lease
USA	400,000	South Sudan	Jarch Management Group, Ltd.	Unspecified lease
Morocco	Unknown	White Nile	Private investor	Unknown
Jordan	170,000	Nile State	Gov-to-gov	Unknown
Total	2,260,000			Source: Babikir 2011:3

domestic investors (Deininger et al. 2010: xiv). However, irrespective of who appropriated the land, the effects upon rural populations were largely the same. It was hardly any consolation to the dispossessed that their land went to domestic investors. Rather, it could be read in terms of an increasing inequality and social differentiation in rural Sudan.

More recently, one of the more important and more extreme drivers of land expropriation in Sudan was oil exploration. As nearly all oil fields are located in what is now South Sudan, the area, as a civil war zone, witnessed the forced displacement of resident populations from their land, leading to serious human rights violations and the loss of means of livelihood (Rone 2003). Furthermore, nomadic migratory routes were severed and water sources polluted, severely disrupting the life of nomadic pastoralists. Although compensation was agreed upon following the signing of the CPA, the trickle down of earmarked funds to local communities was minimal.[17]

As regards recent land appropriation, particularly for foreign investors, it is difficult to know the true extent as the details of land deals are not made public. Babiker (2011), for instance, reports that 2.26 million hectares were leased to foreign investors (see Table 2.1). A year earlier, the Global Land Project estimated that 3.2–4.9 million hectares were contracted for investment (Friis & Reenberg 2010). Similar figures also appeared in GRAIN (2012).

All the above figures, however, could be an underestimation of the amount of land contracted to foreigners. As recently as March and April 2012 it was revealed that government granted 116,000 ha (286,642 acres) to a Qatari company, 168,000 ha (415,137 acres) to a Korean company and 840,000 ha (2.08 million acres) each to Egypt and Saudi Arabia, totalling nearly 2 million hectares (around 4.86 million acres).[18] The land granted to Saudi investors is said to be a freehold (literally a land enclave within Sudan belonging to Saudi Arabia). This particular deal drew angry comments from both the public and newspaper commentators,[19] who pointed out that it is unconstitutional and contradicts even the government's own investment act of 1999, which stipulates that no land should be granted before approval of the feasibility study of the project. Others pointed out that the deal sets a hazardous precedent and that henceforth all investors will demand freehold land rather than a long-term lease. Regarding the above-mentioned land deal, it is worth noting that not a single government official has volunteered to comment on or spell out the actual terms of the deal, despite very specific queries – as though the land taken and allocated to foreigners was private property.

LAND DISPOSSESSION: IMPACTS ON RURAL POPULATIONS

The lands that the government appropriated through its legal instruments are not idle or free, even if they are not in continuous use. Rather, groups of people whose life styles and livelihood depend upon its intermittent use hold claims to this land (Runger 1987). As observed by UNEP, 'land taken by mechanized schemes was generally not vacant. Instead it supported either pastoralism, traditional shifting rainfed agriculture or wild habitats, principally open woodlands and treed plains' (UNEP 2007: 167). Such communal land is owned by rural small farmers and pastoralists.

Nomadic pastoralists are among the most marginalized populations and have little access to state institutions (UNICEF 2008). Still, they are a significant group in rural Sudan (Nuha & Abdel Rahman 2010). The population census of 2008 estimated their number at nearly 2.8 million, roughly 7 per cent of the population, down from nearly 12 per cent in 1983. Furthermore, the census indicated that 35 per cent of the nomadic population likewise engages in small farming, mostly on rain-fed land. The economic activities of small farmers, agro-pastoralists and nomadic pastoralists are based upon usufruct rights to land – rights which by decree were transferred to the government. These rural groups thus are the main losers under the state's land laws which favour mechanized and irrigated farming, and this has been true since the turn of the twentieth century. In fact, it is not only their land that has been grabbed but also their political voice.[20]

These groups were severely affected by such land grabs leading to a quickening and more dynamic pace of disenfranchisement in rural areas. As a consequence, people were alienated from their land, having to abandon small-holder traditional farming to work as seasonal labourers in semi-mechanized farms upon the very land that they had previously farmed on their own account and for their own subsistence, or they were forced to engage in casual labour in an alien and at times hostile urban environment. Sometimes villagers were completely bereft of their land. In Gedaref State in Eastern Sudan, WB (2010) reports that

3,750 families (90.5 per cent) in the area of Umsainat-Samsam were left landless after 'their' land was parcelled and redistributed as land for investors in commercial schemes. Later on, the villages of Um-Maleeha, Tamra, Saraf Saeed, Alam, Daneekola, Babikery and Dokah also lost their land completely (WB 2010:14). It is worth noting that World Bank Group loans (1973–80) financed MF expansion in Umsainat 113,000 ha (279,229 acres), Samsam 85,000 ha (210,039 acres) – in Gedaref area, and also 630,000 ha (1.557 million acres) in Habila – in S Kordofan (Seirab 2007: 52).

This predicament was shared by pastoralists. Nomadic groups affected include both 'Abbala' (camel herders) and 'Baggara' (cattle herders). Some of the Abbala groups encroached upon by large-scale agricultural projects are Rashaida and Shukriyya in Kassala and Gedaref States, Shanabla in North Kordofan State,[21] and Rufaᶜa al-Hoi in Blue Nile State. Affected Baggara are found in South Kordofan State (Hawazma and Missiriyya), Blue Nile, Sennar and Gedaref States (Fellata), and White Nile State (Musallamiyya, Kenana). The expansion of mechanized schemes has also been a primary cause of diminishing natural pastures for nomads. In the Butana area in Eastern Sudan, near Gedaref, camel owners had to purchase failed crops or crop residues to feed their herds during the dry season (Babiker 2011: 5). Previously this fodder was free of charge for nomadic pastoralists migrating to their summer grazing grounds.[22]

Blocked or restricted livestock routes together with the overgrazing of remaining pastures have led to an overall decline of herd sizes. Some nomads have even lost their animal wealth altogether and have turned to other economic options, like small farming, salaried herding, seasonal agriculture or charcoal production. In fact many nomads from the Butana area have abandoned pastoralism as a means of livelihood. The same process can also be seen in Eastern Sudan among the Beja, where many have abandoned pastoralism in order to seek work in Port Sudan and elsewhere.

THE PERFORMANCE OF MODERN AGRICULTURE

Irrigated agriculture was the backbone of the Sudanese economy until the discovery of oil in the 1990s. Its contribution encompassed employment, exports, government revenue, provision of raw materials to industry and the like. Although its contribution to GDP (Gross Domestic Product) was around 12 per cent, its share in exports was on average around 50 per cent before the dawn of the oil exports in the 1990s. By 2008 it had declined to 4 per cent, as a result of neglect.

Mechanized farming contributed substantially to food security through its sorghum production (on average 50 per cent of the total production) and between 40 and 74 per cent of sesame production, an important cash crop for export (Seirab 2007: 9). However, its average contribution to GDP amounted to only 2 per cent. According to some estimates, the sector also accounts for around 50,000 permanent jobs and between one and 1.3 million seasonal labourers during a good cropping season (Seirab 2007, MOA 2009).

Still, the mechanized rain-fed sector, which swallowed most of the appropriated land, did not live up to expectations. First, the productivity of land in the MF schemes was in general very low and not much different from that under traditional cropping methods. Low productivity of semi-mechanized farming, however, seems to be the norm in many African countries, where none of the countries currently attracting investors achieved more than 25 per cent of potential yields (Deininger et al.: xiii). Still, the average yield of sorghum in the past ten years was about 348kg/ha (310 lb/acre), a very low figure when compared with about 1,190kg/ha (1,062 lb/acre) in West Africa and 4,400kg/ha (3,926 lb/acre) in the USA (MOA 2009: 25). This may indicate that the technology employed is outdated and of low quality, or that farmers are reluctant to invest in better appliances in order to minimize the risks associated with mechanized farming. Furthermore, investment levels per feddan are also extremely low, around 10–15 per cent of the amount invested in other countries.

Second, yields are not only low, but also highly unstable. The average yield per feddan of sorghum during the period 1970–2004 fluctuated greatly due to high rainfall variations (El Karouri 2010: 100–102). But poor management also seems to be a problem, as yield fluctuations could be reduced considerably by good management and improved agricultural practices. Unharvested areas were also highly prevalent. Between 1974 and 2004, the mean unharvested area was 21 per cent for sorghum and 17 per cent for sesame (El Karouri 2010: 95). Reasons for this are: shortage of water, damage caused by birds, locusts, rats and insects, low market prices for the produce and yields that are too low to justify the cost of harvesting.

Third, the huge concessions are characterized by a low utilization of land. For instance, agricultural companies with large land holdings in the Blue Nile and Gedaref states use only small portions of the allotted area, usually no more than 20–30 per cent (MOA 2009: 56). This is corroborated by the 2012 decision in the Blue Nile State to reduce the size of areas allocated to companies and individuals by 20–25 per cent.[23] A sample of investment projects in different states estimates the utilization rates as follows: 44 per cent of the total land in private national projects, 25 per cent in joint ventures and 13 per cent in foreign investments (MOI 2011).[24]

Fourth, appropriated land was mostly allocated to scheme owners from outside the area. In Upper Nile State (now in South Sudan) this amounted to 85 per cent of land allocations, in the Nuba Mountains 73–84 per cent, in the Blue Nile 76 per cent and in Gedaref 64 per cent (Ijaimi 2006: 75). These absentee landlords were found to be mostly merchants from major towns, ex-army officers and retired government officials (Umbadda 1990). This has precipitated resentment and later was one of the causes of insurgent movements. While Mosley contends that 'large scale investment in land is not conflict-neutral' (Mosley 2012: 16), Komey strongly argues that grievances over access to land set the stage for further violence, such as the on-going civil wars in Blue Nile, Nuba Mountains and Darfur (Komey 2010a: 354).

Fifth, due to clearing huge tracts of land, MF has resulted in serious environmental degradation. For instance, it has led to overgrazing in adjacent areas, as a result of encroachment upon pastures and livestock routes. In Gedaref area, in particular, as a result of the quick expansion of semi-mechanized farming, the amount of pasture and forest area dropped from 78.5 per cent in 1941 to only 18 per cent in 1991 (Babiker 2011: 4).

Although the semi-mechanized rain-fed schemes were hardly a success, they invariably exerted strong pressure upon natural grazing areas and often blocked seasonal livestock routes (*masarāt*). This squeezed pastoralists into shrinking pastures and forced them to trespass on farming land.[25] The consequence was the spread of local-level conflicts between farmers and pastoralists, which at times escalated into violence and death. In a survey conducted in Kassala, the White Nile and the Blue Nile States, pastoralists viewed mechanized farming schemes as a main cause of rising conflicts between farmers and pastoralists in their areas (MOA 2009: 33).

Therefore, although agricultural investment in the modern sector from a macroeconomic perspective initially contributed considerably to the GDP, exports and food security, its overall successes are rather limited, especially given the modest performance of both sub-sectors. More important for this assessment is that the rural poor shouldered the downsides of the very limited achievements alone: they systematically lost the right to cultivate their customary lands, their environment was damaged and they often had to change their livelihood systems. In many cases the loss of access to land meant impoverishment, and as conflicts spread, so did the disruption of routines, and insecurity.

RISKS AND OPPORTUNITIES OF AGRICULTURAL INVESTMENT

Investment in the modern agricultural sector has not been particularly successful. Its modest achievements should have alerted governments to revise their development strategies, as ILO missions advised as early as the 1980s (ILO 1987). More importantly, the social costs incurred by small farmers and pastoralists, as a result of expropriation of their land, should have strengthened government resolve to undertake such a move. Instead, successive governments seem to be more interested in extracting financial resources from investors, than in evaluating such a strategy or attending to its negative effects, such as the growing conflicts between investors, farmers and pastoralists. To that end, investments acts were amended to extend additional privileges to investors and to give them more protection. Governments believed, encouraged by international institutions, that the country could maximize returns from its only major and available asset – land – and that the opportunities resulting from foreign investments outweighed the risks.

Recent studies (Arezki et al. 2011, Anseeuw et al. 2012b) found that weak land governance and tenure security for current users are more attractive for investors than the quality of the business climate. Similarly, the World Bank detected a connection between foreign investment interests and countries with weak governance, and then concluded that this 'implies that the risks associated with such investments are immense' (Deininger et al. 2010: 102).

In fact, the terms and conditions under which foreign countries and individual investors acquire leasehold land in Africa, Asia-Pacific and South America led many analysts to label the phenomenon as a form of neo-colonialism (Palmer 2010, Alden Wily 2010). According to the Sudanese press and other sources (Anseeuw et al. 2012b: 43), in some contracts between investors and South Sudan, land leases were offered at prices as low as 4 US cents per feddan or less than 10 cents per hectare (3.85 cents per acre). Other reports (Foreign Investment Advisory Services – FIAS – 2006) mentioned Sudan as an example where the duration of leasehold contracts spanned, in some cases, up to 99 years.

Given the underdeveloped agricultural sector and meagre resources of many African countries, foreign investment presents opportunities for agricultural development. Often the investors' home countries also provide incentives for the overseas investments. The Saudi initiative for agricultural investment overseas (King Abdullah Initiative 2009) is a good example of this. The programme promises certain benefits to host countries that negotiate contracts with Saudi investors: providing sufficient capital for investment, contributing to the development of agriculture and associated services by using up-to-date technology and new agricultural methods, assisting in efforts to alleviate poverty and create employment opportunities, contributing to agricultural exports and the reduction of trade and balance of payments deficits, and supporting infrastructural developments in rural areas. Sudan, especially since the South's secession, is in dire need of foreign capital and such promises of benefits could – if realized – contribute to the overall development of the country. International development institutions such as the World Bank thus suggest that such opportunities should be taken (Deininger et al. 2010). However, similar promises were made as part of the breadbasket-strategy in the 1970s, but the realized benefits were minimal.

To protect itself against accusations of exploiting poor host countries, the Saudi initiative advertises that it envisages investment contracts being transparent and just, duly considering the interests of the host country. That, however, seems to be mere lip service as the latest Saudi deal clearly shows. For contracts to be fair and do justice to the host country, the latter's government must have the institutional capacity and negotiators with integrity, ability and skill to gain the greatest benefits or at least to avoid raw deals with investors. In addition to capable institutions and officials, the country needs to utilize model contracts for investments that have been subjected to wide public discussions and consultations with all stakeholders.

But when the government shrouds its deals with foreign investors in secrecy and shields the contract conditions from public scrutiny and debate, it is only reasonable to expect deals and contracts to be harmful for many stakeholders. Many studies have established that official records on land acquisitions are incomplete or lacking altogether. This hinders assessment of the terms and conditions of contracts. Furthermore, it is profoundly difficult to ascertain the location of the allocated land and the actual implementation of contracts. What is more, if the government concerned is known to be venal, it is unrealistic to expect the contract to realize opportunities provided by 'responsible' foreign agricultural investment. Unfortunately, Sudan was ranked the fourth most corrupt country in the world by Transparency International's corruption perception indicator in 2009 and 2010.

Given this, it is more likely that risks rather than opportunities associated with land expropriation will materialize. For instance, unfavourable contracts could result in foreign agricultural investment threatening Sudan's future food security through long-term leases of its fertile land and no restrictions on food exports, the depletion of ground water resources, environmental damage, or violent eruption of local conflicts as a result of confiscation of communally owned land.

Yet, given the low implementation ratio of such projects and the lack of governmental support, the situation looks less bleak, as it is unlikely that all such risks related to land grabbing will occur. For instance, approved foreign investment projects in non-petroleum sectors of the economy during the period 2000–10 amounted to 1,966 projects. Of these only 100 – that is 5 per cent – were in agriculture. While the overall implementation ratio of projects was 26 per cent, that for agriculture was only 17 per cent (MOI 2011). But the lack of implementation does not necessarily mean that there are no territorial impacts. The effects are certainly the same regardless of implementation, if approved projects are fenced-in to exclude small farmers and bar the way for moving nomads. This further complicates drawing any but preliminary conclusions on the outcomes of land grabbing in Sudan. It is necessary to follow these developments closely in the coming years.

Critically examining risks and opportunities emerging from foreign agricultural investment relies on good governance, which explains the dearth of thorough and transparent evaluation of the effects of these investments. A recent report by the World Bank states that, 'according to the Doing Business Report (2007), Sudan ranks twenty-seventh out of 175 countries in ease of registering property (land). This would place Sudan among the best countries in Africa, and indeed, worldwide, on this dimension' (FIAS 2006: 11). Little wonder that Sudan has been classified among a small group of African countries that pay the least respect to communal land rights (Alden Wily 2010: 15).

Despite this, Sudan in the past five years has been ranked very low in the composite index of the Doing Business indicators, namely 154 out of 183 (MOI 2010). Sudan is ranked last (183/183) in closing of business in both 2009 and 2010, 154/183 in investor protection in 2010, 155/183 in hiring project personnel in 2009, and 146/183 in contract enforcement in 2010, among others (MOI 2010). Under these circumstances, the relatively high ranking in land registration alone will not attract investors. Investors are more concerned with the protection of their business ventures or issues like corruption, which raise the cost of doing business. Recently, a Saudi investor complained that State Governors in Sudan would not grant concessions unless they are heavily bribed 'for unspecified services', and this has led some Saudi investors to completely forget about Sudan as an investment destination.[26]

How then to make sense of the progressive distribution of generous concessions for foreign investors and the many exceptional clauses in the investment acts? My contention is that these, coupled with discretionary powers vested in ministers of investment, imply cut-throat competition to attract investors. In view of weak governance, this competition will most likely result in many bilateral project agreements being signed – contracts that benefit a few, while damaging the environment, promoting inequality and stirring contention between both rural and marginalized communities and central authorities. Furthermore, while the cost of attaining external resources in this manner is very high, it is most likely that the resources will not be put to good use, given that recent budgets allocate more than 70 per cent of revenue to security and less than 8 per cent to social services.

The main challenge in realizing opportunities offered by this new wave of foreign agricultural investment is good governance. Following Anseeuw et al. (2012a: 8), 'without transparency, accountability, and open debate, decision-making over land will continue to be swayed by vested interests at the expense of the rural land users. Likewise, without transparency land acquirers cannot be held accountable to contractual obligations, national laws or voluntary guidelines.'

CONCLUDING REMARKS

The issue of land grabbing is highly complicated. On the surface things appear simple: The government, legally in the right but morally questionable, confiscates communally owned land and allocates it to investors without considering the interests of the rural poor (IFAD 2008, 2010). While in effect it may appear that the government is just a fee-collecting lever between its state territory and global agro-business, I argue that this view also has its blind spots. Foreign direct investment in agriculture not only bears risks, but also offers some important development incentives for rural areas and other economic opportunities. The crux of this is that the realization of opportunities is critically conditional on good governance.

It seems that the phenomenal global increase in the demand for land to grow food and plants for biofuel will continue. Sudan will likely remain a destination country[27] for foreign investors, given not only its vast arable land surfaces and subterranean resources, but also the government's unscrupulous dispossession of rural populations. A crucial question, especially for rural communities, is whether Sudan will be able to minimize the risks associated with such opportunities or not.

Many factors challenge the ability of the Sudan Government to exploit the opportunities offered by foreign agricultural investment. First, after losing more than 75 per cent of its foreign exchange earnings and nearly 40 per cent of its budget revenue as a result of the secession of South Sudan, it is in dire need of external resources in the form of foreign direct investment. Government officials roaming the region offering land to foreign investors in return for fresh loans are evidence of this. Second, the government's institutions are dysfunctional, failing and lack credentials of good governance, such as transparent government operations, enforcement of contracts, democratization of decision-making and an independent and fair judicial system. Third, the ousting of qualified personnel over the past two decades and their replacement with government supporters has weakened all state offices and departments and has damaged their institutional capacity. Accordingly, the ability of government institutions to thoroughly screen projects and negotiate contracts is considerably impaired. Fourth, the lack of institutional memory and knowledge and/or disrespect for procedures and ethics of work, coupled with low pay and political association of staff with the ruling party, have nurtured an environment of corruption, which has infested most government operations. Finally, communal land-owners have not been empowered, as their legal rights have been neither recognized nor protected.[28]

In the Comprehensive Peace Agreement of 2005 the parties agreed upon the foundation of a National Land Commission (NLC), which was envisioned as an instrument to redress the historical injustices borne by communal land-owners. The NLC has yet to be established but could potentially turn into a broader platform for the arbitration of conflicting interests.

Nonetheless, the current government (1989 to date) is unlikely to address the issues raised above. By its actions over the past two decades it turned Sudan into a failed state. The Failed States Index 2012 ranks Sudan third, outranked only by Somalia and the Democratic Republic of Congo.[29] Therefore, most likely the government will continue to cheaply expropriate rural people's land to investors, in an unending effort to fill its coffers and perhaps to benefit unscrupulous officials.

REFERENCES

Alden Wily, L. 2010. Whose Land are you Giving Away, Mr. President? Report by Independent Land Tenure Specialist.

Anseeuw, W., Alden Wily, L. A., Cotula, L. ,Taylor, M. 2012a. 'Land Rights and the Rush for Land: Findings of the Global Commercial Pressures on Land Research Project'. Rome: International Land Coalition.

Anseeuw, W., Boche, M., Breu, T., Giger, M., Lay, J., Messerli, P., Nolte, K. 2012b. 'Transnational Land Deals for Agriculture in Global South: Analytical Report based on the Land Matrix Data Base'. The Land Matrix Partnership <http://landmatrix.org>.

Arezki, R.,Deininger, K., Selod, H. 2011. 'What Drives the Global Land Rush?' Economic Research Forum Working Paper 663. Cairo.

Babiker, M. 2011. 'Mobile Pastoralism and Land Grabbing in Sudan: Impacts and Responses.' Paper presented at the International Conference on the Future of Pastoralism, Addis Ababa, March 2011. Organized by Future Agricultures Consortium, University of Sussex, and Feinstein International Centre, Tufts University.

Bell, B. 1930. 'Notes on Land Tenure in the Sudan by Legal Secretary'. Sudan Archive, Durham: SAD 542/23/1-5.

Bolton, A. R. C. 1954. 'Land Tenure in Agricultural Land in the Sudan'. In Tothill, J. D. (ed.), *Agriculture in the Sudan: Being a Handbook of Agriculture as Practised in the Anglo-Egyptian Sudan*. London: Oxford University Press, 187–197.

Deininger, K., Byerlee, D. with Lindsay, J., Norton, A. Selod, H., Stickler, M. 2010. *Rising Global Interest in Farmland: Can it Yield Sustainable and Equitable Benefits*? Washington DC: World Bank.

Egemi, O. 2006. 'Land Tenure in Sudan: Challenges to Livelihood Security and Social Peace'. In Galal el-Din el-Tayeb, ed. with Nimir, B. N., El Hassan, B. A. *Land Issues and Peace in Sudan*. Khartoum: Sudanese Environment Conservation Society, 29–40

El Karouri, M.O. 2010. *Mechanized Rainfed Agriculture in the Sudan*. Khartoum: Alhanna Commercial Printing Press.

El Tahir, A. H. 2006. 'Land Commission in Sudan'. In Galal el-Din el-Tayeb, ed. with Nimir, B. N., El Hassan, B. A. *Land Issues and Peace in Sudan*. Khartoum: Sudanese Environment Conservation Society, 15–27

el-Tayeb, G. el-Din, ed. with Nimir, B. N., El Hassan, B. A. 2006. 'Land Issues and Peace in Sudan'. Khartoum: Sudanese Environment Conservation Society. <www.sd.undp.org/publications/RRBC%20land.pdf>, retrieved 31-07-2012.

Elzubeir, M. K. 2009. '*Al-qurūḍ wal-l-maᶜūnat ad-duwalīya wa 'aṯāruha ᶜala at-tanmīya al-iqtiṣādīya* [Loans and Grants and their Effect on Economic Development]'. Khartoum: Dar Elsadad Printing Press.

Food and Agricultural Organization (FAO) 2009. *From Land Grab to Win-Win*. Economic and Social Perspectives Policy Brief 4. Rome: Economic and Social Development Department, FAO.

Foreign Investment Advisory Services (FIAS) 2006. 'Sudan: Review of Administrative Barriers to Private Sector Investment'. Draft report.

Friis, C., Reenberg, A. 2010. 'Land Grab in Africa: Emerging land system drivers in a teleconnected world'. GLP Report No. 1. Copenhagen: GLP-IPO.

Gordon, C. 1986. 'Recent Developments of the Land Law of the Sudan: A Legislative Analysis'. *Journal of African Law* 30 (2), 143–174.

GRAIN 2012. 'GRAIN releases data set with over 400 global land grabs'.

Barcelona: GRAIN <www.grain.org/article/entries/4479-grain-releases-data-set-with-over-400-global-land-grabs>, retrieved 15-06-2012.
Ijaimi, A. 2006. 'Mechanized Farming and Conflict in Sudan'. In Galal el-Din el-Tayeb, ed. with Nimir, B. N., El Hassan, B. A., *Land Issues and Peace in Sudan*. Khartoum: Sudanese Environment Conservation Society, 69–77.
International Fund for Agricultural Development (IFAD) 2008. 'Promoting Equitable Access to Land and Tenure Security for Rural Poverty Reduction'. Draft report. Rome: IFAD.
IFAD 2010. *Rural Poverty Report*. Rome: IFAD.
International Labour Organization (ILO) 1987. 'Employment and Economic Reform: Towards a Strategy for the Sudan'. Report. Geneva.
Komey, G. K. 2010a. 'Land Factor in Wars and Conflicts in Africa: The Case of the Nuba Struggle in Sudan'. In Falola, T., Njoku, R. C. (eds), *War and Peace in Africa*. Durham NC: Carolina Academic Press, 347–376.
Komey, G. K. 2010b. *Land, Governance, Conflict & the Nuba of Sudan*. Woodbridge and Rochester NY: James Currey.
King Abdullah Initiative for Saudi Agricultural Investment Abroad 2010. El Riad.
MacMichael, H. A. 1954. *The Sudan*. London: Ernest Benn, translated into Arabic by Salih, M. S. O. 2009. Omdurman: Abdel Karim Mirghani Cultural Centre.
Merian Research, CRBM. 2010. The Vultures of Land Grabbing: the Involvement of European Financial Companies in Large-scale Land Acquisition Abroad. Campagna per la riforma della Banca Mondiale, Merian Research. http://farmlandgrab.org/wp-content/uploads/2010/11/VULTURES-completo.pdf
Ministry of Agriculture (MOA) 2008. '*ᶜAzūf al-muzāriᶜīn ᶜan zirāᶜat il-quṭun*' [Why farmers are refraining from cotton cultivation in Gezira]. Khartoum: Republic of Sudan.
Ministry of Agriculture (MOA) 2009. 'Study of the Sustainable Development of the Semi-mechanized Rain-fed Farming', Khartoum; Newtech and Hunting Tech Services for MOA: Republic of Sudan.
Ministry of Investment (MOI) 2005. '*Al-isṭitmārāt az-zirāᶜīya fī s-sūdān wa-r-ru' īya al-mustaqbalīya*'. [Foreign Agricultural Investment in Sudan and the future perspective]. Unpublished report, Khartoum: Republic of Sudan.
Ministry of Investment (MOI) 2007. '*Qānūn tašğīᶜ al-istiṭmār li-sanat 1999*'. [Investment Encouragement Act 1999 (amended 2007)]. Khartoum: Republic of Sudan.
Ministry of Investment (MOI) 2011a. '*Taqrīr ᶜan ḥaṣr wa-t-taḥlīl al-istiṭmār al-'ağnabī al-mubāšir fī s-sūdān*' [Report on the status and analysis of foreign direct investments in Sudan]. Khartoum: Republic of Sudan.
Ministry of Investment (MOI) 2011b. '*Al-taqrīr al-ḫitāmī wa-l-ḫuṭṭa al-qaumīya li-tashīl 'adā' al-'aᶜmāl fī s-sūdān*'. [Final report and plan for the implementation of works in Sudan]. Khartoum: Republic of Sudan.
Mosley, J. 2012. *Peace, Bread and Land: Agricultural Investments in Ethiopia and the Sudans*. London: Chatham House, Africa Programme, AFP BP 2012/01.
Nuha, M. E. A., Abdel Rahman, N. 2010. 'Demographic and Socio-economic Characteristics of Nomadic Population in Sudan'. Khartoum: Sudan Central Bureau of Statistics.
Palmer, R. 2010. 'Would Cecil Rhodes Have Signed a Code of Conduct? Reflections on Global Land Grabbing'. Conference, September 16–19. Oxford: African Studies Association of the UK.
Rone, J. 2003. 'Sudan: Oil and War'. *Review of African Political Economy* 30 (97), 478, 504–510.
Runger, M. 1987. *Land Law and Land Use Control in Western Sudan*. London and Atlantic Highlands NJ: Ithaca Press.

Seirab, M.O. 2007. '*Az-zirāᶜa al-'alīya al-maṭarīya fī s-sūdān – ḥaqā'iq wa 'arqām*' [Mechanized Farming in Sudan: Facts and Figures].

Sudan Data Bank 1986. '*Tā'rīḫ al-intiḫābāt al-barlamānīya fī s-sūdān*'. [History of Parliamentary Elections in Sudan]. Khartoum.

Umbadda, S. 1990. *Colonial Education and the Perpetuation of Regional Imbalances in Sudan 1956–1989*. Discussion paper 88. Development Studies and Research Center, University of Khartoum.

United Nations Environment Programme (UNEP). 2002. *Global Environment Outlook*. Report. Nairobi, etc.: UNEP .

UNEP. 2007. *Sudan: Post-Conflict Environmental Assessment of Sudan*. Nairobi: UNEP.

UNICEF in collaboration with the Federal Ministry of Education, Sudan, 2008. 'The Evaluation of Nomadic Education Project in Kassala, Gedarif, Blue Nile, Sennar and White Nile States'. Report. Khartoum.

World Bank (WB). 2010. 'Social Dimensions of Large-scale Acquisitions of Land Rights.' Sudan draft inception report. Khartoum.

ENDNOTES

1. Egemi (2006) mentions the Land Settlement Act of 1905.

2. Gordon (1986) mentions that there are more than 25 legislative acts related to land up to 1986.

3. This was administered by the (British) Kassala Cotton Company.

4. Others, however, contend that 'colonial authorities never acknowledged that there could be private rights of any kind to land which was used intermittently by communities' (MOA 2009: 9).

5. Land was leased and owners who agreed to become tenants became partners in scheme profits through a sharing agreement with government and scheme administration.

6. According to Gordon (1986: 179), this Ordinance was the reference for all subsequent land legislation until the 1980s, especially regarding compensation.

7. According to Bolton, 'land can be acquired permanently by government for disposal to private persons for development in the public interest' (Bolton 1954: 193).

8. The provisions were retained in the CTA and its amendment of 1990 (MOA 2009).

9. Noronha, R. and Lethem, F. (1983) quoted in Gordon (1986:146).

10. This is stated as 'no court of law is competent to receive a complaint that goes against the interest of the state' (Egemi 2006: 33).

11. Presidential Advisor and secretary general of the Investment Council, Mustafa Ismail, declared that 'nobody (national) will be allowed to take to court any foreign investor'. *Asahafa Newspaper*, 29 November 2011.

12. During the peace negotiations between the NCP and the SPLM, variant positions on land ownership were articulated: the NCP held that 'land belongs to the government' versus the SPLM's charge that 'land belongs to the community'.

This is important because land was and still is one of the factors contributing to the recurring conflicts at different levels in Sudan.

13. See pronouncements of officials from Northern and Gezira States, each offering four million feddan, in *Asahafa* Newspaper, 20 September 2011 and *Alray Alaam* Newspaper, 5 March 2012.

14. This expansion was enabled by the Mechanized Farming Corporation Act of 1968, which provided the government with the legal basis for systematic and aggressive land grabbing for mechanized rain-fed farming schemes – with devastating consequences for rural communities (Gordon 1968).

15. The figure comprises 6.1 million ha of planned mechanized farming and 7.1 million ha of unplanned (illegal) schemes.

16. The cultivated area also fluctuates according to annual rainfall variations.

17. Recently, claiming compensation for displaced populations has become more acceptable, as in the case of villagers of Merowe Dam, but it should be noted that land there is largely privately owned.

18. See, for example, reports in *Alray Alaam* newspaper, 23 March 2012, *Ilaf Economic Weekly*, 11 April 2012, or *Hurriat* 8 April 2012, and *Asahafa*, 20 May 2012.

19. Compare articles in *Asahafa* newspaper, 14–18 April 2012.

20. In both the 1953 and 1958 parliamentary elections, the two leading political parties exported elite candidates from Khartoum to rural constituencies, especially in Darfur and Kordofan, to get elected, and they won (Sudan Data Bank 1986: 24/25–47/53).

21. The Shanabla pastoralists, for instance, after Gezira land was taken by the colonial government in the 1920s, were forced to relocate. They migrated with their herds to the west of the White Nile area and Kordofan, where even after almost a century they are considered as a landless group with only secondary rights to water and grazing resources (WB 2011: 14).

22. The Minister of Animal Resources declared that pasture has been reduced considerably, from 275 million feddan in 1985 to 174 million feddans in 2011. Pasture, according to him, used to provide 75 per cent of herd needs, and currently it fulfils only 26 per cent. *Alray Alaam* newspaper, 7 February 2012.

23. *Alahdath* newspaper, 8 February 2012.

24. Projects in the sample have different approval times in different states and some of them are more than three decades old. Because of secrecy and unwillingness to release information, the author was unable to persuade officials to release the latest information about the total number of projects approved, their location, areas allocated, lease duration or dollar rate per hectare, hence the resort to sampling.

25. For instance, 93 per cent of cases of trespassing reported to courts in Abu Gibeiha, South Kordofan were between pastoralists and farmers (Egemi 2006: 72).

26. See, Alray Alaam newspaper, 3 April 2012. See also *Asahafa* newspaper, 29 November 2011, where MPs said corruption is hindering investment.

27. Anseeuw et al. (2012b: 9) report that Sudan is among the seven most targeted countries by foreign investors in Africa. See also Deininger et al. 2010.

28. Farmlandgrab documents protests in the Gezira, see http://farmlandgrab.org/post/view/18387 and http://farmlandgrab.org/post/view/18583, retrieved June 2012.

29. Failed States Index, Fund for Peace (www.fundforpeace.org/global/?q=fsi2012, retrieved June 2012).

3

Territories of Gold Mining: International Investments and Artisanal Extraction in Sudan

SANDRA CALKINS & ENRICO ILLE

With South Sudan's secession in mid-2011, Sudan was plunged into an economic crisis by the loss of most of its oil resources to the new state. Land and the ability to contract usage rights for land surface and subterranean resources have turned into an important source of revenue for the Government of Sudan. In this chapter, we complement the contributions on disrupting territories which deal with land surface by peering into negotiations over the exploitation of subterranean resources – namely gold.[1]

In recent years the government allocated land parcels of various sizes for gold mining, whereby the largest areas were allotted to foreign private enterprises.[2] We assert that the new wave of investments in mining and agriculture is part of the historical conversion of collective land rights into private property, a process that accelerated again with the spread of neoliberal governance and the internationalization of business ventures. In their spatial consequences, the mining concessions are similar to recent agro-investments: the contracts between the Government of Sudan and foreign investors have alienated rural populations from what they view as their land. Yet, concomitantly artisanal gold mining has turned into a new source of income for thousands of small-scale actors. Based on a case study from north-eastern Sudan, we show that there are various tensions between the legal framework set up by the government which favours industrial mining, the official procedures and practices in the mining sector, and local artisanal mining arrangements. Instead of defusing such tensions, the government is merely pursuing a politics of extracting 'admission fees' to natural resources: On the one hand, legislation clearly supports large-scale investors and the industrial mining sector, which also fills Khartoum's coffers. But on the other hand, the government seldom intervenes to regulate and prohibit artisanal mining being carried out within concession areas and in direct competition with industrial private enterprises. In conclusion, we suggest that the effective control and administration of a territory are secondary aspects in the government's ability to work as a passage point that can allow foreign capital into Sudan (see Callon 1986). Its primary interest is in extracting money for legal rights to territorialized natural resources.

Empirically this chapter is informed by recent ethnographic fieldwork (2008–10) in Eastern Sudan, interviews conducted by the authors, official documents and reports, newspaper reports and other news media for recent developments. The present legal framework will be reviewed as the operational basis for the government's concessions to national and transnational companies. This framework will be contrasted with the practices of artisanal gold miners and the organization of gold markets as interstitial spaces. Finally, a recent governmental assessment of the 'informal' gold mining sector will be analysed to highlight the presumptions and ambiguities of claims for sovereignty in natural resource usage.

APPROACHING THE PROBLEM

With our specific focus on gold mining, we seek to add a perspective on the state's role in organizing the usage of natural resources. We highlight three aspects that qualify the government's role as 'arbiter' between global dynamics and Sudanese territories.

First, it is frequently assumed that a major state function consists in guaranteeing property rights through legitimate means of enforcement.[3] This relates to ideas in political philosophy on sovereignty that generally comprise a certain bounded territory and a particular sovereign actor that is able to control and administer it independently of other (f)actors, rooted in the Westphalian model of state politics (Elden 2005: 8, 9). Space is the abstract grid in maps that emerges out of a certain conceptualization of place, which is mathematically calculable, three-dimensionally extensible and based on geometric co-ordinates. The territory of the nation state figures as the political corollary of this spatial conception and its imposition over places (Elden 2005: 8, 15, 16), which marginalizes other ideas of space and territory. Since we are dealing with foreign capital investments in the territory of the Sudanese state, what should we make of debates on globalization and deterritorialization, which seem to indicate a dissolution of territorial boundedness? Elden argues that ideas of globalization are built on the same conception of abstract calculable space that emerged in Europe between the fifteenth and seventeenth centuries and extended by late capitalism to the entire globe (2005: 16). A problem is that such debates often 'miss the point' by taking globalization increasingly as real physical processes and not shedding light on the conceptions that allow space to be produced, transformed and reconfigured. Therefore Elden (2005: 15, 16) suggests that globalization does not mean deterritorialization in the sense that territories cease to exist, rather it refers to a cognitive operation – the extension of spatial calculation and statistics, which formerly were closely connected to the constitution of the modern state, to the entire globe. This perspective highlights the roles of actors and entities beyond the state – namely globalized actors. These are able to calculate, project, plan and orchestrate their activities across different national settings, in other words 'taking the world as their playground', such as the foreign investors and consortia in Sudanese gold mining.

Second, bodies of literature on flows and entanglements stress the inadequacy of conceptions that are grounded upon fixed territories, such as the nation state, highlighting the connectedness between territories and global capital, power and knowledge flows (Agnew 2009, Appadurai 1996a). Therefore, we emphasize that Sudan has long been integrated into various global flows of people and things. For instance, under Ottoman rule imperial forces extracted slaves for labour, ivory, gum arabic and other precious resources. This south–north flow continued under British rule which exported cotton from large irrigated schemes that it initiated. After independence the nature of such flows altered. Civil war erupted and led to the emergence of financial and aid flows whereby the main agents were international financial agencies, the development industry and UN organizations (Duffield 2001).[4] Furthermore, in the 1970s, related to the breadbasket policies, a Gulf trajectory of flows emerged and in the 1990s mostly Asian companies developed the Sudanese energy and infrastructural sectors; and recently, international business ventures in agriculture and mining have been contracting large surfaces from the Sudan Government for their activities. Our point is not the novelty of such flows into Sudanese territories, but their mediation through the government.

Third, when thinking about the role of the Sudan Government in designing resource politics, it appears significant that Sudan is commonly named among the 'dysfunctional', 'fragile', or 'failing states'.[5] Concepts like 'failing states' are highly controversial and gloss over the fact that 'failing states' work all too well for some, whereas 'functional states' may not. Still, they draw attention to properties that mark the post-colonial state in Sudan, such as the failure to develop institutions that regulate, govern and secure its citizens, or the production of vast marginalized regions outside of the Greater Khartoum region – both socio-economically and socio-culturally (Rotberg 2003, 2004). As a result the Sudanese state is constantly caught in bouts of violent conflict with its own citizens and is unable to control much of the vast state territory, currently Darfur, South Kordofan and the Blue Nile State, for instance. Against this backdrop and inspired by Appadurai's essay on 'sovereignty without territory' (1996b: 49), we show in this chapter that the government's control of the state territory is impaired. Instead, we argue, it works as an 'arbiter' that integrates various global flows into claimed territories. We thereby contribute to a body of literature that challenges common-sense assumptions that good governance and well-functioning institutions are needed to attract foreign capital (cf. Ferguson 2006, Reno 2004, Watts 2004).

Apart from questioning the Government of Sudan's actual ability to control territory and enforce contracts, here we highlight its ability – on paper – to confer a certain legitimacy on the foreign contractors. Often these companies depend upon formal agreements to publicly justify their international business dealings in their respective home countries. The state government as sovereign over the nation-state thence is located at a peculiar passage point in organizing the multifaceted relations between its state laws, territories and capital flows. This involves the

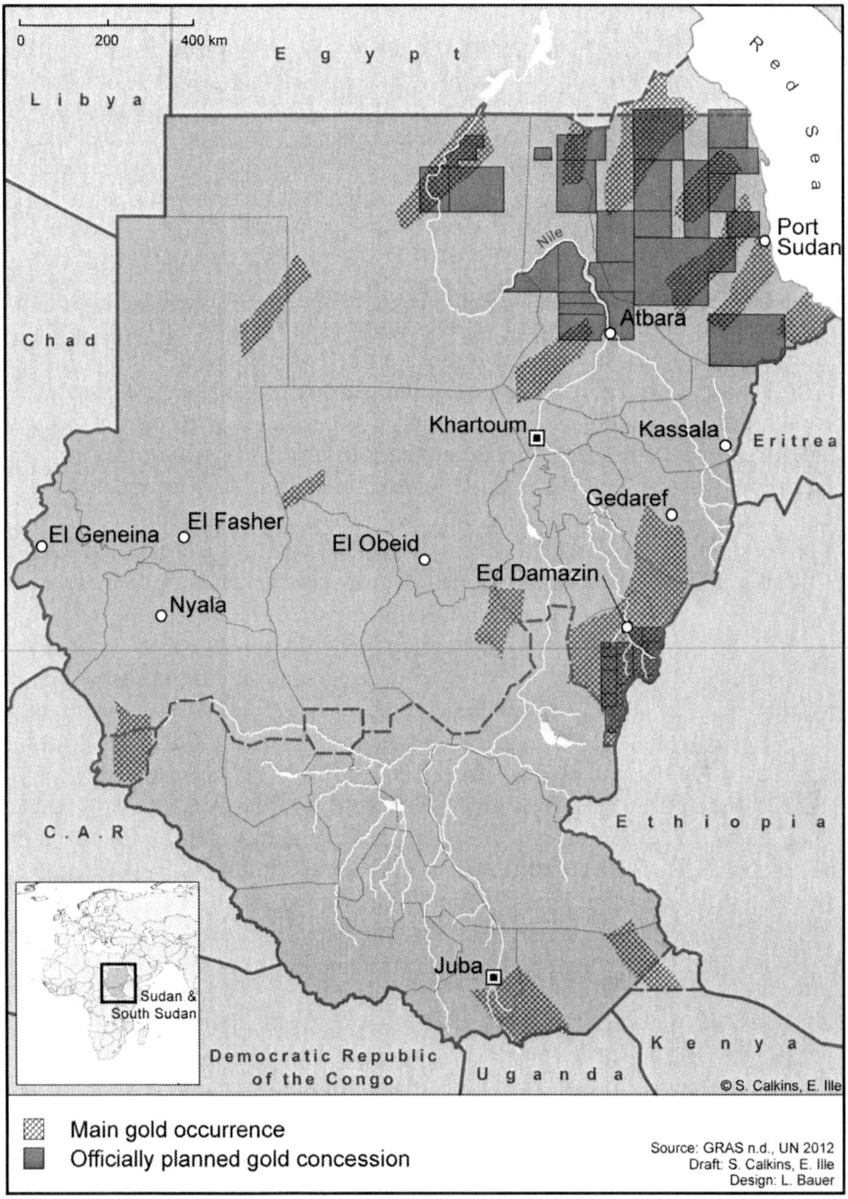

Map 3.1 Official Estimates of Gold Occurrence and Concession Areas

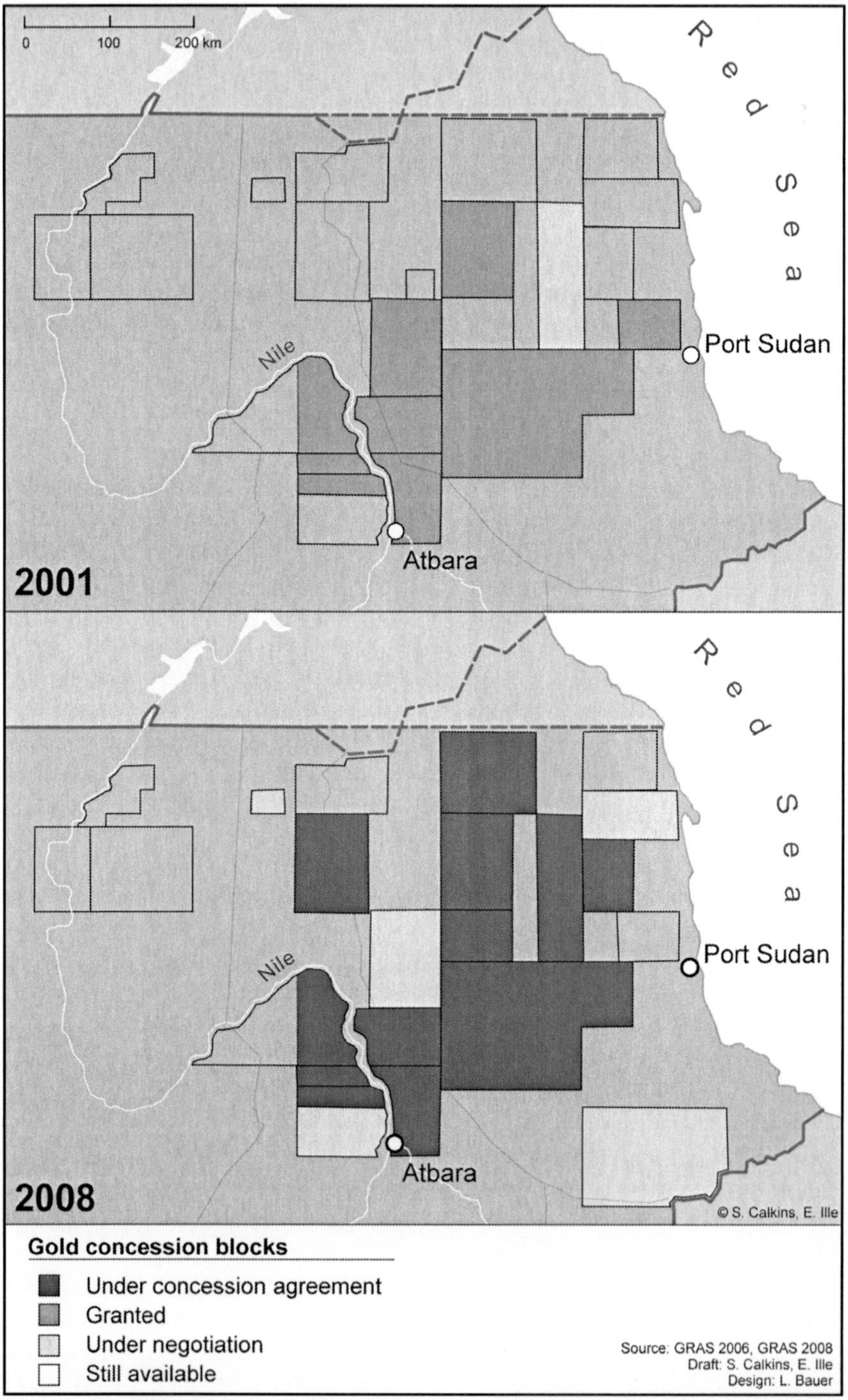

Map 3.2 Gold concessions in 2001 and 2008

negotiation, lease and sale of land rights. The consequences of the governmental reorganizing of land rights materialize first on papers in law texts. The conferral of gold exploration rights on investors next takes a numerical form: numbers are named in contracts, indicating the location and size of concessions. Project maps represent concessions on a map, scaled in relation to other territories. At the last instance this allocation of land rights may affect how the designated land is actually used. However, in contested states, like Sudan, the rights endowed through such governmental contracts compete with other conceptions of rights, which are based on other sources of legitimacy.

DEVELOPING GOLD MINING

After independence (1956), a new phase in gold mining began in the 1970s, when the national government sought to explore the country's mineral resource reservoirs. This led to the identification of more than 50 potential prospects for gold mining. In the 1980s the state-run Sudanese Mining Corporation formed several joint ventures with foreign companies; gold production started in 1987 at the Gebeit mine in north-eastern Sudan and other places (Metz 1991: 164). The amount of gold produced increased significantly with the foundation of a Sudanese-French joint venture, the Ariab Mining Company. In its first year, in 1992, it extracted 982 kg (2,165 lb) of gold. This increased to 5.5 tons in 1999 and 8.6 tons in 2003.[6] The overall production then jumped to 36 tons in 2010 based on a new investment policy which we will detail below (Reuters 18 May 2011). In mid-February 2012, the Sudanese Ministry of Finance announced that the gold exported during the first six weeks had already rocketed to 7.2 tons, generating US $55 million (Reuters 19 February 2012).[7]

Several innovations enabled development of the gold mining sector: a new information infrastructure and new technologies for measurement were introduced. A geological information centre with laboratories and equipment for geophysical measurements was founded, which in 2004 released a first digital geological map (International Business Publications – IBP USA 2011: 44).[8] The process of mapping is central to investments: it represents land as parcelled into clearly delineated and commodifiable territorial blocks – the concessions. A map of contracted concessions from 2001 was presented by the Geological Research Authority of the Sudan (GRAS) at the 2nd International Investment & Trade Conference for Sudan in September 2006 (Obeid & Abdel Rahman 2006). The geological information centre published another map of concessions in June 2008. On comparing these two maps, a clear trend emerges. Both maps only display the area north of Khartoum between the Nile and the Red Sea.[9] Available concessions are coloured light blue and a strong dark red is used for granted concessions. On the map of 2001, 9 of 24 concessions had been granted. In contrast, the map of 2008 is dominated by red and

Table 3.1 Disclosed Gold Mining Licences

Company	License	Source
Ariab Mining Company (Government of Sudan); AREVA Ltd., (France); since 2006 La Mancha Resources Inc. (Canada)	1991	IBP USA 2011: 31 La Mancha 2012
Shirian Al Shamal Company for Engineering and Mining (Sudan)	2002	Yager 2003
Uni-Group Holdings (Pty) Co. (South Africa)	2002	Yager 2003
Advanced Mining Works (Sudan)	2002	Yager 2003
Ansan Wikfs Investments Company Ltd. (Yemen)	2008	IBP USA 2011: 31
Al-Sharif (Sudan)	2008	IBP USA 2011: 31
Manajim Co. (Morroco)	2008	IBP USA 2011: 31, *Sudan Tribune*, September 14, 2008
Dan Fodio Corporation (Sudan)/ Poly Technologies Inc. (China)	2009	*Sudan Tribune*, May 15, 2009
Toro East Africa Ltd. (Toro Gold Ltd., U.K.)	2010	*Bloomberg*, November 7, 2010
Orbit for Multi-Activities Co. Ltd. (Rika Global Impex Ltd., India)	2010	*Bloomberg*, November 7, 2010
Sheikh Musa & Maussane (Chechnya)	2010	*Sudan Tribune*, April 28, 2010
Paramount Mining Company (India)	2010	*Sudan Tribune*, April 28, 2010
Faroun for Indian Metal (India)	2010	*Sudan Tribune*, April 28, 2010
Tahi Global (Turkey)	2010	*Sudan Tribune*, April 28, 2010
ASCOM Precious Metals Mining (Egypt)	2011	Citadel Capital, March 27, 2011

dark orange (awaiting signature) colours; only eight concessions were coloured light blue denoting their availability.

Meanwhile, the main political forces in north-eastern Sudan have begun to resist these mining deals, given that resource extractions in the region have failed to benefit the resident population (Young 2006: 595). A study of the political situation shortly before the Eastern Sudan Peace Agreement of 2006 notes:

> Some Beja leaders commented that the Beja occupy the most strategic piece of land in the country and one of the richest, but do not share any of the wealth which is produced by the region. Similar comments were made by Rashaida leaders who remarked that the Rashaida do not receive any services in return for the levies they pay on their livestock, remittances and trade. (Pantuliano 2006: 711)

Concurrently, thousands of small-scale gold miners undermine the governmental agreements by extracting gold within the areas set aside for state-promoted mining projects. These activities are greatly expanding and spreading. This growing informal gold prospecting is driven by a global dynamic – the steady rise of the gold price.[10] Official sources name the rising gold prices as significant factors in the renewed interest in gold mining – both industrial and artisanal. This is corroborated by artisanal miners from the Lower Atbara area, many of whom began gold mining between late 2008 and mid-2009, when the laborious and potentially hazardous manual gold extraction turned into a lucrative enterprise for local populations. In early 2010 an estimated 40,000 to 50,000[11] people in north-eastern Sudan earned their incomes through artisanal mining and related services; these activities included 1,500 vehicles (pick-up trucks, four-wheel-drive vehicles, lorries and water tankers), over 2,000 metal detectors and 500 diesel-run grinders (Ibrahim & Abdel Baqi 2010). To dig mines, the small-scale miners make local agreements with whoever effectively controls the land. The involvement of Khartoum-based traders, some of whom have links to the ruling party, in small miners' markets, indicates the existence of multiple coexisting flows that need careful scrutiny. In the following, we show how the exclusion of resident communities was formalized by means of regulations and laws that guide governmental contracts with investors. This we set against the actual practices in artisanal mining, which circumvent the legal provisions and thereby resist the exclusionary policies built into Sudan's legal system.

LEGAL FRAMEWORKS FOR GOLD MINING

> [T]he State, in Africa, if not quite a market in the liberal sense of the word is at least an entrepôt governed by a minimal degree of interconnection. (Bayart 1989/2009: 246)

A sovereign nation state paves the way for gold mining investments by passing legislation to convert collective land rights into numerical, calculable and clearly delineated units that can be commoditized (Elden 2005, November et al. 2009). This has been accomplished through a series of land acts in colonial and post-colonial Sudan (cf. Umbadda in Chapter 2, Abdul-Jalil in Chapter 5). Moreover, in its Unregistered Land Act of 1970, the Government of Sudan declared all mineral resources within its (contested) boundaries to be state property, irrespective of how the land at the surface was used. This has given the government sole authority to grant gold exploration and mining rights.

Until 1953 the Government Geologist Office was the authority on mining. Its successor was the Geological Survey Department, until 1978, when the Geological and Mineral Resources Department was formed. This continued its work until 1986 when the name changed to Geological Research Authority of Sudan (GRAS) (IBP USA 2011: 29).[12] Until recently, GRAS' website presented the following documents as legal reference points for prospective investors:

- Mines and Quarries Act 1972
- Mines and Quarries Regulations 1973
- Investment Encouragement Act 1999 (amended 2000)
- Mineral Resources and Mining Development Act 2007
- Procedures for the Acquisition of Exploration and Mining Rights in an Area

- Memorandum of Understanding (as preparation for a concession)
- Final Concession Agreement.

The legal arrangements described in these documents indicate a gradual exclusion of land ownership and usage rights below the state level. The Mines and Quarries Act 1972 follows the stipulations of the Unregistered Land Act of 1970, which declared all unregistered land to belong to the state as represented by the national government. However, the Act preserves the 'existing and recognized customary rights of the native inhabitants of any part of the Sudan to get certain minerals in certain areas for their own benefit without grant or license from the Government' (Mines and Quarries Act 1972 article 12, paragraph a). The Mineral Resources and Mining Development Act of 2007 does not contain any such clause and incriminates any mining of or even search for minerals without a licence, threatening imprisonment and fees (article 24). The Organization of Artisanal Mining Regulation of October 2010 amends the 2007 Act but confirms its spirit and refers to its penalties. It officially allows artisanal mining but only under restrictive conditions and by following official procedures (registration, licence): no use of heavy machinery or equipment (diggers, excavators with belt loaders, etc.), mining may not exceed depths of 10 metres; artisanal miners may only work in designated sites that do not interfere with investors' licences. As well as paying licensing fees, miners are required to hand over 5 per cent of the gold produced to the government. The exclusion of customary claims to land from the 2007 Act and the 2010 Regulation seems to be a significant shift towards a generalized rejection of such claims and towards their practical neutralization by legal regulations and connected fees.

Interestingly, the regulation of 2010 details that land for artisanal mining may be registered 'after making cadastral survey being free from rights of others and encumbrances' (article 13). The reference to cadastres confirms that only certain claims to land – namely those paired with official registration, contracts and licences – are recognized, emphasizing the need to follow certain procedures to engage in gold mining on Sudanese soil. Officials at the Ministry of Energy and Mining in Khartoum in May 2010 described the following: to legally search for gold in Sudan a potential miner needs to acquire a general permit (*ruḫṣat al-baḥṯ al-ᶜāma*) for searching, costing 7,000 Sudanese Pounds (SDG) (then GBP £2,135, US $3,137).[13] A precondition for receiving the permission is a letter outlining the exact location in which the petitioner wants to search, and a bank statement showing at least 50,000 SDG (then £15,250, $22,410) – a discouragingly high sum for people in much of rural Sudan. The Ministry's department of geology then examines the proposal, checking whether concessions for the area have already been issued to avoid an overlap. From January to May 2010, 427 searching permits were issued at the Ministry of Energy and Mining. After receiving the general permit, the miner needs to apply for a mining permit (*ruḫṣat at-taᶜdīn*) which demands another 1,500 SDG (£457, $672 in May 2010). There are two types of mining permits – small concessions up to 10km² and large concessions over this. Further, persons who intend to follow legal procedures to acquire a detector for gold mining need both the general permit and the mining permit. Additionally they must produce evidence, such as a letter, proving that customs duties were paid, ensuring it was not smuggled into Sudan.

In addition to the costs mentioned above, miners holding a small permit must rent the land and renew their contract annually.[14] In contrast, leasehold contracts for large mining permits generally span more than 20 years. In industrial mining, where the initiation of extraction is capital-intensive, such contractual agreements provide investors with the security that enables the set-up of commercial gold extraction facilities. The annual rent in 2010 amounted to 5,000 SDG (then £1,525, $2,241) per square kilometre.[15]

In line with its new investment act (1999, amended 2000), the government in Khartoum fosters large-scale foreign investment in industrial gold mining, from which it derives significant revenues.[16] The vast size of concessions is explained by the lack of geological studies on gold deposits in the northern areas. Yet, as recent news reports indicate, large mining deals signed between the government and foreign private investors are often in a context of bilateral political horse-trading between the government in Khartoum and the enterprise's country of origin, involving loans for the Sudan Government against the promise of favourable investment conditions.[17]

In short, the national government is the only authority legitimated by law to contract concessions. Furthermore, it alone can determine incentives to draw foreign capital investment, such as the vast size of concessions, long duration of contracts or exemption from annual rental fees. This indicates its role as a passage point to Sudan's gold resources in the wider networks of global finance and politics. While the Sudan Government clearly assumes a one-sided mediating role between global capital and its territories, it negates the concerns of people living and using these territories. The mining contracts ignore the fact that the land allocated to foreign investors is not uninhabited and often is used by local populations for seasonal pasture or rain-fed agriculture. Granting private investors rights to land that was previously subject to other usage regulations thus means preventing other groups from realizing their rights to land – at least potentially.

Many of the concessions are vast. They are neither fenced-in nor are they demarcated in the terrain. In many cases mining has not yet been initiated and the concession effects are thus far restricted to their definition on paper – in contracts and maps. In other cases, such as the established Ariab mines, gold extraction is well under way, but not in the entire territory of the concession. The actual mines where gold ore is removed from underground are small and concentrated but penetrate to dozens of metres deep. These sites are also fenced-in and guarded. Thus we stress that the territorial impacts of industrial mining remain to date within a limited surface area – they do not expand across the surface of the large concessions – but penetrate deeply into the ground. Therefore the exclusion of rural peoples from what they consider 'their' land according to customary law largely affects only the legality of people's claims and not the actual use of land.

Still, these transfers of the land entitlements are highly significant, because they open the way to future law enforcement and potential disenfranchisement of resident populations when mining activities are moved to other more productive sites. When companies explore new areas in their concession and leave behind excavated and destroyed spaces, this is likely to impact rural communities more than at present. Above all, legal entitlement declines. Furthermore, as indicated above, local communities in the vicinity of mining sites are beginning to demand compensation for their customary land being taken.[18]

In the following, artisanal gold mining in the Lower Atbara area of northern Sudan will be discussed. Gold mining has flourished there since late 2008 with the rise of the gold price. People from rural communities are hoping for a way out of their overall dismal living conditions. But these small-scale prospectors move quickly and without attending to the boundaries of concession areas and by extracting gold, they upset companies' projections and compete with them for gold resources.[19]

PRACTISING ARTISANAL GOLD MINING

> This government is a good government. It wants the people to benefit (Owner of a very productive mine on the government's seeming tolerance of artisanal mining)

> When they find the detector, that's it. They take it from you. They take your money; they search through your pockets, your car, everything, for gold. If you have money, they will take it and say you have it from stealing gold from the government. Maybe they take you to prison. They say you have to pay so and so much money. So you have to hide it. You don't take it into the market place. You only take it to your house at night (A gold miner working with a metal detector on the dangers of being arrested by the government)

Artisanal gold exploitation in Northern Sudanese mines is similar to what Grätz (2010) and Werthmann (2009) describe for West Africa: gold occurs in alluvial deposits of sand, clay and silt, which are gradually deposited through moving water, typically along river beds or water courses, or deposited in variant associations with rocks, for instance, as inclusion deposits in granite rocks (de Launay 1908: 8–55, Dull et al. 1958a). Artisanal mining in north-eastern Sudan depends upon two technologies of extraction.[20] First, digging mines following gold veins, which involves the laborious process of cutting out gold ore from hard rock veins, crushing the stones, grinding them to powder, washing the ground material and bringing the slurry in contact with mercury where it amalgamates with the gold particles, and heating the amalgamate to separate the gold and the mercury (Dull et al. 1958a, 1958b). Second, searching for surface gold with metal detectors that find nuggets in the ground up to

40–50 centimetres (15–20 inches) deep. However, this kind of search can also lead to new mines being opened.[21]

These two extraction technologies have diverse spatial trajectories: the mines are territorially fixed pits of several metres, usually dug by excavators, whereby individual shafts can reach to depths of dozens of metres. New productive mines usually draw many treasure hunters, leading to a multiplication of mines in the area, and if mining activities are sufficiently large, soon an entire mining infrastructure will follow: market places with grinders, washing pools, restaurants, grocery shops, gas stations, electricians, gold vendors from Khartoum and so forth. The government reports more than 60 sites with informal gold mines (Ibrahim & Abdel Baqi 2010).

Significantly, the opening of such 'informal' mines is organized with respect for customary land rights: in the case of two large mining sites in the Lower Atbara area, Wadi al-ᶜUshar and Wadi ᶜArab, to register a mine under their names, mine owners need to get the permission of sheikhs of the customary landowning Bishariyyn subgroups, Garab and Madhakir respectively. In both cases the sheikhs also hold an administrative office, the presidency of the popular council (*ra'īs al-lağna aš-šaᶜbīya*). Once registered, the sheikhs defend the miners' right to extract gold. If the mine is productive, the local sheikh will demand a so-called *wardīya*, a working shift of varied length that is negotiated with the mine owner. The sheikh puts together a team of workers and extracts gold ore from the mine in the name of the locality for two or three working shifts. Significantly, this arrangement is meant to ensure that local communities earn an income and benefit from the resources on 'their' land. The registration involves seemingly fixed rules, the signing and stamping of registration papers by the local sheikhs in what appears as their official functions. It explains why some artisanal gold miners believe that the federal government tolerates, if not supports, their mining activities at established sites.

In contrast to the organization at gold mines, detector teams search for surface gold mostly along wadis and mountain foothills and depend not only upon the metal detectors but also upon cars for transportation. These teams move quickly and unnoticed through the desert from place to place, have very high mobility and are the most difficult to control. For instance, those using detectors (*'ahl al-ğihāz*) from a rural settlement in the Lower Atbara area at times found large quantities of gold, sparking new construction and investment activity in the settlement.[22] The first detectors were employed from roughly mid-2009 onwards and were smuggled into the country. A government report sees metal detectors as especially threatening, as their overall success encourages imitation and their rapid proliferation (Ibrahim & Abdel Baqi 2010: 1, 2). Here the government has reacted and passed a bill that enables the import of detectors, so as to siphon off some custom duties and extract some money for licensing. Those owning unlicensed detectors are often acutely aware of the danger of confiscation. Before entering market places, detector groups often leave one of their comrades in the desert with the detector or hide the detector in their houses.

Hundreds of mines are being dug by artisanal miners. Yet, most mines are never productive and are discarded after two or three days of unsuccessful digging. These mining activities are transforming the landscape – perhaps more than the rather concentrated and confined industrial mining activities. First, in the Lower Atbara area pastures have been destroyed by the mounds of excavated material as well as the hundreds of ditches and pits. Second, seasonal water courses have been blocked by piles of excavated dirt, impacting herding and farming activities. Third, mercury is used in artisanal mining to amalgamate ground gold particles into one lump but is not handled with care and often leaks in large quantities into the environment, causing pollution and health concerns.[23] Still, rural communities largely refer to mining as *baraka*, a divine blessing, due to the new wealth it creates.

GOLD MARKETS AND NEW INCOMES

While extraction via detectors is increasing, the mining sites in the desert are still much more abundant sources of employment and income for impoverished rural populations. The gold market in Wadi al-ᶜUshar, in the peripheral Lower Atbara area in northern Sudan, is in a large, busy town of makeshift tents and huts, covered with blue plastic sheeting and old cereal or sugar sacks. Wadi al-ᶜUshar is about 20 kilometres south of Wadi ᶜArab, an even younger and smaller market, which emerged around the new excavation sites as people moved northwards from Wadi al-ᶜUshar to search for new mines. In March 2010 the market experienced its first decline, when hundreds of gold miners left for Um Ruweishid, a new mining site in the Butana. However, many miners returned after a few weeks. The Wadi al-ᶜUshar market developed after gold was found in the area in 2008[24] and has facilities to process gold ore, but also figures as a new centre for supply and consumption. At its centre, there are restaurants, grocery and clothing stores. Restaurants in Wadi al-ᶜUshar frequently have their own generators that supply freezers, fans, television and sometimes even game stations, items that are rare in the Lower Atbara area, especially the hinterlands, due to a lack of power generators and electrical networks. Also, camel meat and a variety of fresh fruit can be purchased – goods that are considered luxuries in rural areas.

On the market's south-eastern fringe some electrical and mechanical engineers from Atbara have opened huts, repairing gold detectors, generators and cars. Next to them, some small huts sell tyres, chisels, pickaxes, shovels, hammers and other tools. Several vendors offer petrol (gasoline) from large barrels. As well, a considerable number of men or young boys work as handymen, porters, donkey cart drivers, public transportation drivers with their own cars or as watchmen at the excavation sites or the market. To the south of the camp, large water tankers wait for their turn to sell water brought from the Atbara nearly 70km away, which they sell for 12 SDG (£3.66, $5.38 in May 2010) per *barmīl*[25] to gold miners. To the north-east of the camp, there are more than ten diesel-run grinding machines, operated by three to five workers. They pour pebble-sized stone pieces, delivered to them from the mines in large sugar sacks, into a large funnel. The machine grinds the crushed stones to fine stone dust, which looks like wheat flour but is coarser.[26] The ground stone dust is then transported to the washing pools by porters or donkey carts. There are about 15 to 20 hand-dug square pits just to the west of the grinding machines. Most pits are filled with water and are laid out with plastic covers to prevent the water from seeping away. The pools are used by up to four gold washers, each working in their own corner. They wash the ground material in large round troughs adding mercury. The mercury amalgamates with the gold dust and being heavier than the dirt settles in the troughs, thus the gold can be sifted out from the dirt. The washers generally receive a fixed payment for washing out the gold. In early 2010 the prices in Wadi al-ᶜUshar amounted to 10 SDG (£3.05, 4.15) per *ǧauwāl*[27] of ground material, washing one sack takes a worker around 20 minutes. The government report criticizes this washing technique for only capturing around 50 per cent of the gold, on average yielding between one and five grams of gold per sack (Ibrahim & Abdel Baqi 2010: 2).

The report however overlooks that in Wadi al-ᶜUshar some merchants have specialized in buying washed material comparatively cheaply from the owners of the stones, then washing it a second and a third time. In the centre and to the west of Wadi al-ᶜUshar market, often right in front of gold traders' huts, gold is heated on small fires to separate it from the mercury and it forms one molten lump. Many of the restaurant owners engage in small-scale gold trade. But there are also some large well-armed traders from Khartoum who advance the mercury to gold miners, and the latter are in return obliged to sell their gold to these traders. The mercury price is settled after the gold is weighed and sold. A small police station with three armed officers and huts belonging to the local administrator are located in the west of the camp.[28] There the local administrator, a sheikh of the Garab, a subgroup of the customary land-owning Bishariyyn, registers mines in the name of the mine owner for a fee of 10 SDG, deriving a small income for the rural council aside from the *wardīya* arrangement.

The gold market is not the haphazard agglomeration it first appears, but rather is a structured space with many sub-sectors, organized primarily according to the operational cycle of gold mining: grinding, washing, burning and sales areas. These sub-sectors work with their own sets of rules and organizational patterns. Several such markets operate in north-eastern Sudan. Informal gold mining and the related industry has become a source of livelihood for thousands of people from across Sudan. The absence of state regulations does not mean anarchy and chaos, but rather that a form of social organization of extraction emerges that is largely independent of state interventions and that depends more upon broader societal principles. What stands out as significant, and starkly contrasts with official politics, is that this 'informal' sector respects the landowning groups' customary land rights and the idea that local people should principally benefit from the subterranean resources in 'their' territory.[29] This is expressed in the administrative regulation of registering mines with the local sheikhs and above all the formalization of the informal *wardīya* arrangement.

THE CHALLENGE OF ARTISANAL GOLD MINING

> Hundreds of pick-up trucks, lorries and tankers are crossing the desert, the mountains and intractable terrain searching for gold. These prospectors view the Nubian Desert east of the Nile until the Red Sea hills as an open field for gold mining. (Ibrahim & Abdel Baqi 2010: 10; our translation)

'Many people have left agriculture and herding to search for gold, since the price for one gram rose very much', explains Muhammad Suleiman, director of planning and information of the Geological Research Authority of Sudan (GRAS) in the Ministry of Energy and Mining. In a preliminary report from March 2010,[30] which prepared the Artisanal Mining Regulation of October 2010, GRAS estimates that in early 2010 the number of people working in the informal gold sector had risen to nearly 40,000 in the River Nile State and the Red Sea States. Suleiman estimated nearly 50,000 people by early May 2010. With this, informal extraction had reached a point where it could no longer be ignored by the government.[31] To capture and assess the scope of informal gold mining activities in northern Sudan, the Ministry attempted to count the deployed assets: 1,500 cars including pick-ups, four-wheel drive vehicles, lorries and tankers, 20 excavators and five tractors, over 2,000 detectors of various brands, and nearly 500 diesel-run grinders. Further, it estimated that every week between 50 and 100 kg of extracted gold are sent to Khartoum for black market sale and export (Ibrahim & Abdel Baqi: 3).

GRAS' preliminary report critiqued that miners view the land between the Nubian Desert east of the Nile up to the Red Sea as an 'open field for mining', when in reality the land had been allotted to investors. Two concession areas are singled out as especially affected by the encroaching artisanal miners, first, the Ariab company concession and second, Wadi al-ᶜUshar and Wadi ᶜArab in the Lower Atbara area (Ibrahim & Abdel Baqi 2010: 10). This draws attention to the competition between artisanal and industrial mining: more than 90 per cent of informal gold mining sites are thought to lie within the concession areas of gold extracting companies. The contracts between the government and international investors are threatened by informal mining activities that are hard to control in the vast and isolated terrain. The companies that have leased concessions are challenged by the presence of informal miners, who are accused of taking what the company is entitled to, creating chaos and disturbing the extractive work. They demand the protection of their rights as investors and the prosecution of artisanal miners (Ibrahim & Abdel Baqi 2010: 14).

GRAS' report argues that as well as cheating and stealing, artisanal miners ineffectively wash out the gold, wasting much of the precious resource, a view that circulates among officials and their press releases, and also investment consultancies.[32] It also produces another line of argument against artisanal miners, namely the threat of crime and infectious diseases in mining camps, stressing the need to prosecute illegal mining activities (Ibrahim & Abdel Baqi 2010: 13). Other policy advice was to lay greater responsibility for law enforcement and control of the informal mining sector on the different state governments, and to unite small miners in supervised and delimited sites for gold mining. It also recommends granting gold miners access to sites abandoned by large mining companies where commercial extraction is no longer profitable. Further, it encouraged continuing to grant small concessions of between one and ten square kilometres to artisanal miners, to initiate the formation of miners' unions or cooperatives, and to intensify efforts to confiscate and prosecute the possession of unlicensed detectors (Ibrahim & Abdel Baqi 2010: 14). These suggestions were implemented in the regulation of 2010, but have not at the time of writing had a defining impact on the organization of the informal mining sector. In Sudan, on the ground, the state seems to only marginally affect the practices of artisanal gold mining communities. But as Sudan is undergoing a severe economic crisis and inflation related to the loss of substantial oil revenues, the government is likely to attempt to capitalize on the gold quantities produced by artisanal mining as indicated by the regulation of 2010. There the government's attempt to gain control of the gold produced by artisanal miners is outlined by licensing certain gold traders and banks to engage in this (in)formal sector (Artisanal Mining Regulation 2010 articles 16 & 17).[33]

It is questionable whether the government could suppress artisanal gold mining at all, even if it was not distracted by the ongoing armed conflicts in its southern peripheries and with South Sudan. In Benin in West Africa, after a phase of tolerance, the government attempted to intervene and partially control the informal gold sector through crackdowns, confiscations and displacements, blowing up mines and shafts, or regulating access to mining sites. This had an impact on the social organization of gold mining but not the intended results: instead of suppressing artisanal mining, it led to the emergence of even more transient patterns of organization, like smaller and more mobile camps, the immediate splitting of revenues and faster but more insecure methods of extraction (Grätz 2010: 117–123, 132). Given the mobility and flexibility of miners' camps, but especially of small detector teams in Sudan, it is unclear what effect interventionist policies could have, even assuming the government's commitment to its own rhetoric. But instead of being committed, its position appears somewhat ambiguous. We must ask whether reducing the government's interests to financial aspects is not overly reductive, and if the contradiction between banning artisanal mining on paper, but not enforcing this ban on the ground, does not represent a suitable compromise.

CONCLUSION

> With respect to the question of sovereignty, it should be underlined [. . .] that the core feature of 'sovereignty' of weakly governed African states is not actual or effective control over national territories (and still less a monopoly on the legitimate use of violence). Rather, it is the ability to provide contractual legal authority that can legitimate the extractive work of transnational firms. (Ferguson 2006: 207)

Gold mining is a flourishing economic activity. Artisanal mining is rapidly spreading on the ground, but so are the large government-leased concessions for foreign enterprises. Given the Government of Sudan's ambiguous politics of resource usage that strongly encourage foreign capital investments in gold mining while failing to suppress artisanal mining within the contracted concession areas, we argue that it is not defusing the tensions between these two flourishing mining sectors. Rather, we suggest that the metaphor of the passage point applies to the government in Khartoum to allude to its limited focus on merely extracting fees from global players in exchange for the admission rights to natural resources. This function of the federal government as a passage point between global capital and natural resources, and its ability to confer legitimacy upon foreign contractors, point to a situation where sovereignty does not mean the government's effective control and administration of territory.

For a small share of gold production, the government has passed legislation strongly in favour of the industrial mining sector. But it does not back its investment policies by protecting investors' contracted rights and therefore its own financial interests. Rather, to the chagrin of mining entrepreneurs, artisanal gold mining is spreading unabated and largely is carried out within private enterprise concession areas. The latter increasingly demand that the government crackdown on artisanal miners who extract gold from their concessioned land, but thus far the government has hardly intervened on the ground to halt competition between artisanal and industrial mining, despite its general prohibition of the former. Hence, the flourishing of artisanal gold mining is inconsistent with the official resource politics in Sudan.

Several contradictions stand out, highlighting the government's critical role. While large-scale concessions are encroaching upon the land, investors' rights are likewise encroached upon by artisanal miners. These companies increasingly demand law enforcement and artisanal miners' prosecution for the infringement of their 'assured' rights. At the same time these companies, with government backing, have displaced the collective land rights systems of local communities without offering compensation and frequently without much benefit to local populations. But often their impacts upon the landscape are limited to geographically isolated/dispersed interventions into subterranean matter. The example of informal mining in the Lower Atbara area highlighted that rural communities, although marginalized through such land deals and losing their entitlement to land, do not necessarily lose the actual control over the land or at least not over all of the land. Rather rural communities' customary rights to land are recognized in their mutually supportive relations with small-scale miners. Moreover, these local agreements are not only in step with customary land usage systems but also allow local communities to profit. Furthermore, artisanal mining offers a broad array of economic activities for local populations to generate an income. Although classified as illegal, these activities are highly organized and subject to compromises between various interest groups.

The case studies draw attention to complex entanglements of the federal and state governments and non-state actors, such as private enterprises and artisanal miners as well as local populations in administering, allocating and regulating gold resources. Thus we relate the government's ability to work as a passage point to a broad network of socio-political and legally pluralistic relations in the competition over land and subterranean resources. The privatization of collective property systems in the form of leaseholds for gold exploration is challenged by the practices of artisanal mining, which questions the extent to which the Government of Sudan is able to control territorially-bounded resources, and therewith may also figure as an investment disincentive for future investors in Sudan. But this is not necessarily the case. Political disorder need not be a disincentive for extractive industries. In many parts of Africa the securing of investments of extractive enclaves has been outsourced to private military companies (Ferguson 2006: 205). Such a politically unstable environment as in Sudan, where companies in the long run may need to provide their own security, may even turn out to be advantageous from their point of view: although increasing their expenses, it would have offsetting advantages, such as hindering artisanal miners from extracting gold from the concession area and preventing local communities' claims for a share of resources (Ferguson 2006: 207). In any event, these ambiguous and paradoxical developments need to be followed and scrutinized carefully to capture both their disruptive and constructive dynamics.

REFERENCES

AFP 2010. 'Sudan Gold Miners Vie for Desert Riches'. 23 August, <www.google.com/hostednews/afp/article/ALeqM5gCmQ_KcOqBDUeOvaqdOhPTjAI7tA>, retrieved 15-04-2012.

Agnew, J. 2009. *Globalization and Sovereignty*. Lanham MD: Rowman and Littlefield Publishers.

Appadurai, A. 1996a. *Modernity at Large: Cultural Dimensions of Globalization*. London and Minneapolis MN: University of Minnesota Press.

Appadurai, A. 1996b. 'Sovereignty Without Territoriality: Notes for a Postnational Geography'. In Yaeger, P. (ed.), *The Geography of Identity*. Ann Arbor MI: University of Michigan Press, 40–58.

Bayart, J.-F. 1989/2009. *The State in Africa: The Politics of the Belly*. Cambridge & Malden MA: Polity Press.

Bertram, C., Krätschell, A., O'Brien, K., Brückmann, W., Proelss, A., Rehdanz, K. 2011. 'Metalliferous Sediments in the Atlantis II Deep: Assessing the Geological and Economic Resource Potential and Legal Constraints'. *Resources Policy* 36 (4), 315–329.

Bloomberg 2010. 'Sudan Signs 10 Gold, Iron Mining Exploration Agreements, Minister says'. 7 November, <www.bloomberg.com/news/2010-11-07/sudan-signs-10-gold-iron-mining-exploration-agreements-minister-says.html>, retrieved 15-04-2012.

Callon, M. 1986. 'Some Elements of a Sociology of Translation: Domestication of the Scallops and the Fishermen of St Brieuc Bay'. In Law, J. (ed.), *Power, Action and Belief: A New Sociology of Knowledge?* London: Routledge, 196–233.

Citadel Capital 2011. 'Positive Indications of Gold Mineralization in ASCOM's Ethiopian Concessions'. 27 March, <http://citadelcapital.com/press-releases/positive-indications-of-gold-mineralization-in-ascom's-ethiopian-concession>, retrieved 15-04-2012.

de Launay, L. (Transl. Williams, O. C.) 2010/1908. *The World's Gold: Its Geology, Extraction, and Political Economy*. London: Heinemann; Milton Keynes: Bibliolife Reproduction Series.

Duffield, M. R. 2001. *Global Governance and the New Wars: The Merging of Development and Security*. London: Zed Books.

Dull, C .E., Metcalfe, H. C., Williams, J. E. 1958a. 'Gold – the yellow metal'. In *Modern Chemistry*. New York: Henry Holt, 525.

Dull, C. E., Metcalfe, H. C., Williams, J. E. 1958b. 'Zinc, cadmium, mercury, tin, and lead'. In *Modern Chemistry*. New York: Henry Holt, 535.

Elden, S. 2005. 'Missing the Point: Globalization, Deterritorialization and the Space of the World'. *Transactions of the Institute of British Geographers*. New Series 30 (1), 8–19.

Ferguson, J. 2006. 'Governing Extraction: New Spatializations of Order and Disorder in Neoliberal Africa.' In Ferguson, J., *Global Shadows: Africa in the Neoliberal Order*. Durham NC: Duke University Press, 194–210.

Foreign Policy 2011. 'The Failed State Index 2011', <www.foreignpolicy.com/articles/2011/06/17/2011_failed_states_index_interactive_map_and_rankings>, retrieved 10-06-2012.

Geological Research Authority of the Sudan (GRAS). 2006. Presentation, International Event Partners. 12–14 September. Khartoum.

Geological Research Authority of the Sudan (GRAS). 2008. Gold Concession Map. Khartoum.

Geological Research Authority of the Sudan (GRAS). n.d. 'Gold in Sudan'. Pamphlet. Ministry of Energy and Mining. Khartoum.

Gold Investing News 2011. 'Gold Mining in Sudan'. 6 January <http://goldinvestingnews.com/10826/gold-mining-in-sudan.html>, retrieved 16-04-2012.

Gold Price 2012. 'Gold Price History: 36 Year Gold Price History in US Dollars per Ounce'. 15 April, <www.goldprice.org/gold-price-history.html#36_year_gold_price>, retrieved 16-04-2012.

Grätz, Tilo 2010. *Goldgräber in Westafrika*. Berlin: Reimer.

IBP USA. 2011. *Sudan Mineral and Mining Sector Investment and Business Guide. Volume 1: Strategic Information and Regulation*. Washington DC: International Business Publications.

Ibrahim, M. S., Abdel Baqi, M. A. 2010. '*Raṣd wa taqaīym 'anšāṭ taᶜdīn aḏ-ḏahab al-ᶜašwā'ī – 2010. Wilāyāt naḥr an-nīl – al-baḥr al-'aḥmar – aš-šamālīya*'

[Assessment of artisanal gold mining – 2010. River Nile State- Red Sea State – Ash-Shamaliya]. Ministry of Energy and Mining, General Organization for Geological Studies. Working Paper 03/2010.
IBTimes Gold 2011. 'Sudan Hoping Gold Mining Will Ease Loss of Oil in the South'. 20 October, <http://ca.ibtimes.com/articles/234849/20111020/gold-sudan-ariab-oil.htm>, retrieved 16-04-2012.
Karim, A., Duffield, M., Jaspars, S., Benini, A., Macrae, J., Bradbury, M., Johnson, D. H., Larbi, G, Hendrie, B. 1996. *Operation Lifeline Sudan: A Review*. Geneva: UN Department of Humanitarian Affairs.
La Mancha Resources Ltd. 2011. 'Policy on Ongoing Operations and Investment in Sudan'. Montreal: La Mancha Resources Ltd.
La Mancha Resources Ltd. 2012. 'Reinvent – Transform – Grow'. Annual report 2011. Montreal: La Mancha Resources Ltd.
Metz, H. C. (ed.) 1991. *Sudan: A Country Study*. Washington DC: Federal Research Division, Library of Congress.
Ministry of Minerals (Sudan) 2010. 'The Organization of Artisanal Mining Regulation 2010'. 11 October, <www.minerals.gov.sd/minerals_eng/ahli.php>, retrieved 29-07-2012.
November, V., Camacho-Hübner, E., Latour, B. 2010. 'Entering a Risky Territory: Space in the Age of Digital Navigation'. *Environment and Planning D: Society and Space* 28 (4), 581–599.
Obeid, A.,Abdel Rahman, E.M. 2006. 'The Geological Research Authority of the Sudan (GRAS)'. Presentation at the 2nd International Investment & Trade Conference for Sudan, September 12–14, Khartoum.
Pantuliano, S. 2006. 'Comprehensive Peace? An Analysis of the Evolving Tension in Eastern Sudan'. *Review of African Political Economy* 33 (110), 709–720.
Reno, W. 2004. 'Order and Commerce in Turbulent Areas: 19th Century Lessons, 21st Century Practice'. *Third World Quarterly* 25 (4), 607–625.
Reuters Africa 2011. 'Sudan's Gold Rush Lures Thousands to Remote Areas'. 14 April, <http://af.reuters.com/article/worldNews/idAFTRE73D1GW20110414?sp=true>, retrieved 15-04-2012.
Reuters Africa 2011. 'Sudan Q1 Non-oil Exports Jump 34 pct on Strong Gold Sales'. 18 May, <http://af.reuters.com/article/sudanNews/idAFLAE83347920110518>, retrieved 15-04-2012.
Reuters Africa 2012. 'Sudan Delays China Debt, Exports $400 mln of Gold'. 19 February, <http://af.reuters.com/article/investingNews/idAFJOE81I00620120219>, retrieved 16-04-2012.
Rotberg, R. 2003. *When States Fail: Causes and Consequences*. Princeton NJ: Princeton University Press.
Rotberg, R. 2004. 'Strengthening Governance: Ranking Countries Would Help'. *Washington Quarterly* 28 (1), 71–81.
Spiegel, S. J., Veiga, M. M. 2010. 'International Guidelines on Mercury Management in Small-scale Gold Mining'. *Journal of Cleaner Production* 18, 375–385.
Sudan Tribune 2008. 'Moroccan Company to Explore Gold in Sudan'. 14 September, <www.sudantribune.com/spip.php?article28630>, retrieved 5-11-2013.
Sudan Tribune 2009. 'Sudanese-Chinese Consortium Signs Deal to Explore Gold'. 15 May, <www.sudantribune.com/spip.php?article31181>, retrieved 5-11-2013.

Sudan Tribune 2010, 'Sudan Signs Gold Exploration Agreements'. April 18, <www.sudantribune.com/spip.php?article34920>, retrieved 5-11-2013.

Sudan Tribune 2011. Sudan Tribune 2012. 'Sudan Says it Welcomes Saudi King's Initiative on Arab Food Security'. 11 March, <www.sudantribune.com/spip.php?article41877>, retrieved 5-11-2013.

Sudan Tribune 2011. '50 Gold Mining Contracts Signed in Sudan'. 30 October, <www.sudantribune.com/spip.php?article40579>, retrieved 5-11-2013.

Sudan Tribune 2012. 'Sudan to Offer Gold Exploration Licenses as Collateral for External Loans'. 19 March, <www.sudantribune.com/spip.php?article41972>, retrieved 5-1-2013.

Sudan Tribune 2012. 'UAE Plans to make 'Huge' Investments in Sudan: Official'. 20 March, <www.sudantribune.com/spip.php?article41985>, retrieved 5-11-2013.

Sudan Vision Daily 2003. 'Ariab Gold Mining as an Integrated Investment and Development Project'. 13 September, <www.sudanvisiondaily.com/modules.php?name=News&file=article&sid=7970>, retrieved 15-04-2012.

Sudan Vision Daily 2011. 'Interview with Minister of Mining'. 23 February, <sudanvisiondaily.com/details.html?rsnpid=187070>, retrieved 5-11-2013.

Telmer, K., Stapper, T. 2011. *Reducing Mercury Use in Artisanal and Small-scale Gold Mining: A Practical Guide*. Geneva: United Nations Environment Programme and Artisanal Gold Council.

Trade Precious Metals 2012. 'North Sudan Expands its Gold Mining Sector'. 24 January, <www.tradepreciousmetals.com/north-sudan-expands-its-gold-mining-sector>, retrieved 16-04-2012.

UNEP 2011. *Analysis for Stakeholders on Formalization in the Artisanal and Small-Scale Gold Mining Sector Based on Experiences in Latin America, Africa, and Asia: A Compendium of Case Studies*. Geneva: United Nations Environment Programme.

UNIDO 2007. *Removal of Barriers to the Introduction of Cleaner Artisanal Gold Mining and Extraction Technologies: GMP in Sudan. Final Summary Report*. Vienna: Global Mercury Project, United Nations Industrial Development Organization.

United Nations (UN). 2012. Cartographic Section: Sudan/ South Sudan. New York: UN Department of Field Support, <www.un.org/depts/Cartographic/english/htmain.htm>, retrieved 25-06-2013.

Watts, M. 2004. 'Resource Curse? Governmentality, Oil and Power in the Niger Delta, Nigeria'. *Geopolitics* 9 (1), 50–80.

Werthmann, K. 2009. *Bitteres Gold: Bergbau, Land und Geld in Westafrika*. Köln: Rüdiger Köppe.

Wikipedia 2012. 'Gold Price in USD'. 5 January, <http://en.wikipedia.org/wiki/File:Gold_price_in_USD.png>, retrieved 16-04-2012.

Yager, T. R. 2003. 'The Mineral Industry of Sudan'. In U.S. Geological Survey Minerals Yearbook 2002: 27.1–27.5. <http://minerals.usgs.gov/minerals/pubs/country/2002/sumyb02r.pdf>, retrieved 15-04-2012.

Young, J. 2006. 'Eastern Sudan: Caught in a Web of External Interests'. *Review of African Political Economy* 33 (109), 594–601.

Zeinelabdein, E. 2010. 'Sudan Experience in Using Remote Sensing for Mineral Prospecting'. Paper presented at the 11th Arab Conference for Mineral Resources, 25–27 October, 2010, Tripoli.

ENDNOTES

1. This increasingly includes also submarine resources, as the Atlantis II Deep in the central Red Sea has been identified as a valuable source of minerals (Bertram et al. 2011).

2. In early 2012 as Sudan's economic crisis was deepening, the government's increasing dependence upon foreign currency was expressed in the mounting foreign demand for mining concessions on Sudanese soil in exchange for further loans to the government (*Sudan Tribune*, 19 March 2012).

3. For instance, Max Weber writes: 'The state is that human community, which within a certain area or territory – this area belongs to the feature – has a (successful) monopoly of legitimate physical violence' (quoted in Elden 2005: 9).

4. It is noteworthy that Sudan's territory was partially administered externally, as in the case of the Operation Lifeline corridor (Karim et al. 1996).

5. See, for instance, the annual Failed States rankings of *Foreign Policy*, where Sudan is ranked amongst the top three failing states since 2008.

6. The source quotes information from the government, according to which gold exports amounted to 7 per cent of exports in 1999, but to only 3 per cent in 2001 (IBP USA 2011: 44), probably due to higher oil exports. The figures do not take account of the artisanal mining sector.

7. The article notes, though, that the 'gold output can be hard to verify in Sudan because much of it comes from individual prospectors rather than from regular mines'.

8. The mapping of prospective ores in the Red Sea hills had already been undertaken in the 1990s through the cooperation of the French Bureau de Recherches Géologiques et Minières (BRGM) and the Geological Research Authority of the Sudan (GRAS) with satellite data of Landsat TM and SPOT HRV (spectral ratio technique). Alterations in the satellite pictures were interpreted as mineralized zones and then explored on the ground. Remote sensing was likewise developed and put to use for the digital geological map (Zeinelabdein 2010). In 1981 this cooperation had already produced a 1:2,000,000 geological map of Sudan together with the Saudi-Sudanese Red Sea Joint Commission.

9. Only the concession blocks 18 and 19 were not displayed on the map. In 2010 and 2011, the number of concession blocks multiplied and included seven states, namely the Red Sea, Blue Nile, River Nile, Gezira, North Kordofan, South Kordofan and Northern State; further concessions were prepared for Southern Darfur. On 23 February 2011, the Minister of Mining reported 128 companies mining gold in Sudan (*Sudan Vision Daily*, 23 February 2011). On 30 October 2011, this development climaxed when 50 gold mining contracts were signed in Khartoum with national and international companies. A further indication of the new focus of investment policy since 2010 is the split of the Ministry of Energy and Mining into the Ministry of Petroleum and the Ministry of Mining, paving the way for the prospected transformation from self-regulating small-scale to state-regulated large-scale mining.

10. Most charts indicate a curve with a peak of 850 US$/oz in 1980, connected to oil price hikes, the Iranian revolution, and Soviet interventions in Afghanistan. In the following decades the gold price fell again to between 200 and 400 $/oz, but then in 2008 it again reached the 1980 high of 850 $/oz and has risen since. See <http://upload.wikimedia.org/wikipedia/commons/9/9c/Gold_Spot_Price_per_

Gram_from_Jan_1971_to_Jan_2012.svg> and <www.goldprice.org/gold-price-history.html#36_year_gold_price>

11. These figures are conservative compared to recent reports that estimate 200,000 people engage in informal artisanal mining. See, for instance, *Gold Investing News*, 6 January 2011.

12. International Business Publications' investor guide presents GRAS as 'the guardian of all metals and minerals within the lands, rivers and the continental shelf of the Sudan. It comes under the umbrella of the Ministry of Energy and Mining. It is financially and administratively independent and has its own Board of Directors and its Director General is directly responsible to the Minister. The overriding function of GRAS is to promote development of the mineral resources of the Sudan. This is generally achieved through the identification and systematic inventory of the available resources as a result of geological mapping and geophysical and geochemical exploration programmes. GRAS also engages in cooperation with investors to assist in and enhance the development of identified mineral prospects. In this latter respect GRAS undertakes exploration work in cooperation with international agencies' (IBP USA 2011: 29).

13. The exchange rate we use here is the May 2010 average (1 SDG: GBP £0.3050, US $0.4482) according to <www.oanda.com/currency/historical-rates/> retrieved 5-11-2013.

14. In 2010, the price was at 4,000 SDG (£1,220, $1,793) per square kilometre. When small permits encompass less than one square kilometre, the price then decreases proportional to the size of the rented plot.

15. The contracts contain a clause which enables the government to readjust the price level, provided that land rents in Sudan increase within the contract duration. However, the officials indicated that there may be conditions under which the government decides not to levy the annual rental fees. This, however, is part of the individually negotiated contract conditions, which usually are opaque and kept from public scrutiny.

16. According to the officials interviewed at the Ministry of Energy and Mining in May 2010, in addition to the annual land rents (if applicable, depending on the contract conditions), the government of Sudan receives a share of 25 per cent of the total profit that mining enterprises make, that is nearly 7 per cent of the total production. This concurs with the stipulations of the standard Memorandum of Understanding as established in 2002.

17. See, for instance, articles on Khartoum's ties to UAE (*Sudan Tribune*, 20 March 2012) or the attempts to gain Saudi loans (*Sudan Tribune*, 11 March 2012).

18. Eventually, the public display of these businesses by the government and the companies produces counter-claims. In a Sudan News Agency press release, for example, the Ariab Gold Mining Company was described as 'a model for the economic and development work which has realized all sorts of services [...] in the model village which lies about 35km from the production camp' (*Sudan Vision Daily*, 13 September 2003). La Mancha Resources was very concerned to display both political and social awareness concerning Sudan, which was the only country for which the company had a distinctive 'policy formulation'. Although this formulation was written basically to devalue Darfur-related divestment, it also contained details, how 'the Beja tribe' and regional development benefited from the mining and how environment and workers' health and safety were protected (La Mancha 2011).

19. The following section is based on Sandra Calkins' observations during several one-day visits in Wadi al-ᶜUshar and Wadi ᶜArab, some short conversations with gold miners, mine owners and local administrators but predominantly on her fieldwork in a rural settlement, some 60km south of the Wadi al-ᶜUshar. There she observed the gold miners' traffic – their cyclical coming and going and was able to record the intervals of their trips, their mobility patterns, their successes as well as the constitution and the relations between miners in mobile miner groups.

20. Yet, neither Grätz nor Werthmann mentions the search for gold via detectors. They describe an extractive technology – panning for gold in rivers, which was not mentioned by any of the interlocutors nor was observed. De Launay observes regarding alluvial deposits: 'In any place where man has dwelt for any length of time, he can no longer expect to discover alluvial deposits, the presence of gold in them being too easily detected. ... alluvia only remain today in parts very adversely treated by Nature, under the ice, snow, or marshy turf of the northern regions, in the pestilential forests of the tropics, the deserts, and a few high valleys in mountain chains' (de Launay 1908: 17). The long history of gold exploitation in northern Sudan might explain why panning is not used, although, as several people informed me, it is still used as an extractive technology in South Kordofan. A further major difference from West African gold extraction is that, in Sudan, searching for, processing and trading gold are purely male tasks. Women are even banned from visiting the excavation sites, due to fear of prostitution and immorality. A police officer in Wadi al-ᶜUshar explained that Sandra Calkins' presence was forbidden (mamnūᶜ), urging her to leave the site soon. The visits to Wadi al-ᶜUshar and Wadi ᶜArab were therefore short and drew much attention.

21. Other ways of extracting gold from ores, such as the cyanide process, active carbon adhesion or extraction with moist chlorine gas, are not employed by artisanal miners in Sudan (Dull et al. 1958a, 1958b).

22. Sandra Calkins' fieldwork was done in a new settlement mostly populated by Rashaida. Some of the most daring and most successful detector teams in the area come from among the Rashaida, as they often possess cars for transportation and know the terrain intimately from herding.

23. This is a global issue and was the subject of the Global Mercury Project (2002–07) and informed, among others, subsequent UNEP reports (UNEP 2011, Telmer & Stapper 2011) and discourses around international guidelines (Spiegel & Veiga 2010). According to the Global Mercury Project report, mercury amalgamation has occurred in Sudan only during the last few decades through the influence of immigrants from Ethiopia (UNIDO 2007: 1).

24. The government estimates vaguely that 3,000 to 7,000 people work in Wadi al-ᶜUshar (Ibrahim & Abdel Baqi 2010: 3).

25. Water is sold in *barmīl*. The same volume as a standard oil barrel (200 litres, 55 US gallon), it is often referred to as an imperial barrel.

26. The price for grinding a *ǧauwāl* sack fluctuates between 7 and 9 SDG. The owner of the grinder receives the larger share and pays his workers about 1 SDG per sack.

27. A *ǧauwāl* or *šauwāl* is the volume of a standard cereal, sugar or rice sack. The stones that fit into a ǧauwāl weigh roughly 70kg or 154 lb (Ibrahim & Abdel Baqi 2010: 2).

28. Wadi ᶜArab is administered by a sheikh from a different Bishariyyn subgroup, the Madhakir, whose centre is in Wadi Maᶜasheeb. The sheikh is *ra'īs al-lağna* of the Wadi ᶜArab locality which belongs to the municipality of Haiya.

29. Although the local sheikhs of Wadi al-ᶜUshar and Wadi ᶜArab both hold the office of *ra'īs al-lağna aš-šaᶜbīya*, and are therefore officially integrated into the state's administrative apparatus, they deny having received any guidelines for dealing with gold mining from Khartoum. Khartoum and the state governments (River Nile State for Wadi al-ᶜUshar, Red Sea State for Wadi ᶜArab) consider these mining activities to be illegal, but the police officers there were commissioned from higher administrative levels, indicating the government's awareness of mining activities and its inability to control them.

30. The report's argument has been repeated in interviews with the Minister of Mining throughout 2011 and 2012, where he tried to combine 'the people's well-being' with attracting large-scale investors. In an early interview with the government's *Sudan Vision Daily* in 2011, the Minister stated that 'localities are responsible for traditional mining as this type of mining is not included in the act of mining wealth of 2007'. Asked about taxation and prevention of 'traditional' miners, he claims that '[e]ncouragement of traditional mining doesn't mean negligence of shortcomings accompanying this process. Localities have rights to prevent people from mining in particular areas. The taxes are imposed on services provided by localities not the production.' (*Sudan Vision Daily*, 23 February 2011).

31. He recalls a much shorter but similar flourish of gold mining in 1999 that gradually declined as the gold price fell again.

32. See, for instance, the brief reports on Sudanese mining on the Trade Precious Metals (24 January 2012) and IBTimes Gold websites (20 October 2011).

33. In an interview with AFP, the Minister of Mining ᶜAbd al-Bāqī al-Jaylānī claimed that 200,000 people work in artisanal gold mining, adding that 'we cannot stop the diggers, but we will regulate them'. Another kind of 'resource', archaeological artefacts, is also a source of contention in the Nubian Desert, not just because of damage caused by mining, but also because of a shifting workforce (*AFP*, 23 August 2010). In another interview with Reuters, the Minister mentioned cooperatives as institutional tools towards regulation (*Reuters Africa*, 14 April 2011).

4

Oil, Water and Agriculture: Chinese Impact on Sudanese Land Use

JANKA LINKE

> Sudan is now at a special time in history, the fact of which China fully understands. I want to reiterate that no matter how the regional situation and Sudan's domestic situation may evolve the policy of the Chinese government to develop friendship and cooperation with Sudan will remain unchanged. (...) we will expand practical cooperation for mutual benefit and win-win results. We would like to deepen oil cooperation. We will encourage and support more capable and reputable Chinese companies in investing in Sudan and exploring cooperation opportunities in agriculture, mining, energy, water conservancy, power generation, road and bridge construction, communications and other sectors. At the same time, we will continue to provide assistance to Sudan to the best of our capacity. [...] the We wish to enhance communication and cooperation with Sudan on such major issues as the Security Council reform, climate change and food security to jointly safeguard the legitimate rights and interests of developing countries. We are confident that with the concerted efforts of both sides, our relationship will have an even brighter future.
>
> Chinese Ministry of Foreign Affairs, Yang Jiechi, in July 2011, shortly after the separation of South Sudan and Sudan (MFA 2011)

China is not a new actor in Sudan and Chinese interests in Sudanese resources compete with those of many international stakeholders. Their recent large-scale interventions in the land-based resource systems of oil, water and agriculture dramatically impact on the livelihoods of thousands of nomads and farmers (cf. Large & Patey 2011, Pantuliano 2010).

This chapter adds to recent studies by reviewing official documents, scientific publications, and corporate information published in Chinese[1] and by analysing how they discuss large-scale projects. It focuses on Chinese interventions that are shaping settlement, farming and grazing land in Sudan. As previous scholarship has shown, the introduction of Chinese technologies and capital in combination with the coercive power of the authoritarian Sudanese regime has contributed to the upheaval of the traditional land use system since the mid-1990s. The implementation of large-scale oil and hydro-infrastructure has left visible and at times nearly irreversible imprints upon land (Verhoeven 2011a, Grawert & Andrä 2013). Similarly, agro-businesses managed by the Sudan Government and foreign investors are currently transforming Sudanese agriculture (see Umbadda in Chapter 2). Consequently, rural and pastoralist populations have been expropriated, displaced and resettled from their land, their most important source of livelihood, while representatives of private companies and the Sudan Government have turned a blind eye to the potential implications of large-scale projects.

My analysis draws on James C. Scott's *Seeing Like a State* (1998), which investigates why developmentalist projects to improve society often have gone so fatally wrong. His initial conceptualization rests on four points. First, Scott argues that the 'administrative ordering of nature and society' requires a simplification and standardization of complex realities (1998: 4). What is perceived as illegible and irrational is transformed into 'legible and administratively more convenient format(s)' (1998: 3), whereby slices of reality are remade. The instruments of standardization are various, such as cadastral surveys, concession maps, population registers, and the modern design of resettlement sites.

Second, Scott underlines that administrative tools of rationalization are combined with a high-modernist ideology, i.e. a genuine belief in science, technology and human progress whose representatives 'prefer certain forms of planning and social organization' (1998: 4f.), such as huge dams, centralized communication and transportation hubs, large factories and farms, and grid cities. Only when measures of standardization and high-modernism are added to a third element, namely state power, 'does the combination become potentially lethal' (1998: 5). An authoritarian government or – given the global scale on which standardization has now been implemented – international organizations, such as the World Bank, WTO (World Trade Organization), and the IMF (International Monetary Fund), and transnational capitalist companies (Scott 2009) must be willing and able to actually realize their rationalist plans on the ground.

The fourth element is a 'prostrate civil society that lacks the capacity to resist these plans'. Reasons for a weak civil society, 'the leveled social terrain on which to build', can be war, revolution or economic crisis. Under these conditions, the local population can be forced to give way to the 'administrative ordering of nature' (Scott 1998: 5). In other words, ordinary people in poorer countries often find themselves in a vulnerable situation and with limited capacity to deal with the multiple complexities that penetrate their lives and livelihoods. However, Scott (2009) observes that projects still run the risk of being 'counter-planned': locals develop strategies of coping and adapting to intrusions into their livelihoods. Thus, the affected populations are not considered to be mere victims of modern planning but also agents who might subvert official planning to pursue alternative livelihood strategies.

This conceptual framework allows retracing the top-down mode in which foreign investments often have been planned and implemented. It also represents an analytical tool to comprehend the existing power structures in post-national governance systems (Allen & Cochrane 2010). As Sudan's top trading partner as well as political ally China plays a crucial role. However, as in other African countries (cf. Bräutigam 2013), Chinese activities in Sudan cannot be attributed to a homogeneous state-actor. Instead of reifying the Chinese state as monolithic, my analysis is attentive to a variety of Chinese players pursuing different goals. Even companies formally owned by the Chinese state, such as the China National Petroleum Company (CNPC), have found ways to act independently from Chinese foreign policies (Jiang & Xiao 2011). One should also bear in mind that the Chinese economic development had long been guided by the Maoist planned economy and only recently did it integrate capitalist ideas into official policy when thought to be 'good for China' (Ezzamel 2012). In view of this proclivity to neoliberalism, I will suggest that Chinese investment policies are still missing scientific instruments to generate a more reflexive knowledge production that reckons with societal and environmental costs and integrates this knowledge in overseas business ventures.[2] Against this background my analysis unfolds in four steps: Chinese business cooperation with Sudan is placed in its historical context. Thereafter, Chinese engagement in three sectors of the Sudanese economy is explored, namely the oil industry, the dam programme and agriculture, and I reflect on how three types of Chinese literature appraise these recent large-scale interventions.

THE EMERGENCE OF SINO-SUDANESE RELATIONS

Since the beginning of the twenty-first century, China has been active in almost all African countries with large investments. These activities have been closely monitored and controversially debated by Western scholars, politicians, businessmen and activists.[3] China's engagement in Africa is often represented as being propelled by its demand for resources, such as crude oil (Angola, Sudan), copper (Zambia) or iron ore (Liberia). Countries lacking natural resources were allegedly discovered as markets for Chinese consumer products and textiles (Senegal, Morocco) (Servant 2005). Indeed, Chinese exports of consumer goods to African countries might unfold a larger impact on African livelihoods than the extraction of natural resources (Haugen 2011). Moreover, huge infrastructural projects financed and realized by Chinese donors and companies have been accomplished all over the African continent, at times with irreversible social and environmental imprints.

China is an important political, military and economic partner for many African regimes, constituting an alternative to Western governments and organizations, such as the IMF and World Bank. As Large and Patey (2011: 2) assert, 'in Khartoum, China is seen as having come to Sudan's aid when everyone else had abandoned it'. Its economic prominence on the African continent has been growing in spite of the global economic recession. In 2011, the Sino-African trade volume once again set a new record at more than US $160 billion. China is now ranking first among Africa's top trading partners (*Xinhua* 2012). However, the import-export volume between China and Africa as well as Chinese investments on the continent remain low compared to China's trading relations with other world regions (cf. Statistical Yearbook 2011: 252ff, Corkin 2011: 62); Africa is only one target of the Chinese 'going global' strategy.

Relations between Khartoum and Beijing took off as they did with many African countries in the 1960s–1970s when the People's Republic looked for allies during the Cold War.[4] In 1971, China began to supply medical aid to Sudan, and continues to do so up to today. In addition, a number of aid projects were implemented in the 1970s, such as the construction of the Wad Madani – al-Gedaref road (Bartke 1989) and a bridge in Sinja (ECCO 2003). The erection of the *Friendship Hall* in Khartoum, a textile factory in al-Hasahis and the *Friendship Hospital* in Omdurman also date back to those days (ECCO 2003). From 1981 onward the cooperation continued, according to Chinese sources, with infrastructural projects, building for instance roads, bridges, water and power supply, and apartment houses (ECCO 2003).[5] In the mid-1990s the cooperation tightened when China entered Sudan's oil industry as it required huge energy resources for economic development. China became a net importer of crude oil in 1993. Sudan, for its part, has been under the rule of the military government of Omar al-Bashir and the National Congress Party (NCP, or its predecessor the National Islamic Front) since 1989. Under this influence Western investors in the oil sector gradually withdrew from the country. Potential Islamic investors were well-funded but lacked the technical expertise to continue the work of Western oil companies. Chinese, Indian and Malaysian oil companies stepped in to fill the void. In 1999, oil was first exported from Sudan. The development of the Sudanese oil industry paved the way for the influx of a variety of Chinese companies engaged in infrastructure projects, telecommunications and the pharmaceutical industry. With the global food crisis and South Sudan's secession, agriculture has lately been put on the agenda of large-scale business cooperation. However, after repeated attacks on Chinese workers, their number has dropped from about 30,000 to 10,000 in April 2012 (Shao 2012).

Chinese overseas business activities are regulated by a number of bureaucratic agencies such as the various departments of the Chinese Ministry of Commerce (MOFCOM), which is supposed to concert its efforts with the Chinese Ministry of Foreign Affairs; both are subordinated to the State Council. Chinese state-owned enterprises are expected to enact Chinese foreign policies, but there is room for pursuing their own agendas (cf. Corkin 2011: 82, Jiang & Xiao 2011). The Economic Counsellor of the Chinese Embassy in Sudan (MOFCOM 2009) frames Sino-Sudanese relations in the political context of South–South cooperation (*nannan hezuo*) by which it represents itself as a reliable friend and partner providing 'selfless aid and support' (*wusi yuanzhu he zhichi*), a narrative which is also reproduced in scientific articles (cf. Wang 2012). Economically, Sino-Sudanese cooperation is situated within the political agenda of 'going global' (*zou chu qu*), which in a neoliberal vein has officially encouraged Chinese enterprises to open up foreign markets since 1999. In this context, Chinese publications frequently stress the investment potentials of business in Sudan and that 'there is still much room for future cooperation' (Wang 2012: 67), based on a purported complementarity (*hubuxing*) of the two countries. In this regard, special praise is reserved for Sudan's 'rich natural resources' (*fengfu de ziran ziyuan*) such as more than a dozen different kinds of minerals, and the possibilities of investing in Sudanese agriculture, forestry, animal husbandry and the fishing industry. This led the Economic Counsellor of the Chinese Embassy in Sudan Hao Hongshe to envision Sudan as '(...) a place full of vitality. What I often say is that Sudan's earth is filled with gold, it just depends on whether you're able to bend your waist to choose [from it]. From this you can see that Sudan is a good place for Chinese entrepreneurs to invest in trade and start enterprises' (MOFCOM 2009).

The reports published on the website of the ECCO (Economic and Commercial Counsellor's Office of the Embassy of the People's Republic of China in the Republic of Sudan), which is subordinated to the Chinese Ministry of Commerce and the Chinese Embassy in Sudan, mainly rely on standardized formats of information concerning size, type, costs, projected benefits, and agencies involved in ongoing investment projects. These official reports thus feature abstract numbers and calculations which present 'tidy' realities. They disregard affected people in Sudan and their claims to the same land. These reports are oriented towards pragmatic objectives, namely providing Chinese companies with 'better knowledge about Sudan and a better position to develop trade and business with Sudan' (ECCO 2012c). However, this kind of knowledge production lacks foresight in assessing risks and unintended consequences for societies.

DISRUPTING TERRITORIES: THE CHINESE ROLE IN THE SUDANESE OIL INDUSTRY

Industrial oil production, it is argued here, is one of the main driving forces of transforming Sudanese land use. In recent years, the People's Republic of China has developed into the world's largest oil consumer following the United States. More than half of China's oil demand is covered by imports, which it has been trying to diversify by exploring and investing in countries possessing unexploited oil reserves. When operations in Sudan succeeded, engagements were expanded to other Sub-Saharan states, e.g. Angola and Nigeria, which marked the beginning of the large-scale Africa-wide investment in the new century.[6] In 2011, about two-thirds of Sudanese oil exports were delivered to China, covering about five per cent of that nation's overall oil imports (EIA 2012).

Chinese dominance of the Sudanese petroleum industry has to be placed in historical context (cf. ECOS 2008, Patey 2007): the US-American oil major Chevron took the first steps to explore Sudan's oil potential in the early 1970s. Main discoveries were mapped in the Muglad and Melut basins, markedly at Bentiu (Unity State), Heglig and Adar Yale, all of which are situated along the contested border between the north and South Sudan. Yet, Chevron never made any moves to actually put Sudanese oil on the market, as the political situation continued to be unstable; indeed, the war started anew in 1983. To Chevron, continuing the operations did not seem worth the risk and it completely pulled out of the

Map 4.1 Chinese Land-Based Interventions in Sudan and South Sudan

country in 1992, three years after Omar al-Bashir had taken power. The new regime was in urgent need of funding to fend off a surging Sudan People's Liberation Army and to implement an ambitious Islamization project. But it took the government in Khartoum a few years to find a capable substitute for Chevron, as the potential partner needed to be in command of the necessary funds, experience and technology to advance the Sudanese oil industry. In 1995, China's national oil company CNPC bought its first concession, Block 6, in Western Kordofan. Currently, CNPC holds stakes in five consortia, in all of which it maintains major operating rights. Block 1/2/4, for instance, is operated by the Greater Nile Petroleum Operating Company (GNPOC), a concession which is shared by CNPC (40%), Malaysian Petronas (30%), Indian Oil and Natural Gas Corporation (ONGC, 25%), and Sudanese Sudapet (5%). CNPC holds similar commanding stakes in the other consortia. Its position in the Sudanese oil industry is dominant.[7]

In January 2012, CNPC signed a Transition Agreement of Oil Cooperation with the Ministry of Oil and Mining in Juba, thereby confirming the previous existing contracts with Sudan and acknowledging South Sudan as business partner in the oil sector (ECCO 2012a). 'Today, nearly all the oil produced in Sudan and South Sudan originates from the Muglad Basin (Blocks 1, 2, and 4, Block 5A, Block 6, and Block 17) and Melut Basin (Blocks 3 and 7). Currently, oil produced from Blocks 2, 4, 6, and 17 is counted as Sudan's production, while oil from Blocks 1, 3, and 7 belongs to South Sudan' (EIA 2013).

The implementation of the oil infrastructure spreading across the whole country had a massive impact on the local population, displacing thousands:

> As of March 2002, the total number of displaced persons who fled Western Upper Nile/Unity State [i.e. roughly the location of Blocks 1/2/4 and 5A/5B] to elsewhere in Upper Nile and to Lakes (part of Bahr El Ghazal) alone was estimated at 174,200. This displacement, accomplished through war as the means of control of the strategic and valuable oilfields, was illegal under international rules of war. These civilians were not displaced for one of two permissible reasons under the rules of war: 'imperative military reasons' or the safety of the civilians. They were not allowed to go or to remain at home after the danger of a military campaign was over. They were pushed off their land, in some cases many times, by government army or militia forces, for the purpose of emptying the oil areas of southern civilians whom the central government regarded as 'security threats' to oil development, solely on account of their ethnic origin and therefore presumed rebel loyalties. The government tried to control this 'security threat' by the most extreme means of removal, using military land and air invasions, killing, looting, burning, and destroying the local subsistence economy and killing and injuring civilians. At the same time it cut the area off from humanitarian assistance by imposing relief flight bans and denials of access, while only allowing food into garrison towns, where it could serve as a magnet to draw starving people to crowded areas under government control: a textbook case of a counterinsurgency operation. (Human Rights Watch 2003: 313)

Similarly, probably well above 15,000 people had to flee their homes situated in Block 3/7, while several hundreds were killed (ECOS 2006). All campaigns combined aerial bombardments with a 'scorched earth' tactic on the ground. Villages were looted and burned down, harvests destroyed and cattle stolen, while families were torn apart, women abused and ancestral graves desecrated, thereby destroying important places to which belonging and identity used to refer (ECOS 2006: 3).

All reports place responsibility upon two sets of actors – namely the Sudanese governments and the oil corporations. They illustrate the interaction of powerful parties; the Sudan Government in Khartoum, on the one hand, institutionalized violence in order to open up the lucrative oil fields that promised unprecedented revenues. The foreign enterprises for their part, though not actively involved in the displacement of locals, enabled violent interventions by providing funds and technology. This does not only apply to CNPC but also other South-East Asian and European companies – the list of foreign oil companies in Sudan is long. The Economic Counsellor of the Chinese Embassy in Sudan reiterates the official stance that CNPC's projects are guided by the principle of 'mutually beneficial win-win cooperation and joint development' (*huli shuangying, gongtong fazhan*). 'The establishment of the oil industry played a crucial role in regard to Sudan's economic development. It gave the Sudanese economy the chance to uphold an economic growth rate of more than 8 per cent over several years despite adverse circumstances such as the US economic sanctions' (MOFCOM 2009). Whereas these official reports focus on mutuality and complementarity between Sudan and China, scientific publications tend to address why the tight cooperation between Sudan and China, especially in the oil sector, is perceived so negatively in Western countries and what this denotes of China's image abroad (Jiang & Xiao 2011, Wang 2012: 74). Importantly, while these scientific publications are somewhat self-reflexive they stop short of discussing sensitive issues, such as forced resettlement and other actual damage caused by oil extraction.

One source of discontent among the affected population is the continuing lack of transparency and mismanagement as regards the redistribution of oil revenues. Not only are compensations in oil producing areas completely absent, there also are hardly any signs of the announced 'huge economic and social benefits' of oil production (Wu 2008: 33). 'The large economic growth over the last few years has made a small Northern elite very rich, but most Sudanese people have seen nothing of it' (ECOS 2008: 31). Grawert and Andrä (2013) conclude in their report on the impact of oil exploitation on local communities in Block 3/7, in which CNPC holds a 41 per cent stake, that, while some of the oil investments may have created new livelihood opportunities, these cannot outweigh the destruction of property, land expropriation and pollution. Instead, conflicts over resources and power struggles have been exacerbated. Companies – including CNPC (2011) – have incorporated the establishment of development projects as parts of their contracts, but it remains obscure who actually benefits from them and whether they are sustainable (cf. Moro 2011).

Additionally, oil production potentially has adverse environmental impacts, e.g. the contamination of water and land resources caused by oil spills and the utilization of 'special additives' in the drilling of oil wells

(Cooper 2007). Other indications suggest that oil infrastructure, such as roads, disrupts local drainage and flood patterns, thereby affecting nomads' water supply and mobility, e.g. on the al-Fula–Muglad stock routes which are used by Missiriyya groups:

> Again petroleum road construction has provided an additional and temporary source of water in the construction of borrow pits. Pastoralists claim that the grid of roads has obstructed the stock routes and the natural drainage line, leading to flooding on one side of the road, with negative impacts on the range of plants and tree growth caused by waterlogging. In addition, the obstruction will also increase the incidence of water-borne diseases. To reduce construction costs, the roads of the petroleum grid do not have cross-drainage facilities. (UNDP 2006: 10f)

A glance at the map of the Sudanese oil concessions highlights the materialization and social impact of Scott's argument of 'simplification' (cf. Map 4.1). The straight lines that mark the divisions of oil blocks are detached from any reality in which the land concerned is used as fields and pastures. Accordingly, the map of the oil fields does not merely represent the system of concessions, it creates the system. Block 1/2/4 alone covers an area of 48,388 square km (19,683 square miles) (CNPC 2011) and cuts right through the traditional migration routes of several nomadic Baggara tribes (Lavergne 1989: 38). The demarcation of the oil fields has further fuelled the traditional tensions between nomads and agro-pastoral groups (Dinka) over contracting water and grazing grounds in the region. Second, pointing to Scott's notion of 'counter-planning', there is also evidence of local resistance strategies against these procedures (cf. Patey 2010: 631). For example, the kidnappers who abducted nine Chinese oil workers in South Kordofan in October 2008 were believed to be members of the local Missiriyya nomad tribe protesting against the region having received little benefit from the oil revenues (*Sudan Tribune* 2008). In another more recent attack in January 2012, 29 road workers of the Sinohydro Corporation were kidnapped in South Kordofan. Being one of China's major construction companies operating overseas, Sinohydro has completed major construction works at the Merowe and Roseires Dams. These violent actions demonstrate that large-scale projects bear the risk of damage, not only because of gross simplifications of complex environmental and socio-economic inter-relationships at the planning stage but also because of the negligence of potential counter-strategies. Local people cope with and adapt to large-scale project interventions in ways not anticipated. This equally holds true for recent developments in the exploitation of resources such as gold. Chinese ventures in these fields are considered highly profitable (Wang 2012: 70). Practical steps of joint gold mining in Sudan date back at least to 2006 when agreements were made between the Tianjin North China Geological Exploration Bureau and Sudan's Ministry of Energy & Mining (ECCO 2006) on investments in gold exploration on an area of 6,000 square km (2,317 square miles) in River Nile State. Gold extraction started successfully in 2008 (ECCO 2008a). To date, there is hardly any empirical data on how these transactions affect local livelihoods. An exception is Calkins & Ille's case study (Chapter 3) which shows how small-scale gold miners have thwarted legal provisions designed to exclude resident communities from the gold concessions.

CHINESE ENGAGEMENT IN SUDAN'S DAM PROGRAMME

Since the beginning of the new millennium, China has emerged as one of the biggest players in large-scale infrastructure projects in more than 35 African countries. In terms of the distribution of investment by sector, the main focus is on transport and electricity generation by means of hydropower. Besides Nigeria, Angola and Ethiopia, Sudan is one major recipient of Chinese funds (Foster et al. 2009). Verhoeven (2011a: 120) points out, 'big dams are an integral part of Khartoum's "hydro-agricultural mission", the Al-Ingaz regime's high modernist attempt at recalibrating northern Sudan's political economy'. Chinese investments and construction projects in Sudanese infrastructure are very diverse, comprising electricity, roads, bridges, water supply systems, irrigation and hydropower (cf. Tables 4.1 and 4.2). There are plans to expand the investment scale and cooperation areas (MOFCOM 2009). Even with the recent economic recession due to the secession of the South, optimism prevails in scientific analyses of Sino-Sudanese economic relations. 'There are still many things we can do' (Wang 2012: 75).

On a global scale, large-scale dam projects have experienced an upsurge – China, India and Brazil being the world's top three dam-builders (Verhoeven 2012). Sudan's dam programme aims at electricity generation and large-scale irrigation for the agrarian sector, thus linking the 'blue gold' with recent capital investments into Sudanese agriculture by, for example, Gulf countries. Recently, Chinese investors and enterprises have been engaged in at least five dam projects[8] currently under construction, being the so-called Twin Dam Project at the Upper Atbara (Rumela) and Setit (Burdana). The Roseires Dam Heightening Project, in which the Chinese construction company Sinohydro played a major role, was inaugurated in 2013 (Sinohydro 2013). Chinese companies also signed contracts for the Kajbar and Shereik Dams, both to be built at the Nile (CGGC 2011, International Rivers n.d.b). The Merowe Dam Project was completed after a five-year construction period in summer 2008, and mainly designed for power generation but also to boost Sudan's agricultural sector through irrigation, covering about 300,000 hectares (about 741,000 acres). The large-scale project was realized by a joint venture between the Sudan Government and various investors, mainly from China and the Gulf States. The Sinohydro Corporation and China International Water & Electric Corporation were responsible for the construction of the dam and hydro-mechanical works, while the Harbin Electric Industry Group constructed the electric transmission system. More than 1,700 km of electric transmission lines were laid (DIU 2011).

Table 4.1 Infrastructure Projects Implemented by Chinese Companies (Irrigation and Electrical Generation and Distribution)

Project	Chinese partners	Capacity (as indicated in the sources)	Costs in US$ million	Status	Remarks
Hydropower and irrigation					
Merowe Dam Project	Sinohydro, China International Water & Electric Corporation (CWE), China Three Gorges Corporation (CTGC)	1,250 MW 300,000 ha	886	Fully operating since 2010	70,000 people resettled
Roseires Heightening	Sinohydro, CWE	280 MW 378,000 ha	410	Completed in 2012	20,000 families resettled
Upper Atbara Dam Complex (Rumela & Burdana dams)	CWE, CTGC, Harbin Electric International Co. Ltd.	320 MW 150,000 ha	848	Construction since 2010	30,000 new resettlement houses built
Kajbar Dam	Sinohydro	360 MW	705	Under contract since 2010	12 villages will be flooded, affecting about 10,000 people
Shereik Dam	Gezhouba Corporation	420 MW	711	Under contract since 2010	
Electricity					
Al-Jaili Power Plant, Phase 1	Harbin Power Equipment Company Limited	200 MW	150	Completed in 2001	
Al-Jaili–Shandi–Atbara Transmission Line	China National Machinery & Equipment Import & Export Corporation (CMEC)	261 km	25	Agreement in 2003	
Coal & Gas Power Plants in Port Sudan, Rabak	Shandong Electric Power Constr. Corp.	820 MW	512	Agreement in 2005	
Rabak–al-Obeid Transmission Line	China National Machinery & Equipment Import & Export Corporation (CMEC)	340 km	81	Agreement in 2006	
Al-Jaili Power Plant, Phase 2	Harbin Power Equipment Company Limited	100 MW	97	Completed in 2007	
Al-Fula Gas Power Plant	Shandong Electric Power Constr. Corp.	30 MW	518	Construction in 2007	
Al-Jaili Power Plant, Phase 3, and Transmission Line	Harbin Electric Power Industry Group	540 MW, 187 km	448	Agreement in 2007	

Sources: Foster et al. (2009), www.internationalrivers.org, www.diu.gov.sd/en, http://sd.mofcom.gov.cn, www.cnfol.com (2010).
Note. The table lists a sample of large-scale construction projects; the list is not comprehensive. It is intended to merely indicate the range and scale of Chinese activities in Sudanese infrastructure. The numerous smaller projects, also undertaken by private investors, and development aid projects are excluded. In some cases, official data are disputed or incomplete and unreliable. Costs for dam projects include civil and hydro-mechanical works only. Some projects may have been completed in the meantime without being further mentioned in the press.

In Western countries, the project was criticized by environmental experts and human rights activists.[9] Approximately 170 km of land in length in the area of the Fourth Cataract were swallowed by the reservoir lake, including ancient cultural landscapes and unique archaeological sites (Al-Hakem 1993, Kleinitz & Näser 2011). This destroyed the villages and agricultural spaces of three tribal groups, the Amri, Hamadab and Manasir. Manasir constitute the largest group that had to leave their fertile homeland with its traditional date economy (Salih 1999),

Table 4.2: Infrastructure Projects Implemented by Chinese Companies (Transport, Shipping and Water Supply)

Project	Chinese partners	Capacity (as indicated in the sources)	Costs in US$ million	Status	Remarks
Roads					
Atbara–Haya Road	Chongqing International Construction Company	150 km	–	Completed in 2007	
Dibeibat–al-Fula Road	Chongqing International Construction Company	–	100	Completed in 2010	
Al-Fashir–Umm Kaddada Road	China Poly Group Corp.; China Railway 18th Bureau Group Co. Ltd.	–	96	Completed in 2010	
Water supply systems					
Al-Qadarif/ al-Fashir	China National Construction & Agricultural Machinery Imp./ Exp. Corp. (CAMC)	–	100	Construction in 2005	
Port Sudan	China National Machinery & Equipment Import & Export Corporation (CMEC)	–	509	Agreement in 2009	
Dal (Sennar state)	China CAMC Engineering Co. Ltd.	–	24	Agreement in 2009	
Bridges					
Merowe Friendship Bridge	Jilin International Economy & Technology Cooperation Company (JIC)	396 m	13	Completed in 2007	
Rufaᶜa–al-Hasahisa Bridge	China Poly Group Corp., China Railway 18th Bureau Group Co. Ltd	394 m	23	Completed in 2008	
Others					
Port Sudan container loading berths	China Harbour Engineering Company Ltd	140,000 t	110	Completed in 2009	
Apartment buildings in Sennar, Kassala, North Kordofan, North Darfur etc.	China Poly Group Corp., China Railway 18th Bureau Group Co. Ltd	-	118	Agreement in 2009	

and were resettled in 2009. Although new homes were built for nearly 30,000 Manasir and an agricultural scheme was established in Wadi Mukabrab, 16 km south of the city of Edamer, River Nile State, access to local resources were lost forever.[10] In the course of the Roseires Heightening Project another 20,000 families were resettled in '12 modern cities' (DIU 2012). Both the Merowe Dam implementation and the plans for the construction of the Kajbar dam have provoked many protests by local people (*Sudan Tribune* 2013). The North China Engineering Investigation Institute Company, in charge of geo-technological explorations for half a dozen dams along the Nile, reflected publicly about the difficulties of proceeding with their work in the face of repeated attacks (*xirao*) and 'anti-government protest demonstrations (*fandui zhengfu youxing shiwei*) of a small amount of people' (North China Engineering 2011). These corporate publications point to discontent with Chinese dam building in Sudan but they fall short of discussing the underlying causes of protest. Similarly, CGGC International, the Chinese company which signed the contract over the Shereik Dam, stresses its social responsibility (*shehui zeren*) within the framework of 'going global' and points to various awards it holds in this respect, such as the 'Award for Outstanding Contributions to Sino-African Friendship' (CGGC 2012). However, it remains an open question what exactly the contributions are and who benefits from them. Hence, despite the overly excited representations of the media on its positive outcomes, there is evidence to believe that, similar to the development of the Sudanese oil sector, the dam programme has created islands of 'development' and 'wealth' for groups in proximity to the power centre in Khartoum (Verhoeven 2011b) while simultaneously uprooting thousands of local people and destroying their livelihoods.

Another point of criticism is the poor cost-benefit relation of these massive interventions. Verhoeven's research (2011b: 12) suggests that the costs of sediment removal and flood mitigation amount to millions of US dollars per year. Large-scale irrigation systems require long-term maintenance and expertise on the technologies in use. For example, Calkins (2012) shows how problems surfaced in the so-called resettlement scheme for Manasir in Wadi Mukabrab soon after its construction, namely lacking water supply, the water erosion at the pumping stations and poorly maintained irrigation facilities. Ecological impacts and climate change are equally not taken seriously into account. Scenarios of how changes in precipitation and drought cycles affect the functionality of large-scale irrigated agricultural schemes, for instance, do not exist (cf. Verhoeven 2011b: 9). The Sudanese dam programme is thus – in Scott's line of argument – a prime example of a high modernist intervention for the sake of 'development' which entails large-scale intended and unintended environmental and socio-economic consequences. Chinese companies and financiers – but also some European and Arab stakeholders – act as providers of capital and technical expertise. To them, dams may be good business, while the local population are exposed to changes largely beyond their control. But the Sudanese dam programme also exemplifies an ideology which Scott calls high-modernism. The Sudanese regime draws on the belief in human progress through advanced technology also in order to strengthen its own legitimacy (cf. Verhoeven 2011a: 131–133). Facing the loss of their main source of revenues, the Sudan Government clings to the idea of 'development' through these megaprojects while ignoring their many potential impacts.

SHIFTING THE FOCUS: SINO-SUDANESE AGRICULTURAL COOPERATION

In September 2011, the Sudanese Ministry of Agriculture, once again, announced that agriculture is its economic future. This proclamation has to be judged alongside the recent separation of South Sudan, noting that 80 per cent of the oil fields that had formerly been exploited by the government in Khartoum are now located in the south. Since the agricultural sector is supposed to serve as a vehicle to draw required revenues, it subsequently has been labelled as Sudan's 'everlasting oil' and 'white gold'. The image of Sudan as the 'bread basket of the world' is reemployed, bringing to mind the disastrous consequences of the introduction of large-scale mechanized farming in the 1970s and 1980s (Kaikati 1980, Tetzlaff & Wohlmuth 1980). Utopian ideas to turn Sudan into the 'bread basket of the world' with the help of Sudanese land and Arab capital utterly failed and contributed to the dreadful famines in 1984/5, not to speak of the increasing civil war from 1983. In the 1990s, agriculture and the industrial sector were almost forgotten due to the excitement over the fast-growing oil sector – continuing until the recent turn of interest.

The rediscovery of the agricultural sector echoes the latest interest of banks and states in the acquisition of foreign land. Researchers and activists alike talk of land grabbing, emphasizing potential negative consequences such as the limited capacity of self-supply with staple crops, the impoverishment of local farmers, ecological destruction, etc.[11] For China, Sudan constitutes only one component in an Africa-wide strategy which predominantly reflects a technological approach to agriculture.[12] The renewed interest in African land is framed as being part of a long-standing 'agro-socialist cooperation' between China and Africa (Sautman & Yan 2010: 308). Han (2010) argues that the recent global focus on arable land should be seized as a lucrative business opportunity by Chinese investors. However, contributing to global food security, advancing technological progress and productivity rates in host countries are likewise specified as investment incentives in agriculture, which could lead to socially sustainable development (*kechixu fazhan*) (Han 2011). Scientific discussion of Chinese overseas investment in agriculture in Chinese language captures a broader (historical) context but lacks both theoretical framework and empirical discussion of the micro-level context.

First forms of agricultural cooperation between China and Sudan, limited to development aid, date back to the 1970s. Smaller water utility and irrigation projects followed after 2000 (ECCO 2009h). A wider cooperation in the agricultural sector was initiated with Sudanese President Omar al-Bashir's trip to Beijing in 2005. Recent Chinese statements and publications point to the risks and difficulties investments in Sudanese agriculture might face while simultaneously stressing the great potential (*qianli juda*) for lucrative business in the agricultural sector (MOFCOM 2009, ECCO 2009g, Li 2010, Xu et al. 2010). Sudan is depicted as a traditional agrarian country, whereby agriculture accounts for one third of the GDP. Its rich natural resources are stressed: thus far uncultivated arable land, rich reservoirs of water, livestock, pasture, minerals and oil. Arable land is estimated at as much as 84 million hectares (207.5 million acres) of which 80 per cent remain to be developed. Furthermore, 10 per cent of the Nile water that Sudan is entitled to remains unused. Cotton, gum arabic, sesame and peanuts are recognized to be among the most lucrative crops. An enormous potential for development is also seen in the Sudanese livestock sector, which, comprising 150 million animals, is said to be one of the largest in the world. Despite its potential, Sudanese agriculture is considered to be backward and the country still depends on food imports (ECCO 2009f, Wang 2012: 70–72). The Ministry of Commerce advertises the advantages of engaging with Chinese companies, namely 'China's perfected experience with agricultural production, modern agricultural technology and equipment' (ECCO 2009f). This is said to complement (*hubu*) the abundance of Sudanese natural resources and the backwardness (*luohouxing*) of technological equipment and farming methods (MOFCOM 2009).

The different levels of agency reveal the complexity of Chinese investments in Sudanese agriculture: one emphasis of the agricultural partnership is put on the exchange of agricultural expertise. In 2009, the joint efforts in this field were marked by the first Sino-Sudanese conference on agricultural cooperation held in Khartoum (ECCO 2009a, 2009e). Since then, a number of bilateral visits of agricultural experts have been reported (ECCO 2009c, 2011a, 2011b). The inauguration of the 'Center for Agricultural Technology' in al-Gedaref State followed in 2011 (ECCO 2011c). Chinese technology, such as mowers, is also supplied (ECCO 2008b, 2009b). Second, Chinese state-owned and private enterprises alike have taken an interest in Sudanese agricultural projects. In March 2010 the Chinese company ZTE was allotted approximately 100 square km of land for the commercial production of wheat and maize by the Sudanese Ministry of Agriculture (*Sudan Tribune* 2010). Additionally, the China Shandong International Economic & Technical Cooperation Group, Ltd acquired a contract to utilize 67 square km (26 square miles) of land in the Rahad Irrigation Scheme in May 2012. An investment of US $60 million (GBP £41.5 million in November 2013) in the cultivation of cotton and the construction of a cotton factory is planned. The same company intends to concurrently open up about 667 square km (257.5 square miles) for cotton production in several Sudanese states, including Khartoum and White Nile State (ECCO 2012b). However, it remains difficult to evaluate what is actually realized on the ground and whether such plans are put into practice or eventually end up as 'dead' projects (cf. Verhoeven 2013). Third, there are a number of Chinese private small-scale farm operators, who mainly produce a variety of vegetables, eggs and poultry to serve the demand of Chinese workers in Sudan (Xu et al. 2010).

Regardless of the actual scope of Chinese land deals, the discourse of Sudanese land being vast and full of potential is ominous. These kinds of representations often precede land grabbing by national and international investors (Gertel 2011). This kind of talk potentially introduces processes of standardization (measurement) and commodification (price setting), disintegrating the original relationship between land and the local population for the sake of global players' interests. It largely ignores that 'land has many kinds of use and ownership claims, and a straight purchase or lease under a formal legal system is liable to violate many other traditional uses for the land, and traditional rights' (Bräutigam & Tang 2009: 705).

There also is a lack of transparency concerning how land rights are actually transformed and violated, and to what extent locals have already complained about losses. Moreover, the intended methods of large-scale mechanized farming are questionable. Lessons of the 1970s and 1980s are disregarded: state-run and private agricultural projects of the past have already restricted land access of pastoralists and subsistence farmers, and intensive use has left formerly arable land as wasteland (Elnagheeb & Bromley 1992, Streck 2002, UNEP 2007: 8). In the Nuba Mountains, the unsustainable tendency of rain-fed mechanized farming towards short-term yield maximization resulted in ecological degradation and intensified conflicts over resources (Abdelgabar 1997: 171, Komey 2010).

Agriculture is, Scott argues, an instance of 'a radical reorganization and simplification of flora to suit man's goals' (1998: 2). However, the comeback of large-scale foreign investments in the Sudanese agricultural sector in combination with technology supply adds further dynamics to the basic relationship between people and their land, i.e. power relations that potentially operate top-down, failing to consult local people. The increase of land deals in Sudan represents the materialization of these unbalanced struggles over resources with manifold consequences inscribed into livelihoods and eco-systems.[13]

CONCLUSION

Resource governance in Sudan is a contested field. Its main trajectories are defined by shifting relations between Sudan's authoritarian government and international investors and companies. As the above exploration of investments in oil, water and agriculture illustrated, Chinese companies play a prominent role in Sudan. According to Chinese accounts, Sudan is a 'vast' land and 'rich' in natural resources. Apart from political entanglements, this interest in extracting and marketing resources explains why the Sudan Government seeks partnerships with foreign countries and companies, which provide modern technology and finance, while promising 'development'. I have employed Scott's framework in order to demonstrate how large-scale modernist projects of Chinese companies cause ecological, economic and socio-spatial damage. From the Chinese side there have been no mechanisms in place to calculate risks for local societies and prevent adverse consequences, rather these have been often overlooked or ignored.

Three types of sources were consulted to analyse the types of knowledge produced and circulated in Chinese-language documents about investments in Sudan, namely official business assessments, scientific literature and corporate information. To a certain extent these different actors and agencies can be seen as working in unison, reproducing the use of certain catchwords and phrases such as the emphasis on 'win-win' cooperation, creating social benefits for the affected populations through the implementation of (large-scale) investment projects and envisioning a rich potential for future Sino-Sudanese cooperation. 'Opening up markets' (*kaikuo shichang*) and 'creating a good investment environment' (*chuangzao lianghao touzi maoyi huanjing*) are compelling motifs orienting 'development' practices and limiting projections to economic performance. Such understanding not only fails to anticipate adverse consequences but also to institute scientific mechanisms able to analyse the real and damaging costs of large-scale projects to local communities. Lessons of the past, such as in the case of agriculture modernization, are lessons that have not been learned.

This raises questions regarding the responsibility and accountability of corporations operating in countries like Sudan, without strong state institutions, that do not secure their populations from insecurities. These dilemmas are not addressed. Rather, the politics of resource extraction continues and does so in line with Scott's analysis. Natural resources (arable land, oil, minerals, hydropower) are ordered and classified into manageable schemes with the purpose of redefining their usage, namely turning them into commodities. Subsequently, the terrain formerly utilized by small-scale farmers and pastoralists is transformed into 'resource extraction and construction sites', and 'agricultural zones' for mechanized farming. The very same land that had formerly been unregistered and unmeasured, hence experiences a change of identity by superimposing new foreign topologies of 'productivity' and 'ownership'. Judging from past experiences, many of these intrusions into agricultural and pastoral livelihoods remain irreversible. As James Scott (1998) succinctly noted, even the best of intentions cannot prevent 'certain schemes to improve the human condition' from failure.

REFERENCES

Abdelgabar, O. 1997. *Mechanised Farming and Nuba Peasants: An Example for Non-Sustainable Development in the Sudan*. Hamburg: Lit.

Alden, C. 2007. *China in Africa*. London: Zed Books.

Alden, C., Large, D., Soares de Oliveira, R. (eds) 2008. *China Returns to Africa: A Rising Power and a Continent Embrace*. London: Hurst.

Al-Hakem, A. M. A. 1993. 'Merowe (Hamdab) High Dam and its Impacts'. *Kush* 16, 1–25.

Allen, J., Cochrane, A. 2010. 'Assemblages of State Power: Topological Shifts in the Organization of Government and Politics'. *Antipode* 42 (5), 1071–1089.

Bartke, W. 1989. *The Economic Aid of the PR China to Developing and Socialist Countries*. München and New York: K.G. Saur.

Beck, K. 1997. 'Wer kennt schon Hamdab? Ein Staudammvorhaben im Sudan'. In Pörtge, K.-H. (ed.), *Forschungen im Sudan: Ergebnisse der interdiziplinären Sudantagung im Februar 1996 in Erfurt,* Erfurt: Selbstverlag des Instituts für Geographie der Pädagogischen Hochschule Erfurt, 79–88.

Beck, K. 1999. 'Escaping from Narrow Confines – Returning to Tight Communities: Manasir Labour Migration from the Area of the Fourth Nile Cataract'. In Hahn, H. P., Spittler, G. (eds), *Afrika und die Globalisierung.* Hamburg: Lit, 201–211.

Borras, S.M., Franco, J.C. 2012. 'Global Land Grabbing and Trajectories of Agrarian Change. A Preliminary Analysis'. *Journal of Agrarian Change* 12 (1), 34–59.

Bräutigam, D. 2009. *The Dragon's Gift: The Real Story of China in Africa.* Oxford: Oxford University Press.

Bräutigam, D. 2013. 'Chinese Engagement in African Agriculture: Fiction and Fact'. In Allan, J. A., Keulertz, M., Sojamo, S., Warner, J. (eds), *Handbook of Land and Water Grabs in Africa: Foreign Direct Investment and Food and Water Security.* Abingdon and New York: Routledge, 91–103.

Bräutigam, D., Tang, X. 2009. 'China's Engagement in African Agriculture: "Down to the Countryside"'. *The China Quarterly* 199, 686–706.

Buckley, L. 2011. 'Eating Bitter to Taste Sweet: An Ethnographic Sketch of a Chinese Agriculture Project in Senegal'. Paper presented at the International Conference on Global Land Grabbing 6–8 April 2011 <www.future-agricultures.org/publications/research-and-analysis/policy-briefs/doc_download/1274-eating-bitter-to-taste-sweet-an-ethnographic-sketch-of-a-chinese-agriculture-project-in-senegal>, retrieved 25-04-2013.

Buckley, L. 2013. 'Chinese Land-Based Interventions in Senegal'. *Development and Change* 44 (2), 429–450.

Calkins, S. 2012. 'Agricultural Encroachment in Wadi Mukabrab Area. Policies of Recompense, Differentiation and "Tribal" Belonging'. In Kleinitz, C., Näser, C. (eds), *'Nihna nâs al-bahar – We are the People of the River'. Ethnographic Research in the Fourth Nile Cataract Region, Sudan.* Wiesbaden: Harrassowitz, 229–252.

CGGC 2011. '2010 nian guoji gongcheng youxian gongsi dashi ji' [Record of large-scale ventures of Gezhouba International in 2010], <http://gzbgj.com/article.aspx?menuid=1300&tab=tab_News&tabid=28>, retrieved 15-06-2013.

CGGC 2012. 'Gongsi jianjie' [Company short introduction], <http://gzbgj.com/article.aspx?menuid=1292&tab=tab_News&tabid=5>, retrieved 24-09-2013.

CNPC 2011. 'CNPC in Sudan: Oil and Gas Operations', <www.cnpc.com.cn/en/cnpcworldwide/sudan>, retrieved 25-04-2013.

Cooper, J. C. 2007. 'Sudan Transitional Environment Program: Scoping Statement for a Programmatic Environmental Assessment of Oil Exploration and Production Activities in Southern Sudan'. Washington DC: International Resources Group and USAID, <http://pdf.usaid.gov/pdf_docs/pdacl235.pdf>, retrieved 06-05-2013.

Corkin, L. 2011. 'Redefining Foreign Policy Impulses toward Africa: The Roles of the MFA, the MOFCOM and China Exim Bank'. *Journal of Current Chinese Affairs* 40 (4), 61–90.

Daniel, S., Mittal, A. 2009. 'The Great Land Grab. Rush for World's Farmland Threatens Food Security for the Poor', <www.oaklandinstitute.org/sites/

oaklandinstitute.org/files/LandGrab_final_web.pdf>, retrieved 14-06-2013.

DIU 2011. 'Merowe Dam Project: Transmission Lines', <www.merowedam.gov.sd/en/transp-lines.html>, retrieved 05-05-2013.

DIU 2012. 'Resettlement in Blue Nile Over, Karori', <www.roseiresdam.gov.sd/en/index.php/home_en/show/62#.UY_ov8rDg_w>, retrieved 12-05-2013.

Downs, E.S. 2007. 'The Fact and Fiction of Sino-African Energy Relations'. *China Security* 3 (3), 42–68.

ECCO (Economic and Commercial Counsellor's Office of the Embassy of the People's Republic of China in the Republic of Sudan) 2003. 'Hezuo jianjie' [Brief introduction to Sino-Sudanese cooperation], <http://sd.mofcom.gov.cn/aarticle/zxhz/hzjj/200303/20030300077742.html>, retrieved 16-08-2008.

ECCO 2006. 'Zhongsu liangguo qianshu hezuo kaicai jinkuang de yixiangshu' [China and Sudan sign letter of intent on cooperation in gold mining], <http://sd.mofcom.gov.cn/aarticle/jmxw/200603/20060301684233.html>, retrieved 29-04-2013.

ECCO 2007. 'Sudan ni zai Da'erfu'er diqu da 1000 yan shuijing' [Sudan intends to drill 1000 wells in Darfur], <http://sd.mofcom.gov.cn/article/jmxw/200706/20070604829619.shtml>, retrieved 28-04-2013.

ECCO 2008a. 'Wo zai Su jinkuang kaifa chujian chengxiao' [Chinese companies see first results in exploitation of Sudanese gold mines], <http://sd.mofcom.gov.cn/aarticle/jmxw/200806/20080605606799.html>, retrieved 29-04-2013.

ECCO 2008b. 'Sudan jiang zhubu shixian xiaomai zigei' [Sudan will gradually realize self-sufficiency in wheat], <http://sd.mofcom.gov.cn/article/jmxw/200808/20080805715672.shtml>, retrieved 28-04-2013.

ECCO 2009a. 'Zhongsu di yi jie nongye hezuo luntan kaimu' [Opening of the first Sino-Sudanese forum on agriculture cooperation], <http://sd.mofcom.gov.cn/article/jmxw/200906/20090606348359.shtml>, retrieved 28-04-2013.

ECCO 2009b. 'Beifang gongye gongsi shougeji jiaojie yishi' [Norinco's handover ceremony for harvesting machinery], <http://sd.mofcom.gov.cn/article/jmxw/200903/20090306100544.shtml>, retrieved 28-04-2013.

ECCO 2009c. 'Wo yuan Sudan gaoji nongye zhuanjia di Su' [High-ranking experts on agriculture arrive in Sudan], <http://sd.mofcom.gov.cn/article/jmxw/200908/20090806438885.shtml>, retrieved 28-04-2013.

ECCO 2009d. 'Yuan Sudan Da'erfu'er diqu 30 koushuijing xiangmu huanwen yi qianshu' [Exchange of notes on an aid project of 30 drinking water wells in Darfur, Sudan, has been signed], <http://sd.mofcom.gov.cn/article/jmxw/200907/20090706400829.shtml>, retrieved 28-04-2013.

ECCO 2009e. 'Di yi jie zhongsu nongye hezuo yantaohui shunli bimu' [First Sino-Sudanese symposium on agriculture cooperation ends successfully], <http://sd.mofcom.gov.cn/article/jmxw/200906/20090606348794.shtml>, retrieved 28-04-2013.

ECCO 2009f. 'Sudan nongye fazhan ji liangguo nongye hezuo de jiben qingkuang' [Sudanese agriculture development and basic facts on Sino-Sudanese agriculture cooperation], <http://sd.mofcom.gov.cn/aarticle/zxhz/hzjj/200909/20090906507326.html>, retrieved 14-12-2009.

ECCO 2009g. 'Sudan touzi maoyi huanjing he jingji hezuo zhong ying zhuyi de wenti' [Issues to be considered in Sudan's environment for investment and trade, and economic cooperation], <http://sd.mofcom.gov.cn/aarticle/zxhz/hzjj/200909/20090906504109.html>, retrieved 14-12-2009.

ECCO 2009h. 'Alabo guojia zai Sudan de nongye touzi wenbu zengzhang' [Arab investments in Sudanese agriculture steadily increase], <http://sd.mofcom.gov.cn/article/jmxw/200905/20090506234366.shtml>, retrieved 28-04-2013.

ECCO 2011a. 'Zhongguo nongyebu daibiaotuan fangwen Sudan' [Chinese Ministry of Agriculture sends delegation to Sudan], <http://sd.mofcom.gov.cn/article/jmxw/201112/20111207887060.shtml>, retrieved 28-04-2013.

ECCO 2011b. 'Sudan nongye daibiaotuan fangwen Zhongguo' [Sudanese agriculture delegation visits China], <http://sd.mofcom.gov.cn/article/jmxw/201105/20110507539748.shtml>, retrieved 28-04-2013.

ECCO 2011c. 'Zhongsu qianshu yuan Su nongye shifan zhongxin xiangmu jiaojie zhengshu' [China and Sudan sign handover certificate for agriculture training centre], <http://sd.mofcom.gov.cn/article/jmxw/201106/20110607612790.shtml>, retrieved 24-11-2013.

ECCO 2012a. 'Nan Sudan yu waiguo shiyou gongsi qianshu guodu xieding' [South Sudan and foreign oil companies sign interim agreements], <http://sd.mofcom.gov.cn/article/jmxw/201201/20120107930174.shtml>, retrieved 28-04-2013.

ECCO 2012b. 'Wo qiye zai Sudan daxing nongye kaifa qude shizhixing jinzhang' [Chinese companies achieve substantial progress in Sudan's large-scale agriculture development], <http://sd.mofcom.gov.cn/aarticle/jmxw/201205/20120508139850.html>, retrieved 28-04-2013.

ECCO 2012c. 'Canzan zhici' [Welcoming words of the Counsellor], <http://sd.mofcom.gov.cn/article/about/greeting/201206/20120608201819.shtm>, retrieved 29-09-2013.

ECOS 2006. 'Oil Development in Northern Upper Nile, Sudan', <www.ecosonline.org/reports/2006/melut.pdf>, retrieved 09-05-2013.

ECOS 2007. 'ECOS Oil Map, Colour, Large', <www.ecosonline.org/oilmap/resources/Soedan%20A5%20kleur.pdf>, retrieved 20-10-2012.

ECOS 2008. 'Sudan: Whose Oil? Sudan's Oil Industry: Facts and Analysis, April 2008', <www.ecosonline.org/reports/2008/dossier%20final%20groot%20web.pdf>, retrieved 10-05-2013.

EIA 2013. 'Sudan and South Sudan: Overview', <www.eia.gov/countries/cab.cfm?fips=SU>, retrieved 12-06-2013.

Elnagheeb, A. H., Bromley, D. W. 1992. 'Rainfed Mechanized Farming and Deforestation in Central Sudan'. *Environmental and Resource Economics* 2 (4), 359–371.

Ezzamel, M. 2012. 'The Emergence of Chinese State Capitalism and the Role of Accounting'. Paper presented at the Joint Institutes Colloquium, Max Planck Institute for Social Anthropology and Seminar for Social Anthropology, Martin-Luther University, Halle. November 6, 2012.

Foster, V., Butterfield, W., Chen, C., Pushak, N. 2008. *Building Bridges: China's Growing Role as Infrastructure Financier for Sub-Saharan Africa*. Washington DC: World Bank.

Gertel, J. 2011. 'Konflikte um Weideland: Zwischen Aneignung und Enteignung'. *Geographische Rundschau* 63 (7–8), 4–11.

Gesellschaft für bedrohte Völker [Society for Threatened Peoples] 2006. 'Bau des

Merowe-Großstaudamms im Sudan', <www.gfbv.de/inhaltsDok.php?id=761&stayInsideTree=1>, retrieved 29-04-2013.

GRAIN 2008. 'Seized! The 2008 Land Grab for Food and Financial Security', <www.grain.org/article/entries/93-seized-the-2008-landgrab-for-food-and-financial-security>, retrieved 14-06-2013.

Grawert, E., Andrä, C. 2013. *Oil Investment and Conflict in Upper Nile State, South Sudan*. Bonn: BICC brief 48.

Haberlah, D., von dem Bussche, J. 2005. 'Das Dorf Atoyah auf der Insel Sherari. Wandel der Siedlungsstruktur im Dar al-Manasir'. *Der Antike Sudan. Mitteilungen der Sudanarchäologischen Gesellschaft zu Berlin* 16, 125–135.

Han, Q. 2010. 'Dui Zhongguo nongye duiwai touzi guimo zhuangkuang de fenxi yu sikao' [Analysing the Scope of China's Foreign Direct Investments in Agriculture]. *Guoji Jingji Hezuo [International Economic Cooperation]* 10, 13–17.

Han, Y. 2011. '*Fazhan huli shuangying de zhongfei nongye hezuo*' [Develop the mutually beneficial agricultural cooperation between China and Africa]. *Feizhou Jingmao Yanjiu [Studies on African Economic Relations]* 5, 33–37.

Hänsch, V. 2012. 'Chronology of a Displacement. The Drowning of the Manâsîr People'. In Kleinitz, C., Näser, C. (eds), '*Nihna nâs al-bahar – We are the People of the River*'. *Ethnographic Research in the Fourth Nile Cataract Region, Sudan.* Wiesbaden: Harrassowitz, 179–228.

Haugen, H. Ø. 2011. 'Chinese Exports to Africa: Competition, Complementarity and Cooperation between Micro-Level Actors'. *Forum for Development Studies* 38 (2), 157–176.

Human Rights Watch (HRW) 2003. *Sudan, Oil, and Human Rights*. New York: Human Rights Watch, <www.hrw.org/reports/2003/sudan1103/sudanprint.pdf>, retrieved 22-04-2013.

International Rivers n.d.a. 'Kajbar Dam, Sudan', <www.internationalrivers.org/campaigns/kajbar-dam-sudan>, retrieved 05-05-2013.

International Rivers n.d.b. 'Merowe Dam, Sudan', <www.internationalrivers.org/campaigns/merowe-dam-sudan-0>, retrieved 29-04-2013.

Jakobson, L., Zha, D. 2006. 'China and the Worldwide Search for Oil Security'. *Asia-Pacific Review* 13 (2), 60–73.

Jiang, L., Xiao, J. 2011. 'Zhongguo dui Sudan de shiyou waijiao: zhengqi juese yanjiu' [China's Oil Diplomacy towards Sudan: the State-Enterprise Roles Analysis]. *Alabo Shijie Yanjiu [Arab World Studies]* 5, 40–53.

Kaikati, J.G. 1980. 'The Economy of Sudan: A Potential Breadbasket of the Arab World?' *International Journal of Middle East Studies* 11 (1), 99–123.

Kleinitz, C., Näser, C. 2011. 'The Loss of Innocence. Political and Ethical Dimensions of the Merowe Dam Archaeological Salvage Project at the Fourth Nile Cataract (Sudan)'. *Conservation and Management of Archaeological Sites* 13 (2–3), 253–280.

Komey, G. K. 2010. *Land, Governance, Conflict & the Nuba of Sudan*. Woodbridge and Rochester NY: James Currey.

Large, D., Patey, L. A. 2010. 'Caught in the Middle: China and India in Sudan's Transition'. *DIIS Working Paper* (36). Copenhagen: Danish Institute of International Studies.

Large, D., Patey, L. A. 2011. 'Sudan "Looks East": Introduction'. In Large, D., Patey, L. A. (eds), *Sudan Looks East: China, India & the Politics of Asian Alternatives.* Woodbridge: James Currey, 1–34.

Lavergne, M. (ed.) 1989. *Le Soudan Contemporain. De l'Invasion Turco-Égyptienne à la Rébellion Africaine (1821–1989)*. Paris: Karthala.

Li, R. 2010. 'Kaituo Zhongguo Sudan nongye hezuo xin jumian' [Developing new aspects of Sino-Sudanese agriculture cooperation]. *Nongye jingji [Agriculture and Economy]* (1).

MFA (Ministry of Foreign Affairs) 2011. Foreign Minister Yang Jiechi's Written Interview with Sudanese Press, <www.fmprc.gov.cn/eng/zxxx/t848828.htm>, retrieved 07-05-2013.

MOFCOM (Ministry of Commerce of the People's Republic of China) 2009. 'Zai xian fangtan' [Online Interview], <http://gzly.mofcom.gov.cn/website/face/www_face_history.jsp?sche_no=1452>, retrieved 29-09-2013.

Moro, L. N. 2011. 'Local Relations of Oil Development in Southern Sudan: Displacement, Environmental Impact & Resettlement'. In Large, D., Patey, L. A. (eds), *Sudan Looks East: China, India & the Politics of Asian Alternatives.* Woodbridge: James Currey, 70–86.

North China Engineering Investigation Institute Company 2011. 'Sudan Niluohe shuili shuidian daba baji kancha xiangmu' [The hydropower dam base geotechnical exploration project at the River Nile, Sudan], <www.nceii.com/html/ZhuoYueYeJi/GuoWaiYeJi/17.html>, retrieved 15-06-2013.

OMCT (World Organisation Against Torture) 2007. 'OMCT Action File: SDN 301107.ESCR. Sudan: Ongoing Violence Against Communities Resisting Dam Construction in the Northern Nile Valley', <www.omct.org/files/2007/11/4475/sdn_301107_escr.pdf>, retrieved 29-04-2013.

Pantuliano, S. 2010. 'Oil, Land and Conflict: the Decline of Misseriyya Pastoralism in Sudan'. *Review of African Political Economy* 37 (123), 7–23.

Patey, L. A. 2007. 'State Rules: Oil Companies and Armed Conflict in Sudan'. *Third World Quarterly* 28 (5), 997–1016.

Patey, L. A. 2010. 'Crude Days Ahead? Oil and the Resource Curse in Sudan'. *African Affairs* 109 (437), 617–636.

Raine, S. 2009. *China's African Challenges*. Abingdon: Routledge.

Salih, A.M. 1999. *The Manasir of Northern Sudan: Land and People*. Köln: Rüdiger Köppe.

Sautman, B., Yan, H. 2010. 'Chinese Farms in Zambia: From Socialist to "Agro-Imperialist" Engagement?' *African and Asian Studies* 9 (3), 307–333.

Scott, J. C. 1998. *Seeing Like a State: How Certain Schemes to Improve the Human Condition Have Failed.* London and New Haven CT: Yale University Press.

Scott, J. C. 2009. 'Interview with James C. Scott', <http://voidmanufacturing.wordpress.com/2009/12/17/interview-with-james-c-scott/>, retrieved 27-04-2013.

Servant, J.-C. 2005. 'China's trade safari in Africa'. *Le Monde Diplomatique* (English Edition). 11 May, <http://mondediplo.com/2005/05/11chinafrica>, retrieved 24-11-2013.

Shao, J. 2012. 'Dongdang jushi ling zhongguoren xuanze likai Sudan: renshu yi dafu xiajiang' [Insecure times prompt Chinese citizens to leave Sudan: resident numbers have dropped significantly], <http://news.ifeng.com/mil/2/detail_2012_04/24/14108086_0.shtml>, retrieved 05-05-2013.

Sinohydro 2013. 'Zhongguo shuidian chengjian Sudan Luoseileisi Daba Jiagao Gongcheng juxing jungong qingdian' [Sudan's Roseires Heightening Project contracted by Sinohydro celebrates completion], <http://intl.sinohydro.com/index.php?m=content&c=index&a=show&catid=69&id=1082>, retrieved 06-05-2013.

Statistical Yearbook 2011. *Statistical Yearbook of the Republic of China 2010.* Taipei: The Chinese Statistical Association.

Streck, B. 2002. 'Sudanesische Synthesen: Zu den Hintergründen eines afrikanischen Dauerkonflikts'. *Vereinte Nationen* 50 (3), 104–109.

Sudan Tribune 2008. 'Chinese Oil Workers Kidnapped in Sudan's Kordofan', 19 October. <www.sudantribune.com/spip.php?article28979>, retrieved 15-06-2012.

Sudan Tribune 2010. 'Chinese Firm Given Land Deal in Sudan', 16 March. <www.sudantribune.com/spip.php?article34444>, retrieved 15-06-2012.

Sudan Tribune 2013. 'Sudan Says Dam Project in North Will Flood 12 Villages', 5 May. <www.sudantribune.com/spip.php?article46466>, retrieved 05-06-2013.

Taylor, I. 2006. 'China's Oil Diplomacy in Africa'. *International Affairs* 82 (5), 937–959.

Taylor, I. 2009. *China's New Role in Africa*. Boulder CO: Lynne Rienner.

Tetzlaff, R., Wohlmuth, K. 1980. *Der Sudan: Probleme und Perspektiven der Entwicklung eines weltmarktabhängigen Agrarstaates*. Frankfurt am Main: Metzner.

UN Sudan Information Management Working Group 2010. 'Shapefiles of Settlements, Administrative Boundaries, Rivers'. Geneva: UN Institute for Training and Research, <www.unitar.org/unosat/sudan>, retrieved 20-10-2012.

UNDP (United Nations Development Programme) 2006. 'Pastoral Production Systems in South Kordofan (Study 2)'. Khartoum: UNDP, <http://www.sd.undp.org/publications/rrbc/PASTORAL%20PRODUCTION%20SYSTEMS%20IN%20SOUTH%20KORDOFAN.pdf>, retrieved 25-04-2013.

UNEP 2007. 'Sudan: Post-Conflict Environmental Assessment'. Nairobi: UNEP, <http://postconflict.unep.ch/publications/UNEP_Sudan_synthesis_E.pdf>, retrieved 14-05-2013.

United Nations (UN) 2012. Sudan/ South Sudan. New York: UN Cartographic Section, <www.un.org/depts/Cartographic/english/htmain.htm>, retrieved 25-06-2013.

Verhoeven, H. 2011a. '"Dams are Development": China, the Al-Ingaz Regime & the Political Economy of the Sudanese Nile'. In Large, D., Patey, L. A. (eds), *Sudan Looks East: China, India & the Politics of Asian Alternatives*. Woodbridge: James Currey, 120–138.

Verhoeven, H. 2011b. 'Black Gold for Blue Gold? Sudan's Oil, Ethiopia's Water and Regional Integration'. Briefing Paper. London: Chatham House.

Verhoeven, H. 2012. 'Big is beautiful: Megadams, African Water Security, and China's Role in the New Global Political Economy'. Discussion Paper 1243. Canberra: Global Water Forum.

Verhoeven, H. 2013. 'Sudan and its Agricultural Revival: A Regional Breadbasket at Last or Another Mirage in the Desert?' In Allan, J. A., Keulertz, M., Sojamo, S., Warner, J. (eds), *Handbook of Land and Water Grabs in Africa: Foreign Direct Investment and Food and Water Security*. Abingdon and New York: Routledge, 43–56.

Wang, N. 2012. 'Dui Zhongguo-Sudan jingmao hezuo de zai sikao' [Rethinking Sino-Sudanese Economic and Trade Cooperation]. *Alabo shijie yanjiu [Arab World Studies]* (6), 64–75.

Weinstein, W., Henriksen, T. H. (eds) 1980. *Soviet and Chinese Aid to African Nations*. New York: Praeger.

Wu, F. 2008. 'Sudan de ziran huanjing yu shiyou gongye' [Sudan's Natural

Environment and Oil Industry]. *Alabo Shijie Yanjiu [Arab World Studies]* 87 (4), 31–33.

Xinhua 2012. 'Zhongfei maoyi'e tupo 1600 yi meiyuan maixiang xin taijie' [Sino-African trade volume breaks 160 billion US$ mark, reaching new level]. *Xinhuawang*, 13 June.

Xu, G., Wang, H., Li, R. 2010. 'Zhongguo yu Sudan nongye hezuo xianzhuang yu duice tantao' [Considering the Status Quo of Sino-Sudanese Agriculture Cooperation and Countermeasures]. *Xinan nongye xuebao [Journal of Southwest Agriculture]* (4).

ENDNOTES

1. The three bodies of literature comprise the following analysis. 1) ECCO (Economic and Commercial Counsellor's Office of the Embassy of the People's Republic of China in the Republic of Sudan) focuses on on-going projects, analyses market conditions, publishes legal provisions, reflects on changing market risks and potentials, assesses competition by Arab countries, etc., thus addressing (potential) Chinese investors, operating companies and entrepreneurs, state-owned and private alike, i.e. all kinds of actors who currently invest or are going to invest in Sudan. They mainly deliver standardized information about the involved companies, size of investment, types of projects and duration, but may occasionally also point to 'social benefits' (*shehui liyi*) of the project. 2) Chinese scientific studies on China-Africa and/or Sino-Sudanese economic cooperation shed light on (historical) contexts but remain shallow, lacking empirical research and theoretical insights. Largely descriptive, these studies often establish a pragmatic political reference, providing suggestions and recommendations for Chinese policy makers. They take note of Western criticism of Chinese business practices and therefore reason that only reputable Chinese companies should be encouraged to invest in Sudan (Africa). 3) Company profiles to be found on the internet provide basic information about the scope and type of projects, reflecting on difficulties of proceeding with their projects and sometimes referring to awards for their 'contributions to Sino-African friendship'.

2. China's 12th Five-Year Plan (2011–2015) provides the current overall goals and strategies of Chinese social and economic development. It introduces a discourse on the promotion of a 'green development' (*lüse fazhan*) in China. This kind of rationality has not yet been integrated in the literature dealing with Chinese investments in Sudan.

3. The body of literature on China's role in Africa is steadily growing. Bräutigam (2009) provides an excellent analysis of China's development aid for the continent. Raine (2009) focuses on the challenges to which Chinese policymakers and investors need to adapt while engaging in Africa. Alden (2007, 2008) covers the political economy of China's African engagement, while Taylor (2009) explores China's oil diplomacy in Sub-Saharan states.

4. See Large and Patey (2011) for a review of what 'Looking East' has meant for Sudanese politics, moving from a short flirtation with Moscow to Asian countries.

5. For more detailed information on the beginnings of Chinese development aid to Africa, see Weinstein & Henriksen (1980) and Bartke (1989). The latter also provides a list of Chinese aid projects in Sudan from 1970 to 1987.

6. For more on China's oil diplomacy in general, see, among others, Taylor (2006), Jakobson & Zha (2006), Downs (2007).

7. For detailed information on oil field operators and shareholders, see CNPC (2011).

8. The North China Engineering Investigation Institute Company (2011) reports having conducted geo-technological explorations for hydropower constructions at Kajbar, Shereik, Dal, Sabaloka, Dagash and Mograt, all situated along the Nile.

9. See for instance Gesellschaft für bedrohte Völker – Society for Threatened Peoples (2006), International Rivers (n.d.b), and OMCT (World Organisation Against Torture) (2007).

10. For information on the Dam's effects on the Manasir, Hamadab and Amri peoples, see Al-Hakem (1993), Beck (1997, 1999), Salih (1999), Haberlah & von dem Bussche (2005), and Hänsch (2012); for the resettlement site's effect upon a local pastoral group and other socio-spatial transformations, see Calkins (2012).

11. For an introduction, see, for instance, GRAIN (2008), Daniel & Mittal (2009), Borras & Franco (2012).

12. For critical accounts of Chinese agricultural engagement in Africa, see Bräutigam (2009, 2013). Lila Buckley (2011) shows that Chinese knowledge and technology transfer into African agriculture may not always be disadvantageous for locals. Her case study, revolving around a Senegalese agriculture training centre, reveals that policies are negotiated and performed in practice in different ways by different stakeholders. What actually happens on the ground is the result of a complex process of coping, re-negotiating, and settling conflicts. In the Senegalese case study, agrarian training by the Chinese – one official goal of the Chinese agriculture training centre in question – failed, but off-site training and demonstrations with Senegalese smallholder farmers yielded very positive outcomes. Sautman & Yan (2010: 309) argue that 'Chinese engagement with Zambian agriculture makes small-scale positive contributions to the domestic food market in Zambia'. In general, there is too little scholarly – and ethnographic – research on Chinese engagement in African agriculture (cf. Bräutigam & Tang 2009, Buckley 2011, 2013).

13. Similar conclusions can be made with regard to the drilling of wells on a large scale. In 2007, president al-Bashir called for Chinese investment in the construction of about 1,000 wells in north-western Sudan, especially in Darfur ECCO (2007). Smaller well-drilling projects also come as development aid: after the completion of ten wells in Darfur in 2008, a second project of another 30 wells was approved in 2009 (ECCO 2009d). CNPC engages in well-drilling as part of its development policy: 'CNPC's operation companies in Block 1/2/4, Block 3/7 and Block 6 have dug over 170 water wells for local residents to alleviate their shortage of drinking water' (CNPC 2011). Although the sources allow only partial insights, these kinds of activities remain critical. They are accomplished despite 'a major information gap' on resource management and the environmental situation in general, a fact which 'undermines the ability of decision makers and technical staff to propose and implement feasible projects' (UNDP 2006: 3). Possible long-term ecological and – closely linked to that – social consequences of the intensive well-drilling have not been addressed, let alone assessed. Against the background of regular water shortages in the south-western areas in Sudan, the questions are, accordingly, who will benefit from the new wells and will they meet nomads' and farmers' needs in the long-run?

5

Nomad-Sedentary Relations in the Context of Dynamic Land Rights in Darfur: From Complementarity to Conflict

MUSA ADAM ABDUL-JALIL

The relationship between pastoral nomads and sedentary farmers in the savannah dry-lands of Africa has often been depicted as one of 'polarized opposition' between typical 'herders' and typical 'farmers'. However, in reality one seldom finds communities representing such exact types.[1] The interaction between pastoralists and farmers is so complex that it cannot be adequately understood by using a simple herder/farmer dichotomy. Depending on varying situations such interaction can involve cooperation and complementarities and/or competition and conflict.

Fredrik Barth has suggested three alternative ways to analyse nomad-sedentary relations in the Middle East: understanding nomadic societies in their relations to their total environment, as an outcome of their interconnectedness with sedentary peoples and as a prerequisite for their very emergence and persistence, or by focusing on the total activities of a region (and not on two kinds of society). Regarding this last approach Barth states: 'What I am proposing, then, so as to bring nomadic and sedentary populations into a common analytic framework and understand the forms and variations in the relationships between them is (a) to look at them as participants in a common regional economy, (b) to understand the character of the productive regimes that each is associated with, and (c) to analyze the class relationship between them' (Barth 1973: 11–17).

Following Barth, Babiker (2001) has argued that the focus on the herder/farmer distinction would render the comprehension of complexity and the dynamics of resource competition rather inadequate. He gives two important reasons for objecting to the dichotomous approach. The first reason is that it ignores the importance of scale and multiplicity of analytical levels, on which claims of access and control of resources are usually contested, negotiated and settled (e.g. household, village, region and nation). The second reason is that the approach disregards the importance of processes of social differentiation in the dynamics of resource competition and conflict. I agree that this is a more sensible approach to understanding the dynamics of resource-based conflicts in African dry-land savannah of which Sudan's central regions are the best example.

The issue of nomad-sedentary relations has moved to the centre stage in Darfur in the aftermath of the civil war. Typical media representations depicted the crises as a result of conflicts between pastoral nomads and sedentary farmers. Furthermore, the first are identified as Arabs and the second as Africans. Hence, the Darfur civil war is being portrayed by many as an opposition between two ethnic groups pursuing different ways of life. In this chapter I demonstrate that the two ways of life depicted for Arabs and Africans in Darfur are not inherently polarized. Although certain conditions have led to such recent manifestations of a negative nature, careful consideration of past experiences shows that the two ways of life (that of nomadic pastoralism and sedentary cultivation) tend to interact favourably at other times.[2]

LIVELIHOOD CONDITIONS IN THE SAVANNAH BELT

The savannah covers central Sudan from west to east. It is bounded by semi-desert sandy stretches in the north and by swampy high grass and woodland in the south. Between these there are variations of savannah vegetation with different soil configurations. The northern and southern boundaries of the dry-land savannah are not fixed but shift according to prevalent environmental conditions. Desert encroachment (or desertification) is occurring. Experts believe that desertification is caused by two interacting factors: drought and excessive land use – be it cultivation, grazing or forest cropping (Ibrahim 1984).

There are two major economic activities in the savannah both of which depend on land resources: rain-fed cultivation (sorghum, millet, sesame and groundnuts) and livestock breeding (camels, cattle, sheep and goats). Although the main logic behind the two types of activities is to secure adequate livelihoods for resource users, they have been represented by many as distinct/dichotomous activities. Consequently, the populations living in the savannah are also classified as herders and cultivators and their ways of life as nomadic and sedentary peoples respectively. However, when the everyday practice of the savannah population is observed more closely, various configurations are found that point to less dichotomous patterns and more fluidity. As such, being a nomad or a sedentary person refers only to the predominant economic practice that a given individual or group normally engages in.

Thus from a livelihood point of view both camel- and cattle-herders are considered nomadic pastoralists, as exemplified by the Baggara of South Kordofan and South Darfur (called such because of their cattle-rearing activities). On the other hand, groups depending mostly on agricultural activities are considered sedentary cultivators, as exemplified by the Nuba in South Kordofan and the Fur living in Jebel Marra and its surroundings in Darfur. While such a classification might be supported by direct observation, nevertheless it conceals many dynamic processes that are going on and thus misguides our understanding of the interaction between the two types of activities.

According to Barth's point of view, it is more befitting to see the two activities not as dichotomous but as an open continuum of interaction and management of resources that takes into consideration not only the natural elements of the environment but also the surrounding socio-economic and political factors. Assal underlines that 'sedentary and nomadic people in the Sudan have been interacting since time immemorial. Their interaction has been characterized by ups and downs, depending on the prevalent circumstances that vary according to differences in modes of livelihood, culture and ecological conditions of the environment that supports their subsistence base' (Assal 2006: 6).

Haaland (1969) has even found that nomad-sedentary interactions may sometimes lead to crucial changes in activities and life style. He noticed that some successful sedentary farmers have turned into pastoral nomads (Fur in Western Darfur) and in other instances nomads who lost all of their animals during the 1970s drought have taken to cultivation and become settled (e.g. Zaghawa resettled in southern Darfur). In Gedaref State in Eastern Sudan, where mechanized farming was introduced about half a century ago, many wealthy nomads have become 'farmers'; reversing the Darfur example.

ECOLOGICAL ENDOWMENT AND LIVELIHOOD PATTERNS IN DARFUR

The Darfur region occupies the westernmost part of Sudan and shares borders with Chad, the Central African Republic and Libya. It is characterized by gently undulating to nearly level uplands and plateaus between 600 and 900 m above sea level. However, the topography of the region is interspersed with various hills and mountains. Jebel Marra (c. 3000 m) constitutes a volcanic mountain range of about 115 km long and 45 km wide dominating the mid-western part of the region, while Jebel Meidob constitutes a distinct volcanic mountain in the northeast.

The climate is marked by long hot and dry summers and short mild and dry winters and a rainy season of three to four months (June–October). Rainfall varies between almost zero in the northern parts of the region to 800 mm in the woodland savannah in the southern parts of Darfur. Hence, the region includes a number of climatic zones ranging from desert in the north to rich savannah in the south. Rainfall is not only patchy, erratic and variable, but meteorological data shows an alarming trend towards dry conditions. For example, the total rainfall in El Geneina town was 528 mm in 1980, which dropped to 107 mm in 1984 indicating a lean towards desert conditions. The risk of inadequate rainfall and resulting crop failure is high. It occurs nearly every third year in the central parts of Darfur and twice in three years in the northern parts of Darfur. Only in Jebel Marra area and in the savannah zones is the risk of both rainfall failure and rainfall variability rather low, enabling staple crop production.

The drainage lines in the Darfur region are numerous, all leading from Jebel Marra plateau. The drainage system is either to the south-east to Bahr al-Arab, to the south into the Central Africa Republic and/or to the west into Chad. Most wadis in North Darfur originate from the eastern side of Jebel Marra and drain towards the Nile basin. On the other hand, Wadi Hawar which originates from the highlands on the Chadian border runs towards the Nile, but due to sand accumulation and aridity, the wadi barely flows beyond North Darfur.

Ecologically, Darfur reflects diverse features ranging from a typical desert environment in the north to rich savannah marshland in the south. Environmental experts have not agreed on a unified classification of ecological zones in Darfur. However, for the purpose of appreciating the type of natural resources and associated land utilization patterns, I suggest dividing Darfur into seven ecological zones (Abdul-Jalil 2005): the desert zone (camels and sheep), semi-desert zone (livestock, wadi cultivation), Jebel Marra plateau (intensive agriculture), central plains and hills of sandy soils – or goz (livestock, gum arabic, millet, cash crops), western alluvial plains (perennial horticulture, rain-fed cultivation, camels, cattle), southern plains (cattle, cash crops), and mixed soils (cattle, large-scale agriculture). The ecological conditions are frequently disrupted by a combination of rainfall variability and human interventions. Despite local adaptations based on traditional knowledge and experiences, environmental degradation has become so intense that it triggered conflict between various land users, notably pastoralists and farmers.

LAND RIGHTS UNDER THE CUSTOMARY TENURE SYSTEM

The history of Darfur before the ascendancy of the Keira dynasty to the leadership of the sultanate in the mid-sixteenth century is largely unknown. Therefore, information on land tenure for that period is scanty and unreliable. Nonetheless, it is reasonable to assume that the tribe represented the overarching organizational principle. Membership in tribal groups and their lower components was essential for the formation of local communities. In the pre-state period in Africa, groups living in a given territory frequently owned the surrounding land communally. This implies that land was allocated to each extended family – not to individuals – according to the respective needs within the territory that belongs to a lineage or clan. Families had usufruct rights on their farmland as long as it was continuously utilized. When a household stops cultivating the land for any reason, it reverts back to the community and can be utilized by another family. Normally a community leader, probably the village headman, was responsible for land allocation or recognition of new occupancy.

Uncultivated land was simultaneously utilized by all members of the community for various purposes, ranging from lumber to collection of forest products and hunting. Non-members and visitors had to be accepted in the community, based on which they were given access to natural resources. Since security was an important concern for these communities, they only accepted visitors whom they trusted. In the pre-state period there were vast stretches of unoccupied and hence unclaimed land which was available for newcomers. Historians of Darfur have not recorded any large-scale skirmishes between the indigenous groups and the arriving Arab nomads a few centuries ago. There is enough evidence to show that the infiltration of these groups was gradual and peaceful. The fact that the majority of Arab tribes have their own recognized *dār-s* (homelands) attests to this.

According to Shuqayr (1967), Sultan Musa Ibn Suleiman, the second ruler in the Keira dynasty (1680–1700), is said to have introduced a new system of granting land titles, i.e. estates, called *ḥākūra*, even though the earliest-found documents dated to the time of Sultan Ahmad Bakur, the third sultan in the Keira dynasty (cited in O'Fahey 1980). The granting of *ḥākūra* by sultans was initially associated with the encouragement of Muslim religious teachers to settle in Darfur and teach Islam. Merchants from the Nile valley were also given estates in recognition of their valuable service to the state, which was mainly related to promoting trade with Egypt and riverine Sudan. Despite its connection with the process of the Islamization of Darfur, in later stages the *ḥākūra* system developed into a powerful tool for the consolidation of state power.

The estates granted by Keira sultans fall into two types; an administrative *ḥākūra* which gives limited rights of taxation over people occupying a certain territory, and a more exclusive *ḥākūra* of privilege that bestows upon the title holder all rights for taxes and religious dues. The first type was usually granted to tribal leaders and later came to be known as *dār-s* (literally meaning homeland). Effectively, administrative *ḥākūra* confirmed communal ownership of land for a given group of people who usually make up a tribe or a division of it under a recognized leader. Originally the group had obtained such rights as a result of earlier occupation from the pre-state period. The sultan in this case merely recognized that fact and reconfirmed the position of the group's leader. On the other hand, the *ḥākūra* of privilege (which was relatively smaller) rewarded individuals for services rendered to the state and had limited administrative implications. Both types of estates were managed through stewards acting on behalf of the titleholder (O'Fahey 1980: 51).

Sultans were able to ensure the loyalty and support of tribal leaders by issuing seal-bearing charters, written in Arabic, confirming the authority of a chief over his people and his right to manage the land that falls within the territory of the tribe. Usually such charters also describe the boundaries of the estate being granted. Army leaders and state officials were also granted land titles from which returns they had to meet their expenses, since no regular salary system was in existence. Title holders were able to extract customary dues equal to one tenth of farm yield from those who cultivated their land through a steward or manager, called *sid al-fa's* (master of the axe). The latter managed the estate by allocating pieces of land for settlement or cultivation. Customary dues collected from land were shared by various officials in the administrative hierarchy, which makes a *ḥākūra* less than a freehold.

It seems that Keira sultans succeeded to a great extent in making land tenure a part of the administrative setup of the sultanate. Since not all lands were granted as estates, it meant that the older system of communal tenure continued to exist side by side with the *ḥākūra* system in various places around Darfur. As far as tribal groups were concerned, the land they occupied effectively became synonymous with an administrative *ḥākūra*. In other words, what used to be communal land has now come to be considered as an administrative *ḥākūra* or *dār*. Tribal homelands were named after the tribe e.g. Dar Zaghawa (land of the Zaghawa people) and Dar Rizaiqat (land of the Rizaiqat people). This development introduced a new function to the land other than its economic potential: it became a symbol of group identity. Since the region is open to immigrants from neighbouring areas it follows that newcomers can access land through negotiations with land-holding tribal groups only. This is exactly what nomadic camel pastoralist groups have been doing for the last two hundred years or so.

Because nomadic land use rights are group-based and less individual-specific, they closely resemble the early form of (pre-*ḥākūra*) communal rights. An individual nomad does not need to manage their own particular piece of grazing land because they do not stay in one place anyway. Moreover, the nomadic mode of life requires that pastoralists be given passing rights through special corridors in the tribal lands of sedentary groups. Special arrangements were made between the traditional leaders of each party that aimed at observing customary rights. By means of such relations interdependencies developed between different communities and groups. Many nomads used to keep animals for their sedentary friends. These would reciprocate through gifts and granting access to the remains of agricultural produce which makes good fodder. It is worth mentioning here that while cattle herding Arab groups, occupying most of Southern Darfur State (Rizaiqat, Habbaniyya, Ta'aisha, Beni Halba and Fellata) have their own *dār-s*, the Arab camel nomads of North Darfur (collectively referred to as northern Rizaiqat) do not have *dār-s* of their own. The Ziyadiyya who live around Koma and Melleit are an exceptional case.

When Darfur was finally annexed to Sudan in 1916 the colonial authorities introduced few changes to the existent system of land administration. In the frame of their policy of indirect rule they confirmed tribal leaders as part of a Native Administration system and custodians of land belonging to their tribes. Tribal homelands came to be recognized by the government on the basis of expediency as they helped in controlling the rural population more efficiently. From the perspective of association with a homeland, Darfurian tribes may be classified into land-holding and non-land-holding groups. The first category includes all the sedentary groups plus cattle-herding tribes of southern Darfur. The Ziyadiyya camel nomads and the Bani Husain cattle nomads in North Darfur also fall within the first category. The second one includes the camel nomads of the north plus newcomers from neighbouring Chad, who were driven by drought and/or political instability to seek permanent residence in Darfur. The impact of the different kinds of access to land on the current civil war cannot be overemphasized.

STATE INTERVENTIONS AND THE CONTEST OF LAND RIGHTS

The intervention of the state has displaced relatively stable land relations, opening a Pandora's box. The government of Jaafar an-Nimeiri enacted a law in 1970 called the Unregistered Land Act (ULA) according to which all non-registered lands in Sudan are to be considered government-owned land, hence accessible to all citizens. To make it even worse, it was followed by the abolition of upper-level Native Administration in 1971 and the enactment of the Peoples' Local Courts Act in 1973. These acts drastically reduced the capacity of traditional land managers even when they were later reinstalled after the overthrow of the Nimeiri regime in 1985.

Although the government did not have any means to either map or directly manage all unregistered land in the Sudan, the new law effectively paved the way for later developments affecting land tenure in most parts of the country. The ULA was primarily introduced to provide a legal basis for the expropriation of land for the expansion of the Mechanized Farming Corporation's (MFC) activities. Mechanized farming had been introduced in some parts of the Sudan by British colonial authorities in order to feed soldiers during the First World War (mainly in eastern Sudan). In many parts of the Sudan the expansion of the MFC, which was established by a special act in 1968, has led to the alienation of indigenous populations from their land. The state expropriated the land of these people, serving the interests of rich merchant elites from the large urban centres in riverine Sudan. The Nuba Mountains Mechanized Farming Corporation is a typical example of such processes of disenfranchisement that became the backdrop for resource-based conflict, ultimately culminating in civil war in the mid-1980s (see Suliman 1999).

In Darfur the effect of the ULA has been rather different. The remoteness of the region made it less attractive for the mechanized farming entrepreneurs. However, dynamic land relations in Darfur have been dictated by the movement of people from the arid drought-stricken north to the southern and western parts of the region. Although the customary land tenure system is based on the recognition of the fundamental rights of a major tribe in a given territory, nevertheless tribal authorities are expected to accommodate newcomers. As a general rule the *ḥākūra* system allows for settlement of newcomers whether they are individuals or groups – provided that they adhere to stipulated customary regulations in these matters. The most important of these is to remain subject to the administrative authorities of the host tribe. Grazing, hunting, water and forest use are considered by these regulations as universal rights to be enjoyed by everyone in the community, including temporary visitors. Nomadic people did not have any problem with the system in the past because the migratory system they practised gave them the advantage of exploiting a variety of resources in the different ecological zones to which they moved.

A newcomer usually needs to acquire the right to stay in an area and join the community before they can ask to be allotted farmland. If a person is not accepted in a community, they receive no farmland. The village head first informs his senior native administrator about the arrival of newcomers – whether they plan to settle permanently or are only temporary visitors. When the newcomer is considered harmless to the *dār*, the village headman is allowed to allocate land accordingly. This clearly emphasizes the primacy of community membership over access to land rights, which is only logical since communal land rights have historically preceded the advent of the *ḥākūra* system. The ULA disrupted the way newcomers are incorporated into the host community mainly by establishing rights on the basis of citizenship rather than ethnic/tribal identification.

The migration of many Zaghawa from their home in the extreme north of Darfur due to drought since the early 1970s clearly illustrates the above point. Although they have been allotted land in the new territories according to customary tenure, migrants from northern Darfur, who settled in other places (notably the goz and the southern plains zone), were ready to claim rights to establish their own Native Administration structures in their new homes since the land they occupy belongs to the government. Such claims would have been unthinkable in the past when newcomers remained as 'guests' of the host tribe and had to abide by its customary rules regarding land tenure and Native Administration. The many conflicts involving the resettled Zaghawa in the goz in the areas south of El-Fasher in the mid-1980s attest to the negative effects of the 1970 act (see Abdul-Jalil 1988). The current tension between the Zaghawa and their host group (the Birgid) in the areas east of Nyala can be largely understood as a manifestation of the contested legitimacy of land and associated political rights. When they migrated in small numbers in the beginning, the Zaghawa accepted the supremacy of Birgid political leadership, but when their numbers increased, they wanted to be independent from Birgid domination. Although the two groups had several skirmishes before, the fighting that occurred after the signing of Darfur Peace Agreement (DPA) in Abuja Nigeria in 2005 was the most brutal to date.

However, despite the developments that added further complexity to the system, customary land tenure persisted because it was flexible enough to adapt to new situations. The 1970 ULA affected mainly uncultivated land since most agricultural land was already formally claimed and the government could only redistribute unclaimed land. In partial recognition for the time-tested customary acquisition of land, the government issued a Civil Transactions Act (CTA) in 1984, which states that local communities have usufruct rights over land they occupy although legal ownership rests with the government. The result is that different land tenure systems coexist in the same area. Nonetheless, diverse factors have impacted land use patterns in Darfur in the past three decades, which in turn affected customary land tenure and put its adaptive capabilities to the test. The failure to regulate the relationship between nomadic pastoralists and sedentary cultivators in a manner that inhibits the frequent occurrence of violent conflicts poses a challenge. Pastoralists have also begun to contest the rights of the original *dār* owners. However, this does not mean that the sole responsibility for rising conflict lies with the pastoralists. The practices of the cultivators have also altered, thus it is an interactive situation.

TWO DISTINCT BUT COMPLEMENTARY WAYS OF LIFE

Nomadic pastoralism and sedentary cultivation have often been perceived as cultural polar opposites not only by researchers but often by the actors themselves who openly admire their own way of life while being dismissive of 'the other'. Village dwellers in Darfur express their own stereotypical views of 'herders' while the latter also have their own perceptions about 'cultivators'. Sedentary people consider village life as more comfortable and sociable. It is also associated with good food, cleanliness and religious worthiness. At the same time, they attach opposite values to nomadic life. By the same token, nomadic people believe their lives to be more comfortable, healthy and involving greater freedom. Unhesitatingly they despise village life for its laborious agricultural tasks, bad health and limited freedom.

Such polarized views should be understood as expressions of ideological preference for certain cultural values and their associated lifestyle. In no way do they correctly reflect the realities of everyday life. Ideological perceptions about opposed life styles develop into communal reference points for the construction of the 'We' and 'They'. Subsequently they constitute the basis for ethnic classification of livelihood patterns. Certain ethnic groups are considered cultivators while others are classified as pastoralists. The former category includes the Fur, Berti, Masalit, Tunjur and Dajo and the latter includes camel nomads of the north (northern Rizaiqat) as well as various Baggara cattle nomads of South Darfur (mainly Rizaiqat, Habbaniyya, Ta'aisha, Beni Halba and Fellata).

It is difficult to find many villagers or nomads who fulfil the expected stereotypical pattern of economic activity. In fact most people in Darfur carry out mixed economic activities. Animals are not only kept by nomads. Sedentary people keep all sorts of animals (camels, cattle, sheep, goats, horses and donkeys). In this regard, three types of pastoralism can be distinguished:

1. Nomadic pastoralism: people are always on the move with their animals, wandering throughout the year searching for water and pastures. Herding and watering are the major activities. They usually inhabit arid areas, raise camels as their preferred animals and live in tents in temporary locations and camps. The tents are made of cloth, plastic material or straw. Groups of extended families of the same kin usually move together to secure themselves against raiding. An example of such a group is the northern Rizaiqat of North Darfur.

2. Transhumance: people stay in villages during the rainy season and engage in small-scale subsistence cultivation and maintain their herds around the area. In the dry season, they migrate to seek water and pasture following definite and well-recognized routes. Cattle and sheep

are usually herded far away from the villages by members of the family or by paid labourers. These usually receive payments in kind, e.g. a small animal every year. The Baggara tribes of South Darfur (as well as the Hawazma and the Missiriyya of South Kordofan) constitute typical examples.

3. Agro-pastoralism: people are permanently settled and engaged in agriculture as the major economic activity but are also involved in some livestock breeding. Animals are maintained around their villages and movements outside the settlement domain are very limited. The Tunjur and Berti tribes of North Darfur provide an example of such practices.

The relationship between the three types of economic activities in the past was generally characterized by complementarity. Gunnar Haaland (1969, 1972, 1977) has extensively documented the pattern of activities and relationships between various economic sectors in Darfur and their intersection with ethnic group identity. Depending largely on economic analysis he argued that a given life style is not maintained because of ideological preferences but rather as a result of value management of alternative strategies enabled by ecological conditions. Relationships between groups also follow the same logic of interaction. Cultural preference is mainly used as ideological justification for otherwise purely rational actions. Thus, to explain how the pastoral system evolves in relation to the surrounding environment Haaland argues: 'This context is constituted by constraints imposed by the natural habitat, by available technology, and by the relationships between economic units. In the actions and reactions of such units to the natural environment and to each other, systematic interdependencies emerge. The nature of these interdependencies is significantly structured by cultural values and social commitments' (1977: 179).

When Haaland looked at the life of the Fur and their Baggara neighbours he found that they do not only depict distinctive livelihood patterns, each of which is supported by a clear rationale of value management, but also they complement each other in some respects. Referring to this relationship he observed:

> Fur-Baggara contact is regulated by shared codification of the reciprocal statuses that were appropriate for members of the two groups respectively. Both the Fur and the Baggara are Muslims and may thus interact on ritual occasions. A Baggara may camp in the Fur area in the dry season, but is then subject to the jurisdiction of the Fur local chief (sheikh or omda). In the market place they provide complementary goods: the Baggara supply milk and livestock, and the Fur supply agricultural products of which millet is of major importance to the Baggara. The herding contract is another basis for Fur-Baggara transactions. Persons in Fur villages may own cattle, but ecological conditions make it risky to keep them in the villages in the Fur area in the rainy season. Cattle-owning Fur farmers may avoid this problem by handing their cows over to Baggara nomads. The Baggara keeps the cows in his own herd and drives them to his *dār* in the rainy season. He gets the milk from the cows while the owner gets the calves. The Baggara is not responsible if predatory animals or disease kill the cows. (Haaland 1972: 59)

The above quotation shows the complementary nature of relations between typical pastoral nomads and sedentary cultivators in Darfur up to the early 1970s especially in the Jebel Marra area and the western plains which represent the home of the Fur people. Since then conditions have steadily changed. The nature of that relationship has transformed from complementarity to conflict. The same nomads that the sedentary used to invite to camp on their farms so that the soil would benefit from animal manure are now barred from passing by the village. For their part, nomads trek through with their animals devastating crops and gardens, causing great economic damage to farmers. When they meet resistance, they may use their semi-automatic firearms and kill whoever dares to defend themselves.

THE ROOT CAUSES OF CONFLICT: WITHIN AND WITHOUT

From the mid-1980s onwards Darfur witnessed a gradual increase of violent interactions between various groups. Some of these conflicts took place between nomads, others between sedentary peoples but the most vicious conflicts involved the largest sedentary group – the Fur – against the largest nomadic group – the Arabs. This has put an end to a pattern of complementary interactions and peaceful coexistence that characterized the relationship between the two sides for decades. Access to land and natural resources has been directly associated with the majority of violent confrontations between various ethnic groups in Darfur so far. Out of about 40 major incidents of inter-tribal fighting that have taken place between 1932 and 2000, 31 of them resulted from conflicts over grazing and water rights. The remaining nine were related to political competition and contest of customary administrative boundaries. It is also noticeable that Arab camel nomads have been involved in 13 of these incidents and the Zaghawa in 14 incidents. Both groups are pastoralists from North Darfur which is the driest part of the region (Abdul-Jalil 2006). One wonders therefore about the main causes of conflict in the region in general. While some may concentrate on the descriptive accounts of specific violent encounters to explain the spread of violence in Darfur, I prefer to emphasize the importance of factors operating at the macro level.

Admittedly, there are many factors that are associated with the escalation of conflict in Darfur. However, not all of them play the same role in triggering intertribal fighting. Moreover, some factors are of a structural nature pertaining to political and economic relations within the country at large. Other factors are more directly related to the events leading up to violent confrontations between groups. For this reason, I consider it more useful to classify factors associated with the escalation of conflict in Darfur into two main categories: root causes and direct factors.

Root Causes

These factors are generally associated with the performance of the state. As a country, Sudan has failed to adequately perform state functions properly. This has affected the management of conflict both at micro and macro levels. It is therefore possible to argue that even purely local fighting incidents can be linked to central national factors of state governance (Abdul-Jalil 2009). For this reason, I prefer to identify root causes of conflict as those existing at the macro (central/national) level. Four root causes have been identified as listed below:

- *Underdevelopment* (indicated by poor infrastructure, lack of development projects, unemployment, poor basic services).
- *Marginalization* (indicated by poor representation in decision making, little influence on national policies, unbalanced regional policies).
- *Lack of democratic governance* (indicated by ineffective public administration and rule of law institutions, totalitarian politics and ethnic polarization).
- *Poverty* (indicated by the dominance of a subsistence economy, dependence on natural resources, recurring food shortages, comparative low income).

Direct Factors, or Triggers

All conflicts are associated with descriptive accounts of incidents immediately taking place before the outbreak of violent interactions. Although most people consider these as the causes for the given conflict, I prefer to assign them the secondary role of triggers or direct factors. They are on the whole related to the immediate environment where the events take place. Nine such factors are mentioned below:

1. *Drought and desertification.* Drought is an inherent feature of the arid regions of western Sudan, Darfur and Kordofan. There have been five drought disasters over the last hundred years. Two of these, however, have occurred in the last 20 years alone. In these regions – lying between the 100mm and 600mm isohyets – a mere 100mm decline in the mean annual precipitation could bring people and livestock to the brink of disaster. Rainfall data covering the period 1950–90 reveal three major spans of drought, a relatively mild one in the mid-1960s, and two severe droughts in 1972–74 and 1982–84. In all three cases the drought was accompanied by flaring of skirmishes, the worst of which took place in the mid-1980s and assumed the form of inter-tribal war. The correlation of rainfall data to conflict intensity over a 30 year period (1957–87) reveals two interesting patterns: an increase in incidents of conflict with the corresponding decrease in rainfall and a lag between minimum rainfall and maximum conflict intensity of roughly one year, corresponding to a relaxation period before the impact of the drought takes its full effect (Suliman 1999).

Natural population increase has meant that each year new farmland has to be secured for newly founded families. Darfur's population has multiplied nearly five times since 1973 (from 1,350,000 to 6,480,000) according to the 1973 census and 2003 estimates from the central bureau of statistics. This has resulted in decreased wasteland and disregard for the practice of fallowing. Moreover, nomad migratory routes and rest places have also been turned into farmlands. Out of 11 migratory routes in the

1950s only three are functioning today and only a few new routes have been created.

2. *Increased animal population.* Animal population has likewise increased drastically in the same period for different reasons. Because Sudan started exporting meat and live animals to Arab Gulf countries, livestock breeders invested more in animal health care. Sedentary farmers were also lured to increase their stocks since farming can no longer satisfy their growing need for cash.

3. *Population movements.* Darfur witnessed two types of migration that directly affected land use patterns. A decade of mostly dry years (mid-1970s to mid-1980s) triggered internal migration from northern Darfur. The displaced sought refuge in the eastern goz to the south of El-Fasher as well as in the southern zone. These places soon began to show signs of over-use. As mentioned above, pastoralists from Chad were tempted to cross the border and seek permanent settlement in Darfur. Many tribes extend across the border and this complicates the task of the Sudanese authorities to monitor such cross-border migrations.

4. *Increased commercialized farming.* With the spread of education and increased urbanization people in rural areas became acquainted with new consumption patterns. As their need for cash increased their strategies in agriculture gradually became market-oriented. Oil seeds production (peanuts, sesame and water melon seeds) on the eastern goz was greatly expanded to meet the needs of a growing export market. Vegetable and fruit cultivation is increasingly practised wherever conditions permit. Small urban centres provide excellent marketing opportunities for such ventures. As a result, farmland, orchards and vegetable gardens are extending into pastoral spaces.

5. *Increased market-oriented livestock breeding.* Because the growing Sudanese livestock export market favours sheep, many nomadic pastoralists in northern Darfur started changing the structure of their herds by concentrating more on sheep and less on camels. Accordingly, migratory routes and patterns have been altered as an adaptive mechanism to the new trend. Moreover, sedentary farmers also took to sheep raising and thereby competing with pastoralists. Some of them have even become pastoral transhumants. Accurate figures have yet to be produced by reliable authorities in order to substantiate such observations.

6. *Increase of cultivated areas and fodder enclosures.* Millet is the staple food crop in Darfur. Farmers are obliged to put more land under millet cultivation for two main reasons. First is the decreased productivity of agriculture. A farmer cannot expect the same amount of grain from the same area each year, therefore increasing the area under cultivation is an important coping strategy. Second, with an increased number of new families needing to have their own farms, new land has to be cleared even if it is marginal and may be unproductive. Extended families cannot

continue to secure the needs of their members from the same land as before. Such expansion comes at the expense of land previously available for grazing animals. Pastoralists therefore continue to be disadvantaged.

7. *Blocking of livestock migration routes.* Blocking of animal migration routes has become more frequent. Some researchers have noticed that nomads often complain about such practices which go against customary land tenure arrangements (Fadul 2004). The better pieces of land that lie around watercourses are utilized by farmers to grow fruit and vegetables resulting in the blockage of livestock routes. Blocking of routes has become a permanent item on the agenda of tribal reconciliation conferences convened during the last two decades to solve inter-ethnic disputes in Darfur. It is one of the common causes of resource-based grass-roots conflicts.

8. *Spread of small arms.* The last two decades witnessed a huge increase in the number of small arms in the hands of civilians in Darfur although no statistical evidence is available to prove it. Supplies flow from army stores (corrupt practices) and neighbouring countries (mainly Libya and Chad). The availability of arms does not in itself represent a conflict factor but rather a catalyst which, in the presence of hostilities, contributes to rapid escalation of violent confrontations. Small arms have nurtured the spread of armed robbery in Darfur, which has led to interethnic violence.

9. *Overspill of cross-boundary conflicts.* Conflict in Darfur is strongly connected to the region's border situation with Libya and Chad, which have either been at war with each other or supported insurgent groups working across their respective borders. Since the 1960s Chad has constantly experienced various episodes of its long-lasting civil war. Most of the actors involved in the Chadian civil war share common ethnic identity with groups in Darfur. Both Zaghawa and nomadic Arab groups have kindred in Chad. The phenomenon of arbitrary boundaries that divide ethnic groups across international boundaries is a part of colonial legacy in most African countries. In the current war, Darfurian armed movements depend on Libya and Chad for their critical supplies. The Sudan Government retaliated by hosting Chadian rebels hoping to change the regime that backs the insurgency in Darfur. In addition to the political issue, many Chadian nomads actually have direct interest in the natural resources of Darfur. Some of them have exploited the current situation and joined the government-backed Arab militias (commonly known as Janjawid). This tendency resulted in the occupation of vast areas in West Darfur state, where the sedentary indigenous population – mainly from Fur and Masalit ethnic groups – have been displaced and are currently living in refugee camps.

A related critical issue in this regard is the position of those groups without *dār*-s (practically landless). The northern Rizaiqat Abbala (camel pastoralists) have no *dār* of their own. This was in part because the granting of tribal *dār* favoured larger tribes, and in part because at that time land was not an issue – there were no shortages and the prosperity of Arab tribes depended on nomadic pastoralism and trade, not land ownership. More recently in Western Darfur there were additional pressures from the influx of Arab groups from Chad, many of whom have close ties with Sudanese nomadic groups. The issue of the *dār* became more pressing as a result of the ecological degradation of natural resources combined with expanding rain-fed and wadi cultivation. El-Amin confirms:

> With the pressure of the drought and in their quest for pasture and water, pastoralists violated customary arrangements that organize access to pasture and their passage during seasonal movements. While peasant and commercial farming expansion (both goz and wadi cultivation) encroached on pastoralist and transhumant grazing rights, pastoralists also have tended to deviate from defined and agreed upon seasonal movements routes, grazed on farms and damaged crops. Competition over resources created conflict among pastoralists on the one hand and between farming communities and pastoralists on the other, with negative implications for the environment and social peace within and between communities. (El-Amin 1999: 82)

FROM COMPLEMENTARITY TO CONFLICT: OSCILLATING NOMAD-SEDENTARY INTERACTIONS

In Darfur most households mix cultivation and herding. Usually sedentary families keep some livestock as well as cultivating, and nearly all herders, except some camel owners, also practice crop cultivation. Whereas in the past most of these activities have operated in a more or less complementary fashion, new factors have led to a complete crisis in the relationship between nomadic pastoralists and sedentary farmers.

One factor is that in the past two decades Sudan's export of livestock (mainly sheep) and meat has increased. There is a tendency among sedentary cultivators to invest more in livestock breeding for commercial purposes, thus they compete with nomadic pastoralists. Moreover the population growth of small urban centres has led to the increased consumption of fruit and vegetables, promoting a trend of investment in horticultural activities by utilizing land near watercourses. Today, the relations between nomadic pastoralists and sedentary cultivators in the savannah dry-lands of the Sudan generally reflect competition rather than complementarity.

This situation is neither new nor unique to Darfur. History tells us that during the heyday of the Keira sultanate in Darfur there was an uneasy relationship between the Fur rulers and various Baggara tribes that ended in violent confrontation with the state several times. The camel nomads of the north had their animals confiscated by the sultan more than once. It seems that whenever livelihood options are reduced, nomad-sedentary relations move towards competition. However, the reverse is true. What has happened in the past was being replicated again in the recent crisis although the particularities are different. Moreover, there were new factors making the ongoing situation more complex. Factors from outside the region now have a leading part in the ongoing crisis. The role of the central government has remained crucial in this respect.

In the face of such evidence, the chapter argues that relations between the two dominant livelihood patterns – nomadic pastoralism and sedentary cultivation – tend to oscillate between the two poles of complementarity and conflict. Factors that affect the environment in a broad sociological sense tend to cause such relationships to tilt towards one pole or the other. For this reason it is of great importance to identify the most relevant and crucial factors and classify them into root causes and direct factors or triggers. This can facilitate a better understanding of the nature of the crises that Darfur is witnessing at the moment. According to such a scheme, it becomes clear that factors related to the role of the state are mostly responsible for the escalation of conflict. Discussing the 1980s Fur-Arab conflict, Harir summarized the general argument pertaining to the explanation of ethnic conflicts when he concluded:

> Environmental conditions, such as those which were dominant in Dar Fur and the Sudan, in general, created suitable preconditions for ethnic conflicts. However, were it not for the prevalent local, regional, and national political situation, in addition to the geopolitics of the area which made the continuous supply of "cheap" arms possible, this conflict might not have been so brutal a war as it became in Dar Fur'. (Harir 1994: 184)

CONCLUSION

Users of natural resources in the savannah belt of the Sudan have a long experience of complementary relations in various economic activities. What determines the relationship between pastoralists and cultivators is not only the immediate ecological conditions but also a host of other factors such as population increase, expansion of agriculture, national policies, insecurity arising from conflict and civil wars and the failure of governance in general.

Since the Sahelian drought of the 1970s, more pressure has been put on the savannah dry-lands of the Sudan. Cultivators from North Darfur resettled in South Darfur. Camel nomads of the semi-desert ventured deeper into the savannah, competing with cattle nomads for pastures which have in turn degraded as animal numbers have increased. Land productivity also decreased, forcing farmers to put more land under cultivation. In other words the accumulated effect of human activity resulted in desertification. These conditions resulted in more grass roots (local) conflicts regarding rights of use over natural resources, mainly land and water. It is true to say that minor skirmishes between groups with regard to natural resources always existed. But there were traditional mechanisms for settling such conflicts amicably in the past. The heightened conflicts of the last two decades are rather extraordinary in that external factors have more strongly interfered transforming these local conflicts into wide-scale communal antagonisms ending up in war (Suliman 1999).

The current situation of interlocking conflict between pastoralists and farmers, in many hot spots like Darfur in the savannah belt in Sudan, is not insurmountable but it takes more than the application of traditional mechanisms for conflict resolution, which are incapable of handling these conflicts at the moment. Instead, efficient and effective governance at the national and state levels needs to be reinstalled in a proper manner. A responsible, accountable and efficient system of governance is needed in Sudan for a better management of the public domain.

It is important to highlight the fact that pastoral nomadism does not exist as an independent economic system, but as an economic activity interacting with sedentary agriculture. The history of relations between the people pursuing these alternative livelihoods is characterized by dynamic tensions and mutually beneficial interactions. Actual herder/farmer interactions can be quite varied based on contextual factors such as local government, environmental differences, migrations, etc. Access to land is an issue according to which many of these conflicts are perceived. When these rights are contested it should not be considered simply as a matter of legal rights of land ownership. Contesting land rights is not only an expression of a complex history of relationships between groups but also a register of shifting coping strategies and involvement of external forces. The Darfur case illustrates all these complexities.

REFERENCES

Abdul-Jalil, M. A., Umbadda, S. 1988. 'Some Political Aspects of Zaghawa Migration and Resettlement'. In Ibrahim, F., Ruppert, H. (eds), *Rural-Urban Migration and Identity Change: Case Studies from the Sudan*. Bayreuth: Bayreuther Geowissenschaftliche Arbeiten, Volume 11, 13–36.

Abdul-Jalil, M. A. 2005. 'Land tenure and inter-ethnic conflict in Darfur'. In African Centre for Technology Studies *(ACTS), Report of the conference on land tenure and conflict in Africa: prevention, mitigation and reconstruction,* 9–10 December 2004. Nairobi: ACTS Press.

Abdul-Jalil, M. A. 2006. 'The Dynamics of Customary land Tenure and Natural Resource Management in Darfur'. *Land Reform, Settlement and Cooperatives* 2006/2, 8–23.

Abdul-Jalil, M. A. 2009. 'Intertribal Conflicts in Darfur: Scarcity of Resources or Crises of Governance?' In Laroy, M. (ed.), *Environment and Conflict in Africa: Reflections from Darfur*. Addis Ababa: University for Peace, Africa Programme.

Assal, M. 2006. 'All about History Repeating Itself: The State and the Involution of Conflict in Darfur.' *Journal of Darfurian Studies* 1 (1), 6–22.

Babiker, M. 2001. 'Resource Competition and Conflict: Herder/Farmer or Pastoralism/Agriculture?' In Salih, M. A., Dietz, T., Ahmed, A. G. M. (eds), *African Pastoralism: Conflict, Institutions and Government*. London: Pluto Press, 135–144.

Barth, F. 1973. 'A General Perspective on Nomad-Sedentary Relations in the Middle East'. In Nelson, C. (ed.), *The Desert and the Sown: Nomads in the Wider Society*. Berkeley CA: University of California Press, 11–21.

El-Amin, K. A. 1999. *Drought, Adjustments in Economic Activities, Changes in Land Use and Land Tenure Forms in Darfur, Sudan*. (DSRC Monograph Series 42). Khartoum: University of Khartoum Press.

Fadul, A. A. 2004. 'Natural Resources Management for Sustainable Peace in Darfur.' Paper presented at a workshop on Environmental Degradation and Conflict in Darfur, 15–16 December 2004, U N University for Peace & University of Khartoum Peace Research Centre, Khartoum.

Haaland, G. 1969. 'Economic Determinants in Ethnic Processes'. In Barth, F. (ed.), *Ethnic Groups and Boundaries*. London: George Allen & Unwin, 58–73.

Haaland, G. 1972. 'Nomadism as an Economic Career among the Sedentaries in the Sudan Savannah Belt'. In Cunnison, I., James, W. (eds), *Essays in Sudan Ethnography*. London: Hurst, 148–172.

Haaland, G. 1977. 'Pastoral Systems of Production: The Socio-Cultural Context and Some Economic and Ecological Implications'. In O'Keeve, P., Wisner, B. (eds), *Land Use and Development*. London: International African Institute, 179–193.

Harir, S. 1994. "Arab Belt" versus "African Belt": Ethno Political Conflict in Dar Fur and the Regional Cultural Factors'. In Harir, S., Tvedt, T. (eds), *Short Cut to Decay: The Case of the Sudan*. Uppsala: The Scandinavian Institute of African Studies, 144–185.

Ibrahim, F. N. 1984. *Ecological Imbalance in the Republic of the Sudan – with Special Reference to Desertification in Darfur*. Bayreuther Geowissenschaftliche Arbeiten 6. Bayreuth: University of Bayreuth.

O'Fahey, R. S. 1980. *State and Society in Darfur*. London: Hurst.

Shuqayr, N. (1967). 'Ǧiyuġrāfiyā wa tarīḫ as-Sūdān' [*Geography and History of the Sudan*]. Beirut: Dar al-Thaqafa.

Suliman, M. 1999. *The Sudan: A Continent of Conflicts – A Report on the State of War and Peace in the Sudan*. Geneva: Swiss Peace Foundation.

ENDNOTES

1. I thank Richard Rottenburg who helped me with this work by providing financial support and editing an earlier version.

2. The chapter depends on secondary material (both published and unpublished) as well as on a personal long-term association with Darfur as my homeland. More recently, I had a chance to visit Darfur in the capacity of a land tenure adviser with the Darfur Joint Assessment Mission which was managed by UNDP and aimed at facilitating the implementation of the Darfur Peace Agreement (DPA) signed in Abuja, Nigeria in May 2006. Although the data collected for the mission is not included in this review I have certainly benefited from the insight gained.

6

Sedentary-Nomadic Relations in a Shared Territory: Post-Conflict Dynamics in the Nuba Mountains, Sudan[1]

GUMA KUNDA KOMEY

Sudan's civil war (1983–2005) is the longest and bloodiest conflict in post-colonial Africa. Though land was not a prime factor of the war in southern Sudan, it was one of the key causes of its extension into northern Sudan (see Komey 2009a, 2009b, 2010a, 2010c). As detailed elsewhere (Komey 2010b) the extension of the war from the south to the Nuba Mountains region from the mid-1980s was the greatest event in the region's recent history. It reshaped its entire public space and brought about new dynamics with significant repercussions on the historical, political, economic and territorial relationships between the state and society and equally between the various communal groups in the region. Most destructive was the collapse of the coexistence of the sedentary Nuba and the nomadic Baggara, where the failure of the symbiotic relationship that had always existed between them in a shared territory led to a near complete breakdown of their market and economic complementarities, social interactions and ties. The question of communal land rights' claims and counter claims in the region was and still is a bone of contention between these two co-existing groups, particularly after the Comprehensive Peace Agreement (CPA) was signed on January 9, 2005.

After peace was achieved, the commonly held conviction was that the underlying root causes of Sudan's civil war, including the land question, had been diagnosed, negotiated and finally transformed into sustainable resolutions. Thus, two closely related questions have arisen. First, to what extent has the CPA been successful in addressing the land question as one of the root causes of the civil wars, particularly in the Nuba Mountains region? Second, how will the conflict between the nomadic Baggara and the sedentary Nuba people of Southern Kordofan/ Nuba Mountains and the contradictions between traditional land rights and modern civil land rights be resolved in practice? The issue of land rights involves aspects of governance, state legality, social legitimacy, territoriality, ethnic identities and conflicts, together with their political, economic, cultural and ecological dimensions.

In view of these core questions, the main objective of this chapter is to examine some post-war dynamics – which since the region's return to war in 2011 also figure as pre-war dynamics – in the relation between the nomadic Arabs of the Baggara and the sedentary Nuba of the region.

It explores local discourses and practices of social and political belonging and attachments of these two groups in the region since the early 1980s, during the civil war, and thereafter. The questions of access, control, and/or use rights for land and water are the main focus of this study of autochthonous identity politics. Emphasis is placed precisely on the autochthonous/customary claim to land rights by the sedentary Nuba and the persistent questioning of those rights not only by the nomadic Baggara in the region but also by the state. The contentious issue here is that most of these claims are articulated in terms of autochthonous rights.

The concept of autochthony is a key analytical tool in this discussion. It is the claim to collective rights on the basis of belonging to an indigenous group with strong ties to an ancestral homeland (see Rosivach 1987, Geschiere & Nyamnjoh 2000, Geschiere 2005, Geschiere & Jackson 2006, Ceuppens 2006, Komey 2008a, 2009a, 2010a). Autochthony is a notion associated with an ever-increasing articulation of collective rights in categories difficult to reconcile with the principles of modern statehood. In most rural communities, the land rights claims are presented within categories of ethnicity, culture and religion, among others. The difficulty of reconciling these categories with the principles of the modern state stems from the fact that all these categories have doubtful references, are far from being clear, and do not simply exist to be used but instead emerge when invoked. Thus, the claim of autochthony, as a tie between territory and collective identity, is always not only contested, but also difficult to prove empirically. There are no clear-cut social and territorial boundaries, coupled with constant situational or strategic shift in identities, alliances or enemy making (see Manger 1994, 2001, 2001/02, 2003, Mohamed Salih 1998a, 1998b, Schlee 2001, 2002a, 2002b, 2008, Komey 2010b).

In view of the above reasoning, the following core questions are of great significance in directing the content of this overall discussion:

1. Why and how have the traditional relations between the sedentary Nuba and the nomadic Baggara groups witnessed such a drastic shift from amicable coexistence, complementarities, and self-management of local conflicts, towards large-scale civil war, coupled with growing exclusionary tendencies along ethnic lines?

2. Why have these two major groups, previously coexisting in the Nuba Mountains region been unwilling to pursue jointly what is apparently their clear common interest and to confront the central government's systematic policy of land grabbing of farming and grazing lands alike for public and private mechanized farming and oil investment?

3. Why do they not jointly resist the government, given the fact that the state has consistently placed both of them, as social forces, on the periphery of social space by means of a broader centre-periphery dynamic process of unequal economic, social and political relationships?

THE NUBA MOUNTAINS: AN OVERVIEW

As an ecological field, the Nuba Mountains region lies in the geographical centre of the former undivided Sudan. Following the separation of South Sudan in July 2011, the relative location of the region has shifted from a central zone to a borderland with an international boundary. It is situated between longitudes 29° and 31°30'E and latitudes 10° and 12°30'N and covers an area of approximately 88,000 square km (roughly 34,000 square miles) within the savannah summer rain belt. It is bordered by North Kordofan in the north, White Nile State in the east, South Darfur State in the west and Upper Nile, Warrap, Jonglei, and Unity States in South Sudan.

The Nuba region's mountainous topographical features give it unique physical characteristics in relation to its surroundings. Several mountain masses and isolated hills, which represent 18.5 per cent of the total area, are separated by plains of various sizes that are the distinct topographic features of the region. The plains areas are covered with muddy, cracking and/or non-cracking soils with some alluvial deposits at the edges, close to the Bahr al-Arab River in the south and the White Nile in the east. The fertile clay and alluvial soils account for about 45 per cent of the total land area in the region. A second land type of sandy soils covers the western and northern parts of the region and composes approximately 32 per cent of the total land area of the region (see March 1944, 1954, Tothill 1954, Babiker et al. 1985, Komey 2010a).

Generally, arable land in the region constitutes 15 per cent of the total arable land in the Sudan. It is divided into the fertile clay soils of the plains known locally as *ha-aba* (black cotton soils), the sandy/clay pediment soils found at the foot of the mountain known as *qardūd*, broad wadi as well as small wadi soil systems known as *baṭ-ḥa* or *fāw*, and the rocky mountain soils known as *karkar*. Over 20 per cent of the total area of the region is grazing land, whereas 14–22 per cent of the area is either cultivated or lies fallow (Harragin 2003: 4, March 1944: 1–3, see also Colvin 1939, Bolton 1954, Hassan 1963, Babiker et al. 1985, Komey 2010a). These distinctive ecological features have a bearing on patterns of human settlement, land use, and overall socio-economic activities and their organization.

There are two predominant, co-existing subsistence systems of land use in the region: rain-fed cultivation, practised chiefly by the sedentary Nuba, and pastoralism, which is the main way of life for the nomadic Baggara. These complementary traditional modes of life are supplemented by the cultivation of gardens, irrigated by seasonal water courses or shallow aquifers. Since the 1960s, there has been a successive introduction of modern mechanized rain-fed farming systems in the region (Saeed 1980, Battahani 1980, 1983, Salih 1982, Ibrahim 1988). Mechanized rain-fed farming and trade businesses are in the hands of small but extremely influential groups of the Jellaba, from northern and central Sudan, and the Fellata who are migrants from West Africa (Kursany 1983, Battahani 1986, Manger 1984, 1988).

As a promising agricultural region strategically located between equatorial southern Sudan and the northern desert areas, this region is one of the major economic bases for the country's agrarian economy. Moreover, rich oil fields recently discovered and exploited in the south-western portion in the 1980s have added more economic, political and strategic significance to the region at national as well as global levels (see Suliman 2001, Mohamed & Fisher 2002, Johnson 2003, International Crisis Group 2002, Rone 2003, Patey 2007, Komey 2010b).

NUBA AND BAGGARA SETTLEMENT HISTORY AND LAND USE PATTERNS

The region is predominantly inhabited by a cluster of Nuba peoples who identify themselves as indigenous to the area. Classic literature attests to the undisputed status of the Nuba as the first-comers (Pallme 1844, Seligmann 1910, Seligmann & Seligmann 1932, Lloyd 1908, Sagar 1922). The Nuba are composed of more than 50 different ethnic groups (Nadel 1947: 1) and constitute ten distinct linguistic groups (MacDiarmid & MacDiarmid 1931: 160–161). They are of African origin and followers of Islam, Christianity and traditional religions. For a long time, the Nuba enjoyed a period of comparative tranquillity and peace, which allowed them to cultivate huge tracts of land with 'their crops stretching for miles into the plains around their Jebels' (Lloyd 1908: 55, Sagar 1922: 139). This pattern continued until the arrival of the Baggara into the Dar Nuba from the west in the 1780s (Lloyd 1908, Henderson 1935, 1939, Cunnison 1966).

In 1927, the Nuba population was estimated at 270,000, representing 72 per cent of the total population in the region, at that time including the former Nuba Mountains Province (1914–28), part of Jebel al-Dair, and the Nuba hills of al-Haraza, Um Duraq, Abu Hadid and Kaja (Gillan 1931: 8) in the present North Kordofan. In the 1955 population census, the Nuba population was estimated at 572,935, representing six per cent of the total population of the Sudan (Republic of the Sudan 1958).

Since independence, however, population censuses in the region have become a highly contested topic, due to ethno-politics that tend to manipulate statistics for various interests. In view of this, in the 1983 census, the population of the region was described as 'more than a million, nearly five per cent of the total population of Sudan, before war engulfed the region in the early 1990s' (Meyer 2005: 25). In 1993, the Sudan Government estimated the total number of Nuba in the region to be 1.1 million, while a UN census in 1998 put the figure at 1,025,772. Later, in 2006, the Government estimated the total population in the region to be 1.7 million (Republic of Sudan 2006: 06), with Nuba peoples representing about 70 per cent of that total. Johnson (2003: 131) cites a range between 1.3 and 1.6 million for the Nuba population, excluding internally displaced peoples and refugees. In 2008, the Minority Rights Group International estimated the total number of Nuba to be around

3.7 million (see Ylönen 2009: 14). According to a fifth population census conducted in 2009, the total population of the region stands at 1,406,404. The process and results of this last census were controversial, and it was officially rescinded and an agreement reached to repeat the census. In 2010 the new census revealed that the total population of the region amounts to more than 2,508, 000 people.

Despite their statistical majority, the Nuba 'constitute a political minority due to their social and economic marginalization' (Mohamed Salih 1999: 10). The history of the Nuba reviewed below shows that their political struggle has been characterized by a series of violent phases. These rest consistently on two main pillars: identity and territory, both of which contribute to a constant striving on the part of the Nuba for sovereignty and for the right to manage their own development (Manger 2007: 72).

Due to major historical and contemporary dynamic forces, the indigenous Nuba peoples were forced to retreat to the hilly parts of the region, while the fertile plain was forcibly occupied by others, mainly the Baggara. Historical forces are, among others, the influx of Baggara Arabs into the region and their effective participation in pre-colonial slave raiding; the Turko-Egyptian regime and its successive slavery campaigns against the Nuba (MacMichael 1912, Sagar 1922, March 1954); and British colonial rule and its closed districts policy (Gillan 1931, Nadel 1947, March 1954, Stevenson 1965, Salih 1982, 1990, Mohamed Salih 1995, 1999). Contemporary forces include both the post-colonial state associated with two separate, yet interrelated dynamics, namely: the Jellaba domination of national politics and the outright appropriation of land by the government for public and private mechanized schemes (Roden 1972, Manger 1984, 1988, Battahani 1986, 1998, Ibrahim 1988, Suliman 1998, 1999, 2002, Komey 2008a), and the central government's war, associated with mass displacement, ethnocide and genocide (Mohamed Salih 1995, 1999, African Rights 1995, Komey 2008a, 2009a, 2010a).

The Baggara, who arrived in the area of the Nuba Mountains over 200 years ago as pastoral nomadic peoples, represent the major sub-ethnic group of Arab origin in the region (see Lloyd 1908, 1910a, 1910b, MacMichael 1912, 1922, Yunis 1922, Henderson 1935, 1939, Cunnison 1966, Adams 1982). They are part of larger nomadic Arab tribes in Africa who collectively occupy a zone extending from the left bank of the White Nile to Lake Chad, covering in the Sudan the plains of Kordofan and Darfur as far south as the Bahr al-Arab. The term 'Baggara' ([pl., 'Baggari' (sg.)] means 'cattlemen' and applies to 'an Arab who has been forced by circumstances to live in a country which will support the cow but not the camel' (Henderson 1939: 5). The Baggara in the region are typical of the pastoral and nomadic groups that roam across Africa's arid and semi-arid lands. In their well-defined and rhythmic spatial mobility, an integral part of their life-style, they constantly adopt different strategies and coping mechanisms to survive changing ecological and human situations (see Henderson 1939, Cunnison 1966, Haraldsson 1982, Abdel-Hamid 1986, Michael 1987a, 1987b, 1998, Azarya 1996, Mohamed Salih et al. 2001, Gertel 2007, Komey 2010a).

According to Cunnison (1966: 1) and Henderson (1939: 52), after the Arabs' invasion of Egypt, groups which later became the Baggara drifted westwards along the North African coast to present-day Tunisia, then headed south-east to the Chad region, Bornu and Wadai, and later spread eastwards in the direction of the Nile, via Kordofan. Others, such as MacMichael (1912: 276), favour the view that the Baggara formed part of the Guhayna Arab group who spread in large numbers over the Nile valley in the first half of the fourteenth century and in the following centuries appear to have pushed westwards as far as Bornu. By 1803, they were already well established in Darfur (Henderson 1939: 58).

The Baggara of South Kordofan consist primarily of three main groups: Missiriyya, Aulad Himaid and the Hawazma. According to Gillan (1931: 8), the Arab population in the region in 1927 was estimated at between 65,000 and 70,000, representing 28 per cent of the region's total population. In the first population census (1955/56), the figure totalled 351,393, including the Arabicized Nuba of Tegali (see Republic of the Sudan 1958: 48).

Out of these three main groups, the focus here is on the Hawazma sub-groups because of their relevance to the study. The word Hawazma originates from an Arabic term meaning 'tie together'. During the sixteenth century, there were numerous tribal clashes and many small tribes in Kordofan needed to cooperate. They formed the Hawazma by swearing on the Qur'ān that they would always give up their own claim to independence if needed for the sake of the whole tribe; since then, many groups and individuals have sworn the Hawazma oath (Haraldsson 1982: 26).

Over time, the Hawazma has become more than a tribe or even an ethnic group. Today, it is a conglomerate of ethnic groups, as it has flexibly extended its alliances to integrate other non-Arab ethnic groups. For example, the six tribes of Zunara, Takarir, Jellaba, Hawara, Jawama'a, Bidayrriyya and slaves are part of Halafa. None of these six tribes forming Halafa is genealogically Arab, as are most Hawazma groups. These non-Arab groups were integrated into Hawazma in the mid-eighteenth century upon swearing an oath that bound them to the Hawazma alliance (MacMichael 1922: 151–2).

The Baggara move seasonally southwards during the dry season between the hilly Nuba areas towards the traditional homelands of the peoples of South Sudan and then return northwards during the rainy season. Although they are historically known to be nomadic, a great number have acquired a more sedentary mode of life today, as they move gradually from nomadism to an agro-pastoralist mode of life that depends on both animals and cultivation on the plains of the Nuba Mountains. Moreover, some of these agro-pastoralists have been completely transformed into sedentary groups with progressive engagement in trade and farming in the Nuba Mountains (see Henderson 1939, Adams 1982, Abdel-Hamid 1986, Battahani 1980, 1986, 1998).

THE CIVIL WAR AND ITS IMPLICATIONS FOR TERRITORY AND ETHNIC RELATIONS

The extension of the civil war from the southern Sudan to the Nuba Mountains in 1985 brought about new dynamics that came to have significant repercussions on land ownership rights or access rights. First, the normal coexistence of the sedentary Nuba and the Baggara nomads ceased as the bulk of the Nuba supported the Sudan People's Liberation Movement/Army (SPLM/A) while the Baggara sided with the Islam-oriented central government.

Second, as the war intensified, the Nuba Mountains territory was progressively divided into two geopolitical and administrative parts: areas either controlled and administered by the Islamic Government of the Sudan, where the Baggara had the upper hand in political affairs and where the Nuba were alienated from their land; and areas controlled and administered by the Nuba-led SPLM/A, with effective land management by the Nuba peoples, who in turn denied the Baggara Arabs the access to grazing lands and water.

Third, the two warring parties pursued two different policies pertaining to land rights in their respective territories. In the SPLM/A controlled areas, customary practices of communal land rights were recognized as legal rights and strengthened further. The SPLM/A initiated a Land Action Strategy (2004) intended to empower the Nuba communities in administering their claimed land at different levels of social and spatial organization. The strategy, which is still in the making, recognizes two different types of customary land rights in the SPLM/A controlled areas: customary ownership rights for the indigenous Nuba people; and customary use and access rights for nomadic groups with long-standing seasonal access to the same lands (Manger 2006: 13). The government, in contrast, continued to appropriate arable land for public and private investments based on the 1970 Unregistered Land Act, disavowing the legal recognition of individual or communal customary land rights (African Rights 1995, Mohamed Salih 1999, Harragin 2003, El-Imam & Egemi 2004, Manger 2006, Komey 2010a).

THE COMPREHENSIVE PEACE AGREEMENT AND THE QUESTION OF CUSTOMARY LAND

The Comprehensive Peace Agreement (CPA) addressed the land question in the Wealth Sharing Protocol, as well as in the South Kordofan/ Nuba Mountains and Blue Nile States Protocol. However, looking critically at the passages related to land issues, it is apparent that 'land policy issues are not fully addressed in the Comprehensive Peace Agreement' (Polloni 2005: 21) and that the core land issues were not explicitly resolved despite the centrality of the land question in the civil war.

The main institutions stipulated in the CPA to deal with land issues during the interim period are Land Commissions at national, Southern

Sudan, Southern Kordofan and Blue Nile States levels. The Protocols offer no direct guarantees for securing ownership rights for communally-owned lands, or for incorporating customary land rights, practices and laws in expected new legislation. The final settlement of land issues was left to the discretion of the Land Commissions. In the absence of clear-cut guarantees or solutions in the CPA on issues related to customary land rights, uncertainties have emerged concerning the nature of laws upon which arbitration will be based, the recognition of customary law, the enforceability of verdicts on land and alternatives for redress in case a commission refuses to consider a claim (Polloni 2005: 21).

Despite the fact that the transitional period of the CPA (2005–2011) has ended, Land Commissions at various levels have not been established. Therefore, no progress has been made in incorporating customary land rights into legislation at different levels. This implies that the land related conflicts between the sedentary Nuba and the nomadic Baggara and the government policy of appropriating lands customarily owned by rural peoples in the Nuba Mountains continue to persist during the CPA period and beyond.

In a nutshell, the war intensified antagonism between the two divided territories along ethno-political lines leading to recurrent massive displacements, mostly among the sedentary Nuba. It also stimulated the articulating of ethnic identities in the struggle for land as a source of socio-political identity and economic survival. It thereby accelerated the rate and the scale of local conflicts along ethnic lines. This war-imposed situation continued in the post-conflict era despite the CPA, as demonstrated by the following ethnographic case study from Keiga Tummero locale.

Keiga Tummero Communal Land-Based Social Organization

Keiga Tummero is a cluster of interconnected homesteads, about 42 km north of Kadugli, and less than 5 km east of the Kadugli-Dilling asphalt road at al-Kweik settlement point. It is a hill community which is part of the Keiga sub-ethnic group. The structure of the social system of the Keiga Tummero and its territorial boundaries were studied through direct interviews and participatory observations during my fieldwork. The Keiga Tummero area, with its four villages of Kolo, Keidi, Tummero and al-Joghba, represents a typical example of Nuba hill communities, where each hill or sub-hill community represents a clan or a lineage with loosely defined social and territorial boundaries in settlements and farmlands. Each clan or lineage is, in turn, ruled by one or two sheikhs, depending on the size of the households. The total population of the Keiga Tummero is about three thousand, governed by one omda and several sheikhs. The author's interview with the omda and a group of sheikhs of Keiga Tummero, Keidi, on 4 December 2006, resulted in a description of this area as loosely organized territorially and socially as follows:

- Kolo sub-hill, a territory for the Kolo clan, is composed of the four lineages – Ghamile, Gum Swadi, Gado De Madi and Ghardik – with a total of 63 households. The omda of Keiga Tummero in 2009, al-Yias Ibrahim, comes from this Kolo sub-hill community.

- Keidi sub-hill, a territory for the Keidi clan, is composed of the six major sheikh-headed lineages of Kasmago, Danadudri, Kadak, Keidi, Ghadbrug and Kafuk with a total of 68 households. The Kafuk lineage has disappeared in the area, but some elderly people still remember some of its remnants in urban areas.
- Tummero sub-hill is a territory for the Tummero clan and is composed of the five major lineages Ghadidi, Kosobidi, Kadimidogo, Kashadi and Kadingre with a total of 129 households.
- Al-Joghba sub-hill is the territory of al-Joghba clan and is composed of the four main lineages Gasmo, Godmile, Kaduk, and Kasslu with a total of 78 households.

Each of these clans represents a sub-hill community or village with its own perceived settlement and farming land. However, the spatial overlap of settlements and farm zoning patterns, and of social ties from intermarriages between these four sub-hill communities, are all evident. The whole system of social organization is fluid and dynamic, with some form of continuous change in the titles, structures and powers of leadership at each social level, i.e. lineage, clan, tribe or ethnic group.

Territorial and social boundaries exist but are flexible, a feature of the social and spatial boundaries that allows the people of Keiga Tummero to act to some degree as a collective social entity when it comes to communal land and its imagined boundaries with 'others'. Depending on the source and magnitude of the perceived or actual threat, this collective action can be initiated at a single family level, then pushed up to clan level or even higher up to Keiga (tribal level) and, on rare occasions if necessary, to the Nuba (ethnic level) as a unified ethno-political entity.

The four sub-hill communities of Kolo, Keidi, Tummero, and al-Joghba, who represent the Keiga Tummero sub-tribe, are situated at the foot of Keiga Tummero hill. Before them lies a wide plain of arable land that continues to their perceived borders with the Laguri and Saburi hill communities. This open land constitutes a farming zone during the rainy season and a grazing land for nomads' livestock during the dry season.

Two major water courses run through the plain, providing a permanent water source known as *baṭ-ḥa*, but there are also numerous seasonal water points known as *mašaqqa*. They provide a water supply for humans, livestock and horticulture during the dry season. Within both these natural and constructed settings nomadic and sedentary peoples constantly encounter one another, with frequent disputes over limited land and water resources.

Baggara Agro-Pastoralists in Keiga Tummero

Several agro-pastoral groups of Arabs and Fellata with their own Native Administration also live on the land traditionally claimed by the Keiga. At present, part of the Baggara of Dar Jamaiᶜ, a sub-tribe of Rowowga of Hawazma, have established their *'imāra*[2] (Native Administration) in the Keiga Luban territory Queik as their politico-administrative seat, under the leadership of omda[3] Bushra Somi of Dar Jamai[c] and Akbar Abdella of the Salamat tribe. Although the origin of the Salamat tribe can be traced back to Darfur, they allied with the Dar Jamai[c] of Hawazma on Keiga Luban territorial land and formed two interrelated omodias, which are currently part of the Dar Jamai[c] *'imāra* under the paramount chieftainship of Amir Musa.

In addition to the Dar Jamai[c] and Salamat Arab agropastoral groups, there are other smaller but influential Arab groups including: (i) part of the Awlad Nuba sub-tribe of Rowowga of Hawazma, who are mostly based around their *'imāra* at Tecksowna in Laguri area, although some of them have extended their settlements northwards into Keiga Tummero agricultural land at its southern border near the Hajar el-Tash and el-Darot areas; (ii) the Zunara Arabs, who recently migrated from North Kordofan and are currently concentrated in a fertile area in the Keiga Tummero territory called al-Jughan, although without any Native Administration; (iii) some Bedeyria from North Kordofan; and (iv) several nomadic Arab groups, namely Dar Na'yla, Shenabla, Humr, Missiriyya and Dar Shalango, who only come to the region with their cattle during the dry season. These groups practise agro-pastoralism, mechanized farming and trading, with a recently growing tendency towards claiming land ownership, contesting the autochthonous claims of the Nuba of Keiga.

The Keiga Tummero Autochthonous Land Claims: Narratives and Practices

The people of Keiga Tummero, like so many Nuba tribes, believe that they are the indigenous population who inherited their present territory from their forefathers a long time ago. Therefore, others who have lately joined them by way of settlement, grazing, farming and trading, only enjoy rights of access to their autochthonous land, and no rights of ownership. In this respect, the people of Keiga Tummero have several legends and stories related to land autochthony. For instance, they narrate how the Dar Jamai[c] Arabs of Rowowga-Hawazma were hosted, for the first time, upon their arrival in Keiga territory.

Several elders from Keiga Tummero stated that, according to stories narrated by their forefathers, there were intertribal conflicts between two sections of Arab tribes of Dar Betti and Dar Jamai[c] in a place called Baraka at el-Qoz in North Kordofan several generations ago. Having lost the battle, the Dar Jamai[c] were forced to flee southwards to Nuba lands, seeking refuge and protection. Upon their arrival, they divided into groups with each one targeting specific Nuba communities in their respective hills. A group led by Sheikh Tawir (the founder of Dar Jamai[c] in the area) approached Keiga Tummero hill at Kolo point. They were well-received by the Keiga Tummero leaders and, for security reasons, were settled on top of the hill together with their horses, where some of their material culture still exists today.

In time, however, and with the assistance of various state powers, these latecomers started to strengthen their presence as settlers as well as nomads on land claimed by the Keiga. Today, historical and contemporary evidence on the ground suggests that Keiga Tummero autochthonous claims have progressively been contested by this group of Sheikh Tawir, which maintained its name as Dar Jamai[c] within the Rowowga-Hawazma federation in the region. The annual Nuba road clearing campaigns, under supervision of their native leaders during the Turko-Egyptian and the colonial periods, is one of the widely shared arguments among the Nuba of Keiga Tummero supporting their collective ownership rights of their customary land as indigenous territory.

My informant, Omda al-Yias Ibrahim Koko of Keiga Tummero, argued that during the British colonial period, people under the leadership of the local chiefs used to annually clear the Dilling-Kadugli road, which in those days passed through Keiga Tummero. In the process of the campaigns to clear the bushes along the road after each rainy season, the people of Keiga Tummero used to receive work from the Nuba of Debri at el-Ganaiya point, and hand it over to the people of Keiga Luban, who, in turn, passed it over to those of Saburi. They claim that there were no borders between them and any Arab group despite their seasonal presence. In other words, Nuba perceive the Baggara as users – not owners – of land in the region although they co-existed for a long time. The Nuba argue that these Arabs never participated in the annual road clearing campaigns; and whenever they were asked to participate, they used to say to the British inspector or administrative officer in front of the Nuba native leaders that they had nothing to do with Nuba land, and that they were not inhabitants of this territory but merely seasonal nomads passing through. Their homeland, they claimed, was in Kordofan. From the Nuba point of view, this was recognition of their autochthonous land ownership rights by the Arabs, who are contesting these same rights today because of several ecological, ethno-political and socio-economic changes. The emerging agro-pastoral Arabs' attitude towards claiming ownership rights over some of the Nuba historical homeland territory has intensified the recurrent conflicts at grass root levels between the sedentary Nuba and the nomadic Baggara in the Nuba Mountains.[4]

The Keiga Tummero people were also able to narrate numerous historical and current cases of land-related conflicts between them and some agro-pastoral Arabs in the area. For example, it was claimed that in 1952 a land-related conflict arose between the Baggara of Awlad Shadad of Dar Jamai[c], known locally as Takarir,[5] and the Nuba of Keiga Tummero in the arable area of el-Tash south of Keiga Tummero. The conflict resulted in human losses on both sides. The victim from Keiga was seen as a martyr who sacrificed his life to defend the collective rights of the Keiga people. Despite this incident, the family members of one of the Arab victims continued to practise traditional farming in the area. After they had accumulated some wealth, they were able to shift to mechanized farming on the same disputed land. By this time the Awlad Shadad family were backed by the government and got its approval for a mechanized farming project despite the Keiga customary ownership claim to the land. From the Nuba perspective, all these actors, including the relevant government institutions are acting jointly, and represent the dominant ingredients of state formation in South Kordofan throughout the post-colonial period but most markedly during the civil war.

Another narrative worth mentioning is regarding a conflict dated to the early 1980s, before the civil war in the Nuba Mountains. Serious tension arose between Nuba farmers from Keiga Tummero and the Baggara of Awlad Nuba of Rowowga over arable land in the al-Jughan area on the southern border of Keiga Tummero territory with Laguri. As a result of government intervention, a fact-finding committee was formed to visit the area and try to verify the claims of the contesting parties. After thorough investigation, the committee's verdict was in favour of the Keiga farmers and official documents were given to both parties confirming the contested land to be customarily part of Keiga territory. The verdict was based on the fact that the disputed area was part of the Keiga Tummero cotton production zone during the colonial period and thereafter. However, later the Arabs of Awlad Nuba appealed against the verdict and the case was reopened. This time, the original verdict in favour of the Keiga was overturned. My informant believes that some officials and Baggara native leaders hid a certain document in court files that supported the Nuba claim. By so doing, they were able to jeopardize the Keiga claim over the contested land.[6]

The alienation of farmers from their land by the courts, among other institutions, has been widely reported by different sources. For example, in its summary findings, the UN-sponsored Nuba Mountains Programme Advancing Conflict Transformation (NMPACT) concluded that 'tension and discrimination, including in the court system, between nomads and settled farmers, between Arab and Nuba remained one of the root causes of the conflict which remain unaddressed in the region' (NMPACT 2002, 21). The people of Keiga Tummero claim that the land currently occupied by the Arabs of Awlad Nuba in the border area between them and the Laguri tribe was their ancestral land until the 1940s. It is an arable fertile zone that includes the areas of Hejir el-*c*Ajal, et-Tash, Khashm el-Girba, el-*c*Eriq and Shaq el-Gideil. The area has been famous for Keiga Tummero cotton production since the 1940s. Gradually however, Baggara of the Awlad Nuba started to systematically settle into the area from Laguri territory. At the same time, they began to claim ownership over the territory, while the Keiga peoples perceived them as users and not owners of the land. An elder from Keiga Tummero stated:[7]

> These Arab peoples came to us and our grandfathers gave them our land, in good faith, after they took an oath to respect our coexistence and mutual respect to our indigenous land. But they have betrayed this oath and have by now grabbed most of our arable land. Also, those who recently came from Kordofan are deliberately encouraged by their leaders to expand territorially at the expense of our customarily owned lands. As these peoples continue to create many problems including claiming lands, we cannot continue the peaceful relationship with them; unless all of our land-related grievances are fairly redressed and all of our inherited territory is restored.

AGGRAVATING FACTORS OF NOMADIC-SEDENTARY CONFLICTS

Based on the Keiga Tummero case, three separate but closely interrelated processes have been identified as major factors systematically triggering and/or accelerating local land-driven conflicts. First, the state's imposition of seasonal livestock routes through Nuba farming and settlement lands; second, the forced displacement, migration, and resettlement of some nomads from North Kordofan due to the severe ecological changes that hit the African Sahelian dry zone, including the northern parts of western Sudan; and third, the state's establishment of privately owned, mechanized farming schemes on communal territories with no consideration of local people's claims, interests and priorities. It is worth noting that all these factors have been externally imposed on both the sedentary and the nomadic populations.

Imposed Livestock Routes

The Keiga Tummero territory is classified by the government as a formal route of passage and a water-point for nomads during their seasonal migration. According to the Southern Kordofan State Act No. 3, 2000, entitled Agricultural and Grazing Regulation Act, Keiga Tummero's *baṭ-ḥa* (permanent water source) is recognized as a farming and horticultural zone as well as an 'Id point', i.e. a water source for livestock during dry season migratory movements. The same Act prohibits farmers from blocking water points during the entire dry season. However, the dilemma here is that orchard cultivation, practised at these same water points, is an important income generating activity for many farmers during the dry season. The result is severe competition over water resources coupled with unavoidable and recurrent water-based conflicts.

Arab nomads cling to their water access rights described in the Act. At the same time, the sedentary Nuba people feel that this is their own communal land and that therefore they have first rights to utilize its resources, including water. Sheikh Makin al-Wakil al-Zubayr of the Kolo sub-hill community in Keiga Tummero spoke in grief when he said:[8]

> We want to develop our rich lands around the water sources and transform them into large-scale horticultural schemes. But we are not able to do so partly because of the nomads' intrusions into our land during the dry season. Their intrusions are backed by the Act and various government institutions and policies. The government is favouring nomads while preventing us, the farmers, from using our fertile lands around the water sources. It wants us to remain underdeveloped in our rich territory. This is unfair.

Several sedentary–nomad conflicts are related to the frequent intrusion of livestock onto fields before they are harvested. During my six weeks of participatory observations in Keiga Tummero in 2006, I observed and documented 35 instances of farmer–nomad conflict during the harvest season in Kolo village due to livestock intrusions that caused partial or at times total crop damage. Another 23 cases occurred and were recorded in Keidi village in the same period. These repeated cases took place not only during the day but also at night. Previously, the intrusion of livestock onto a farm was always reported to the relevant native leader by a livestock owner, a farmer or even a third party. Today, this is no longer the case, as both parties tend to resort to violence to settle their disputes. With the ascendancy of a culture of war and the dwindling of the culture of peace and tolerance, traditional institutions that used to manage these conflicts effectively are unable to do so today.

The tendency to violent action and reaction was demonstrated when some young farmers from Keiga Tummero bypassed their native leadership and resorted to force to put an end to recurring livestock intrusions into their fields before their crops could be harvested. They decided to block all access of Arab nomads' livestock to grazing or water within Keiga farming and horticultural areas. In retaliation, the nomads also resorted to force. The situation remained highly confrontational until the nomads reluctantly accepted a negotiated written agreement with some harsh conditions. One of these was that as of the following year (2007) the Dar Na'yla livestock would not approach any part of the Keiga area before the crops were completely harvested. In spite of this, during the 2007 dry season, the nomads managed to cooperate peacefully in sharing water resources.

Although this particular confrontation was resolved peacefully through a direct and locally negotiated agreement, similar cases escalated when pursued along ethno-political lines. At times this has resulted in fatal skirmishes involving automatic weapons, as was the case in the Debri area near Keiga Tummero, between the sedentary Ghulfan and the nomadic Aulad ᶜAli of Dar Na'yla in 2005, 2006, and 2008. The conflict spilled over into the neighbouring Keiga Tummero. As a result there was an excessive presence of weapons in the hands of young people day and night in the area throughout the conflict period. However, it is interesting to note that some conflicts were settled by direct negotiation, mediation or court settlements while other similar cases resulted in confrontation on a limited or even a widespread scale. Moreover, some of these local conflicts certainly escalated when ethno-political factors came into play and were caught up in larger, more complex dimensions. The distribution of weapons among sedentary and nomadic people alike is a stimulating factor, leading to the frequent use of force to resolve some of these recurrent conflicts, which, historically, were resolved quite simply by peaceful means through intermediary, socially accredited, local institutions.

Ecological Changes

In the 1970s and 1980s, dry regions in northern Sudan, particularly northern Kordofan and Darfur, experienced a series of severe droughts as part of the African Sahelian zone's desertification (see Adams 1982: 268, Azarya 1996: 39, Abdul-Jalil 2005: 63). Several nomadic groups in the drought-affected zones moved south into more fertile areas, increasing the pressure on arable land and causing conflicts with local farmers. In this context, South Kordofan was subjected to two new processes.

First, due to the negative ecological changes caused by drought, nomads were forced to respond by adapting their coping mechanisms.

Accordingly, their rhythmic north-south-north movement was radically altered, in terms of route and timing. It is vital to understand that the nomads' seasonal migratory movement is not a matter of choice; rather, it is a function of year-by-year ecological variations. For example, as their northern base (*maḫraf*) started to dry up earlier than usual due to less rainfall, the nomads found themselves having to start their southwards migration earlier, in search of water and grazing lands. By doing so, they arrived in the Nuba Mountains while the harvest was at its peak. Also, it is worth noting that the Nuba traditional farmers' decision to harvest their crops is not a matter of choice but a function of rainfall patterns every year. In short, the lower the amount of rainfall, the earlier the journey of the nomads southwards; likewise, less rainfall delays the Nuba farmers' harvest. This earlier movement of the nomads, coinciding with the late harvest of the farmers, leads unavoidably to recurring conflicts between the sedentary and nomadic groups entirely due to ecological factors.

Second, the 1970s and 1980s droughts led to an influx of successive waves of displaced Arab nomads from North Kordofan to the Nuba Mountains. On arrival, they became partially sedentary and engaged in farming while maintaining such livestock as remained after their drastic reversals. Several local farmers in Keiga Tummero complained that, despite the fact that the government had demarcated passage routes for nomads' livestock, some of these displaced nomads had settled down and established permanent hamlets along the official migratory routes. In this way, they blocked traditional migration movements, forcing regular nomads to deviate from the prescribed routes. Thus, they frequently encroached on farming zones, causing destruction and damage to agricultural production.

Empirical evidence has shown that several cases of conflict in the area can be ascribed to this drought-driven situation. For example, the al-Darut plain areas, south of Keiga Tummero hill, and the al-Jughan area along the Keiga Tummero-Umm Heitan border, comprise the main 'far farm' lands for the people of Keiga Tummero. Several migratory nomadic routes pass through these farming zones. However, due to the change in climate patterns, the area has been gradually transformed into a settlement by the Zunara nomads, who fled from drought conditions in the al-Guz area of North Kordofan. The Keiga people claim that they have frequently hosted these Arabs as they fled southwards with their livestock from the parched fields of their homeland. Some returned home voluntarily when the situation improved, while others did not.

These newly settled Zunara created problems by claiming ownership of the most fertile areas in Keiga Tummero. This claim became a practical reality during the civil war in the 1990s, when the people of Keiga Tummero felt threatened and retreated from their plains areas towards the foothills of their region. This temporary retreat persuaded several Arab groups, namely Dar Jamaiᶜ, Aulad Nuba, Zunara and Jummuiyya, to expand their settlements and farming activities into Keiga Tummero lands. Thus, they started developing a sense of ownership of the land, albeit only through their recent usage and control of the land. After the Nuba Mountains Ceasefire Agreement of 2002, the people of Keiga Tummero intended to resume cultivation of their 'far farm' land in the al-Jughan area. However, they found that the area had been occupied for good and was being farmed by these newcomers. The result was conflict and confrontation, with far-reaching implications for the local sedentary Nuba.

First, the permanent settlements of the newcomers, associated with their farming activities inside the Keiga Tummero's land, have alienated the local people from their traditional livelihood base. Second, as mentioned above, these new settlements blocked the designated migration routes, forcing the actual routes to be modified at the expense of the local farmers' arable lands resulting in recurrent tensions and conflicts between the sedentary Nuba people and the agro-pastoral Arabs. Third, these newly sedentary Arab groups were supported by some state institutions in fostering a sense of ownership of the land in the course of their settlement, and began mechanized and traditional farming activities.

Some of my informants in Keiga Tummero believe that this demographic and territorial restructuring in favour of Arab groups (nomads, sedentary, and merchants) is happening with the support of regional and central governments. As the Nuba see it, this is part of a government plan aimed at empowering the Baggara while weakening and eventually endangering their own livelihood and, indeed, their very survival. As a result, government interventions have been met with strong resistance among different Nuba groups. One recent study (Pantuliano et al. 2007: 27) reported that, in 'areas like Keiga al-Khayl, Nuba communities resented what they perceived as government attempts to resettle Baggara pastoralists on Keiga lands.'

Bad State Governance and Disguised Development Interventions

Mechanized farming schemes have been discussed at length elsewhere (see Saeed 1980, Battahani 1980, 1983, Manger 1981, 1984, 1988, Komey 2010c, Umbadda Chapter 2 this volume). In summary, it has been shown how the government's allocation of mechanized farming schemes, taking no account of the interests and priorities of the local communities, has aggravated farmer-nomad tensions. Indeed, members of both groups tend to be squeezed out as the mechanized farms expand systematically at their expense.

From the Nuba farmers' perspective, any land allocated by the government to the mechanized farming scheme customarily belongs to certain sub-hill communities as an essential part of their shifting cultivation zone. From the nomads' standpoint, the mechanized farming projects are a major obstacle to their rhythmic movements. This is so because, unlike traditional farming, the activities on mechanized farms, particularly harvesting, usually continue throughout the dry season. This situation inevitably forces nomads to deviate and pass through some traditional farming zones. From the government standpoint, all unregistered lands are government property, and it maintains its own rights, based on civil law and regulations, to determine their utilization as it deems appropriate. Thus, despite their claims and counter-claims, both the Nuba and the Baggara share one common challenge related to the legal framework of the modern state as it pertains to land policy. The law has consistently undermined both sides' communal claims based on their respective historical and/or contemporary customary legitimacy.

In the 1990s, the government initiated a plan for land redistribution in the region (El-Imam & Egemi 2004). Within that plan, Small Farmers' Collective Schemes (SFCSs) were introduced as part of a wider agricultural investment plan. In theory, the initiative was meant to transform customarily owned communal lands into individually registered land rights. Towards that end, a process of surveying, allocation and registration based on modern state land laws was pursued in the area. In the process of allocations, state authorities publicized that priority would be given to members of households constituting a community, i.e. a tribe, clan or lineage, in their specific claimed territories. The state has promised to fund the mechanization of agricultural operations of the proposed SFCSs in order to raise productivity per land unit and household. But the bulk of Nuba and Baggara leaders alike have been suspicious and unenthusiastic about the initiative.

Nuba suspicions were reinforced by two other factors. First, most Nuba feared that the process would result in some of their claimed communal land being handed over to local Arabs, who perceived the Nuba as land users without ownership entitlement. This concern stems from the fact that the local Baggara supported the central government against the Nuba-led SPLM/A in the region during the war. Second, some Nuba leaders were convinced that the timing of the initiative was inappropriate since most of the Nuba, at that time, had been forcefully displaced from their homelands while other people had moved in and occupied their lands. The plan should have been pursued when peace was fully restored and internally displaced Nuba had returned to their respective homelands.

Soon after the implementation of the initiative, all the above-mentioned fears proved correct. In an interview, Muhammad Ibrahim al-Digayl[9] confirmed the opposition of some Nuba ethnic groups, including the Keiga, to the process of land allocation proposed by the government, because the process involves distributing some of their customarily owned land to other ethnic groups, whom they do not recognize as having rights of ownership. As a government official, al-Digayl confirmed that the government recognizes that all the coexisting ethnic groups in any given territory have equal rights in terms of land ownership or use. Based on this principle, all the people inhabiting the region, Nuba and non-Nuba, have equal rights to land entitlement subject to a package of administrative, financial and legal procedures and conditions.[10] In this respect, al-Yias Ibrahim Koko, the omda of Keiga Tummero affirmed that 'right from the start I opposed the proposed small farmers' collective scheme being carried out in Keiga Tummero because it is another form of land grabbing by the state'.[11]

Table 6.1 Allocation of Small Farmers' Collective Schemes in Keiga Land, 1994

Community	Allocated schemes by serial numbers	Total (%)
Keiga Tummero	1 , 2 (partial), 4, 5, 10, 11 and 12	7 (15.7)
Debri (Nuba Ghulfan)	2 (partial), 6, 7 and 13	4 (8.9)
Fellata Takarir and others	3	1 (2.2)
Baggara Dar Jami'	8, 9, 14, 15, 20, 23, 26, 27, 30-35, 38, 39 and 40	17 (39.5)
Baggara Aulad Nuba	24, 28 and 29	3 (6.7)
Keiga Luban	35 and 36	2 (4.4)
Fellata of Al Bardab	37, 42, 43, 44, 45, 46, 51 , 52, 53 and 54	10 (22.6)
	Total	44 (100)

Source: compiled by the author from data obtained from Land Use and Water Section, Ministry of Agriculture, Kadugli, South Kordofan State, 21–22 February 2007. (See also Table 7.1 in Komey 2010: 209.)

In the same way, some of the Dar Jami^c community leaders expressed similar grievances, feeling that the government is undermining their traditional communal land rights while trying to regulate the land on a private basis. My key informant, al-Bushra Somi Tawir of Dar Jamai^c, complained bitterly about the government's practice of land grabbing from local communities. He revealed that 'most of the allocated schemes went to government officials and their supporters inside as well as outside the area. Some of these outsiders are from places like al-Rahad and other towns in North Kordofan.'[12] Equally, 'Usman Bilal, the paramount nazir of Rawawqa, seems disappointed about the initiative as a process and the final outcome of land distribution:

> From the outset, I was in disagreement with the government in the way it allocated the schemes. I was of the opinion that distribution should be confined at this stage to the land actually farmed by the respective households. The remaining land should be maintained as communal property for future expansion. The problem is that the government allocated some of these schemes to people who are not part of the local communities.[13]

In spite of opposition from the bulk of the Nuba and the Baggara communities alike, the government continued with the survey and allocation of the schemes to the designated households. Within Keiga communal land, 65 schemes were accomplished on a total land area of about 50,000 to 60,000 feddans[14] (52,000 to 62,000 acres, 21,000 to 25,000 hectares in a fertile plain that stretches from north-west to north and north-east Kadugli. These are known collectively as *az-Zelataiyya* schemes. The average size of each household's allocation varies from 500 to 1000 feddans (519 to 1038 acres, 210 to 420 hectares). The distribution patterns of the schemes depicted in Table 6.1 reveal the following:

1. The majority of the schemes were allocated to the local Arabs of Dar Jamai^c (39.6 per cent), Aulad Nuba (6.8 per cent), the Fellata Takarir (2.3 per cent) and the Fellata of al-Bardab (22.7 per cent), amounting to a total of about 62 per cent of the schemes.

2. The Nuba Keiga of Tummero and Luban received nine schemes representing 20.4 per cent of the 44 schemes as shown in the table.

3. This author's key informants[15] confirmed that the total schemes in the area described amount to 65. This implies that as well as the 44 shown in the table, there are another 21 that the author was not able to trace.

In the process of allocating these schemes, enormous problems arose between the state and local communities and between the local Arabs and the Nuba. In 2001, a joint complaint letter was submitted by Ahmed Musa Haren, the amir of the Eastern Imara (the Nuba of Keiga and Saburi-Laguri), and Musa Somi Rahma, the amir of Dar Jamai[c] to the Minister of Agriculture and Irrigation, Southern Kordofan State. The two amirs demanded that the government take the following steps, among others, in order to redress the grievances of the local communities affected by the scheme:

1. Cancellation of the social survey performed unilaterally by the government officials with no involvement of the community-based committees as agreed beforehand.

2. Replacement of the chief surveyor because he was the main source of discontent among the different communities, farmers and nomads alike.

3. Conducting a new social survey with effective participation from the local communities' representatives at all stages of the process in order to establish a socially accredited base for the distribution of the schemes among the members of the different communities inhabiting in the area.

Due to the growing tension between the two competing local communities and between the state and local communities, the execution of the plan was delayed for three years. In the end, some wealthy new owners, mostly among the Baggara and the Takarir outside the area were able to secure some schemes inside the communal traditional farming zone in Keiga land.[16]

It was only later that the Keiga people discovered that the government had allocated some schemes inside their claimed communal land to Takarir households, particularly the Shadad family, with whom they had a long history of land-based disputes. After the CPA, in June 2006, 49 Keiga farmers protested against the state plan and claimed customary rights over the area allocated to the Shadad family. As a result of this dispute, the latter was unable to invest in practical terms in the assigned land.[17] Thus, officially recognized owners such as Shadad could not exercise their legal rights to the disputed land. From the local community perspective, these new owners are, in fact, state-assisted land grabbers. The state's legality has been challenged by the local community on the basis of their customary legitimacy, and to an extent they have won. However, this has happened in response to the state policy of land grabbing that persistently undermines communal customary rights and the legitimacy of local people, with no consideration for interests and priorities connected with their livelihood.

In concluding this part, two key points deserve emphasis. First, this field-centred analysis reveals the contradiction between communal customary rights and practices of two traditional communities (farmers and nomads), and the wayward application of modern state laws with no recognition of customary land rights. Other studies, such as that of Egemi (2004, 2006), Pantuliano et al. (2007) and International Crisis Group (2008) have come to the same conclusion. Pantuliano et al. reported that 'in Southern Kordofan access to and ownership of land are central issues, both for the reintegration of returnees and for sustainability of the peace process. Customary land rights are generally not recognized by the government, and statutory legislation has often been used to bypass local customs'. Second, ecological changes and state-driven factors, including distorted/underhand development interventions and the failure of the CPA to redress the question of land in the region, have resulted in an upsurge of land-related conflicts among different stakeholders in the region in the post-conflict period.

EMERGING AUTOCHTHONOUS LAND CLAIMS AT THE NUBA CONFERENCES: THE KEIGA CASE

Autochthonous land claims have become widely popularized among the Nuba people including those of Keiga Tummero. A communally initiated land committee was formed in Keiga Tummero in 2005. It was entrusted with the task of tracing, identifying and fixing local communal territorial boundaries. The first Keiga Conference (Tummero, Luban, Demik, El-Kheil and Jerru) held on 12–14 April 2006 in Keiga Tummero, reinforced this initiative. In fact, issues related to autochthonous land claims were the central subject of the conference deliberations and its final communiqué. The conference was organized and facilitated by urban-based Keiga elites, local community leaders and youths. The elites mobilized their people through the Keiga Council, a newly established, community-based organization (CBO) with its headquarters in Khartoum. According to the Council's chairperson, Shamsūn Khamis Kafi, land-related problems were the primary driving force behind the formation of this Council. This is manifested in its mandate, which aims at uniting all Keiga people, identifying and fixing Keiga territorial boundaries, laying out a strategy for dealing with other ethnic groups that have or have not shown feelings of belonging to Keiga territory, and establishing a separate Native Administration for the Keiga sub-ethnic group (Kafi 2006, cited in Komey 2010c: 196).

In its introductory section, the communiqué of the first Keiga Conference demonstrated the solidarity and will of the Keiga people, as a sub-ethnic group, to organize collective action for development and to protect their land. It expressed the commitment of the conference participants to their autochthonous land claims: 'With all our consciousness and free will, we, the people of Keiga Tummero, Luban, el-Kheil, Demik and Jerru, have determinedly decided to totally adhere to our communal unity, to respect democratic practices and principles, to recognize citizenship as a base for rights and obligations, and to work collectively for the sake of developing Keiga while protecting its land territory, people and resources' (Keiga Council, 1st Conference, 12–14 April 2006). The communiqué enumerated several land-related recommendations and resolutions, with the following being the most relevant to this discussion:

1. Formulation of a high commission for Keiga land;
2. Affirmation of complete ownership over communal land and its boundary fixation;
3. Nullification/cancellation of all contracts related to the sale of any Keiga land;
4. Compensation of the Keiga people, who have been affected by the construction of the oil pipeline, at levels equal to that paid to other groups;
5. Representation of Keiga people in the Southern Kordofan State's Land Commission;
6. Reconsideration of the overlapping native administrations on the same territory within Keiga land;
7. Reviving the indigenous Nuba names among the Keiga peoples and the names of places within the Keiga territory;
8. Prevention of the intrusion of nomads' livestock into the farming areas until the harvesting of the crops is completed, i.e. not before March. Severe punishments should apply in cases of violations against people's property or dignity;
9. Confirmation that the displacement of the Keiga peoples and their alienation from their land, which has since been effectively controlled by others, was due to the civil war (Keiga Council 2006).

The conference and its resolutions, which centred on ethno-political identity and land autochthony, are similar to numerous other regular tribal conferences among Nuba groups.[18] These conferences seem to be inspired by the All Nuba 1st and 2nd Conferences held under SPLM/A patronage in 2–4 November 2002 and 5–8 April 2005 in Kauda in the Nuba Mountains, the political and military regional headquarters of the SPLM/A. The emerging movement among Nuba ethnic groups focused on forming themselves as unitary cultural and political communities. This is based on a perceived 'Nuba territoriality' as an ancestral homeland, source of livelihood, ethno-cultural identity and political heritage as well as a dynamic of a comprehensive nation-building. The movement is expressed in different forms, including Nuba identity and cultural revival, with strong ties between ethnicity and territoriality as manifested in the recent process of renaming of all tribes, places, natural and human features using original Nuba names on new maps and records and, therefore, the purging of all names that are not related to the roots of the Nuba peoples.[19]

BAGGARA PARALLEL CONFERENCES AND LAND-RELATED DISCOURSES

In reaction to this emerging collective Nuba position, the Baggara of Rowowga-Hawazma decided to hold parallel conferences. The Nuba's ongoing attempt to articulate their ethno-political identity in their struggle over land is perceived by the Baggara as a deliberate move aiming at ethnic exclusion of all non-Nuba groups from land entitlement in the region. The Baggara argue that all non-Nuba groups are indispensable ingredients of the Nuba Mountains' demographic, economic, cultural and ethno-political landscape. Therefore, their exclusion is just not a possible or a practical option. This discourse is manifested in the two consecutive Rowowga conferences held in Kurchi in Moro, 20–21 May 2005 and in Kadugli, 21–23 June 2006.[20] Nuba-Baggara coexistence and land-related concerns and issues were the central themes of the conferences. Their resolutions emphasize the following issues:[21]

1. The need for renewing the long-standing pre-war Nuba-Baggara alliances based on new principles of coexistence, mutual understanding and respect;
2. The need for the other ethnic groups in the region to recognize and accept the reality that the Baggara of Rowowga are part of the indigenous community in the Nuba Mountains region;
3. The need for South Kordofan State's Land Commission to reflect the ethnic, cultural and religious diversity of the region;
4. The need to re-open seasonal migratory routes and provide necessary social and security services as well as water and animal health services;
5. The need to guarantee the rights of all citizens to secure lands for farming, grazing and settlements;
6. The need for the representation of nomads in legislative and executive institutions at state and local levels during the transitional period;
7. The need for mobilizing local institutions such as native leaders, singers, artists and various socio-cultural festivals to promote a climate of peace and coexistence.

Contrary to the Nuba position, which perceives the Baggara nomads in the region as users and not owners of the land and its resources, the conference resolutions demonstrate that the Baggara perceive themselves as indigenous inhabitants of the region with full land entitlements and political representation based on the citizenship principle. They also reflect a strong desire for rebuilding Nuba-Baggara interethnic ties, which were disrupted by the civil war, as the only way to ensure sustainable and peaceful coexistence between these ethnic groups in the region.

CONCLUSION

Ethnographic analysis of this selected village has shown that the most dominant cultural feature of South Kordofan/Nuba Mountains region is the coexistence of sedentary Nuba and nomadic Baggara communities, with constant competition over the land resources and water. This coexistence has been characterized by intensive and long-standing relations, with various forms of cooperation and conflict at different levels of their social organizations. In the process of competition over land resources, various social institutions are mobilized and often eventually instrumentalized along ethno-political lines, especially when ordinary competition escalates into violent confrontation. The land rights claims, whether the Nuba's customary ownership claims or the Baggara claims for access rights to land resources, are usually articulated in terms of autochthonous rights on the basis of belonging to an indigenous group with strong ties to ancestral land. The ancestral land itself, especially from the Nuba point of view, is perceived as a basis for collective ethno-cultural and political identity as well as a source of economic well-being. This implies that the contested autochthonous claims are multi-dimensional in nature, leading to a range of diverse conflict lines, such as between nomadic and sedentary groups over natural resources, and between settled Arabs and Nuba over land ownership.

One major recent development in the Nuba-Baggara territorial relations is the emerging Nuba movement to reconstruct themselves as one unified ethno-political group in order to be able to take collective socio-cultural and political action, including their restless effort to consolidate their claim of autochthonous land rights. However, this emerging collective Nuba position is being contested, persistently and systematically, by the Baggara and other ethnic groups in the region, by means of different forms of alliances, solidarity, and power control at various levels of governance, including the manipulation of the Native Administration and the mobilization of relevant government institutions to support their response.

Despite these conflicting claims between Baggara nomads and sedentary Nuba, it is also evident that various forms of economically motivated cooperation and interdependency exist, discernible in intermediary spaces and among intermediary actors such as local market institutions, socio-cultural events especially wrestling, watering points and mixed or neighbouring settlements and farming activities. These long-standing historical forms of differentiation, adjustment, conflict and cooperation in the relations of the sedentary Nuba and the nomadic Arab people of South Kordofan have undergone significant changes during and since the civil war. Several pre-war forms of coexistence and complementarities between nomadic and sedentary groups have ceased to exist, with one party losing its control over land ownership or access rights. After the war, the return of various stakeholders to their land has been a tense process. This is due to the fact that each party exerts tremendous pressure to practically consolidate its control over land under its actual use while contesting others' claims. This new repositioning is evident in the struggle of the people of Keiga Tummero to regain their far farms land, which has been occupied by newly settled nomads displaced by recent ecological changes in northern Sudan.

With the recent violent conflict in the region in June 2011 continuing unabated, relations between the sedentary Nuba and nomadic Baggara have entered another stage of tension and polarization along ethno-political lines. This last development and its impact on the Baggara-Nuba spatial, socio-economic and political relations deserve a separate analysis, being beyond the scope of this chapter.

REFERENCES

Abdel-Hamid, M. O. 1986. 'The Hawazma Baggara: Some Issues and Problems in Pastoral Adaptations'. Unpublished M.A. Thesis, University of Bergen.

Abdul-Jalil, M. A. 2005. 'Land Tenure and Inter-Ethnic Conflict in Darfur'. In ACTS (ed.) *Report of the Conference on Land Tenure and Conflict in Africa: Prevention, Mitigation and Reconstruction.* 9–10 December 2004. Nairobi: ACTS Press, 53–71.

Adams, M. 1982. 'The Baggara Problem: Attempts at Modern Change in Southern Darfur and Southern Kordofan (Sudan)'. *Development and Change* 13 (2), 259–89.

African Rights. 1995. *Facing Genocide: The Nuba of Sudan.* London: African Rights.

Azarya, V. 1996. *Nomads and the State in Africa: The Political Roots of Marginality.* Leiden: African Studies Centre.

Babiker, A. A., Musnad, H. A, Shadad, M. Z. 1985. 'Wood Resources, and their Use in the Nuba Mountains'. In Davies, H. R. J. (ed.), *Natural Resources and Rural Development in Arid Lands: Case Studies from Sudan.* Tokyo: United Nations University Press, 30–59.

Battahani, A 1983. 'A Strategy for the Modernization of Traditional Agriculture in Southern Kordofan'. In Awad, M. H. (ed.), *Socioeconomic Change in the Sudan.* Graduate College, Monograph 6, Khartoum: University of Khartoum, 67–79.

Battahani, A 1998. 'On the Transformation of Ethnic-National Policies in the Sudan: the Case of the Nuba People'. *Sudan Notes and Records* 2, 99–116.

Battahani, A. 1980. *The State and the Agrarian Question: a Case-Study of South Kordofan 1971–1977.* Khartoum: University of Khartoum.

Battahani, A. 1986. 'Nationalism and Peasant Politics in the Nuba Mountains Region of Sudan, 1924–1966'. Ph.D. Thesis, University of Sussex.

Bolton, A. R. C. 1954. 'Land Tenure on Agricultural Land in the Sudan'. In Tothill, J. D. (ed.), *Agriculture in the Sudan. Being a Handbook of Agriculture as Practised in the Anglo-Egyptian Sudan.* London: Oxford University Press, 187–197.

Ceuppens, B. 2006. 'Allochthons, Colonizers, and Scroungers: Exclusionary Populism in Belgium'. *African Studies Review.* Special Issue: Autochthony and the Crisis of Citizenship 49 (2), 147–86.

Colvin, R. C. 1939. *Agricultural Survey of Nuba Mountains.* Khartoum: McCorquodale and Co.

Cunnison, I. 1966. *Baggara Arabs: Power and Lineage in a Sudanese Nomad Tribe.* Oxford: Clarendon Press.

Egemi, O. 2004. 'Land Tenure in Sudan: Challenges to Livelihood Security and Social Peace'. Unpublished paper. Khartoum: UNDP.

Egemi, O. 2006. 'Land and Peace Processes in Sudan'. Accord Conciliation Resources. <www.c-r.org/accord-article/land-and-peace-processes-sudan>, retrieved 23-11-2013.

El-Imam, A. E., Egemi, O. 2004. *Addressing Land Questions in the Nuba Mountains: Capitalizing on Previous Experiences.* Khartoum: UNDP.

Gertel, Jörg. 2007. 'Mobility and Insecurity: The Significance of Resources'. In Gertel, J., Breuer, I. (eds), *Pastoral Morocco: Globalizing Scopes of Mobility and Insecurity*. Wiesbaden: Reichert, 11–30.

Geschiere, P. 2005. 'Autochthony and Citizenship: New Modes in the Struggle over Belonging and Exclusion in Africa'. *Quest: an African Journal of Philosophy* XVIII (1–2), 9–24.

Geschiere, P., Jackson, S. 2006. 'Autochthony and the Crisis of Citizenship: Democratization, Decentralization, and the Politics of Belonging'. *African Studies Review* 49 (2), 1–7.

Geschiere, P., Nyamnjoh, F. 2000. 'Capitalism and Autochthony: The Seesaw of Mobility and Belonging'. *Public Culture* 12 (2), 423–52.

Gillan, J. A. 1931. *Some Aspects of Nuba Administration.* Sudan Government Memoranda No. 1. Khartoum: Sudan Government.

Government of the Republic of Sudan and the Sudan People's Liberation Movement/ Army. 2005. 'The Comprehensive Peace Agreement 9 January 2005,Naivasha,Kenya'.<http://reliefweb.int/report/sudan/comprehensive-peace-agreement-between-government-republic-sudan-and-sudan-peoples>, retrieved 23-11-2013.

Government of the Republic Sudan and the Sudan Peoples' Liberation Movement/ Nuba. 2002. The Nuba Mountains Cease-Fire Agreement. Bürgenstock, Switzerland, January 19, 2002. <http://reliefweb.int/report/sudan/sudan-nuba-mountains-cease-fire-agreement>, retrieved 23-11-2013.

Haraldsson, I. 1982. *Nomadism and Agriculture in the Southern Kordofan Province of Sudan.* Uppsala: Sveriges lantbruksuniversitet.

Harragin, S. 2003. *Nuba Mountains Land and Natural Resources Study: Part 1 – Land Study.* Columbia MO: University of Missouri, International Agriculture Programs and USAID.

Hassan, S. G. 1963. 'Land Use Problems in the Nuba Mountains'. In *Proceedings of the Ninth Annual Conference on Surveying for Development in Sudan.* Khartoum: Philosophical Society of the Sudan, 47–57.

Henderson, K. D. D. 1935. 'Nubian and Nuba'. *Sudan Notes and Records* 18, 325–26.

Henderson, K. D. D. 1939. 'A Note on the Migration of the Messiria tribe into South-West Kordofan'. *Sudan Notes and Records* 22 (1), 49–74.

Ibrahim, H. E. 1988. 'Agricultural Development Policy, Ethnicity and Socio-Political Change in the Nuba Mountains, Sudan'. Ph.D. Thesis, University of Connecticut.

International Crisis Group. 2002. *God, Oil, and Country: Changing the Logic of War in Sudan.* Africa Report 39. Brussels: ICG.

International Crisis Group. 2008. *Sudan's Southern Kordofan Problem: the Next Darfur?* Africa Report 145. Brussels: ICG.

Johnson, D. H. 2003. *The Root Causes of Sudan's Civil Wars*. Oxford: James Currey.

Kafi, Shamsūn Khamis 2006. 'Keiga First Conference's Final Resolutions'. Keiga Council, Khartoum. Sudaneseonline.com, 23 June.

Kauda Conference Communiqués. 2003. All Nuba First Conference, December 3–4. Kauda, Nuba Mountains, SPLM/A-controlled areas, Sudan. <www.nubasurvival.com/Nuba%20Vision/Vol%202%20Issue%202/7%20Kauda%20Conference%20Communiqu%E9.htm>, retrieved 4-03-2008.

Keiga Council. 2006. 'The Final Communiqué of All Keiga'. Keiga Luban, Nuba Mountains.

Komey, G. K. 2005a. 'Regional Disparity in National Development of the Sudan and its Impact on Nation-Building: with Reference to the Peripheral Region of the Nuba Mountains'. Ph.D. Thesis, University of Khartoum.

Komey, G. K. 2005b. 'Dynamics of the Marginalization Process in Sudan: the Nuba Mountains Case'. In Abdel Ati, H. (ed.), *The Sudan: Challenges of Peace and Redressing Marginalization.* Khartoum: EDGE and Heinrich Böll Foundation, 54–87.

Komey, G. K. 2008a. 'The Autochthonous Claim of Land Rights by the Sedentary Nuba and its Persistent Contest by the Nomadic Baggara of South Kordofan/ Nuba Mountains, Sudan'. In Rottenburg, R. (ed.), *Nomadic–Sedentary Relations and Failing State Institutions in Dārfur and Kordofan, Sudan.* Halle: University of Halle-Wittenberg, Orientwissenschaftliche Hefte 26, 101–27.

Komey, G. K. 2008b. 'The Denied Land Rights of the Indigenous Peoples and their Endangered Livelihood and Survival: The Case of the Nuba of the Sudan'. *Ethnic and Racial Studies* 31 (5), 991–1008.

Komey, G. K. 2009a. 'Autochthonous Identity: its Territorial Attachment and Political Expression in Claiming Communal Land in the Nuba Mountains Region, Sudan'. In Kath, R., Rieger, A-K. (eds), *Raum – Landschaft – Territorium. Zur Konstruktion physischer Räume als nomadischer und sesshafter Lebensräume.* Wiesbaden: Reichert, 203–27.

Komey, G. K. 2009b. 'Striving in the Exclusionary State: Territory, Identity and Ethno-Politics of the Nuba, Sudan'. *Journal of International Politics and Development* 7 (2), 1–20.

Komey, G. K. 2010a. 'Ethnic Identity Politics & Boundary Making in Claiming Communal Land: Nuba Mountains after the CPA'. In Grawert, E. (ed.), *After the Comprehensive Peace Agreement in Sudan,* Oxford: James Currey, 110–29.

Komey, G. K. 2010b. 'Land Factor in War and Conflicts in Africa: the Case of the Nuba Struggle in Sudan'. In Falola, T., Njoku, R. C. (eds), *War and Peace in Africa.* Durham NC: Carolina Academic Press, 351–81.

Komey, G. K. 2010c. *Land, Governance, Conflict and the Nuba of Sudan.* Woodbridge and Rochester NY: James Currey.

Kursany, Ibrahim. 1983. 'Peasants of the Nuba Mountains Region'. *Review of African Political Economy* 10, 26: 35–44.

Lloyd, W. 1908. *Appendix D: Report on Kordofan Province. Sudan.* Sudan Archives: SAD783/9/40-86. Durham: University of Durham.

Lloyd, W. 1910a. 'Kordofan'. *Bulletin of the American Geographical Society* 42 (7), 521–24.

Lloyd, W. 1910b. 'Notes on Kordofan province'. *Geographical Journal* 35 (3), 249–67.

Macdiarmid, P. A., Macdiarmid, D. N. 1931. 'The Languages of the Nuba Mountains'. *Sudan Notes and Records* 14 (1), 149–62.

MacMichael, H. A. 1912/67. *The Tribes of Northern and Central Kordofan.* London: Frank Cass.

MacMichael, H. A. 1922/67. *A History of the Arabs in the Sudan and Some Account of the People who Preceded them and of the Tribes Inhabiting Dār Fur.* Vol. I. London: Frank Cass.

Manger, L. 1981. *Public Schemes and Local Participation: Some Remarks on the Present Situation in the Southern Nuba Mountains Area of the Sudan.* Bergen: University of Bergen.

Manger, L. 1984. 'Traders and Farmers in the Nuba Mountains: Jellāba Family Firms in the Liri Area'. In Manger, L. (ed.), *Trade and Traders in the Sudan.* Bergen: University of Bergen, 213–42.

Manger, L. 1988. 'Traders, Farmers and Pastoralists: Economic Adaptations and Environmental Problems in the Southern Nuba Mountains of the Sudan'. In Johnson, D. H., Anderson, D. M. (eds), *The Ecology of Survival: Case Studies from Northeast African History.* London and Boulder CO: Westview Press, 155–72.

Manger, L. 1994. *From the Mountains to the Plains: The Integration of the Lafofa Nuba into Sudanese Society.* Uppsala: The Scandinavian Institute of African Studies.

Manger, L. 2001. 'The Nuba Mountains: Battlegrounds of Identities, Cultural Traditions and Territories'. In Johannsen, M.-B., Kastfelt, N. (eds), *Sudanese Society in the Context of Civil War.* Papers from a Seminar at the University of Copenhagen. Copenhagen: University of Copenhagen, 49–90.

Manger, L. 2001/02. 'Religion, Identities, and Politics: Defining Muslim Discourses in the Nuba Mountains of the Sudan'. *Journal of Arabic and Islamic Studies* 4, 132–152.

Manger, L. 2003. Civil War and the Politics of Subjectivity in the Nuba Mountains, Sudan. The XV ICAES Congress, Florence, July 5–12. Florence: F. de Beer.

Manger, L. 2006. 'Understanding the Ethnic Situation in the Nuba Mountains in the Sudan. How to Handle Processes of Group-Making, Meaning Production and Metaphorization in a Situation of Post-Conflict Reconstruction'. The 1st International Colloquium of a Commission on Ethnic Relations (COER) for IUAES, 7–9 July. Florence, Italy.

Manger, L. 2007. 'Ethnicity and Post-Conflict Reconstruction in the Nuba Mountains of the Sudan: Processes of Group-making, Meaning Production, and Metaphorization'. *Ethnoculture* 1, 72–84.

Manger, L. 2008. 'Building Peace in the Sudan: Reflections on Local and Regional Challenges'. In Shanmugaratnam, N. (ed.), *Between War and Peace in Sudan and Sri Lanka: Deprivation and Livelihood Revival.* Oxford: James Currey, 27–40.

March, G. F. 1944. Report of the Soil Conservation Committee: Appendix XX: Note on the Nuba Mountains Area of Kordofan. Khartoum: Sudan Government, 133–37.

March, G. F. 1954. 'Kordofan Province'. In Tothill, J. D. (ed.), *Agriculture in the Sudan. Being a Handbook of Agriculture as Practised in the Anglo-Egyptian Sudan.* London: Oxford University Press, 827–50.

Meyer, G. 2005. *War and Faith in Sudan.* Cambridge and Grand Rapids MI: William B. Eerdmans.

Michael, B. J. 1987a. 'Cows, Bulls and Gender Roles: Pastoral Strategies for Survival and Continuity in Western Sudan'. Ph.D. Thesis, University of Kansas.

Michael, B. J. 1987b. 'Milk Production and Sales by the Hawazma (Baggara) of

Sudan: Implications for Gender Roles'. *Research in Economic Anthropology* 9, 105–41.

Michael, B. J. 1998. 'Baggara Women as Market Strategists'. In Lobban, R. (ed.), *Middle Eastern Women and the Invisible Economy*. Gainesville FL: University of Florida Press, 60–73.

Mohamed Salih, M. A. 1995. 'Resistance and Response: Ethnocide and Genocide in the Nuba Mountains, Sudan'. *Geo-Journal* 36 (1), 71–78.

Mohamed Salih, M. A. 1998a. 'Other Identities: Politics of Sudanese Discursive Narratives'. *Identities: Global Studies in Culture and Power* 5 (1), 5–31.

Mohamed Salih, M. A. 1998b. 'Political Narratives and Identity Formation in Post-1989 Sudan'. In Mohamed Salih, M. A., Markakis, J. (eds), *Ethnicity and the State in Eastern Africa.* Uppsala: Nordiska Afrikainstitutet, 72–85.

Mohamed Salih, M. A. 1999. 'Land Alienation and Genocide in the Nuba Mountains'. *Cultural Survival Quarterly* 22 (4), 36–38.

Mohamed Salih, M. A., Dietz, T., Ahmed, A. M. 2001. *African Pastoralism: Conflict, Institutions and Government.* London: Pluto Press.

Mohamed, M. A., Fisher, M. 2002. 'The Nuba of Sudan'. In Hitchcock, R. K., Osborn, A. J. (eds), *Endangered Peoples of Africa and the Middle East: Struggles to Survive and Thrive.* Westport CT and London: Greenwood, 115–28.

Nadel, S. F. 1947. *The Nuba: An Anthropological Study of the Hill Tribes of Kordofan.* London: Oxford University Press.

NMPACT Coordination Unit. 2002. *NMPACT Report of the Baseline Data Collection Exercise – Summary Findings*. Khartoum: UNOCHA.

Pallme, I. 1844. *Travels in Kordofan.* London: J. Madden.

Pantuliano, S., Buchanan-Smith, M., Murphy, P. 2007. 'The Long Road Home: Opportunities and Obstacles to the Reintegration of the IDPs and Refugees Returning to Southern Sudan and the Three Areas – Report of Phase 1', A Report Commissioned by the UK Department for International Development, London: Humanitarian Policy Group, Overseas Development Institute.

Patey, L. A. 2007. 'State Rules: Oil Companies and Armed Conflict in Sudan'. *Sudan Tribune*, July 18, 2007. <www.sudantribune.com/spip.php?article22901>, retrieved 09-09-2008.

Polloni, D. 2005. 'Land and the Sudan Transition to Peace'. *Forced Migration Review* 24. Oxford: University of Oxford, the Refugee Studies Programme, 21–22.

Republic of Sudan. 2006. *South Kordofan State's Transitional Five Year Plan.*

Republic of the Sudan. 1958. *First Population Census of Sudan 1955/56. Notes on Omodia Map*. Khartoum: Ministry for Social Affairs, Population Census Office.

Roden, David. 1972. 'Down-Migration in the Moro Hills of Southern Kordofan'. *Sudan Notes and Records* 53: 79–99.

Rone, J. 2003. 'Oil and War'. *Review of African Political Economy* 30 (97), 504–10.

Rosivach, V. J. 1987. 'Autochthony and the Athenians'. *The Classical Quarterly* 37 (2), 294–306.

Saeed, M. H. 1980. 'Economic Effects of Agricultural Mechanization in Rural Sudan: the Case of Habila, Southern Kordofan'. In Haaland, G. (ed.), *Problems of Savannah Development: the Sudan Case.* Bergen: University of Bergen, Department of Social Anthropology, 167–184.

Sagar, J. W. 1922. 'Notes on the History, Religion and Customs of the Nuba'. *Sudan Notes and Records* 5, 137–56.

Salih, K. O. 1982. 'The British Administration in the Nuba Mountains Region of Sudan 1900–1956'. Ph.D. Thesis, University of London.

Salih, K. O. 1990. 'British Policy and the Accentuation of Inter-Ethnic Divisions: The Case of the Nuba Mountains Region of Sudan, 1920–1940'. *African Affairs* 89 (356), 417–36.

Schlee, G. 2001. *Regularity in Chaos: The Politics of Difference in the Recent History of Somalia.* Working Paper No. 18. Halle: Max Planck Institute for Social Anthropology.

Schlee, G. 2002a. *Taking Sides and Constructing Identities: Reflection on Conflict Theory.* Working Paper No. 43. Halle: Max Planck Institute for Social Anthropology.

Schlee, G. 2002b. *Imagined Differences: Hatred and the Construction of Identity.* New York: Palgrave Macmillan.

Schlee, G. 2008. *How Enemies are Made: Towards a Theory of Ethnic and Religious Conflicts.* Oxford and New York: Berghahn Books.

Seligmann, C. G. 1910. 'The Physical Characters of the Nuba of Kordofan'. *The Journal of the Royal Anthropological Institute of Great Britain and Ireland* 40, 505–24.

Seligmann, C. G., Seligmann, B. 1932/65. 'The Nuba'. In Seligman, C. G., Seligman B., *Pagan Tribes of the Nilotic Sudan.* London: Routledge & Kegan Paul, 367–412.

SPLM. 2004. SPLM Nuba Land Action Strategy. Nuba Mountains Region: Governor's Workshop of Land Security Strategy, Kauda-Lwere, November 4–5, 2004. Kauda-Lwere: SPLM Land Office.

Stevenson, R. C. 1965. *The Nuba People of Kordofan Province: an Ethnographic Survey.* Graduate College, Publications Monograph 7. Khartoum: University of Khartoum.

Sudan Government. 1912. *Anglo-Egyptian Sudan Handbook Series* 2. *Kordofan and the Region to the West of the White Nile.* London: His Majesty's Stationary Office.

Sudan Tribune 2005. 'Final Communiqué – The 2nd All Nuba Conference'. <www.sudantribune.com/spip.php?article9487>, retrieved 10-03-2008.

Suliman, M. 1998. 'Resource Access: A Major Cause of Armed Conflict in the Sudan. The Case of the Nuba Mountains'. International Workshop on Community-Based Natural Resource Management, May 10–14. Washington DC: World Bank.

Suliman, M. 1999. 'The Nuba Mountains of Sudan: Resource Access, Violent Conflict, and Identity'. In Buckles, D. (ed.), *Cultivating Peace: Conflict and Collaboration in Natural Resource Management.* Ottawa: IDRC & Washington DC: World Bank Institute, 205–220.

Suliman, M. 2001. 'Oil and the Civil War in the Sudan'. Institute for African Alternatives. <http://new.ifaanet.org/wp-content/uploads/2011/12/oil_sudan1.htm>, retrieved 23-11-2013.

Suliman, M. 2002. 'Resource Access, Identity, and Armed Conflict in the Nuba Mountains, Southern Sudan'. In Baechler, G., Spillmann, K. R., Suliman, M. (eds), *Transformation of Resource Conflicts: Approach and Instruments.* Bern: Peter Lang, 163–183.

Tothill, J. D. (ed.) 1954. *Agriculture in the Sudan. Being a Handbook of Agriculture as Practised in the Anglo-Egyptian Sudan.* London: Oxford University Press.

Ylönen, A. 2009. *Marginalization and Violence: Considering Origins of Insurgency and Peace Implementation in the Nuba Mountains of Sudan.* ISS Paper 201 (October). Pretoria, South Africa.

Yunis, N. E.1922. 'Notes on the Baggara and Nuba of Western Kordofan'. *Sudan Notes and Records*, 200–207.

ENDNOTES

1. This chapter is an edited excerpt from the author's book *Land, Governance, Conflict and the Nuba of Sudan*. Woodbridge and Rochester NY: James Currey, 2010.

2. '*Imāra* is a term introduced by the Islamic-oriented government led by the National Congress Party in the early 1990s as part of its Islamization programme among native leaders. Though it is associated with social leadership, the term also connotes that this social leader, by virtue of his leadership position in a time of peace, is also a commander (amir) of the Islamic fighters during war. In the past this native administration unit was termed nazarah for the Arabs or mekship for the Nuba; the native leaders were called nazir or mek respectively.

3. Derived from Arab tribal organization, each tribe is ruled by a nazir, beneath whom there are a number of omdas, each responsible for an omodia (a group of villages, numbering from two or three up to thirty or more) and beneath the omda is the sheikh, who is the headman of a small group of families if the people are nomadic, or often of a village if the people are settled (see Population Census Office 1958).

4. Author's interview with al-Yias Ibrahim Koko, Keiga Tummero, 5 June 2005.

5. All Fellata and other tribes that come from the west and pass through Kordofan on their way to Mecca for the hajj are subsumed under the umbrella term Takarir (MacMichael 1922/67, 152). They are part of the Dar Jamai[c]'s Native Administration in South Kordofan despite their being of different ethnic genealogies.

6. Author's interview with Makein el-Wakeil, Keiga Tummero, 8 June 2005.

7. Author's interview with Adam Abu Shok, Keiga Tummero, 9 June 2005.

8. Author's interview with sheikh Makin al-Wakil al-Zubayr, Keiga Tummero, 6 June 2005.

9. A survey engineer in Land Use and Water Department, Ministry of Agriculture, Kadugli, South Kordofan State. He was in charge of surveying, mapping, and plotting the 'small farmers' collective schemes' in 1994. He was interviewed in Kadugli, 21 and 22 February 2007.

10. Author's interview with Muhammad Ibrahim al-Digayl, Kadugli 21 February 2007.

11. Author's interview with al-Yias Ibrahim Koko, Omda of Keiga Tummero, Keiga Tummero, 14 February 2007.

12. Author's interview with al-Bushra Somi Tawer, al-Kweik, 13 February 2007.

13. Author's interview with Usman Bilal Hamid al-Likha, Kadugli, 22 February 2007.

14. One feddan equals 1.038 acres or 0.42 hectare.

15. (i) Muhammad Ibrahim al-Digayl, Kadugli, 21 February 2007; (ii) Nazir al-Bushra Somi Tawer, al-Kweik, 13 February 2007; and (iii) Nazir 'Usman Bilal, Kadugli, 22 February 2007.

16. Author's interview with Muhammad Ibrahim al-Digayl, Kadugli, 21 February 2007. In the same interview, my informant revealed that one wealthy Takarir man came from the Gulf States and paid, on behalf of the Takarir community, all fees required for the registration of their allocated 4,000 feddans.

17. Author's interview with Sheikh Sulayman Shirra, Keiga Tummero, 14 February 2007.

18. See, for example, the Abol 3rd Conference in Kobang, 13–16 April 2005; the Leira 3rd Conference in Hagar Bago, 16–18 April 2005; the Irral Payam Conference in Shwai, 21–22 April 2005, and the Korongo-Messakin tribes Conference in Farandella, Buram County, 29 May – 1 June 2005.

19. This issue of Nuba identity and cultural revival with strong ties to territoriality was listed as resolution No. 27 in the All Nuba 2nd Conference in Kauda, 5–8 April 2005. It was then discussed and put into practice in a number of community-based conferences. For example, the Korongo-Messakin tribes Conference held in Farandella, Buram County, 29 May – 1 June 2005, resolved that the Arab names of the Buram, Reikha and Teis areas were henceforth to be known by their original Nuba names as Tobo, Tolabi, and Tromo respectively.

20. See the Khartoum-based daily newspaper *Al-Adwaa*, Issue No. 996, 25 June 2006, p. 8.

21. These points have been extracted and translated from Arabic to English from the final documents of the Rowowga 1st and 2nd Conferences held in Kurchi in Moro 20–21 May 2005 and in Kadugli 21–23 June 2006.

7

Entangled Land and Identity: Beja History and Institutions

SARA PANTULIANO

This contribution highlights the interconnections between land as a source of livelihood and land as a source of identity from the perspective of 'the Beja' in Eastern Sudan. But who are 'the Beja'? The chapter traces how nomadic people with claims to certain territories in Eastern Sudan came to be identified as Beja. Foreign interests in Beja territory have a long historical trajectory: Egyptian pharaohs, Roman and Arab armies have all invaded to extract gold and mineral resources. The territory later formed part of the pilgrimage route to Saudi Arabia, which led to multiple foreign contacts and intermarriages. Under colonial rule, land tenure and the political system were reformed, marginalizing customary claims to land as well as political institutions. Agricultural schemes encroached upon Beja lands, especially in the Gash and Tokar deltas. The marginalization of people in Eastern Sudan was further aggravated by post-colonial politics that instead of promoting state-building through diversity fostered homogenization through its Arabization politics. In the past few decades, pressures on rural livelihoods have increased. Together with the eruption of armed conflict, successive droughts and famine, the granting of large concessions for foreign investors in agriculture and mining (cf. Umbadda in Chapter 2 and Calkins & Ille in Chapter 3), and the inability of successive Sudanese governments to govern, regulate and secure their citizens, have led to the disruption of the multi-layered relationships between people and their land. This chapter argues that the growing need to protect both land and identity has resulted in a process of ethnic mobilization of different tribes whereby the label Beja was accentuated. This added political weight to their claims for inclusion and enabled their representation through an ethnic political party, the Beja Congress. Therefore, what appear as 'traditional' and 'indigenous' institutions, namely the constriction of land rights to the *diwab* system in the frame of customary law (*silif*), need to be read against a long history of struggle against external interests and encroachments upon the very land from which local nomadic and agro-pastoral communities gained their livelihoods.

This chapter begins with some more general reflections on who are designated as Beja. Then it traces four phases linking the history of the people to their territories: the early history up to the Arab invasion,

Turko-Egyptian rule and the Mahdiya, British colonial rule (1899–1956), and post-independence governments until the signing of the Eastern Sudan Peace Agreement of 2006. The subsequent sections are devoted to analysing the present configurations of territories, identities and livelihoods of TuBedawiye speaking groups. To argue that the increasing pressure on land and associated livelihood systems resulted in accentuating 'Beja' identity, the reinterpretation of the principles of *diwab* and customary law (*silif*) in line with urban Islamic contexts will be discussed.

APPROACHING 'THE BEJA'

Travellers and colonial administrators in the past few centuries have identified and described five tribes as Beja: Ababda, Bishariyyn, Amar'ar/Atmaan, Hadendowa and Beni Amer (Palmisano 1991: 7). Other authors (Morton 1989a, Environmental Research Group Oxford –ERGO 1990) limit this list to the three largest groups, Amar'ar/Atmaan, Bishariyyn and Hadendowa, an interpretation that is also prevalent among these communities. Whereas Beni Amer are sometimes viewed as kinsfolk, the Ababda largely are not. However, the Beja do not share a common genealogy as a group and it is more appropriate to describe them as a confederation of tribes united by a common language and segmentary structure. Importantly, each of these tribal segments is intimately intertwined with ideas of a home territory. The word Beja is not commonly used by local people in their ethnic identifications, instead people use the name of their own group and lineage. Collectively, the Beja refer to themselves as TuBedawiye speakers. TuBedawiye is unwritten and represents the northernmost language of the Cushitic family, one of the Semito-Hamitic linguistic groups, also known as Afro-Asiatic (Greenberg 1963). Other Cushitic languages are mainly spoken in the Horn of Africa and include Afar, Galla, Oromo, Saho and Somali.

The Amar'ar/Atmaan, the Bishariyyn and the Hadendowa mostly live in north-eastern Sudan between the Egyptian and the Eritrean borders, speaking similar dialects of TuBedawiye. Although an increasing number of men, especially in Port Sudan and the coastal area, also know Arabic, they consider it of secondary importance. The Ababda, who occupy an area between Aswan and the northern Red Sea coast, speak Arabic as their first language and only a few know TuBedawiye. For this reason, and also because many Ababda claim to be pure Arabs (Paul 1954: 143), other groups do not refer to them as Beja. Some literature (Palmisano 1991) classifies them as Beja because of their constant interaction and frequent intermarriage with the Bishariyyn (Morton 1989a: 11).

The Beni Amer inhabit a wide region between South Tokar, Khor Baraka and Northern Eritrea. The majority of them originate from Eritrea, but the Eritrean-Ethiopian wars have driven many Beni Amer across the Sudanese border and today it is possible to find large groups settled in or around Kassala, Tokar town and Port Sudan. Most Beni

Amer speak Tigré, a Semitic language related to Tigrinya and Amharic, and only a few lineages, known as the Hadareb, are native speakers of TuBedawiye (ERGO 1990: 19). The Beni Amer also differ from main Beja groups due to their social and political organization (Palmisano 1991: 59). Their society is not based on a segmentary system but rather on a caste system where lineages are in a serf/client-master relationship (Nadel 1945, Paul 1950). The aristocratic group is called *nabtab*, while the serfs are called *tigré*, the *nabtab* also call them Arabs when speaking to outsiders (Nadel 1945: 57). The *nabtab-tigré* relationship is characterized by a series of strict behavioural rules and prohibitions that enforces the idea of subalternation of the serfs/clients to the masters, but also highlights the dependency of the *nabtab* on the *tigré* to satisfy practical needs, e.g. milk or ground sorghum, since the *nabtab* are not allowed to milk cattle or grind sorghum. Palmisano (1991: 61) talks about an 'articulated complex of mutual obligations/exchanges' which cannot be simplified as a unilateral relationship of *tigré* subordination to the *nabtab*. Nevertheless, the relationship between the two groups differs substantially from the type of social organization characteristic of Beja groups, which is based on a segmentary patrilineal lineage structure linked to common ownership of land (Morton 1989a: 16).

Based on these observations and on discussions with several Amar'ar/Atmaan, Bishariyyn, and Hadendowa communities over the years, it seems a more widely held opinion of the Beja themselves that the Beja consist of the Amar'ar/Atmaan, the Bishariyyn and the Hadendowa and other minor related groups like the Arteiga, the Ashraf, the Kemeilab, the Halanga and the Shayaab. It is important to stress that the word 'Beja' is used here only as a simplification to describe TuBedawiye speaking groups, with some shared features, such as social organization and its interconnectedness with land ownership. While they are able to reflect upon the label Beja and to discuss its significations, the Amar'ar/Atmaan, the Bishariyyn and the Hadendowa do not usually employ the term Beja to identify themselves. The Beni Amer are therefore not included in the general perception of what constitutes being Beja, although there have been moves by Beja politicians over the years to bring them into the Beja fold under the umbrella of the Beja Congress.

EARLY HISTORY

Records of the Beja in north-eastern Sudan date back to reports of Egyptian expeditions of c.2500 BCE looking for gold under the Fifth Pharaonic dynasty (Paul 1954: 21). The Egyptians established relations with the ancestors of the Beja and these contacts remained frequent because of Egyptian interest in gold and precious stones that could be found in Beja territory. Later records mention the Beja as allies of the Meroitic twenty-fifth dynasty against Persia (290 BCE), when they fought in exchange for 14 years of tax exemption (Paul 1954: 31), and opponents of the Ptolomies (217 BCE), who tried to expand their control southward

(Paul 1954: 32). During this time the Beja were referred to as 'the Blemmyes', a name that was widely used also throughout the early Greek and Roman literature on them (Herodotus, Olympiodorus, Vospicius). For Roman writers, the word Blemmyes designated a range of nomadic tribes scattered about the eastern desert between Abyssinia, Egypt and the Red Sea, whose geographical limits, tribal divisions, nomadic patterns and livelihood systems are similar to those of contemporary Beja (Kirwan quoted in Paul 1954: 55). The name Beja appears for the first time towards the end of the third century BCE in royal inscriptions of the kingdom of Axum to describe these people as a northern tribe and as subjects of the kingdom (Paul 1954: 44).

During Roman domination of Egypt, 'Beja' engaged in continuous raids against Roman and Nubian settlements (300–400 CE) and they even became a threat to Roman rule over the Thebaid region, as they occupied a section of the Nile south of Aswan and controlled a number of towns until they were forced out in 276 CE. However, the raids continued until they were ultimately expelled from their settlements in the Nile valley in the sixth century and had to withdraw into the eastern desert (Paul 1954: 57, 62). Still, in the sixth century, attempts were made by emissaries of the Emperor Justinian and Empress Theodora to convert the Beja to Christianity. Some of them eventually became proselytes of Monophysite Christianity, but as the influence of Rome declined, they returned to 'pagan' beliefs that they had perhaps never really abandoned (Paul 1954: 62).

In the seventh century Beja territory was subject to continuous invasions from Arab groups coming from southern Arabia. Later on, after the Hegira, Muslim peoples also started to arrive both from the Arabian Peninsula and from Upper Egypt. These groups frequently intermarried with the Beja, promoting their gradual conversion to Islam between about 1000 and 1300 CE (Newbold 1935: 149). According to the historian Yagubi (891 CE), at the time of the Arab invasion there were six separate Beja kingdoms between the Nile and the Red Sea, although other sources indicate that there were only four kingdoms (Gaffar Baamkar, personal communication, 1998). The Amar'ar/Atmaan are the only group still known today among those mentioned by Yagubi; the Hadendowa and the Bishariyyn had not yet become separate tribes (Newbold 1935). Relations between Beja and Arabs were characterized by continuous fighting. In 831 the Beja signed a treaty with caliph Mamun, agreeing to pay a tribute to the caliph and to grant Arabs safe passage in Beja territory, where they were looking for gold and emerald mines. However, the Beja broke the treaty a few years later, refusing to pay the tribute. The Arabs reacted with a massive military expedition and subjugated the Beja. Some Arabs, especially the Rabi'a and the Juhayna tribes, intermarried extensively with Beja and stayed in the Red Sea Hills, even when the rest of the army returned to Egypt (Palmisano 1991: 67–72).

The Arabs remained dominant in the region for a few centuries and under their control the small port of Aydhab (near Abu Ramad) became an important pilgrimage station and trading centre for goods coming from India and China. Aydhab benefited particularly from the closure of the Sinai during the Crusades that forced all North-African Muslim pilgrims to cross Beja territory on their way to Mecca. The Beja started to escort the caravans across the desert and engaged in petty trading of milk, butter and honey around towns; they also controlled a camel market in Bukht, where they traded camels with other nomadic populations (Idrisi 1864: 27, quoted in Hjort af Ornäs & Dahl 1991: 23). In 1426 the port was destroyed by the Mamluks, who protected the newly established port of Suakin, from where slaves and ivory from inner Africa as well as camels and ghee from Eastern Sudan were exported to Mecca. The destruction of Aydhab gradually led to the decline of the Hadareb, the powerful Arab group that controlled it, enabling the territorial expansion of the present Beja tribes until the eighteenth century. The Bishariyyn, who had started to emerge as a tribe in the Elba district between 1000 and 1400 (Newbold 1935), pushed the Arabs out of the Atbai (a large region of north-eastern Sudan situated between Jabal Elba and Ábrag) towards the end of the fifteenth century. The Hadareb were then defeated by the Funj from central Sudan near Suakin in the late sixteenth century. Later on, the Hadendowa, who had become a united tribe under Wail ᶜAli in 1600, drove them out of the Sinkat area in the early seventeenth century (Morton 1989a: 7).

During the eighteenth century the Amar'ar/Atmaan, who originally lived just around the area where Port Sudan exists today, began their expansion northwards, achieved primarily through a deliberate intra-ethnic intermarriage policy, while the Bishariyyn expanded westwards towards the Atbara river to occupy an area that has been their territory ever since. In the meanwhile the Hadendowa pushed alien tribes out of the Gash area (in central Kassala State today) but later on started to fight against the Bishariyyn. However, the two groups soon united their lineages against Mohammad Ali's army that had been sent from Egypt to destroy the Funj kingdom and occupy Sudan in 1821, in the hope of finding gold and to procure safer channels for the slave trade (Schultze 1963: 279).

TURKO-EGYPTIAN RULE AND THE MAHDIYA

During the first few years of their occupation of Sudan, the Turko-Egyptians paid very little attention to the hilly parts of the eastern provinces and most Beja were left largely undisturbed, since the Turks concentrated on taxing coastal peoples, especially in the form of slave confiscation (Hjort af Ornäs & Dahl 1991: 30). In 1831/32, however, a massive tax-gathering expedition was launched against the Hadendowa. On this occasion the Turko-Egyptian troops were defeated, but a second attack in 1840 proved more successful and the Hadendowa were eventually forced to submit. To secure the payment of the tribute, the Turkish governor attempted to dam the Gash river, though his plan failed when the dam burst and the Hadendowa fled into the bush (Holt & Daly 1979: 66). The Hadendowa seem to be the Beja group most affected by the Turko-Egyptian tax policy, since the Bishariyyn and the Amar'ar/Atmaan were living in areas that were less accessible to the local administrators. Nonetheless, the Amar'ar/Atmaan had to provide the Turko-Egyptian troops with camels, which was felt to be extortionate (Hjort af Ornäs & Dahl 1991: 33).

Taxes were not the only external pressure imposed by the foreign administration on the Beja. Rather, the Turko-Egyptian administrators introduced agricultural schemes in areas that were devoted to grazing or subsistence cultivation. The Hadendowa were once again the most affected since the schemes were introduced into their territory, occupying land they used as pasture reserves in times of drought. The schemes were set up around Kassala and Tokar, to produce cotton, sugar cane, roses, vines and even jasmine. They were first introduced by the Turkish governor of Suakin in 1870, but although his aim was to put 6.7 million hectares (16.55 million acres) under cotton, a much more limited area was eventually cultivated, in 1871: 50 acres (20 hectares) in Tokar and 2,500 acres (1,011 hectares) in the Gash (Schultze 1963: 44). The Mahdist insurrection halted the development of the scheme, which resumed when the east was occupied by the Anglo-Egyptian forces in 1891, eight years before the final re-occupation of Sudan led by Lord Kitchener with the battle of Omdurman. However, it was not until around 1905/6 that the Tokar area came to be heavily developed, with an average of 50,000 acres being sown annually and a peak of 120,000 acres in good years (Paul 1954: 123). The Gash scheme was opened in 1926 by the Kassala Cotton Company to produce cotton over an area of 250,000 feddans (about 260,000 acres, 105,000 hectares) (Abdel Ati 1996: 110). It is reported that the Hadendowa were also forced to work without payment on the schemes (Cumming 1940: 229ff quoted in Palmisano 1991: 16).

Meanwhile, in the more northern areas the Amar'ar/Atmaan and the Bishariyyn had continued to be involved in caravan-escorting and camel-supplying along the route from Suakin to Berber. In the mid-1850s Bishariyyn and Amar'ar/Atmaan started to fight for control of the business, with the latter eventually coming out on top. Goods imported at Suakin were transported by camels across the Beja territory. This offered the Beja a chance to sell their pastoral products such as butter, water skins and other leather products in demand in the Arabian markets (Hjort af Ornäs & Dahl 1991: 35).

The different circumstances of the Beja tribes under the Turko-Egyptian domination subsequently led to different attitudes being adopted towards the initial expansion of the Mahdist movement. The Hadendowa, who were in open conflict with the government because of the agricultural schemes, supported the Mahdi from the beginning and were a decisive factor in bringing about Gordon's demise in Khartoum in 1885. They obstructed the Suakin-Berber route, contributed to the fall of Suakin and to the British defeat at at-Teb (Palmisano 1991:17). The Amar'ar/Atmaan and the Bishariyyn welcomed the Mahdi's emissary Osman Digna less enthusiastically, especially because they feared that a conflict in the area would disrupt their trade. For this reason they never declared open support to Osman Digna and, although some lineages temporarily chose his side when he was more successful, they remained neutral or pro-British most of the time. Amar'ar/Atmaan relations with Osman degenerated into open conflict in 1886, when he sent an emissary with some troops to claim the payment of tribute and his men were attacked by the Amar'ar/Atmaan. Osman's reaction was very harsh: a large number of Amar'ar/Atmaan were captured and left to die of starvation and, their nazir was executed together with the sheikh of the Nurab lineage (Jackson 1926: 116). As a result, Osman lost the support of most of the Beja sections that had stood by his side, and at the battle of Omdurman (1898) only a few Hadendowa fought with him in defence of the Mahdist project against the British troops.

The years of the Mahdiya were also characterized by severe epidemics and ecological disasters that, combined with the ongoing fighting, reduced the Sudanese population dramatically (*sana sitta* period, 1889–90). Records estimate that in 1870 in the Kassala Province (which today comprises the whole of the Red Sea State) there were about 500,000 people, of whom 300,000 died from disease and 120,000 because of war, reducing the population to around 80,000 in 1903 (McLoughlin 1966: 11 quoted in Hjort af Ornäs & Dahl 1991: 38). The most widespread diseases were cholera and smallpox, but the situation was aggravated by locust attacks and outbreaks of rinderpest among livestock. In addition, food production declined dramatically during the Mahdist war as severe drought affected many parts of Africa. The Beja economy was also hit by the cessation of the export trade and the abolition of pilgrimages to Mecca ordered by the Khalifa, the Mahdi's successor.

BETWEEN THE COLONIAL GOVERNMENT AND THE MODERN STATE

The British ruled Sudan jointly with the Egyptians between 1898 and 1956, although the Egyptian involvement in the administration of the colony was negligible, following the murder of Sir Lee Stack, the governor-general, in Cairo in 1924 (Voll & Potts Voll 1985: 58). During the first 25 years of colonialism the British did not pay much attention to eastern Sudan. As a result the Beja were largely overlooked by the new rulers. Following the creation of the Anglo-Egyptian Condominium in the 1920s, a new system of administration was adopted based on the model of Indirect Rule elaborated by Lord Lugard during his governorship in Nigeria. The implementation of this model of governance in Sudan, however, had peculiarly complex features due to the political situation at the time. The British selected their native agents in Sudan not only for financial reasons (i.e. to reduce administrative costs), but also to offset the power that the Mahdist movement still held in many areas (Bakheit 1974: 25).

Local tribal leaders were appointed from amongst the Beja to collect and deliver taxes and guarantee security along the trade routes in the east. The leaders were organized into a hierarchy of administrative units (*ḥiṣṣa*-s, omodias and nazarahs) that were supposed to conform to the existing tribal patterns of social organization. However, in most cases the units identified did not mirror the indigenous ones, mainly because the Native Administration system required a permanent structure, with a fixed number of people and a minimum size. This prerequisite could not be met by existing patterns of organization, since group membership was subject to constant change for political reasons and its size varied significantly in line with historical or ecological conditions (Morton 1989a: 234). Consequently, the British administration created units whose size and nature were artificial, but functional to their own administrative needs. These structures, especially at the higher level (nazirs), were endowed with an unprecedented level of authority and power among Beja groups. In some cases, lineages that had never submitted to a nazir were administratively placed under the authority of one nazir. This measure aimed to consolidate colonial control over the Beja, whom the British found extremely difficult to govern, largely because they were scattered over a vast and sometimes inaccessible territory (Paul 1954: 122). The nazirs were given ample judicial and tax-collecting powers in addition to administrative rule and became privileged intermediaries of the colonial administration. This was backed by economic incentives (salaries, ratios of revenue collected, etc.) and political powers which continued until recently for the families that inherited those titles and positions.

The nazarahs were created or reinforced notwithstanding the plea made in 1901 by several minor Beja sheikhs to be entitled to pay the tribute independently (as they had been doing with the Turko-Egyptians), instead of being placed under the control of an alien paramount structure (Hjort af Ornäs & Dahl 1991: 39). Separate nazirs were appointed for the different Beja groups and in all cases the criterion followed was to choose a 'ruling family' (Newbold 1935: 160), instead of respecting the local logic based on territorial ownership and descent. The major consequence of this British policy was to create small family elites with power over whole tribes in a society traditionally characterized by a relative absence of multi-levelled hierarchies. Thanks to the economic and social power they had gained over the years, these elites were in many cases able to maintain their dominance over the rest of the tribe, even after the abolition of the system of Native Administration by the Nimeiri regime in the early 1970s. Moreover, they were able to use their influence to ensure significant representation in local government councils throughout the 1970s and beginning of the 1980s. This phenomenon had a negative impact on the Beja as a whole since the elites were more preoccupied with infighting for control of tax revenues, rather than securing land and water resources in the interests of the communities they represented (Morton 1989a: 236, Abdel Ati 1996: 115). As a reaction to the power of the native administrators and the central authority, in 1958 a group of urban-based educated Beja united to form the Beja Congress, an organization whose main aim was to coalesce the different Beja groups in an attempt to create a stronger political unit that could advocate for people's needs at a higher level. However, the Beja Congress was initially ineffective in its endeavours, given that many of its members kept resorting to tribal leaders to obtain access to sources of power (Abdel Ati 1991: 115).

The impact of the British colonization went beyond the political level, materializing in Beja territories. The British greatly expanded the size of farming schemes in Sudan to increase agricultural production, especially cash crops such as cotton, sesame, groundnuts and gum Arabic for the international market and food for emerging urban centres. These schemes encroached upon the land of small farmers and pastoralists throughout the country, such as in Gezira, Nuba Mountains and Gedaref (Salih 1989: 106). In the Beja territory, this policy was developed in two main ways: the first was the closure in 1922 of the old port of Suakin, which became only a base to serve pilgrims, and the opening of a new and bigger port at Shaikh Barghut, which later became Port Sudan. The need for a bigger port was due to the increase in the export of crops, especially cotton. Cotton became the monoculture to which the British geared Sudanese agriculture. Sudan's development became focused on the agricultural sector and the high potential of pastoral resources was utterly overlooked. The expansion of the cotton schemes implemented by the Turko-Egyptians in the Gash Delta was the second feature of British development policy in the Red Sea area. The Hadendowa were alienated from much of the land and it was given to the Kassala Cotton Company, through a concession by the government to grow cotton in the Gash Delta in 1924/25. This caused the loss of crucial pasture reserves that had been used by the Hadendowa and other Beja groups, like the Amar'ar/Atmaan, in drought years when the rains had failed elsewhere and laid the basis for the decline of their pastoral economy (Niblock 1987: 148).

The Amar'ar/Atmaan and the Bishariyyn were affected in a different way by British colonization. The area in which they lived was not suitable for large-scale cultivation, but was rich in gold and other minerals, for which speculation soon began. As a result many pastoralists were drawn to work in the mines, while others started to leave the hills to work in Port Sudan as dock labourers or in the Delta for cotton-picking. Their involvement in such activities was strongly encouraged by the British (Hjort af Ornäs & Dahl 1991: 41), but it caused major alterations in Beja traditional coping strategies. When in the late 1940s a severe drought killed most of the livestock in the Atbai, this led to an increase in the number of Beja men moving to Port Sudan to look for paid work. Their families often followed them after a few years and the number of Beja in town increased very rapidly, leading to a situation of 'over-urbanization' (Milne 1974: 72) marked by vast areas of squatter settlements mushrooming all around Port Sudan towards the end of the 1950s.

POST-INDEPENDENCE YEARS

Sudan became independent from Great Britain in 1956 and the colonial authority was substituted with a parliamentary government that stayed in power until 1958 when General Abbud overthrew it with a military coup. The first two independent Sudanese governments did not pay much attention to the situation in the Red Sea area and the Beja were completely overlooked in national politics. This led to a group of educated Beja coming together in October 1958, resulting in the formation of the Beja Congress. The Congress's main aim was to draw attention to the underdevelopment and the marginalization of the Beja area and to advocate for more autonomy at administrative and political levels. However in November the same year, its leaders were arrested and imprisoned when the parliamentary government was overthrown by Abbud (Niblock 1987: 149). In 1964 the Abbud regime was brought down by a popular uprising and parliamentary elections were held the following year with the Umma Party winning in most constituencies. The Beja Congress decided to stand for the elections as a separate party and it managed to win ten seats in the new parliament. Its main agenda was to promote a regionalization process in the country. In this endeavour the Congress was joined by southern and Nuba elements that resisted the homogenizing Arabization project (Morton 1989b: 67). However, the high number of Congress MPs was mainly due to the People's Democratic Party (PDP) boycotting the elections. When in 1968 the PDP contested elections in alliance with the National Unionist Party (NUP), the number of seats for the Beja Congress declined to three only (Morton 1989b: 67).

Greater regional autonomy was granted throughout the country by the military regime of Ja'far Mohammad an-Nimeiri that took power in 1969. Nimeiri soon turned the country into a one-party state centred on the Sudan Socialist Union, suppressing any other political organization, including the Beja Congress. The regime instituted regional governments (Rural District Councils), whose members were appointed by the central authority, with limited powers and a restricted independent revenue base. To appease the Beja, a high proportion of posts at the provincial and the regional levels were filled with Beja politicians loyal to the one-party system. This was consistent with Nimeiri's policy of promoting ethnic minorities in order to keep the regime's popularity high in more remote areas. In 1973 the former Kassala Province was divided, with the northern part becoming the Red Sea Province. Later, in 1980, the two were reunited as the new Eastern Region. Thanks to the efforts of some Beja politicians, the northern Nile valley was not included in the new region that hence became strongly Beja dominated (Morton 1989b: 68). Nimeiri succeeded in his attempt at increasing the popularity of his regime among the Beja, and many of them still remember the first years of Nimeiri positively for granting the Beja greater powers in local politics. However, the needs of the Beja population were never seriously represented in Khartoum, not even when a dire famine struck at the beginning of the 1980s and relief was needed to cope with the emergency. Whereas

Beja politicians had been quite successful in securing the provision of some health and education services for their own people in the 1970s, at least in the urban areas, they were unable to organize a response to the famine. This reflected an approach, retained from the colonial past, of advocating immediate benefits rather than long-term strategic interests. It was also a consequence of a more general policy adopted by Nimeiri at a national level, namely to pretend that the emergency did not concern Sudanese people, but was a problem only faced by Chadian or Ethiopian refugees (Morton 1989b: 69).

Nimeiri was overthrown in early April 1985 by a military coup led by his army chief of staff General Siwar al-Dahab. The coup followed ten days of demonstrations in the streets of Khartoum, which broke out after increases in the price of bread and sugar had been announced by President Nimeiri. His downfall marked the end of Beja political control over Eastern Sudan. The regional, provincial and district councils that they controlled were eliminated and power was taken by the military or given to Local Government Officers who were mostly non Beja (Morton 1989b: 69). There was general dissatisfaction with Beja politicians within the local population, especially the Arabs, who perceived them as corrupt and untrustworthy.

At the parliamentary elections held in April 1986, the Beja Congress reappeared 17 years after it had been banned, although its political platform was substantially different. In the 1960s the Congress's main objective was to draw attention to the marginalization of the Beja and to advocate for their needs and demand more administrative autonomy from the central government. At the end of the 1980s the situation looked completely different. The Eastern Region was facing new challenges, mainly because of the demographic transformation due to the arrival of refugees from southern Sudan and Eritrea and the migration of northern Sudanese to Port Sudan. For this reason, the Congress' main concern became the preservation of the Beja identity and the control over the land they had traditionally inhabited. To strengthen the Beja political clout, a common identity between the Beja and the Beni Amer began to be forged by the Beja Congress leaders, although ordinary Beja would still not recognize this broader definition of Beja identity. The Congress was successful in 1986 in using its influence to negotiate with the central government that the governor of the Eastern Region be chosen from the Beja, while the deputy had to be elected from among the northern population (Verney 1995: 28). The retired Bishariyyn general Mohammad Karrar was soon appointed as governor for the region and he stayed in power for most of the duration of the democratically elected government of Sadiq al-Mahdi.

The al-Mahdi government was overthrown by the coup led by Omar Hassan Ahmed al-Bashir in June 1989. Relations between the Beja and the new government were difficult from the beginning, particularly because of the regime's discriminatory attitude towards non-Arab minorities. They worsened after Governor Karrar was summarily executed in April 1990, following an accusation of his plotting a coup attempt.

Some members of the Karrar clan attacked government and security personnel in Port Sudan, after which relations between the Beja and the new regime degenerated (Verney 1995: 28). The Beja Congress was banned soon after the coup, like all other political parties, but it remained active underground and was repeatedly accused by the government of plotting to destabilize the political situation in the East. In August 1994 the Beja Congress in Cairo reported that a 'terror' campaign had been undertaken by the government against Beja people in Eastern Sudan. The repression against Beja dissidents in Eastern Sudan worsened and the Khartoum regime also denounced Eritreans for training Sudanese Beja in camps in their country (Verney 1995: 28). Conversely, the Eritrean government severed diplomatic ties with Sudan in December 1994 on the grounds that Islamic terrorists had been training in Sudan and then infiltrated into groups of Eritrean returnees. Fighting between Sudanese troops and opposition groups allegedly supported by the Eritreans started along the Sudan-Eritrea border in 1995, when the Beja Congress joined the National Democratic Alliance (NDA), a coalition of former mainstream political parties from the north side-lined by the 1989 military coup – the Umma Party, the Democratic Unionist Party (DUP) and Sudan Communist Party – as well as the main military and political force in southern Sudan, Sudan People's Liberation Movement/Army (SPLM/A), and a number of other smaller political parties, trades unions and professional associations. For the first time in its history the Beja Congress became involved in military operations in collaboration with other NDA forces. Military operations largely consisted of guerrilla strikes against government military installations as well as the Khartoum-Port Sudan highway and the oil pipeline. The border was mined and this had a terrible effect on traditional pastoral migration. In 1996 the Beja Congress was charged with having backed a failed coup attempt in August of that year and fighting between the parties intensified in the southern area of the then Tokar and Kassala Provinces, with the opposition groups eventually occupying most of the area between the border and Tokar and the town itself in spring 1997. Tokar was retaken by government forces shortly afterwards, but the NDA kept control of much of the border region, including the towns of Telkuk and Hamashkoreb, until the redeployment of the SPLA following the signing of the Comprehensive Peace Agreement (CPA) in 2005.

With the negotiations for the CPA moving towards a successful conclusion, the Beja Congress leaders worked to expand their political platform to other groups living in Eastern Sudan. This led to the formation of the Eastern Front in February 2005. The Front is a political alliance between the Beja Congress, the Rashaida Free Lions (a group created in the late 1990s with a similar agenda centred on the marginalization and the underdevelopment of Eastern Sudan, cf. Calkins in Chapter 8) and representatives from other small ethno-political groups belonging to the Shukriya and the Dabaina. The formation of the Front was an attempt by the Beja Congress and the Rashaida Free Lions to de-ethnicize their political agenda and appeal to other communities in Eastern Sudan, though this ambition was never fully realized. The Front briefly became the main protagonist in the conflict in Eastern Sudan, following the signing of the CPA. Peace negotiations aimed at bringing an end to the conflict and meeting the political and developmental concerns of actors in the region began in Asmara in July 2006 and were concluded with the signing of the Eastern Sudan Peace Agreement (ESPA) between the Eastern Front and the government of Sudan in October 2006. The negotiations and the signing of the ESPA, as well as the years that followed, were, however, marked by the rise of intra- and inter-tribal tensions between different Beja groups, with strong divisions between the Beni Amer and other Beja groups, especially Hadendowa, and between the Beja and Rashaida in particular (cf. Calkins in Chapter 8).

Parallel to these political processes, in post-colonial Sudan, national governments promoted irrigated agriculture under the bandwagon of 'national development', appropriating enormous tracts of land through discriminatory land reforms for commercial production (cf. Umbadda in Chapter 2, Komey in Chapter 6, Abdul-Jalil in Chapter 5). This series of land acts disregarded pastoralists' claims to land, which like in the Beja case, are built upon a collective property system. The Land Acts were displaced by legislation that encouraged privatization of land rights, causing losses of pasture and rain-fed land and the closure of pastoral transhumance routes due to encroaching schemes (Pantuliano 2006: 718). To sum up, historical grievances, such as the marginalization of Beja communities by exploitive governments and the overall unjust resource distribution, have led to demands for political power, socio-economic inclusion and a fair representation. This has been the breeding ground for various processes of ethnic mobilization and resistance to the central government; the Beja movement in Eastern Sudan is one example of these processes that cut across Sudan. Following this historical introduction, the chapter will now detail some of the contemporary configurations of territories, identities and livelihoods among TuBedawiye speaking groups, indicating how recent territorial transformations have affected identifications and livelihood portfolios.

TUBEDAWIYE SPEAKERS – EXTERNAL PERCEPTIONS AND SELF-REPRESENTATIONS

The different TuBedawiye speaking groups of Eastern Sudan have often been viewed as one indistinct tribe by external observers (travellers, researchers, administrators), who have also frequently stereotyped them on the basis of a superficial analysis of their social customs and livelihood patterns. Since Roman times, the Beja have been associated with the idea of 'ferociousness and cruelty, timelessness and absence of any type of social structure' (Palmisano 1991: 19). In his work on Beja ethnicity, Palmisano accurately illustrates how this cliché has been reiterated by European travellers and administrators over the past five centuries, whereas the image of the Beja that Arab travellers offered to the public was less prejudiced and more informative, since their main aim was to report on the possibilities of exchanging trade relationships with them.

References to the Beja by European writers can be found as early as 1540, when a Portuguese traveller and administrator, Don Joao de Castro, stopped in the Red Sea while travelling to the Indies. Many other European travellers and orientalists crossed Beja territory in the following centuries and most of them described the Beja as 'real savages ... who had surprisingly survived up to our days and kept their own primordial social, economic, political and religious order unaltered' (Palmisano 1991: 23). The most famous description of the Beja is contained in a poem published by Rudyard Kipling in 1925, whose title 'Fuzzy-Wuzzy' refers to the traditional hairstyle of Beja men. Kipling, moving away from images of the Beja as untrustworthy and cruel, focuses on the military ability of those Beja who stood up bravely against the British during the fight to oust the Mahdist rule.

However, both the disparaging and the eulogistic images are based on superficial analyses and do not reflect Beja self-representation in any way. As indicated above, it is inappropriate to talk of 'the Beja' as one unified group, but it is nonetheless possible to identify common features shared by the different TuBedawiye speakers in Sudan. These features have in recent times been used by Beja politicians to argue for a single ethnic identity, as this mobilizes more people in support of the political claims for inclusion. Therefore, I argue that in the light of various marginalizing policies and territorial interventions on 'Beja' land, which have disrupted their livelihood systems and often forced people to migrate to the towns, the claim to one shared identity is slowly spreading, not only in representations in the political arena but in the very self-identifications of TuBedawiye speakers especially in urban contexts, such as Port Sudan. Conversely, in rural areas people still tend to identify themselves as belonging to a specific group or lineage.

BISHARIYYN, AMAR'AR/ATMAAN, HADENODOWA – TERRITORIES, IDENTITIES AND LIVELIHOODS

Of the three major Beja groups, the Bishariyyn are the smallest, although they occupy the largest territory. They inhabit the area between the former administrative border with Egypt and Dungunab Bay along the Red Sea coast. Towards the west they occupy the region called Atbai and extend their control as far as Tamarab grasslands, west of Musmar, and to the area around the river Atbara southwards (Pantuliano 2000). The Egyptian administrative border was established by the British in 1902, but it was never recognized by Egypt which has always claimed its sovereignty over the border town of Halaib and the surrounding area. The border was drawn by the British to coincide with the tribal border of the Bishariyyn and has later become the *de facto* border (Morton 1989a: 42). In 1957/58, soon after Sudan became an independent state, Egypt attempted to annex the north-eastern part of the Bishariyyn area, also known as the Halaib triangle. Although agreement was soon reached between the two countries, Egypt kept army posts in the area that were never dismantled. The situation degenerated when the present Sudanese regime took over: fighting over the border resumed at the beginning of the 1990s and Halaib (with the surrounding area) was eventually seized by the Egyptians in 1994 and it remains under Egyptian control to date. This created enormous disruption to the Bishariyyn traditional seasonal transhumance movements and to their profitable camel trade across the Sudan-Egypt border.

The Bishariyyn land is very arid and for this reason they mainly raise camels or goats that are better adjusted to dryland than are cows or sheep. Their camels are widely known to be very light-coloured and speedy; they are considered the best riding camels in Sudan. The two finest strains, the *Ba Nagir* and the *Kiliewau,* are famous race camels and are in great demand in the Saudi markets. The Bishariyyn also used to breed camels for meat that was exported to Egypt (Palmisano 1991: 46), but the closure of the border has virtually stopped official commerce, although a good number of camels are still smuggled to Egypt. Camel-breeding and herding is the main economic activity for the Bishariyyn, who also market their milk and hides, but it is increasingly complemented by small stock-keeping (especially goats). Subsistence agriculture (mainly sorghum) and fishing are also practised wherever this is possible. Yet, the decline of pastoral activities in the past few years has led many Bishariyyn men to look for wage work elsewhere in order to meet their family needs. Some of them have taken up work as lorry drivers along the Egypt–Sudan route and many have sought employment as dock labourers in Port Sudan.

Like the rest of the Beja groups, the Bishariyyn can be sub-divided into smaller sections. The name Bishariyyn refers to the largest unit, the *qabīla*, an Arabic word meaning 'tribe', which has been completely assimilated into TuBedawiye. Sometimes this word is also used to indicate lineages, but never to indicate 'the Beja' as a whole. The plural *qabā'il badawīya* (in Arabic) or *bedawiêti tegabila* (in TuBedawiye) is instead used to refer to them collectively. The next sub-unit is called *fari*ᶜ in Arabic, but people also use the TuBedawiye expression *gau*. The *fari*ᶜ is in turn sub-divided into *diwab*s (lineages), which constitute the smallest and most important unit of the Beja segmentary lineage structure. People always refer to their *diwab* together with the *qabīla* when describing their ethnic affiliation, whereas the *fari*ᶜ is rarely even mentioned.

The Amar'ar/Atmaan are the second largest tribe after the Hadendowa. They occupy the area north of Port Sudan along the coast as far as Mohammad Qol. In the hills, they live between Khor Arbaat and the inland plateaux of Atbai and Aulib, with some sections dwelling north of this area in Khor Oko and Khor Amur (Pantuliano 2000). Port Sudan itself lies within the Amar'ar/Atmaan territory and south of the town the Amar'ar/Atmaan control an area that goes as far as Musmar. Many Bishariyyn and Hadendowa also live in this area, but to receive grazing and farming rights they need to refer to the customary landowning

Amar'ar/Atmaan (Hjort af Ornäs & Dahl 1991: 45). Although they are not the biggest Beja group, the Amar'ar/Atmaan control a large portion of territory. This is mainly the result of a targeted expansionist policy that they have been pursuing since the eighteenth century, especially through intermarriages with bordering groups like the Arteiga, the Ashraf and the Bishariyyn and the Hadendowa themselves (Palmisano 1991: 50).

The Amar'ar/Atmaan have been referred to in most of the traditional ethnographic and colonial literature simply as Amar'ar, a name that only applies to two small *faric* of the tribe, who were numerically dominant until some time ago. Today the Atmaan are said to be more numerous (reportedly 85 per cent of the total group) and they no longer call themselves Amar'ar (Hjort af Ornäs & Dahl 1991: 46).

Like the Bishariyyn, most of the Amar'ar/Atmaan are pastoral nomads and mainly raise camels, differentiated in three categories: *shallagêa*, *ararīt* and *matiāt*. The *shallagêa* camels are the best milk producers and they are especially bred on the coastal strip, since they are adapted to browse salty grass. The *ararīt* also give a good quantity of milk, but they are better known for their ability to carry weight and are therefore used for transport; they are mainly bred in the Aulib and Atbai plateaus. The *matiāt* are the fastest of all the Amar'ar/Atmaan camels and they can be found along the khors (seasonal streams) and in the hilly areas, where they feed almost exclusively on the *araak* tree (*Salvadora persica*, or *Hiib* in TuBedawiye), a plant that would not be eaten by the *shallagêa* and the *ararīt* unless forced, since it causes heavy diarrhoea (Hjort af Ornäs & Dahl 1991: 46). The *matiāt* are known among the Beja to be very resistant to drought, since the *araak* tree on which they feed can survive without rain for a long time (Almotalib Ibrahim, personal communication). The difference between the three types of camel stems from the need to adapt the herd to varied environmental conditions and nature of the pasture. Patterns of transhumance and therefore the degree of mobility of the different camels also vary according to the area in which the single *diwab* is based. Some sections of the Amar'ar, e.g. the Nurab, also breed cattle, but their number is steadily decreasing together with the number of camels. As a result, an unremitting trend common to all Beja groups towards herding small stock (especially goats) can be observed throughout the Red Sea area.

Livestock keeping is in many cases complemented by subsistence agriculture along the khors, aimed at producing sorghum for household consumption. Coastal *diwab*-s, like the Kurbab, are also increasingly taking up fishing and pearl marketing, while in the mountains the cAliab have been working as day labourers in the Gebeit gold mine. However, the main alternative activity for all sections of the Amar'ar/Atmaan has traditionally been dock work as day labourers in Port Sudan. The Amar'ar/Atmaan have been affected more than any other Beja group by the opening of the port on their land in 1905, since the great majority of Amar'ar/Atmaan young men have been attracted by the prospect of earning ready cash over the years. This has caused a drain of resources away from the rural areas and as a result has hindered the ability of the *diwab*s to cope with crises over the long term.

The Hadendowa are the largest and most well-known Beja group. Their territory extends from Tokar south-westwards to the north of Kassala and from there to the eastern bank of the river Atbara. To the north they occupy an area that goes from Suakin to Kambosanha Station through the Red Sea Hills and thence south-west as far as Musmar, bordering the Amar'ar/Atmaan area. Hadendowa territory offers better environmental conditions than the rest of north-eastern Sudan (Palmisano 1991: 54, Pantuliano 2000). Therefore, the economic portfolio of the Hadendowa differs in some important aspects from that of the Bishariyyn and the Amar'ar/Atmaan. Although the northern lineages keep camels, they are more intensely involved in agriculture than the rest of the Beja groups, thanks to the slightly higher rainfall in the region. Therefore, the majority of Hadendowa are primarily agro-pastoralists. A major role in the Hadendowa economy is played by the irrigated agricultural schemes that have been established in their area, in Tokar and the Gash. Many migrate regularly to the schemes for wage labour as well as to the towns (especially Port Sudan). Recent research suggests that these movements have dramatically risen in the past two decades (Egemi 1996: 39, Pantuliano 2006).

Beja livelihood systems, i.e. pastoralism and farming, were strongly framed by the access to various natural resources, above all land and water. That people in the past decades were forced to search for new means of livelihood in the urban centres or agricultural schemes relates strongly to diverse encroachments upon 'their' land, alienation of land rights and environmental disasters. This importance of land resources as means of survival also explains the strong emotional bond between land and identity among Beja communities. The following sections are devoted to exploring the changing role of Beja institutions in managing land resources and thus social life.

BEJA INSTITUTIONS – DIWAB IDEOLOGY

The use of TuBedawiye is not the only feature that these three Beja groups share. A major aspect that structures Beja society and characterizes Beja groups is the link between descent and territoriality. This inextricable interweaving of descent and land also provides the framework for land use regulations. Although men own and inherit land individually, they can only aggregate the different portions within a 'structure of segmentary patrilineal descent' (Morton 1989a: 43). As a result, a certain spatial conception emerges: land is conceived of as a collective property belonging to a specific *diwab* (lineage). All members of a lineage have the right to access pasture and water sources on the *diwab* territory, leading to a strong identification of people with both their 'own' lineage and territory. Both for the Bishariyyn and the Amar'ar/Atmaan *diwab* membership is a fundamental principle defining their identity, that is not only based on ideas of shared descent, but also entails material benefits, namely 'sharing affiliation to a territory and its productive resources' (Hjort af Ornäs & Dahl 1991: 52).

The *diwab* institution confirms and guards the shared access to and control over both material and symbolic resources. The most important resource is the collective title to land and the associated rights to pasture and wells found within the *diwab* territory. Interests in livestock and other economic resources are also shared. The *diwab* institution is not only organized by a territorial principle but also a principle of patrilineal descent, which act together in regulating aspects of living together. I will focus here on three areas organized by the *diwab* institution, namely inheritance, marriage and leadership structures.

First, although there is no prescriptive rule about patrilinearity within the Beja groups, the dominant lineage ideology is nonetheless associated with patrilineal descent. Women are normally excluded from land and animal inheritance to retain property within the *diwab*. Women can inherit land and livestock in exceptional cases, for instance in the absence of brothers, but the tendency is to transmit the *diwab* wealth only patrilineally. This prescription clashes with Muslim sharia laws on inheritance, according to which all sons and daughters inherit in a ratio of 2:1. Aware of the discrepancy, the Bishariyyn and the Amar'ar/Atmaan prefer to stick to their customary rules.

Second, *diwab* ideology also permeates marriage customs: all Beja groups have a distinct preference for close endogamy, although this pattern is undergoing significant changes in urban areas. Unlike most Sudanese Arab groups, the Beja do not have a particular prescription for patrilateral parallel-cousin marriages, as cross-cousin marriage is also contemplated. The order of preference is the following: FBD (Father's Brother's Daughter), MBD (Mother's Brother's Daughter), FSD (Father's Sister's Daughter), MSD (Mother's Sister's Daughter), but any girl of the *diwab* is thence considered (Hjort af Ornäs & Dahl 1991: 93). Intra-ethnic marriages were frequently contracted by the Amar'ar/Atmaan in the past, especially with the Hadendowa, and some inter-ethnic marriages also took place, but they never undermined the integrity of the Amar'ar/Atmaan society. Instead they were used to expand their territory and increase the wealth of the Amar'ar/Atmaan *diwab*s (Palmisano 1991: 72). Marriage is never sought by the Beja to create alliances between clans, but it is rather seen as a frail institution that needs to be reinforced by 'brotherly solidarity' (Hjort af Ornäs & Dahl: 107). As a result of such close endogamy, women often end up spending all their life with the same group of women, to whom they are often linked by multiple kinship ties.

Third, Beja political organization also reflects the importance of their *diwab*-based system. The leadership of the sheikhs is based on a territorial principle directly expressing the segmentary lineage system and it has survived despite the presence of the territorial administrative system (nazarah and omodia) created in colonial times. The political importance of the patrilineal system is not limited to rural areas, but it is as powerful and active in the urban milieu, where it has also become a significant source of tribal identity.

The increasing pressure on land and associated livelihood systems resulted in a resistance movement, which accentuated Beja identity. Therefore, in recent years in spite of the decline of pastoral production and urban migration, it has to be emphasized that, perhaps counter intuitively, the loss of land has not ushered in the demise of the *diwab* institution. Rather, the importance of the *diwab* model was reinterpreted along with the more unified Beja identity and has been perpetuated outside the tribal territory.[1] *Diwab* figures as one institution in a complex of rules, so-called *silif*, which will be discussed below.

SILIF – BEJA CUSTOMARY LAW

The life events of all Beja groups (birth, marriage, death, conflict) are regulated by a customary law known as *silif*, a complex but flexible body of rules based on Beja traditional values. Access to land and other resources is guided by *silif*, which differentiates between the rights of three groups: *diwab* members, other Beja people and travellers. In the Red Sea Hills, *silif* is used to regulate access to and control reciprocal use of environmental resources i.e. grazing land, water points, arable land and firewood. The aim is to protect the environment against overexploitation. Rules are not codified but flexible and are negotiated between the Beja through alliances and agreements within or between the different groups, clans or lineages. The sheikhs usually constitute the 'management group', which provides the institutional framework to negotiate such rules. These arise as a result of a process aimed to ensure that consensus among all participants is reached and good relations are maintained (Morton 1989a: 104).

The vast majority of the Beja profess to be Muslim, but the Islam they observe is far from orthodox. Where Muslim prescriptions differ from customary rules, Beja behaviour tends to adhere to *silif*. The *diwab* ideology has supremacy in Beja life, but it is not perceived as antagonistic to Islam and sharia. On the contrary, customary rules have in some ways been harmonized with the religious system and are perceived as licit and legitimate. Within this framework, the Beja custom that does not allow women to inherit land and animals or to take part in public meetings or speak to non-kin males is interpreted to be consistent with Islamic precepts.[2]

Silif also plays a major role in conflict resolution: the leaders of the different groups between which the conflict has occurred sit together and discuss the matter until they reach a *silif* agreement. Very rarely do they fail and have to refer to the local juridical authority. Conflicts are dealt with in this way both in the rural areas and in towns, where disputes are usually settled by sheikhs that live in the different *deims* (suburbs). Other events regulated by *silif* are social occasions, like weddings, funerals and childbirth, in which all *diwab* members and their Beja neighbours take part, contributing money or goods to the family concerned. Economic support is also given through *silif* to the poorest members of the community, but this aspect of *silif* is being increasingly challenged in Port Sudan, where the economic conditions of many Beja are very bad and people find it difficult to share any part of their meagre and irregular income with other members of the *diwab* (Pantuliano 2000: 61).

Although the economic dimension of *silif* seems to be losing prominence in urban areas, its social meaning has been reinforced. *Silif* is used to maintain and strengthen relationships between individuals and between different Beja groups who have settled in Port Sudan. In both urban and rural contexts, the degree of reciprocity under the *silif* system determines the strength of people's relationships. Another important function of *silif* is to preserve memories of past events and transmit them to future generations. Sitting together to narrate old stories is one of the most important forms of *silif*. In this way crucial information (e.g. about past coping strategies in drought times) is passed on to younger generations, whereby group identity is strengthened (Pantuliano 2000: 138).

Silif rules bind people to assist one another with mutual support and exchange news and information that could be useful. This is done through a prolonged greeting ritual that the Beja call *sakanab*. The most important news concerns rain and grazing, information that is crucial to the survival of Beja pastoralists (Morton 1988: 431). People rely on such information for their movements and therefore their informants are obliged by *silif* rules to provide reliable and trustworthy information. News is, for example, also exchanged about the demand for labour in the Gebeit gold mine and prices of the main staples in Port Sudan market, regulating the economic life of Beja groups in the hills. Likewise, young men's migration to Port Sudan relates to information about the availability of work on the docks.

Women's roles and position in the community are also defined within the framework of *silif* rules. Women are not allowed to take part in men's affairs and even if they are directly concerned with a legal case, this will be dealt with by one of their male kin (Lewis 1962: 37). Moreover, they are excluded from public decision making and politics as well as the access to land and large livestock herds. If they do manage to gain access to such resources, they are not allowed to exercise any control over them. However, some of these restrictions are slowly loosening up in the coastal area and in Port Sudan, where women are more exposed to outside views and their daughters have more access to education. A restriction that shows very little sign of waning and that the Beja perceive as 'ethnically distinctive to them' (Hjort af Ornäs & Dahl 1991: 99) is the prohibition on women milking any kind of livestock. The same habit is common to the Hima of Uganda, where milk bears a symbolic linkage with semen (Hjort af Ornäs & Dahl 1991: 99). This linkage does not seem to be the case with the Beja, but the prohibition appears to be more related to the fact that the first sip of milk should always be offered to another man, even if this implies walking for miles to find one. Beja women are not allowed to meet men who are not their kin, and therefore it would be difficult for them to fulfil this requirement that is culturally linked to the important role that hospitality plays in Beja life. Furthermore, it reinforces the traditional division of labour within the household, where the man is the primary provider of food (Hjort af Ornäs & Dahl 1991: 99).

Silif regulates much of Beja social and economic life. These rules include, among others, mechanisms of solidarity and reciprocity, such as herd redistribution. As in many other pastoralist societies, animals are generally redistributed through inheritance or payment of bridewealth. Among the Beja *silif* rules also exist to encourage wealthy livestock keepers to transfer some stock to *diwab* members in need of support, especially during periods of drought or food insecurity. Three main practices can be identified: *lahagen, tait* and *dangeit* or *yahamot. Lahagen* is called the gift of animals that a young man receives or can ask for from his friends or relatives when he gets married: these animals are added to those he receives from his father which constitute the bulk of the bridewealth. Animals can also be donated to a new owner in absence of a marriage: this arrangement takes the name of *tait.* A *tait* gift bestows upon the new owner full authority over the animals as well as all of their offspring. It also creates a long-lasting relationship between the people involved in the transaction. The third arrangement, *dangeit* or *yahamot* allows for the loan of animals, especially milking goats, to poorer households between *diwab* members or neighbours. In this case, unlike the others, the borrower can only use the milk and must return the animals and the offspring to the original owner once the period of difficulty is over or their agreement has come to an end. *Yahamot* is not limited to milking goats: riding camels are also lent to dispossessed herders when they need a means of transportation to move to far away pastures or to go to urban markets (Pantuliano 2002: 17).

Other *silif* rules concern ownership and use of grazing and cultivable land. Beja land rights can be divided into two main categories: *aṣl* and *amara* rights. *Aṣl* is the Arabic word (also used in TuBedawiye) that describes the customary right over a certain piece of land and its natural resources inherited from the ancestors by the entire *diwab. Amara* refers to the usufruct right given to non-lineage members to use pasture, water or cultivable land on the *aṣl* land of another lineage against the payment of a tribute called *gwadab. Aṣl* land rights are transferred collectively to male lineage members in the line of patrilineal descent; women have no claim to land. This rule has been challenged by some women, who advocate for the application of the sharia law that entitles women to inherit from their fathers. The land inherited through the *aṣl* right constitutes the *damar* (home area) of the *diwab* and cannot be sub-divided or alienated. Lineage members are entitled to use all the natural resources on their given territory. Springs, streams and pools are used collectively while there are certain acknowledged individual rights to wells, cultivable plots, residential sites and in some cases even single Acacia trees (Salih 1980: 119).

The use of all resources is regulated by strict principles which aim to preserve the environment from overexploitation. Green trees cannot be cut for firewood by anybody, including *diwab* members, but pollarding them for fodder is allowed. Conversely, dry wood can be picked freely. Trees can be browsed by everybody's animals, but they cannot be used for wood or charcoal production, if permission is not given by the owner. Permission is also needed by non-lineage members to dig a well or cultivate on another *diwab*'s land. When permission is given it is usually formalized through the payment of the *gwadab*. As Manger has pointed out, the economic value of the *gwadab* is normally nominal but it still is a highly significant symbolic gesture: by paying the tribute the non-lineage member recognizes and confirms that the land he is about to use belongs to the *diwab* and is not his own (Manger 1994: 9).

THE EROSION OF *SILIF*

Although the body of *silif* rules has not changed, the gap between 'traditional' norms and actual behaviour has been widening in recent years. Fewer and fewer people today are in a position to lend animals and even customs regarding the giving and exchange of camels as part of the bridewealth are changing. Young grooms used to be able to buy camels to be donated to the bride's family at a reduced amount from other *diwab* members, usually at 10 or 20 per cent of the market price. This custom is changing. *Silif* camels, as the Beja call them, are now bought at more or less the equivalent of the market price, although significant differences from place to place can be observed. The decline of *tait* and *yahamot* arrangements has made the rebuilding of the stock more difficult. People in rural towns, like Gebeit and Mohammad Qol, used to be granted loans for household commodities or fodder by merchants or local shop-keepers, especially during the dry season or in a time of drought. Merchants or shop-keepers counted on the animal wealth of the borrowers and the whole *diwab* for the repayment: the *silif* livestock arrangements acted as a guarantee that the debt would be repaid even in time of crisis. The general decrease in livestock numbers and the subsequent breakdown of the borrowing mechanisms have created a vicious circle that forces people to sell small stock during the dry season and even more during droughts to meet family needs, slowing down, and at times hampering, the reconstitution of the herd. This erosion of mechanisms of solidarity relates to the overall dismal living conditions that people are experiencing.

Silif rules over land are also increasingly being ignored. Refusal to pay the *gwadab* is becoming more and more common and conflict over land has also intensified since there is less recognition of owner's rights over their land. One of the worst consequences of the weakening of rules over land has been the progressive deterioration and depletion of natural resources, particularly trees. In the khor (river streams) areas trees are cut to clear land for cultivation, to which people are increasingly resorting as a source of livelihood. This has created tension with the local herders, also because tree or shrub clearing (particularly *Suaeda fruticosa*) has hastened erosion and sand dune migration (Hjort af Ornäs 1992: 169).

Cultivation is not the only reason for tree cutting. Firewood collection and charcoal making seem to be the main factors responsible for the rapid degradation of vegetation cover in Halaib Province. Charcoal and firewood have been important cash sources for the Beja for quite some time, as indicated in records available from Sandars (1935: 218) and Winkler (1938: 290). However, the scale of these two activities, and the number of practitioners involved, significantly increased during the late 1960s and early 1970s famine, when the trade in wood and charcoal became more commercialized, as Bishariyyn herders intensified their migration to Port Sudan (English 1987: 8). The 1983–85 famine then hastened the process of tree cutting which has become very widespread today. Hjort af Ornäs and Dahl (1991: 170) report that during their fieldwork in 1980, Beja people would say that it was acceptable to take dead trees to make charcoal, but immoral to cut from green trees. In 1986, shortly after the great Sahelian famine, the response they received was significantly different, since people no longer analysed the issue according to moral rules, but underlined that blame could not be attached to anyone for mobilizing all resources available to generate cash in times of crisis. El Siddig (1992 quoted in Harir 1996: 87) reports that many of the people involved in charcoal production evade 'the social ban on cutting living trees by cutting the bark around the trunk of the tree in order to kill them so that they can legitimately be used for charcoal production'.

The increase in the cutting of trees is not only a consequence of the Beja need for cash: urban demand for fuel and building materials both from small rural towns and larger ones like Port Sudan or Kassala has also accelerated the rate of destruction of trees in the surrounding rural areas. Both in squatter settlements in Port Sudan and in rural towns, houses are made of wooden planks or branches (often *dom* palm wood, *Hyphaene thebaica*). As a consequence, tree cover in the more immediate vicinity of the towns has significantly decreased and people now have to walk towards the hills for hours to find trees that can be used to make charcoal.

The degradation of the tree cover in Red Sea State has generated an increase in the price of firewood and charcoal and as a consequence more people have been attracted to economic activities related to these. Herders who have lost hope of rebuilding their stock find charcoal an easy and remunerative alternative to pastoral production. Although people, especially the elders, are aware of the risk of exhausting natural resources in the long term, there does not seem to be a reversal in this trend at the moment. The breakdown of *silif* thus has a negative impact on the entire region's environmental sustainability.

CONCLUSION

For Beja communities land, livelihood and identity are inseparably entangled. The life of Beja groups has been regulated by the customary law called *silif*, a complex but somewhat flexible set of rules based on

Beja values. The most significant Beja institution, the *diwab* principle, embodies the codes of land rights and prescribes their mediation by tribal authorities. *Diwab* and the superordinate *silif* have regulated the access to natural resources as well as the careful reciprocal use of grazing land, water points, farming land and various trees, but also conflict resolution and reciprocal exchanges at important life stages such as birth, marriage and death (Pantuliano 2006: 709). *Diwab* leaders, who based their authority on an interlacing of the territorial and patrilineal principle, managed communal rights, ensured the environmental sustainability of land and minimized conflicts. However, in recent decades *silif* and its traditional mediators have been severely undermined by successive governments' discriminatory policies, which have disenfranchised Beja communities from much of their land and have left them in precarious livelihood circumstances.

This gradual weakening of Beja livelihood security had already begun under British colonial rule with the imposition of the rigid hierarchical Native Administration system. This administrative system was ill-adapted to Beja social organization and did not take into account that the flexibility of Beja leadership structures was attuned to pastoral life. Traditional leaders were side-lined and powers were handed to an artificial hand-picked ruling elite, which pursued its own interests and only rarely represented Beja interest and needs.

Simultaneously, Beja communal lands were gradually encroached upon by agricultural schemes. The earliest of these in the Gash and Tokar deltas date back to Turko-Egyptian rule. Agricultural projects then greatly expanded their surface under British colonial rule, a development that was carried further after independence in 1956 (Bolton 1954: 189–191, Kapteijns & Spaulding 1991: 95, 96). Especially as Sudan pursued the so-called breadbasket strategies in the 1970s to attract investors in agriculture from the Gulf, it has reformed its land tenure system and abolished all communal forms of land ownership (i.e. pastures, rain-fed land). In the course of such legal/political developments, the Beja were alienated from their land and it was made available for investment by largely non-resident landowners. One example is the Saudi Osama Bin Laden, who in the 1990s was allotted large portions of Beja territory as training camps for Islamic organizations and farming schemes (Johnson 2003: 137).

Apart from political exclusion and the gradual appropriation of their claimed territories, Beja culture and language were discriminated against by governmental Arabization policies. Instead of being coerced into uniformity, different groups responded by highlighting their 'Beja' identity and strove to preserve their language TuBedawiye. The loss of their productive resource, land, dissatisfaction about the lack of political representation for Beja, socio-economic and socio-cultural marginalization as well as the lack of public services (health, education, infrastructure) were amongst the reasons which led to the formation of the Beja Congress in 1958.

Thus, there is a long historical trajectory of external interests in Beja territory and external political pressures on the Beja, dating back to the early Pharaonic and Arab invaders, through the colonial periods, then continuing in the shape of post-independence government interventions and policies (or the lack of them), and further complicated by the stand-off between the Beja Congress and the government until the signing of the ESPA. Together these interventions have contributed to the disruption of how most Beja relate to land through their (agro-)pastoral livelihood systems. These external pressures have led to broad livelihood transformations and have highlighted the need to protect both land and identity. This has changed the way people have interpreted the building blocks of their identity, whereby the identification as Beja (instead of lineage or clan affiliations) has emerged as a relatively novel signifying practice. Through its ability to assemble a large proportion of the citizens of Eastern Sudan, this ethnic label has added force to political claims for inclusion. The fact that people still strongly identify with the values of *diwab* and that *silif* continues to exercise a strong influence on people's lives is an expression of this rather new emphasis on Beja identity.

Therefore, the perpetuation of 'traditional' and 'indigenous' institutions (*diwab, silif*) connects to a long history of struggle against external interests and encroachments upon the very land from which local nomadic and agro-pastoral communities gained their livelihoods. Whilst the economic dimensions of *silif* have been challenged both in the rural areas and to an even greater extent in town, the cultural dimensions remain strong. People still make remarkable efforts to contribute money to celebrate weddings, child births and funerals whenever related households are involved, especially if they belong to the same *diwab*. These social occasions appear to have assumed stronger significance for the migrants in Port Sudan than they have for the people in the rural areas, since they constitute a means of cohesion and unity for the Beja in town. Some of these occasions are said to be able to transcend political divisions amongst the Beja that have increasingly become apparent along sub-tribal lines following the rift within the leadership of the Eastern Front.

The attachment to *silif* values does not seem to differ on the basis of age or gender nor does it seem to be affected by the length of permanent urban residence, although the elders complain that moral rules are no longer being strictly observed by the younger generations. For all the different groups it is evident that even if it has become difficult to fulfil economic obligations and political stances differ, the *silif* system has not lost importance. Rather, it seems that its cultural dimension has been emphasized and *silif* has assumed a specific role in defining the identity of the Beja in the urban milieu where their weak economic position makes them feel marginalized by other groups.

REFERENCES

Abdel Ati, H. 1991. 'The Development Impact of NGO Activities in the Red Sea Province of Sudan'. RESAP Technical Paper 3. Khartoum: Khartoum University Press.

Abdel Ati, H. 1996. 'Beyond the Locality: Urban Centres, Agricultural Schemes, the State and NGOs'. In Manger, L., Abdel Ati, H., Harir, S., Krzywinski, K., Vetaas, O. (eds), *Survival on Meagre Resources. Hadendowa Pastoralism in the Red Sea Hills*. Uppsala: Nordiska Africainstitutet, 103–119.

Bakheit, G. M. A. 1974. 'The Condominium and Indirect Rule'. In Howell, J. (ed.), *Local Government and Politics in the Sudan*. Khartoum, 25–32.

Bolton, A. R. C. 1954. 'Land Tenure on Agricultural Land in the Sudan'. In Tothill, J. D. (ed.), *Agriculture in the Sudan. Being a Handbook of Agriculture as Practised in the Anglo-Egyptian Sudan.* London: Oxford University Press, 187–197.

Cumming, D. C. 1940. 'The history of Kassala and the province of Taka' (p.I). *Sudan Notes and Records* 23, 1–55.

Egemi, O. A. 1996. 'From Adaptation to Marginalisation: The Political Ecology of Subsistence Crisis among the Hadendowa Pastoralists of Eastern Sudan'. In Ahmed, A. G. M., Abdel Ati, H. (eds), *Managing Scarcity: Human Adaptation in East African Drylands.* Proceedings of a Regional Workshop on August 24–26, 1995, Addis Ababa: OSSREA, 30–49.

El Siddig, M. O. O. 1992. 'Coping with Drought and Famine: Strategies Adopted by Three Communities in Sinkat District, Red Sea Hills'. M.Sc. Thesis, Department of Sociology and Social Anthropology, University of Khartoum.

English, J. 1987. *The Oxfam Targeting and Monitoring Operation in Halaib District, Red Sea Province, Sudan, 1985–1986*. Port Sudan: Oxfam.

ERGO – Environmental Research Group Oxford. 1990. *Integrated Livestock Surveys of Red Sea Province, Sudan*. Oxford: Oxfam.

Greenberg, J. H. 1963. *Languages of Africa.* Bloomington IN: Indiana University Press.

Harir, S. 1996. 'Adaptive Forms and Processes among the Hadendowa: Coping with Unpredictability'. In Manger, L., Abdel Ati, H., Harir, S., Krzywinski, K., Vetaas, O. (eds), *Survival on Meagre Resources: Hadendowa Pastoralism in the Red Sea Hills.* Uppsala: Nordiska Africainstitutet, 81–102.

Hjort af Ornäs, A., Dahl, G. 1991. *The Responsible Man: The Atmaan Beja of North-eastern Sudan.* Stockholm Studies in Social Anthropology 27. Uppsala: Nordiska Africainstitutet.

Hjort af Ornäs, A. 1992. 'Dryland Management for Food Production: a Shift in Paradigms'. African Arid Lands. Working Paper Series 2/ 92. Uppsala: The Scandinavian Institute of African Studies.

Holt, P. M., Daly, M. W. 1979. *The History of the Sudan: From the Coming of Islam to the Present Day.* 3rd edition. London: Weidenfeld and Nicolson.

Idrisi, M. A. A. 1864. *Ṣifatu 'l-maġrib wa' s-sūdān wa miṣr wa' l-Andalus* (English: Characteristics of the Maghreb and the Sudan and al-Andalus). Leiden: Brill.

Jackson, H. C. 1926. *Osman Digna*. London: Methuen.

Johnson, D. 2003. *The Root Causes of Sudan's Civil Wars.* Oxford: James Currey.

Kapteijns, L., Spaulding, J. 1991. 'History, Ethnicity and Agriculture in the Sudan'. In Craig, G. M. (ed.), *The Agriculture of the Sudan.* Oxford: Oxford University Press.

Kirwan, L. P. 1937. 'Studies in the Later History of Nubia'. *Liverpool Annals* 24.

Lewis, B. A. 1962. 'Daim el-Arab and the Beja Stevedores of Port Sudan'. *Sudan Notes and Records* 43: 16–49.

Manger, L. 1994. 'Managing Pastoral Adaptation in the Red Sea Hills of the Sudan: Challenges and Dilemmas'. *Drylands Networks Programme* 52. London: International Institute for Environment and Development.

McLoughlin, C. 1966. 'Labour Market Conditions and Wages in the Gash and Tokar Deltas, 1900–1955'. *Sudan Notes and Records* 47: 111–126.

Milne, J. 1974. 'The Impact of Labour Migration on the Amar'ar in Port Sudan'. *Sudan Notes and Records* 55: 70–87.

Morton, J. 1988. 'Sakanab: Greetings and Information among the Northern Beja'. *Africa* 58 (4), 423–436.

Morton, J. 1989a. 'Descent, Reciprocity and Inequality among the Northern Beja'. Ph.D. Thesis, University of Hull.

Morton, J. 1989b. 'Ethnicity and Politics in Red Sea Province, Sudan'. *African Affairs* 88 (350), 63–76.

Nadel, S. F. 1945. 'Notes on the Beni Amer Society'. *Sudan Notes and Records* 26, 51–94.

Newbold, D. 1935. 'The Beja Tribes of the Red Sea Hinterland'. In Hamilton, J. A. (ed.), *The Anglo-Egyptian Sudan from Within.* London; Faber & Faber, 140–164.

Niblock, T. 1987. *Class and Power in Sudan: The Dynamics of Sudanese Politics 1898–1985.* London: Macmillan.

Palmisano, A. 1991. *Ethnicity: The Beja as Representation.* Ethnizität und Gesellschaft. Occasional Paper 29. Berlin: Das Arab Buch.

Pantuliano, S. 2000. 'Changing Livelihoods: Urban Adaptation of the Beja Pastoralists of Halaib Province (NE Sudan) and NGO Planning Approaches'. Ph.D. Thesis, University of Leeds.

Pantuliano, S. 2002. 'Sustaining Livelihoods across the Urban-Rural divide: Changes and Challenges facing the Beja Pastoralists of North Eastern Sudan'. *Pastoral Land Tenure Series* 14. London: International Institute for Environment and Development (IIED).

Pantuliano, S. 2006. 'Comprehensive Peace? An Analysis of the Evolving Tension in Eastern Sudan'. *Review of African Political Economy* 33 (110), 709–720.

Paul, A. 1950. 'Notes on the Beni Amer'. *Sudan Notes and Records* 31, 223–245.

Paul, M. A. 1954. *A History of the Beja Tribes of the Sudan.* Cambridge: Cambridge University Press.

Salih, M. A. M. 1989. 'Political Coercion and the Limits of State Intervention, Sudan'. In Hjort af Ornäs, A., Salih, M. (eds), *Ecology and Politics: Environmental Stress and Security in Africa.* Uppsala: The Scandinavian Institute of African Studies, 101–116.

Salih, M. S. 1980. 'Hadendowa Traditional Territorial Rights'. *Sudan Notes and Records* 61, 118–133.

Sandars, G. E. 1935. 'The Amar'ar'. *Sudan Notes and Records* 18, 195–219.

Schultze, J. H. 1963. *The Eastern Sudan: Development between Desert and Rain Forest.* Berlin: Dietrich Reimer.

Verney, P. 1995. *Sudan: Conflict and Minorities.* London: Minority Rights Group International.

Voll, J., Potts Voll, S. 1985. *The Sudan: Unity and Diversity in a Multicultural State.* Boulder CO: Westview.

Winkler, H. A. 1938. *Rock Drawings of Southern Upper Egypt.* Oxford: Oxford University Press.

Yagubi, al. 891. 'Kitab al Buldan'. In de Goeje, M. J. (ed. 1892), *Bibliotheca Geographorum Arabicorum* 7.

ENDNOTES

1. In Port Sudan, for instance, dock labour is arranged between several work groups that often mirror the different *diwabs* of the Bishariyyn and the Amar'ar/Atmaan. A fundamental element of the *diwab* ideology is the normative idea of group solidarity and honour: each member of the *diwab* should be prepared to defend the honour of and to physically protect any other member, as well as to support the collective name of the *diwab* (Hjort af Ornäs & Dahl 1991: 75).

2. Old animistic beliefs in spirits and other divinities have been reinterpreted by the Beja under Islam and these spirits have become a more friendly intermediary to access the monotheistic Muslim God (Milne 1974: 85). Known among the Beja as *ğinn* (Arabic) or *winay* (TuBedawiye), these spirit creatures are organized into the same segmentary lineage structure as the Beja themselves and are thought to inhabit 'marginal places' (Palmisano 1991: 67), like graveyards, old house courtyards, empty or decrepit homes, walls and toilets. Beja refusal to use latrines in Port Sudan (especially women who think that *ğinn*-s will make them barren) has been the focus of specific development programmes implemented by Save the Children Fund UK and others, which aim at educating people to the use of facilities in order to reduce health hazards in the area, particularly for children. *Ğinn*-s can also cause illness and death. They can possess people and be induced to work magic, for this reason they are much feared both in rural and urban areas. Although in Port Sudan people have more access to education and Islamic teaching, belief in *ğinn*-s is sometimes even stronger and has become an important means to preserve 'ethnic identity and coherence of the tribal group in an urban situation' (Milne 1974: 85). The particular combination of Islamic and animist elements and the predominance of customary laws over the Islamic code are common to all the different Beja groups. The peculiarity of this form of religious practice, along with the use of TuBedawiye and the centrality of *diwab* ideology and *silif*, are the fundamental elements that define the Bishariyyn, the Amar'ar/Atmaan and the Hadendowa as ethnically related.

8

Gaining Access to Land: Everyday Negotiations and Rashaida Ethnic Politics in North-eastern Sudan

SANDRA CALKINS

In view of recent foreign interests in Sudan's arable land and its subterranean resources, the hold of rural people over this crucial resource is insecure. Land is not only a productive resource for rural people, but also in principle enables an access to other spatially fixed state resources, such as education, water and health services. This chapter analyses how landless pastoral people, 'the Rashaida', articulated a need for land and gained an access to it. Their classification as a newcomer tribe without a homeland (*dār*), based on their immigrant and occupational backgrounds, profoundly affected how these people organize access to land, even after having lived in Sudan for generations.

This chapter focuses on a process of land appropriation from below and links it to social stratification and processes of group formation. To develop my argument, I juxtapose people's land relations in two regions, the Lower Atbara area and Kassala, focusing attention on the entanglements between regional economic opportunities, political mobilization and the modes in which belonging is articulated. I will argue that processes of social stratification, which resulted in the formation of an elite in Kassala, are fundamental to representing 'the Rashaida' as an ethnic group in the Sudanese political sphere. This affects the modalities of land access. In the Lower Atbara, where people are still largely disconnected from the benefits of recent political developments in Eastern Sudan, individuals have to make sense of their situations and find their own pragmatic arrangements with landowning groups. In Kassala, through a process of ethno-political mobilization, specific land-related grievances were translated into a concern of the ethnic group, resulting in an access to some resources (settlement land, government offices).

To theorize this jump in scale from individual to collective organization of land access, I draw upon Thévenot's notion of 'investments in forms' (1984), which highlights the difficult and arduous work of establishing/maintaining any form that could facilitate co-ordination against a background of uncertainty. Invested forms are conceived as the things that hold together in situations and enable co-ordination, such as rules, classifications, codes, habits, laws, etc. In this case ethnicity figures as invested forms, a label that is (re)established and stabilized through arduous and repetitive semantic investments. Yet, ethnicity as a form, while effective in mobilizing Rashaida as a group, is insufficient to claim access to land, given that Rashaida were classified as latecomers. Political leaders therefore legitimized their claims to land and other resources by invoking the rights of 'the Rashaida' as Sudanese citizens. The invocation of citizenship rights is connected to the inability of Rashaida leaders to claim access to land by reference to autochthony, a normative claim in Africa that connects being first in a territory to ethnic ideas (Komey 2010 and Chapter 6 this volume, cf. Mbembe 2001, Geschiere & Nyamnjoh 2000, Geschiere 2005, 2009, Hilgers 2011).

GROUPS, TERRITORIES AND 'LATECOMERS' IN NORTH-EASTERN SUDAN

> We, the Rashaida, acknowledge that the land on which we graze and water our animals is the property of the Hadendowa tribe. We have no right to claim ownership for ourselves. (...) Should the rains be poor and the pastures not sufficient for the animals of the Hadendowa tribe, we have no right to put forward any claims for pastures or for cultivation. (Salih 1980, quoted in Kibreab 2002: 48, 49)

This pledge was allegedly made in the late 1920s or early 1930s after Rashaida had clashed with Hadendowa and sought to enter their tribal land (*dār*). It is a significant testimony to the land rights situation of Rashaida and newcomers in Sudan in general. Further background to the specific challenges Rashaida faced in north-eastern Sudan is provided here.

North-eastern Sudan here refers roughly to the area north of Khartoum, east of the Nile, up to the Egyptian border in the north, and the Eritrean border in the east. Dominant geographical features are the Nile and its arid hinterlands. The northern Nile valley is home to an agrarian, overwhelmingly Muslim and Arabic-speaking population (Holt & Daly 2000: 2–7, Fadlalla 2004: 18–22). Nomadic pastoralists roam the rich grasslands of the Butana plains, between the Blue Nile, Nile and the Atbara river. The Red Sea Hills, and parts of the plains sloping to the Nile, as well as the Gash and Tokar basins between the Red Sea and the Eritrean border are home to camel herding and agro-pastoral Beja groups, such as the Hadendowa, Bishariyyn, Amra'ar, and Beni Amer (Holt & Daly 2000: 7, Manger et al. 1996).[1]

Dār rights used to be an important institution for rural people, linking communal rights to certain territorially bounded resources to a group of people, conceived as tribe. They enabled the exclusion of others, a provident management of seasonal resources, and provided a mechanism to resolve intergroup conflicts (see Kibreab 2002: 19–29). In the twentieth century legal reforms and novel practices in agriculture led to a gradual erosion of the communal ways of organizing land access in rural Sudan. Five state initiatives had far-reaching territorial consequences, as follows:

1. In the early twentieth century, the British colonial authorities employed technologies of governance, such as the collection of census data, historiography and legal acts, to prescribe certain delineated populations to territorial units (Mamdani 2009: 146, Kapteijns & Spaulding 1991: 94, cf. Hilgers 2011: 36, 37). Harold MacMichael, who was crucial in defining the census categories, for instance, designated the Rashaida as Arabs in the Sudan and as 'recent immigrants from Arabia' (MacMichael 1922: 345). With this classification as a settler tribe, Rashaida were endowed with subordinate rights when compared to native tribes with customary rights to tribal land (*dār*) and a Native Administration (Mamdani 2009: 151, 166–169).[2] Overall, colonial rule led to the institutionalization of an unequal land rights system, which favoured people classified as autochthones in a territory, while disenfranchizing all others as allochthones and immigrants (Mamdani 2009: 167, 168, cf. Bolton 1954). This especially affected camel nomads who are always on the move and 'meant that they had no *dār*, or tribal homeland, anywhere' (Mamdani 2009: 167).

2. Colonial rule did not only materialize in legal texts, but changed the landscape. The most significant territorial intervention was the establishment of huge agricultural schemes in the Gezira, the Gash and Tokar deltas from the 1910s onward (Kapteijns & Spaulding 1991: 95, 96, Bolton 1954: 189–191).

3. The late colonial and early independent governments also fostered rain-fed mechanized farming in the Gedaref belt. The promotion of irrigated and mechanized rain-fed farming drew an ethnically diverse fleet of labourers from across Sudan into these expanding areas, which prior to their commercial agricultural development had been mainly used by rural populations as pasture or for rain-fed sorghum cultivation (Kapteijns & Spaulding 1991: 96, 97).

4. In post-colonial Sudan, in the 1960s after the construction of the Aswan high dam, the New Halfa agricultural scheme was constructed in the Butana for the resettlement of the Nubians, swallowing much – mainly Shukriyya claimed – pasture land (Sørbø 1985, Salem-Murdock 1989).

5. To encourage private investment in Sudan's agriculture, the post-colonial government in 1970 passed the Unregistered Land Act (ULA). This act converted all unregistered land into government land, that is, most of the land used by small farmers and pastoralists.[3] This land act thus provided the legal footing for the allocation of large tracts of land to private investors, and also the current new wave of foreign investments in Sudan. For example, land in the Gash and Tokar basins was appropriated from Beja groups for the extension of mechanized farming. In the mid-1990s in line with Khartoum's Islamist policies, large training camps and agricultural spaces were used by foreign Islamic organizations (Johnson 2003: 137, Young 2007a: 15–19).

In short, the successive governments of Sudan, from the colonial to the present, have reformed the land tenure system, first by differentiating between 'newcomers' and 'natives' and circumscribing autochthonous groups to territorial units, and second by decreeing all land as state property to facilitate its commodification. While land was only appropriated for certain large-scale agricultural schemes and in many places in spite of the legal acts is still negotiated according to customary law, agriculture sprawled on former small farming and grazing lands, often associated with farmer-herder conflicts (cf. Schlee & Osman in this volume). Territorial structures in north-eastern Sudan have not only been continuously renegotiated between different local land users but have also implicated displaced people, government bureaucrats, agricultural agendas, infrastructural elements, such as oil pipelines, pumping stations and new roads. Since independence, the eruption of civil war, drought and hunger have also resulted in the settlement of internally displaced people in urban and agricultural areas of north-eastern Sudan. Furthermore, thousands of Eritrean refugees have crossed the border to Kassala in Eastern Sudan, fleeing war and destitution (Kok 1989, Kibreab 1996).

It is commonly held that 'the Rashaida' entered the north-eastern Sudanese setting in the mid-nineteenth century, originating from somewhere in the Gulf States (MacMichael 1922: 345, Young 1996: 101–106, Bushra 2005: 277, 278, Pantuliano 2005: 12). Soon after their appearance in Sudan, clashes with other groups over grazing land were reported (Pantuliano 2005: 15, 16, Young 1996: 104, 105; 2008). Rashaida 'as latecomers or strangers were unable to acquire dar rights irrespective of their stay in the area concerned' (Kibreab 2002: 23). As a consequence of difficulties in accessing land, but also of getting caught in political upheavals during the Mahdiya and the colonial encounters, Rashaida remained on the move for a long time (Young 2008). Those who still engage in pastoral production today continue to migrate in often small and highly mobile herding units across north-eastern Sudan (Young 1988: 15–20). A hodgepodge of people in diverse situations was recently assembled by the label 'Rashaida' in Eastern Sudan. The people concerned are distributed across six Sudanese states: Kassala, the River Nile State, the Red Sea State, Gedaref, Gezira and Khartoum State. Their presence is most concentrated in Kassala, where the earliest permanent Rashaida settlements can also be found and currently many more are mushrooming between New Halfa and Kassala along the tarmac road. There the proximity to Eritrea enables cross-border trade. In other localities Rashaida are more or less mobile, earn their livelihoods from pastoralism, rain-fed farming, trade, day-labour and international labour migration, and live in diverse habitats, such as tents, huts of wood and cloth, or mudbrick houses (Young 1996: 26–31, Calkins 2009). A recent dynamic that has pulled many 'Rashaida' into new areas is the burgeoning of artisanal gold mining in north-eastern Sudan, especially in the peripheral Lower Atbara area (RNS) and the northern Butana. The dispersion, the pursuit of diverse economic activities, different levels of wealth and education, as well as various lifestyles and relations to mobility and settlement, highlight a problem: given this heterogeneity it is difficult to conceive of what holds these people together as 'Rashaida'. Yet, in view of the difficulties that individuals faced in accessing land, a need emerged to reinterpret the discriminatory colonial classification of Rashaida as a landless settler tribe – a need that has been increasingly felt in times of crisis.

SOCIO-ECONOMIC DIFFERENTIATION: DROUGHT AND COPING MECHANISMS

As new immigrants to Sudan, Rashaida have faced opposition in accessing pasture land. Local pastoral groups frequently contest their right to free access and demand the payment of tributes[4] (Bushra 2005: 283–285). This situation of competition for pastoral resources was sharpened during a series of droughts in the 1970s and 1980s, especially the devastating drought of 1984/5. This drought led to a massive loss of livestock in Eastern Africa, resulting in the impoverishment of pastoralists and a general atrophy of pastoral production (Ahmed et al. 2002, De Waal 2005). Rashaida pastoralists relate that in many places they were denied access to sparse pastures by local groups (Calkins 2009, 2011). Many lost their herds, experienced destitution and hunger. Connected to regional circumstances and alternative income options, regional disparities grew, as well as disparities between the impoverished and the well-off, materializing in new (or dramatically reduced) mobility patterns, and unequal access to monetary resources, especially migrant remittances (Calkins 2009: 63, 64). The destitute, having lost their herds, reduced their spatial mobility patterns: they sought settlement near urban centres or in agricultural areas to search for wage labour in the markets or in cultivation, or in the wadis to grow subsistence rain-fed sorghum. But when impoverished pastoralists wanted to settle on or cultivate land that was claimed by other groups, they were often denied access to land based on their classification as members of a 'landless tribe' (Pantuliano 2005: 15). In a classical Marxist sense, the devastating drought, by leading to a decline of the ownership of means of production (livestock) and by forcing the impoverished to sell their wage labour for a living, was a mechanism that triggered social differentiation in Eastern Sudan. At the same time, by accentuating the problematic land access based on the shared classification as latecomers, the drought-related circumstances contributed to diverse people perceiving themselves as in the same situation.

How people responded to the great drought had a strong effect upon social stratification amongst Rashaida pastoralists and was fundamental for the formation of a commercial elite. Related to cultural and symbolic ties to the Gulf States as the alleged ancestral homeland of 'the Rashaida', a large number of men migrated to Saudi Arabia, Kuwait and the United Arab Emirates to cope with the drought. In the Gulf States, Rashaida men, who are renowned as camel herders, frequently found employment as herders or worked as traders in the livestock markets, which was much more lucrative than employment in Sudan. Migrant remittances were often used to reinvest in means of pastoral production, mainly livestock, after the famine. This led to a renaissance of pastoralism among migrant households (Calkins 2009: 61–63). Further processes of differentiation unfolded as many households disposing of long-term remittance flows diversified into other economic branches in Sudan, purchasing pick-up trucks or other transport vehicles to engage in cross-border trade or to take up public transportation services.[5] Yet, international labour migration among Rashaida was not a new phenomenon (Young 1996: 32, 33); instead the drought disaster led to an extension and acceleration of the dynamic, which has – with a short disruption during the Gulf War (1990/1) – increased ever since. Only after the emergence of gold mining as a livelihood option from late 2008, has the number of migrants seemed to abate. Therefore the unequal ownership of means of production has moulded the direction of social stratification amongst Rashaida pastoralists and enabled the formation of a new commercial and political elite. These processes are connected to how people responded to drought crises, whether they were able to engage in labour migration, as well as the stability of migrant remittances.

The significance of remittances is underlined by a reversal of circumstances between Rashaida and customary landowning pastoral groups like the Hadendowa, Bishariyyn, or Shukriyya.[6] Often these groups now herd the livestock of wealthy Rashaida households instead of their own. The drought of 1984/5 struck many pastoralists severely, leading to impoverishment and permanent settlement. Lacking remittance flows from the Gulf, many were unable to rebuild their flocks after the drought disaster (Pantuliano Chapter 7 this volume, Johnson 2003: 137). Hence, in the aftermath of this drought, which many refer to as the great drought or hunger, competition for pasture and water stalled, as many pastoralists had abandoned the range land, leaving space for wealthy Rashaida to restock their herds (Johnson 2003: 137).

REGIONAL OPTIONS: ORGANIZING LAND ACCESS

In spite of setting off new dynamics of social differentiation, the drought also (re)activated a feeling of sameness in view of experiencing the same situation amongst Rashaida. Being classified as a landless settler tribe, people in the most diverse situations experienced the same difficulties in claiming their share of land. This sentiment formed the basis for the success of investing in the ethnic label 'Rashaida', as I will enlarge further below. But this label does not neatly define what evidently belongs together, rather Rashaida are dispersed across six Sudanese states. There they are subject to diverse administrative and legal frameworks, to various political dynamics, and are party to disparate demographic, socio-economic, and ecological situations. Far from suggesting that a thing like 'the access' to land of 'the Rashaida' exists, local and regional differences have a bearing on the organization of land use. To make this point, I will compare patterns of land access in two unlike regions in north-eastern Sudan – the Lower Atbara area and Kassala. This will reveal that regional settings frame the relationships between socio economic differentiation, political mobilization and articulations of attachment.

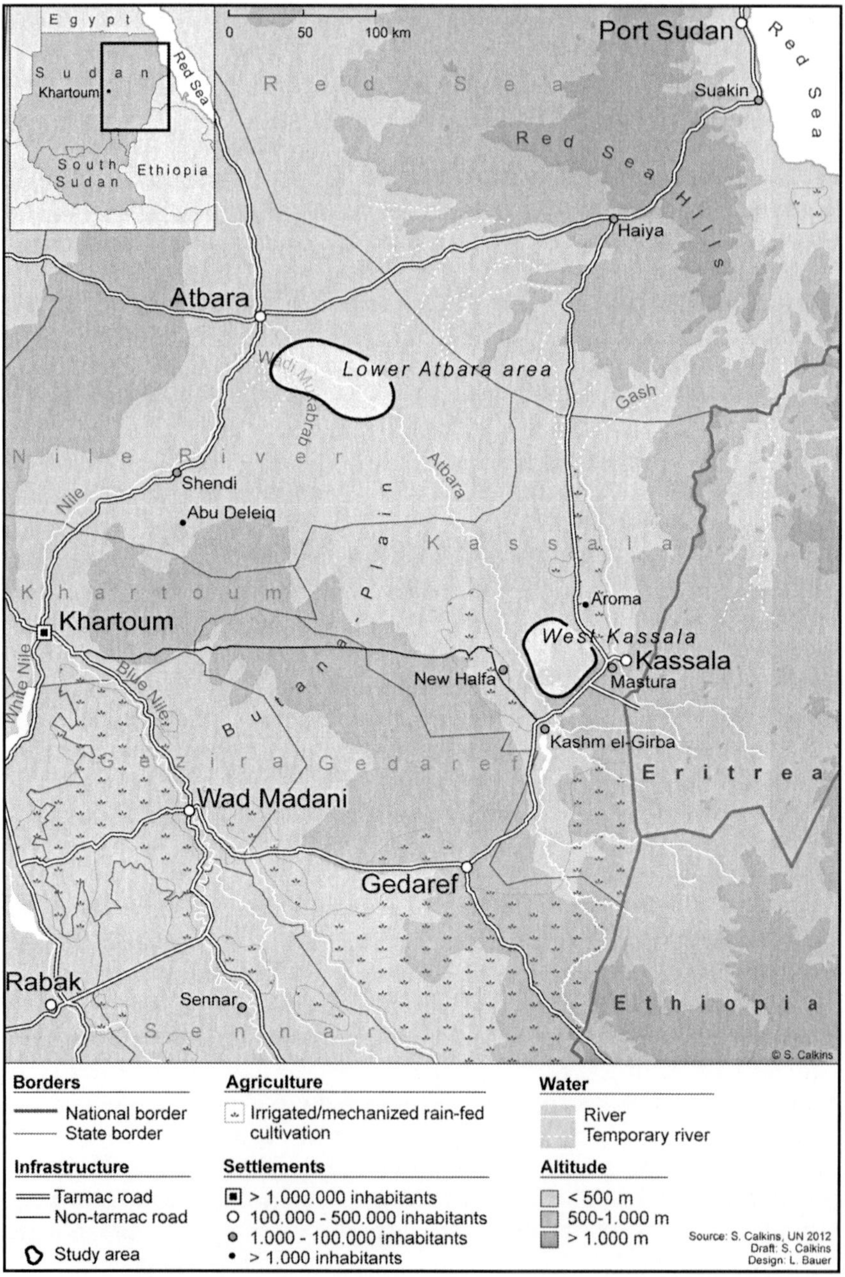

Map 8.1 Lower Atbara and West Kassala

The compared regions have diverse environmental and economic features: The Lower Atbara area is a peripheral region in the River Nile State (cf. Abdel Ati 1985). Most people are struggling to meet their daily needs through subsistence agriculture and pastoralism. The customary land owning group are Bishariyyn. To settle or engage in rain-fed agriculture, landless people need to negotiate a price or share-cropping agreement with the landholding Bishariyyn. Kassala, in contrast, has abundant grazing lands and water sources, enabling the raising of large herds. Kassala city is a busy market town, close to the border with Eritrea and offers many opportunities to make a living and even acquire some wealth. Different groups have customary claims to land in Kassala, but the largest landowning group are agro-pastoral Hadendowa. Significantly, land access is organized between landless and landowning individuals in the Lower Atbara area, whereas in Kassala individuals can connect their claims to land to the collective political negotiations of 'the Rashaida' in Eastern Sudan.

EVERYDAY PRACTICES: HOW TO GAIN ACCESS TO LAND?

In the following I will show how two individuals I met during 2008 and 2009 make sense of their landless situation and how they approach the problem of gaining access to land resources in their respective regions. One person is a newly settled trader and agro-pastoralist from Kassala, the other an impoverished pastoralist from the Lower Atbara area. Considering the livelihood configurations of these two pastoralists will shed light on how land access is organized in the everyday practices of households and what this means for local economic strategies. I will also attempt to define which mechanisms cut across the different regions in times of crisis, and how the diverse livelihood configurations are related to the respective regional economic and political contexts. In our conversations both men explicitly identified with their lineage affiliations. The pastoralist from the Lower Atbara area only mentioned his individual agreements with the Bishari landowner; the trader from Kassala, in contrast, when talking of conflicts or the issue of settlement referred to 'the Rashaida'. This aspect is important for the argument that the jump in scale from individual to collective organization of land access is associated with the 'invested form' ethnicity, which was reinterpreted in Kassala and presupposes someone who could articulate a common cause.

Kassala: Bureik Abdallah

Bureik Abdallah[7] (58 years) is a wealthy herd owner and trader, who identifies as member of a section of Bara^{c}sa branch. Bureik has a large family, including several working sons. In 2006 the family along with several members of their lineage settled next to the tarmac road between Gedaref and Haiya, roughly 10km from Kassala city. Bureik owns two herds – one of 120 camels and a mixed flock of 80 sheep and goats. He also trains four racing camels:

> The herd always was the reason to move. We followed the rains everywhere and milk was abundant. I never wanted to settle. The only time I ever thought about it was during the drought [1984/5]. It was a disaster! The drought swallowed 40 camels and 150 sheep and goats. I had only ten camels and some 30 goats left over – no real herd, no wealth. ... The children were hungry, they were crying. The animals had no milk. Grain was so expensive. Our herd continued to disappear as we kept buying grain.

In 1988 as a consequence of the drought, Bureik migrated to Saudi Arabia and worked as a shepherd near Riyadh until 1990. Upon his return he married again and invested in livestock. For the next eight years he developed a cyclical migration between Sudan and Riyadh, where he worked as a livestock trader. He married a third wife and invested in more livestock. Soon he expanded his trading activities to livestock markets in Eastern Sudan and purchased two cars:

> My sons used them to buy cheap things in Eritrea and then sold them here for a little bit more. They made some money, but then everybody bought cars and brought things [from Eritrea]. Nobody wanted to pay a good price any more. At the same time, the government became aggressive, sometimes killing young men like my sons, only because they work to feed their families. ... We still trade but it's not as lucrative anymore.

Bureik also expanded his agricultural activities. He relates how his father occasionally grew rain-fed sorghum, but he now cultivates 30 feddans (12.6 hectares, 31 acres)[8] in Wadi Abu Talha every rainy year to have some grain in stock in case of drought. In the 2008 drought, he thus was able to sustain his family and to avoid fetching expensive grain from the market. Bureik explains that his life has changed. He now relies predominantly upon trade and agriculture, which added motivation to settle:

> When the omda [Bureik's father's brother] said that the Rashaida should settle after peace [the Eastern Sudan Peace Agreement signed in 2006], we listened. A fair number of us [clan] pitched our tents here. The place is good. It is close to the market in Kassala, to the pastures along the Atbara and the Butana and also to the road [Gedaref-Haiya]. I built a *rakūba* [hut of wood and cloth] here in 2007, but when the rains came we moved away with the herd. In 2008 we built three *quṭṭīya*-s [round adobe houses with a straw roof] after they made it a village. (...) I decided to settle here, because my uncles said it was time to get a good piece of land and let our children go to school, so that they can be doctors. But I am disappointed. We need schools, mosques and doctors, and above all water. Every day we have to buy water from by-passing water tankers to drink. There is no well .(...) We all helped in paying for a mosque. The doctors in Kassala are close, but everything comes from our own pockets. We even paid for the school building ourselves, there is no help from the government. It wants taxes but when we want something, where is this government?

Bureik begins to express his relations with the land by stressing that he never wanted to settle. He buffered the great drought's effects by engaging in labour migration to Saudi Arabia and reinvesting in livestock. In later years, the family further diversified into trade and breeding racing camels, all the while moving with its livestock. Instead of mentioning negotiation with landowners, he explains as the reason for settlement that the sheikhs decided the time had come to claim a piece of land after the Eastern Sudan Peace Agreement and to be able to access governmental educational and health services. The omda designated a place and there Bureik pitched his tents. Meanwhile he has built three mud-brick houses. Yet, due to the household's livestock wealth only a part of the family stays in the settlement permanently, the rest is still mobile with the livestock.

Lower Atbara Area: Hamdan Suweili

The situation of Hamdan Suweili (60 years) is quite different. He is an impoverished pastoralist from the Lower Atbara area. Hamdan has wanted to settle since the great drought but he has neither the money to construct a mud-brick house nor access to land. He views this as his individual plight and does not connect his lack of land access to his lineage Dhuwi Salaam (associated with a clan of the Zinaimat branch). Hamdan is head of a family of ten. His eldest sons, although married family fathers themselves, still depend upon their father for a living. Hamdan relates:

> When I was a young lad, my father had a large herd. Eighty camels and 100 sheep and goats or something like this. ... In those days we drank milk all the time. There was no hunger, we were singing and dancing. ... Then dry years came and the great drought.

The drought led to the loss of all small stock and the survival of only a few camels. Hamdan migrated to Saudi Arabia for three years and worked milking stock. He did not earn enough to save for larger investments – except something like ten goats and ten sheep – but spent his earnings on covering his family's sustenance. Now Hamdan derives a small income from the sale of young animals from his mixed herd of 15 sheep and goats:

> We don't migrate far any more. We live in the desert like animals, but we have lost our livestock. We have no reason to migrate anywhere. We only move our tents from one well to another, from the trees and to the fields. (...) Of course, we want to settle, we want houses, and schools for our children, doctors and wells, but nobody helps us.

In the surroundings mud-brick houses are being built, but Hamdan has neither the money to pay for the construction (400–500 SDG, GBP £128–£160, US $185–$232 in January 2009) nor to buy a plot (80 SDG, £26, $37) from a local Bishari landowner. After his return from Saudi Arabia, Hamdan started to cultivate sorghum. However, he complains that the Bishari landowner will not rent more than two feddans to him and that costs are high at 10 SDG (£3.20, $4.64) per feddan. He is frustrated that even when his field produces little, the landowner collects a tenth of the produce, and that he has no choice but to cooperate with him.

Everyday Organization of Land Access and Social Differentiation

Related to their economic activities, Bureik and Hamdan use land either as seasonal pasture, agricultural land or permanent settlement land.

Their everyday practices are strongly shaped by the disparate regional opportunities. The cases of Hamdan and Bureik thus accentuate that the general process of differentiation between wealthy and poor encompasses a regional element: due to the absence of economic opportunities in the Lower Atbara area, many impoverished pastoralists still live in precarious circumstances, lacking access to the most basic services. Hamdan lives in a shabby, repeatedly patched tent in the dry hinterland of Seidon. With his small herd, he lacks motivation for long distance migration and has adopted a very small range of movement. His household has to keep on the move because they lack the rights to land and to use water sources permanently, which are claimed by other groups. His example indicates how precariously some formerly nomadic people dwell in the Lower Atbara area. In contrast, Bureik's case illustrates how households in Kassala easily combine herd mobility and permanent habitats with diversified patterns of land use: farming on agricultural land in the wadi, settlement near Kassala, pasture land between Kassala and the Eritrean border and even involving agricultural spaces in Gedaref.

By complaining that nobody helps them, both men implicitly express the moral understanding that somebody should be in charge of providing social services. Bureik places responsibility directly upon the Sudan Government, which likely relates to the more politicized environment in Kassala. Furthermore, while both men complain about being left in the lurch, only Bureik has the financial resources to participate in funding a school and mosque, and is able to pay for doctors and to buy water daily. While there are wealthier households than Hamdan's in the Lower Atbara area, none of the households I encountered were as wealthy as Bureik's, in which migration, trade and pastoralism were merged. I think this is due to the profitability of smuggling goods from Eritrea into Sudan, which figures as an attractive livelihood option in the border region of Kassala. Bureik's household belongs to the higher income strata among people of Kassala, but overall more people there have achieved a higher standard of living.

In spite of different regional settings, both Hamdan and Bureik were hard-hit by the drought of the mid-1980s. Their examples indicate that although the drought had diverse repercussions upon the respective households, there was a drought-inherent mechanism at work across different regional settings. The explosion of grain prices, the loss of livestock to death and sales, and the hunger that was experienced, ushered in the decline of nomadic pastoralism and led to a search for other sources of income. Bureik's and Hamdan's livestock wealth was similar before the drought. But their abilities to respond to the drought and to diversify economically were not alike. Hamdan migrated abroad for only three years and saved enough to purchase a small flock, whereas Bureik worked in the Gulf for ten years, accumulating capital to reinvest in livestock herding and buy a car. As regards the further differentiation, this is where regional economic opportunities come into play. Even if Hamdan had had the means to buy a car, he still could not have engaged in lucrative smuggling, given the distance from the border and his unfamiliarity with the terrain.

For rural people, assets – among them land resources – are essential in developing diverse economic strategies (Gertel 2007: 22–25), therefore the question of how access is organized is crucial. Pasture land was one of the central resources for pastoral production, but it is not individually owned and is characterized by transient land-people relations. As livelihoods were transformed after the drought, access to land resources for settlement and agriculture, that is, more permanent land usage, gained importance. Hamdan and Bureik face disparate situations: field sizes in Kassala vary but are generally much larger than those of pastoralists in the Lower Atbara area, as mirrored by Bureik's cultivation of 30 feddans in Kassala compared to Hamdan's two feddans in the Lower Atbara area. There, individual households depend upon their relations to a Bishari landowner, often a sheikh of the dominant local group, who claims the land based on customary rights. Landowners usually limit the amount and size of plots accessible to landless households for cultivation, forge sharecropping agreements, and often entertain patron-client relations with the sharecroppers. Significantly, while Hamdan bemoans his dependence upon a Bishari farmer to get access to land resources, as well as the costs involved in renting land and the sharecropping contracts, Bureik makes no mention of negotiations with customary landowners as regards agriculture or settlement. Rather his uncle, the omda, motivated him to settle in the Western Kassala administrative unit, where households can principally obtain available agricultural and settlement land free of charge. The administrative unit is dominated by people qualified as 'Rashaida'. Land is distributed between different groups of claimants, most of whom embrace Rashidi identity, along agnatic and affinal ties. Analogous to the Bishariyyn, they employ a system of land rights based on customary usage, according to which households can claim usufruct rights on land, which they have farmed before. Bureik thus also belongs to the new settlers, whose arrival led to a process of population concentration in the vicinity, as is evidenced by the mushrooming of settlements in the southwest of Kassala city.[9] The fast and unbureaucratic recognition of the new settlement as a village enabled the local distribution of plots and the erection of adobe houses, giving the inhabitants hope that infrastructural and social services would soon be delivered. In contrast, settlement of pastoralists in the Lower Atbara area, as Hamdan's case highlighted, depends upon the household's relations with the landowning group and their personally negotiated agreements regarding the size of plots and the costs. The access to land resources is more constricted and based on face-to-face negotiations between two contract parties. In the West Kassala administrative unit, in contrast, land access is organized between leaders of kin groups and local authorities and then is subdivided along kin lines. Clearly then, how people like Hamdan and Bureik make sense of their relation to land and organize access to it is informed by regional political contexts.

COLLECTIVE ORGANIZATION OF LAND ACCESS – ETHNICITY AND BELONGING

The different modes of access to land between Kassala and the Lower Atbara area are striking. The variant ecological and economic contexts shape social practices. Processes of social stratification seem to have a bearing on levels of political activism in both regions and on how belonging is articulated in the respective settings. This section discusses ethnic belonging as an 'invested form'. The concept of 'investment in forms'[10] denotes the costly work of coding or classifying, which produces commonality and equivalence of heterogeneous things and people and enables actors to jointly direct their activities towards a contingent future (Thévenot 1984, Blokker & Brighenti 2011: 358).[11] The investment I am interested in is how certain actors, a small commercial elite, managed to define the roles and problems of a category, 'the Rashaida' in Sudan since the 1990s, and how this 'invested form' gained some stability, that is, how people came to apply this definition of the ethnic group, and its concerns as a marginalized, landless tribe, to themselves. This section begins by a more general presentation of emic understandings of belonging and related mechanisms of inclusion/exclusion. Then it investigates how ethnic belonging to 'the Rashaida' was invested in to organize the access to land more collectively in Kassala, showing how certain actors used the notion to translate the everyday struggle for land politically in terms of ethnicity and marginalization.

Ethnic and Regional Dimensions of Belonging

In this section I will argue that the sentiment of belonging to the 'Rashaida' (as opposed to less general forms, e.g. family, lineage, clan, etc.) emerged after the ethnic category was reinterpreted and mobilized in a context of marginalization by the government and resource competition with other groups, leading to a more rigid definition of the boundary between Rashaida and non-Rashaida. The position for which I argue is neither essentialist nor social constructivist: the people subsumed under the category of Rashaida do not display common features. Likewise the existence of the tribe or ethnic group cannot be reduced to a mere colonially fabricated classification. Rather, 'Rashaida' as a category or label endures through time, but it must be adapted, performed and reinvested in line with situational pragmatics or, in other words, that which the label designates as changes at different rates in diverse periods (Schlee 2009: 1, 2, Bayart 2009: 50, 51).

The Lower Atbara area and the north-western Butana are predominantly inhabited by pastoral people who invoke a sense of belonging to the Zinaimat tribal branch[12] and the smaller Gazaiza, ᶜAuwazim and ᶜUraynat tribes. Kassala, the Red Sea and Eritrea, in contrast, are mainly roamed by the Baraᶜsa and Baratikh tribal branches (Bushra 2005: 280). When talking to people and leaders of the Zinaimat, Baraᶜsa and Baratikh tribes, they generally conceive of themselves and the two other tribes as each descending from an agnate, Zunaym, Bureyᶜas and Bartikh respectively, who in turn are said to somehow descend from the eponymous ancestor, Rashid or Rashid az-Zol (Young 1996: 86, 87). Without elaborating on representations of the agnatic kinship system of Rashaida, which lies beyond the scope of this chapter, the frequency with which people mention and refer to these differences appears significant, as does the associated understanding of certain group-specific spatial realms.

The relationships between the main branches were often tense, marked by a series of internal rivalries and continuous leadership struggles within the Baraᶜsa and between the Baraᶜsa and Zinaimat branches for the representation of the entire confederation (Bushra 2005: 292–305). According to Bushra (2005: 291), the latter were the only tribal branch to migrate to Sudan under their paramount chief, Mabrouk Abdallah, who due to his negotiating skills and clever marriage alliances with local groups soon emerged as chief spokesman and leadership figure for all Rashaida. However, this ruling family's spokesmanship and leadership was undermined with the official appointment of the nazir[13] from a nouveau riche clan, the Dhuwi Amri that identifies with the Baraᶜsa branch. Many Zinaimat, especially Abdallah's lineage, to this day reject the Dhuwi Amri leadership and claim an independent nazir.

While the government-acknowledged leaders of the Rashaida invoke a unified tribe, long-standing leadership struggles are reflected in the political organization. Zinaimat, Baraᶜsa, and Baratikh had their own omodias and remained politically and economically autonomous, while claiming common descent as indicated by the metaphor of branches (*furūᶜ*) in the tribal pedigree (Bushra 2005: 288). Given that people generally stress the affiliation to 'their' branch as well as identifying with their lineage, and thus discursively reproduce these differences, it seems reasonable to assume that this sense of belonging to a certain branch can work as a principle of in/exclusion. For instance, in the Lower Atbara area people of the Dhuwi Salaam (Zinaimat) complained about their precarious land access and the various costs attached to it. Responding to why they do not move and settle on a parcel of land in the newly found *maḥalīya* of West Kassala, they replied that it was not possible for them to go and that their *'ahl* (kin) were not there and thus they could not claim any land. In line with this, it stands out that access to land in the Lower Atbara area and the Butana – areas in which people understand themselves as Zinaimat (not Baratikh and Baraᶜsa) – is often still insecure. These people seem largely isolated from the political sphere and other recent developments in Eastern Sudan, where the mobilized notion of Rashaida-ness has materialized in some concrete resources. Even if people refer to their own branches, they implicitly invoke a sense of Rashaida-ness as some superordinate original category, but how closely people relate to it depends upon regional and political contexts.

However, the unfolding social differentiation and regional divides indicate that being a member of 'the Rashaida' does not translate into networks of reciprocal solidarities and only to a limited degree expresses a feeling of belonging to a specific cultural group. Further, the cases of Hamdan and Bureik affirm the contemporary consensus on ethnicity as a relative, elastically constructed and situationally circumscribed category. As Barth (1969) asserted in his classical work, ethnic groups must be treated as units of ascription and identification by the actors themselves and by others, which organize the interaction between people. A main focus is thereby placed on social boundaries which generate and ensure the persistence of groups, constituting the particular characteristics by which membership is signalled and also the cultural standards to judge if ethnic co-members are 'playing the same game' (Barth 1969: 6, 10–16). In line with this, Rashaida-ness refers to an investment in a predominantly cognitive form that was invoked and renegotiated in a series of political contests for access to resources. This competitive setting in Kassala, which involved the drawing and hardening of boundaries between groups, directly connects to Bureik's identification with the Rashaida in narrating the organization of land access.

The Formation of 'Rashaida' Tribal Politics and the Armed Fight for Land

Two dynamics led to a reassembling of 'the tribe': the occupational reorientation after the drought of the mid-1980s, which crystallized the need for access to land, and stricter governmental anti-smuggling measures, which profoundly hurt the business interests of wealthy traders. First, as outlined above, after the series of droughts, which culminated in the great Sahelian drought of 1984/5, many Rashaida who wanted to settle permanently or engage in cultivation were resisted by sedentary populations with autochthonous claims to the land. This bred widespread discontent among people labelled as Rashaida. Second, governmental interventions affected the trade of contraband goods. During the Gulf War (1990/91), several hundred migrants (Sudanese Rashaida) had joined the Kuwaiti army in fighting the Iraqi forces, while the Sudan Government had sided with Iraq. The Kuwaiti government rewarded this support by giving 400 off-road vehicles to Rashaida, which many imported to Sudan, engaging in cross-border trade. Opposition to the government mounted in the mid-1990s when a ban on private ownership of off-road vehicles was introduced as part of stricter anti-smuggling measures in Eastern Sudan, resulting in the confiscation of a large number of such cars (Young 2007a: 21, Pantuliano 2005: 15, 16). This profoundly hurt the business interests of wealthy traders among Rashaida. The interplay of the widespread need for land access and the disturbance of the lucrative cross-border trade was crucial for ethnic mobilization in resistance to the government. Some among this trading elite not only saw the widespread need of perennial access to land for settlement and as a basis for the development of more extensive trade infrastructure, but also realized that the dispersed demands for land access had to be bundled together. Moreover, some in this small commercial elite had both the financial power and political will for a costly and laborious 'investment in form', namely invoking and reinterpreting the ethnic category Rashaida. They began to organize resistance to the Sudan Government, accusing it of launching hostilities aimed at undermining the livelihoods of 'the Rashaida'.

The subsequent mobilization of people and the design of tribal politics was spearheaded by Mabrouk Mubarak Salim, a former DUP member of parliament and a wealthy trader from the Baratikh tribal section. Salim not only managed to assemble people in opposition to the marginalization of 'the Rashaida', but also by founding the Rashaida Free Lions (RFL) political party in the late 1990s prepared a position for himself as a key spokesperson for 'the Rashaida' in Sudan[14] (Young 2007a: 21). By breathing life into a notion of Rashaida-ness that cut across intra-tribal distinctions between the branches and certain lineages, he managed to mobilize a considerable number of young men to join the armed opposition in Eastern Sudan and Eritrea. The state of belonging to 'the Rashaida' was propagated in political discourses, speeches, songs and poems, as well as in the publications of diverse sheikhs and leadership figures. Today they are perpetuated in diverse lay platforms of self-representations, such as YouTube and Facebook. Importantly in this context, leaders argued that 'the Rashaida' were fighting for their fair share of resources, a share to which they, as a marginalized Sudanese tribe, were entitled. Hence, the RFL developed the same goals as the Beja Congress (BC),[15] the enduring ethnic opposition party of Eastern Sudan, namely an end to marginalization. This meant and 'continues to mean the overwhelming poverty of the region, the government in Khartoum refusing to pursue development, or even provide basic services such as health and education in the East, and the government undermining local economies and traditional authorities' (Young 2007a: 11, 1).[16]

While the goals of the RFL were similar to the BC, their arguments and justifications of violence differed. While the BC can argue in ethnic terms and simultaneously invoke the related principle of autochthony, the Rashaida with their classification as latecomers cannot. Leaders therefore needed to adjust and translate the land issue differently: they referred to the contradictory principles of ethnicity and citizenship, thereby drawing up two irreconcilable common goods. For one, ethnicity demands a prioritizing of 'Rashaida' and ranking according to the position in a chain of kin ties, and second, citizenship requires reneging discrimination in favour of the fundamental equality and neutrality of all human beings (cf. Boltanski & Thévenot 2006).

Nonetheless, the Beja Congress and diverse local opposition groups, prominently the Rashaida Free Lions and the Beni Amer, allied in 2005, forming the Eastern Front (Young 2007a: 11, 12).[17] Before the Eastern Front was formed, Khartoum had attempted to divide the opposition under the wing of the NDA across ethnic lines, by signing a separate agreement in 2000 with the RFL in Tripoli, Libya. This agreement represented an important step towards the formalization of an ethnically-based land access but, as it was not implemented, the RFL soon re-allied with opposition forces to form the Eastern Front. Hostilities ended in 2006 when the Eastern Sudan Peace Agreement (ESPA) was signed between the government of Sudan and the Eastern Front, significantly also endorsing the Tripoli agreement of 2000. This designated several benefits for the Rashaida: an independent administration of the Rashaida with a nazir as head, the establishment of nomadic councils in the Red Sea and River Nile States, the establishment of model villages for Rashaida pastoralists and political offices in the three eastern Sudanese states, the appointment of Mubarak as state minister of transport, roads and bridges, and finally the return of or compensation for lands around Baratikh village, where Mubarak's kin had settled, which the government had destroyed during the armed conflict (Abdel Ati 2009: 31, Ahmed & Egemi 2009: 101).

Outcomes of the Political Struggle for Land

One of the most outstanding benefits of the struggle for land was the long pending and divisive recognition of a nazarah for Rashaida. In Sudan political representation and the land question are entangled: the title nazir, the highest tribal representative and chief of an independent Native Administration, is linked to a tribal territory. Lacking access to land, Rashaida have been grouped administratively amongst the Beja and for a long time were subject to the authority of the Hadendowa nazir (Population Census Office 1958: 42, Pantuliano 2005: 15). By the mid-1980s some leaders of the Baracsa in Eastern Sudan began to demand their own nazir from Khartoum. In 1989, though, the new government wanted to grant Rashaida a nazarah, but backed down after violent Beja protests, reappointing the designated nazir to the rank of president of the Rashaida Administration (Al-Hardallu & El Tayeb 2005: 56, 57, Bushra 2005: 165, Pantuliano 2005: 15,16, Young W. 2007a: 30).

Significantly, Khartoum did not address the land issue directly in the peace agreement, but rather chose an underhanded strategy to grant Rashaida land by recognizing a nazir (without a tribal homeland) and granting them the right to administer the *maḥalīya* West Kassala. This administrative unit was founded before the ESPA, but the settlement process therein received a new impetus after the agreement. Many Rashaida settled there directly after this, since it is mainly inhabited and administered by Rashaida. Bureik's settlement highlights, for one, how leaders encouraged people to settle in the *maḥalīya* and, second, how this was motived by the promise of benefits and services (Ahmed & Egemi 2009: 101).

The Hadendowa felt defrauded: in conversations in Kassala and Khartoum several dignitaries expressed their disappointment at how the government let Rashaida 'foreigners' steal their customary land.[18] In line with this accusation, it is crucial to note that the government denies that Rashaida have received any land at all. It argues that a local-level administrative unit was founded that is part of the federal system, open to all Sudanese citizens and clearly does not bear any distinct ethnic character. However, the influx and a concentration of Rashaida, who secure land by settling on it and then demand recognition of their settlement by the *maḥalīya,* is a major tool in creating territorial facts. Rashaida leadership discursively negates these spatial practices by repeating the government's rhetoric that all Sudanese citizens are equally entitled to access land, arguing that customary land rights of other groups should be abolished all together and made accessible to all Sudanese citizens. The practices in the *maḥalīya* of Western Kassala, however, contradict these claims of equal access: the administration is mainly composed of Rashaida. They oversee cultivation in the wadis, grant land rights to local 'Rashaida' lineages often based on arguments of customary use, are in close contact with security organs, administer the mushrooming settlements and rapidly grant them village status. Other groups, even Zinaimat who during the conflict were mobilized as Rashaida in political discourses, are practically excluded from receiving land in this administrative unit, which many more or less openly call the land or *dār* of the Rashaida.[19]

CONCLUSION

The situation of Rashaida pastoralists exemplifies the struggles of both newcomers to Sudan and other landless groups (people without a territory). The drought crisis of the 1980s was a watershed. It marked widespread insecurity, increased economic diversification, the demise of pastoral mobility, and accelerated the unfolding of processes of social differentiation. In many places in Eastern Sudan, as in Darfur, this resulted in an identity-related land appropriation which upset extant socio-spatial patterns and prompted land conflicts, materializing as disrupting territories. But this encroachment cannot be conceived as a grassroots movement only. Rather as the Kassala example has shown, another pattern becomes apparent: the government rewards its landless supporters for taking its side with an administrative unit and justifies this by taking recourse to the principle of citizenship.

Rashaida are just one among many landless 'latecomer' groups, but the socio-economic and cultural articulations with the Gulf States, the scattering across north-eastern Sudan, the comparative livestock wealth, the cross-border habitat (Sudan-Eritrea) and related trade also add up to a unique set of circumstances. Some Rashaida were able to cope with crises and to diversify into new lucrative economic branches. These prospered, while others are still struggling to meet their most basic needs.

Related to these patterns of socio-economic differentiation, the cases of Hamdan and Bureik demonstrated how access to agricultural and settlement land is organized in different regional settings, involving individual agreements with landowning groups or more-collective negotiations. I have argued that the reinterpretation of these everyday arrangements between different landless people and people controlling/administering the land into ethnic terms was a significant investment of forms, demanding political foresight. This investment in the ethnic category assembled and mobilized heterogeneous but landless people around a concern, namely gaining access to land as an ethnic group. While Hamdan and Bureik express a sense of belonging to certain lineages ahead of the 'Rashaida', Bureik also pragmatically refers to the ethnic category in situations in which claims to membership in the tribe enables access to concrete resources. In Kassala the ethnic category, therefore, emerged as a more stable and durable form than in the Lower Atbara area. This is an achievement of the continuous and protean 'investments in forms' especially by Mabrouk Mubarak Salim and other members of the Rashaida Free Lions. With Bayart (2009), I argue that processes of social stratification and specifically the formation of an economic and political elite in Kassala were a prerequisite for the mobilization of 'Rashaida' as a group by means of ethnic belonging.[20]

This political mobilization of Rashaida was spearheaded by wealthy traders and some tribal leaders in Kassala who are also among the main profiteers of the formalized land access in the *maḥalīya* West Kassala, contradicting the claim to represent all Rashaida in Sudan. The high degree of socio-economic stratification among the people represented as Rashaida resonates with Asad's point 'that the group which is able to participate in the making of political decisions is not necessarily coterminous with the group in whose name, or with reference to which, such decisions are made' (Asad 1970: 232, see also Schlee 2004: 137). This draws attention to the process of translation, how the situation came about in which 'a few obtain the right to express and represent the many silent actors ("the Rashaida") and natural worlds they have mobilized' (Callon 1986: 224). Investments in the label Rashaida then appear as efforts to establish an equivalence, in the sense of Thévenot (2007), between people who are stratified and deeply divided along regional, (intra-)tribal and socio-economic lines and pursue diverse interests, even if they have not yet succeeded in creating sameness in the understandings of all the peoples mobilized.

The surge of ethnic political movement in Sudan connects to the government's divide-and-rule politics, as in many authoritarian regimes (Hutchinson & Smith 1996: 8, 9, cf. Geschiere & Nyamnjoh 2000: 438, 439). Still, the conflict was not about identity issues.[21] Rather, the invested form 'ethnicity' here combined political and economic interests but also sentiments of a common heritage, mobilizing people to end marginality and exact access to vital resources. A case in point was made by Casciarri (2006) when she showed how the recent reinvention of the Ahamda tribe was related to claims for economic resources and political representation. In line with this, ethnicity can be viewed as a social, political and cultural resource, reinvigorated and reinterpreted by influential people to mobilize people and to accumulate wealth and political power (cf. Bayart 2009: 55).[22]

A tension emerges between the different normative claims with which the claim to land was justified. On the one hand, spokespersons of 'the Rashaida' as part of the peace agreement appealed to their rights as Sudanese citizens to settle in the area, explicitly referring to civil law whilst negating Hadendowa claims to customary landownership. On the other hand, instead of treating all claimants to land equally as citizens, land access in the *maḥalīya* West Kassala is largely organized according to the ethnic principle, prioritizing kin ties and excluding foreigners. This contradiction underscores the accomplishments of the translation processes performed by Rashaida leaders in order to claim access to land. The intimate association between ethnicity and autochthony, which worked as discursive resources for 'native' groups to maintain control over their territories (cf. Komey 2010), could not be tapped in the Rashaida case, as they were classified as allochthones or settler groups. The interpretative achievement was to couple ethnicity and citizenship, and to legitimize claims to land access based on a situation of marginality in the Sudanese state.[23] Given that ethnicity and citizenship are founded on contradictory common principles (hierarchical relations of personal dependence, equality of all citizens in the nation state) that are not akin as ethnicity and autochthony are, this necessitated the decoupling of political claims from actual land-related practices.

All over Sudan, political groups have emerged that articulate their opposition to the government in terms of ethnic criteria; some of the ramifications are what has been called an ethnically-motivated land grab. In modern Sudan, the role of ethnic groups is relevant in the political sphere and is closely linked to the distribution of resources. The government itself by its biased policies directly promotes the formation of ethnic divides along dubious and unclear categories that are irreconcilable with the principles of modern statehood it allegedly seeks to promote. This leads to a paradoxical situation: the rise of ethnicity-based movements and the fact that there is no space for ethnic autonomy in the national state, which requires of all its members to integrate into it on the basis of citizenship. The case of Rashaida from their position as newcomers who could not jump on the bandwagon of autochthonous claims, shows how local leaders dealt creatively with such contradictions by embedding their claims into discourses of marginality and shifting between ethnic identity and citizenship as frames of reference when they deemed it convenient.

REFERENCES

Abdel Ati, H. 1985. *Lower River Atbara Area (Nile Province)*. Khartoum: Institute of Environmental Studies, University of Khartoum.

Abdel Ati, H. 2009. 'Eastern Sudan: Socio-economic and Political Developments and Research Responses 1993–2007'. In Ahmed, A. G. M., Manger, L. (eds), *Peace in Eastern Sudan: Some Important Aspects for Consideration.* Bergen: University of Bergen Press, 15–31

Ahmed, A. G. M., Azeze A., Babiker, M., Tsegaye, D. 2002. 'Post-Drought Recovery Strategies among Pastoral Households in the Horn of Africa'. *Development Research Report 3.* Addis Ababa: OSSREA.

Ahmed, A. G. M., Manger, L. (eds), *Peace in Eastern Sudan: Some Important Aspects for Consideration.* Bergen: University of Bergen Press, 95–124.

Ahmed, A. G. M., Egemi, O. 2009. 'Peace and development in Eastern Sudan: Research challenges and priorities'. In Ahmed, A. G. M., Manger, L. (eds), *Peace in Eastern Sudan: Some Important Aspects for Consideration.* Bergen: University of Bergen Press, 95–124.

Al-Hardallu, A., El Tayeb, S. 2005. 'A Case Study of the Eastern Region'. *Inter-Communal Conflict in Sudan. Causes, Resolution Mechanisms and Transformation 4.* Omdurman: Ahfad University.

Asad, Talal 1970. *The Kababish Arabs: Power, Authority and Consent in a Nomadic Tribe.* London: Hurst.

Barth, F. 1998 (1969). *Ethnic Groups and Boundaries: The Social Organization of Culture Difference.* Long Grove IL: Waveland.

Bayart, J.-F. 1989/2009. *The State in Africa: The Politics of the Belly.* Cambridge & Malden MA: Polity.

Blokker, P., Brighenti, A. 2011. 'An Interview with Laurent Thévenot: On Engagement, Critique, Commonality and Power'. *European Journal of Social Theory* 14 (3), 383–400.

Boltanski, L., Thévenot, L. 2006. *On Justification: The Economies of Worth.* Princeton NJ: Princeton University Press.

Boltanksi, L. 2011. *On Critique: A Sociology of Emancipation.* Cambridge and Malden: Polity.

Bolton, A. R. C. 1954. 'Land Tenure in Agricultural Land in the Sudan'. In Tothill, J. D. (ed.), *Agriculture in the Sudan: Being a Handbook of Agriculture as Practised in the Anglo-Egyptian Sudan.* London: Oxford University Press, 187–197.

Brubaker, R. 2004. '"Civic" and "ethnic" nationalism'. In Brubaker, R. (ed.), *Ethnicity Without Groups.* Cambridge MA: Harvard University Press, 132–146.

Bushra, E. 2005. 'Local-Level Political Dynamics in Kassala State: The Rashayda'. In Miller, C. (ed.), *Land, Ethnicity and Political Legitimacy in Eastern Sudan: Kassala and Gedaref States.* Cairo: Centre d'études et de documentation économiques, juridiques et sociales (CEDEJ), 277–307.

Calkins, S. 2009. 'Transformed Livelihoods in the Lower Atbara Area: Pastoral Rashayda – Responses to Crisis'. *Nomadic Peoples* 13 (1), 45–68.

Calkins, S. 2011. 'Dürrejahre im Sudan: Neue Formen nomadischer Mobilität'. In Gertel, J., Calkins, S. (eds), *Nomaden in unserer Welt: Die Vorreiter der Globalisierung – von Mobilität und Handel, Herrschaft und Widerstand.* Bielefeld: Transcript, 52–59.

Calkins, S., Komey, G. K. 2011. 'Umkämpfte Weiden: Landzugang und Überleben im Sudan'. *Geographische Rundschau* 63 (7–8), 28–35.

Callon, M. 1986. 'Some Elements of a Sociology of Translation: Domestication of the Scallops and the Fishermen of St. Brieuc Bay.' In Law, J. (ed.), *Power, Action and Belief: A New Sociology of Knowledge?* London: Routledge, 196–233.

Casciarri, B. 2006. 'Readapting the Gabīla: The Ahamda Pastoralists of Central Sudan and the State. Tribal Federalism Politics in the Mid-1990s'. In Chatty, D. (ed.), *Nomadic Societies in the Middle East and North Africa: Entering the 21st Century.* Leiden: Brill, 205–239.

Delmet, C. 2005. 'The Native Administration System in Eastern Sudan: From its Liquidation to its Revival'. In Miller, C. (ed.), *Land, Ethnicity and Political Legitimacy in Eastern Sudan: Kassala and Gedaref States.* Cairo: CEDEJ, 146–172.

De Waal, A. 2005. *Famine that Kills: Darfur, Sudan.* Revised Edition. Oxford & New York: Oxford University Press.

Ḥasan, Y. F. 1967. *The Arabs and the Sudan from the Seventh to the Early Sixteenth Century.* Edinburgh: Edinburgh University Press.

Fadlalla, M. H. 2004. *Short History of Sudan.* Bloomingtin IN: iUniverse.

Gertel, J. 2007. 'Mobility and Insecurity: The Significance of Resources'. In Gertel, J. and Breuer I. (eds), *Pastoral Morocco: Globalizing Scapes of Mobility and Insecurity*. Wiesbaden: Reichert, 11–30.

Geschiere, P. 2005. 'Autochthony and Citizenship: New Modes in the Struggle over Belonging and Exclusion in Africa'. *African Journal of Philosophy/ Revue Africaine de Philosophie* XVIII (1–2), 9–24.

Geschiere, P. 2009. *The Perils of Belonging: Autochthony, Citizenship, and Exclusion in Africa and Europe*. Chicago IL: University of Chicago Press.

Geschiere, P., Nyamnjoh, F. 2000. 'Capitalism and Autochthony: The Seesaw of Mobility and Belonging'. *Public Culture* 12 (2), 423–452.

Hilgers, M. 2011. 'Autochthony as Capital in a Global Age'. *Theory, Culture & Society* 28 (1), 34–54.

Holt, P. M., Daly, M. W. (1961/2000). *A History of the Sudan: From the Coming of Islam to the Present Day*. 5th edition. Harlow and New York: Longman.

Hutchinson, J., Smith, A. D. 1996. *Ethnicity*. Oxford: Oxford University Press.

Johnson, D. 2003. *The Root Causes of Sudan's Civil Wars*. Oxford: James Currey.

Kapteijns, L., Spaulding, J. 1991. 'History, Ethnicity, and Agriculture in the Sudan'. In Craig, G. M. (ed.), *The Agriculture of the Sudan*. Oxford: Oxford University Press.

Kibreab, G. 1996. *People on the Edge in the Horn: Displacement, Land Use and the Environment in the Gedaref Region, Sudan*. Oxford: James Currey.

Kibreab, G. 2002. *State Intervention and the Environment in Sudan, 1889–1989. The Demise of Communal Resource Management*. Lewiston, Queenston ON & Lampeter: Edwin Mellen.

Kirk, M. 1994. 'Changes in Land Tenure in the Butana'. In Bittner, A. (ed.), *Animal Production in Semiarid Regions: An Example from the Eastern Sahel (Butana, Republic of Sudan). Animal Research and Development*, Vol. 39. Tübingen: Institute for Scientific Co-operation.

Kok, W. 1989. 'Self-settled Refugees and the Socio-Economic Impact of their Presence on Kassala, Eastern Sudan'. *Journal of Refugee Studies* 2 (4), 419–440.

Komey, G. K. 2010. *Land, Governance, Conflict and the Nuba of Sudan*. Woodbridge and Rochester NY: James Currey.

Mamdani, M. 2009. *Saviors and Survivors. Darfur, Politics, and the War on Terror*. New York: Doubleday.

MacMichael, H. A. 1922. *A History of the Arabs in the Sudan: And Some Account of the People who Preceded Them and of the Tribes Inhabiting Dárfũr*. Cambridge: Cambridge University Press.

Manger, L., Abdel Ati, H., Harir, S., Krzywinski, K, Vetaas, O. R. 1996. *Survival on Meagre Resources, Hadendowa Pastoralism in the Red Sea Hills*. Uppsala: Nordiska Afrikainstitutet.

Mbembe, A. 2001. 'Ways of Seeing: Beyond the New Nativism'. *African Studies Review* 44 (2), 1–14.

Miller, C., Abu-Manga, A. A. 2005. 'The West African (Fallata) Communities in Gedaref State: Process of Settlement and Local Integration'. In Miller, C. (ed), *Land, Ethnicity and Political Legitimacy in Eastern Sudan: Kassala and Gedaref States*. Cairo: CEDEJ, 375–423.

Morton, J. 1989. 'Ethnicity and Politics in Red Sea Province, Sudan'. *African Affairs* 88 (350), 63–76.

Pantuliano, S. 2005. *Comprehensive Peace? Causes and Consequences of Underdevelopment and Instability in Eastern Sudan*. Report. London: Save the Children UK.

Population Census Office. 1958. *First Population Census of Sudan 1955/56. Notes on Omodia Map.* Khartoum: Ministry for Social Affairs, Republic of Sudan.

Salem-Murdock, M. 1989. *Arabs and Nubians in New Halfa: A Study of Settlement and Irrigation.* Salt Lake City: University of Utah Press.

Salih, A. 1999. *The Manasir of Northern Sudan: Land and People – A Riverain Society and Resource Scarcity.* Köln: Köppe.

Schlee, G. 2004. 'Taking Sides and Constructing Identities: Reflections on Conflict Theory'. *Royal Anthropological Institute* 10 (1), 135–156.

Schlee, G. 2009. *Territorialising Ethnicity: The Political Ecology of Pastoralism in Northern Kenya and Southern Ethiopia.* Working Paper 121. Halle (Saale): Max Planck Institute for Social Anthropology.

Schlee, G. (forthcoming). 'Competing forms of land use and incompatible identifications of who is to benefit from policies in the South of the North: Pastoralists, agro-industry and farmers in the Blue Nile region.' In Ille, E., Calkins, S., Rottenburg, R. (eds), *Emerging Orders in the Sudans.* Bamenda: Langaa.

Sklar, R. 1967. 'Political Science and National Integration: a Radical Approach'. *Journal of Modern African Studies* 5 (1), 1–11.

Smith, A. D. 1991. *National Identity.* Harmondsworth: Penguin.

Sørbø, G. 1985. *Tenants and Nomads in Eastern Sudan: A Study of Economic Adaptations in the New Halfa Scheme.* Uppsala: Nordic Africa Institute.

Thévenot, L. 1984. 'Rules and Implements: Investment in Forms'. *Social Science Information* 23 (1), 1–45.

Thévenot, L. 2001. 'Pragmatic Regimes Governing the Engagement with the World'. In Schatzki, T., Knorr-Cetina, K., von Savigny, E. (eds), *The Practice Turn in Contemporary Theory.* New York & London: Routledge, 56–73.

Thévenot, L. 2007. 'The Plurality of Cognitive Formats and Engagements: Moving between the Familiar and the Public'. *European Journal of Social Theory* 10 (3), 409–423.

United Nations (UN). 2012. Sudan and South Sudan. <www.un.org/depts/Cartographic/english/htmain.htm>, retrieved 25-06-2013.

Young, J. 2007a. *The Eastern Front and Its Struggle against Marginalization.* Geneva: Small Arms Survey, <www.smallarmssurveysudan.org/pdfs/HSBA-SWP-3-Eastern-Front.pdf>, retrieved 08-10-2010.

Young, J. 2007b. *Armed Groups along Sudan's Eastern Frontier: An Overview and Analysis.* Geneva: Small Arms Survey. <www.smallarmssurveysudan.org/fileadmin/docs/working-papers/HSBA-WP-09-Eastern-Frontier.pdf>, retrieved 23-11-2013.

Young, W. C. 1988. 'The Days of Joy: a Structuralist Analysis of Weddings among the Rashaayda Arabs of Sudan'. Unpublished dissertation. Los Angeles CA: University of California.

Young, W. C. 1996. *The Rashaayda Bedouin: Arab Pastoralists of Eastern Sudan.* Fort Worth TX: Harcourt Brace.

Young, W. C. 2008. 'The Rashāyida Arabs vs. the State: The Impact of European Colonialism on a Small-Scale Society in Sudan and Eritrea'. *Journal of Colonialism and Colonial History* 9 (2).

Zenker, O. 2011. 'Autochthony, Ethnicity, Indigeneity and Nationalism: Time-honouring and State-oriented Modes of Rooting Individual-Territory-Group Triads in a Globalizing World'. *Critique of Anthropology* 31 (1), 63–81.

ENDNOTES

1. For more on how Beja are classified/classify, see Pantuliano 2005.

2. See Kibreab (2002) for a treatment of how the institution of *dār* rights was eroded in post-colonial Sudan.

3. The colonial Land Settlement Ordinance of 1905 had already converted unoccupied lands into state property. The Unregistered Land Act went beyond that by declaring unregistered but occupied land to be government land 'with no chance of any recognition, settlement, or eventual private or communal registration of such land, or of an alternative fair compensation as previously' (Komey 2010: 66, 67).

4. Conflicts continued to flare up between Rashaida and Hadendowa, whereby the former were seen as intruders in the latter's *dār*. As a result of a bloody clashes, Rashaida were forced to formalize their own status as guests on Beja land in 1929 by forming a covenant regarding resource sharing and borders, according to which Rashaida had to pay a symbolic tribute for land and water use and agreed not to graze east of the Gash river (Kibreab 2002: 46, Al-Hardallu & El Tayeb 2005: 56, 57, Pantuliano 2005: 15).

5. This is corroborated by the fact that cross-border trade with Ethiopia/ Eritrea reached a new level after the early 1990s as did governmental counter-smuggling measures, which soon led to confrontations between Khartoum and 'the Rashaida' (Young 2007a: 18, 21, Pantuliano 2005: 15, 16).

6. I do not intend to reiterate the position of Sklar (1967) that class differences are masked by adherence to different ethnic groups. While differentiation between groups plays a role, my main emphasis is on social stratification among people who were assembled under the same ethnic label, a process that I see as constitutive of the political mobilization of that ethnicity.

7. All names of private individuals, their lineages and specific places that would allow identification have been either omitted or changed due to an overall tense political situation.

8. One feddan corresponds to 0.42 hectares and 1.04 acres.

9. Aside from these recent settlements in the West Kassala *maḥalīya*, there are a number of surveyed villages of formerly nomadic Rashaida with private plots and even stone houses but also shanty towns in the *maḥalīya* of Kassala city; the first and largest is Mastura from the early 1970s (Young 1996: 29–32, 1988: 27).

10. A similar approach would be to take Callon's (1986) moments of translation – *intéressement, problématisation, enrôlement, mobilisation* – to get around ethnicity, not taking ethnic group as the given unit of analysis, but looking at what was enrolled by the ethnic label. A similar approach can be found in Callon (1986) where he defines four moments of translation in a sociological sense.

11. Forms in this sense could be habits, customs, codes, classifications, rules, standards, qualifications, authentications, legal acts and other institutions (Thévenot 2007: 412, 413). A common feature of these forms is that they reduce the effort of co-ordination and in principle enable people to move quickly from their specific situations to more public situations (Thévenot 2001: 58). The solidity of the equivalences that have been invested in depends upon their duration in time, their spatial trajectory, and their material support (Thévenot 2007: 413, 1984: 10–16).

12. Rashaida are thought to be a conglomerate of different 'tribes' originating from various places including the Gulf States, Libya and Sinai (Young 1996: 101–106, Bushra 2005: 277, 278). The much criticized term 'tribe' here does not suggest a stable, clearly delineated unit based on agnatic descent, rather it mirrors the uncomfortable attempt to find an English equivalent to the vernacular Arabic *qabīla*, which is so ubiquitously used by people in Sudan when referring to the social organization of rural societies. However, the word *qabīla* is applied to the entire tribal confederation of Rashaida, just as it is to the three main tribal branches (*furūᶜ*): *qabīlat* az-Zinaimat, *qabīlat* al-Baracsa, and *qabīlat* al-Baratikh. I assume that the notion of tribe or ethnic group only exists in the context of oppositions and relativities. In spite of these caveats, for people in Sudan 'the tribe' is part of how reality in this part of the world presents itself. In this sense, as elements of constructed reality that still have tangible consequences, I therefore at times refer to 'the tribe' and 'tribal'.

13. Nazir is the highest position within a government-appointed Native Administration, which was reintroduced in Sudan in the 1990s (cf. Delmet 2005). Since the British introduced the Native Administration system, the nazarah was tied to a tribal land. Hence the landless Rashaida were connected to the administration of the Hadendowa until their own administration (*'idārat 'ahlīya li-qabīlat ar-rašaiyda*, – Native Administration of the Rashaida tribe) was granted in the frame of the Eastern Sudan Peace Agreement as expounded below.

14. Importantly, the Rashaida Free Lions work closely with an ethnically-oriented charity (the Kuwaiti welfare organization for the Rashaida), which in some localities has provided crucial public services for communities and has distributed goods for the disadvantaged.

15. The Beja Congress has been dominated by the Hadendowa, the largest group that identifies as Beja, who are traditionally linked to the Ansar order. Other Beja groups are said to follow the Khatmiyya Sufi order. Morton points out that the allegiance to an order tends to coincide with identity issues (Morton 1989: 63, 70).

16. In addition to land access and counter-smuggling measures, the formation of Rashaida tribal politics was fuelled by other political developments: the National Islamic Front (NIF) takeover in 1989, its promotion of a single Arabic culture and its fundamentalist version of Islam, resulted in the consolidation of diverse Sudanese opposition groups, uniting under the umbrella of the National Democratic Alliance (NDA) in Asmara in 1991. From its foundation, the NDA was nurtured by the Eritrean and Ethiopian governments and soon embraced the SPLM/A; in 1993 the Beja Congress (BC) joined the NDA (Young 2007b: 27–29). The front in eastern Sudan never turned into a full-fledged war, like the wars in southern Sudan, the Nuba Mountains or the southern Blue Nile. Rather, military operations in eastern Sudan took the form of a low level insurgency with occasional strikes on oil pipelines, roads and mechanized farming schemes (Johnson 2003: 138, Young 2007a: 39, 44, 45). The defeat of the Eritrean army in the Eritrean-Ethiopian war (1998–2000) led to the loss of bases and material supplies in Eritrea, weakening the NDA, which further disintegrated with the SPLM/A withdrawal after the Comprehensive Peace Agreement of 2005, leaving eastern Sudanese groups alone with their struggle (Young 2007a: 11, Johnson 2003: 138, 139). Consequently, the BC abandoned an ethnic rationale for a regional one, allying with diverse local opposition groups, prominently the Rashaida Free Lions and the Beni Amer, to form the Eastern Front in early 2005 (Young 2007a: 11, 12).

17. By supporting and favouring diverse groups along ethnic lines, like the Beni Amer, or setting up ethnic parallel organizations, such as the Beja Congress for Reform and Development, the National Congress Party (NCP, formerly NIF) tried to encourage tribal tensions and thus to subvert the Eastern Front (Young 2007a: 31) – the pattern of divide and rule it has also frequently employed in other regions.

18. See Pantuliano (this volume Chapter 7) and Morton (1989) for more on the strong cultural and emotional interrelations between identity and land among the Beja.

19. Fears of a territorial expansion of Rashaida and widespread frustration with the ESPA, have added to the rise of ethnic and tribal politics in eastern Sudan (Ahmed & Manger 2009: 109, Young 2007: 27–32). Tribal antagonisms have been fostered by the ESPA-negotiated distribution of power on a purely tribal basis: 18 parliamentary seats were allotted to Hadendowa, 16 to Beni Amer, 14 to Rashaida and 12 for other tribal groups (Ahmed & Egemi 2009: 108, 109). This ignores the demographic set-up of eastern Sudan and grants the Rashaida and Beni Amer disproportionate benefits to the disadvantage of Hadendowa. But other people also excluded from the peace process are learning their lessons and beginning to frame their claims to a share of power and resources in ethnic terms, such as people of diverse West African origin, who are now ascribing to a common identity of Fellata (Miller & Abu-Manga 2005).

20. Bayart (2009: 57) argues that ethnicity emerges from the paradoxical actions of certain social strata or categories: 'one could even say that the role of these categories in the enunciation of ethnicity is probably determinant, as the ethnic community is a channel through which redistribution is demanded, as well as being a means of accumulation'.

21. See Schlee's perspective on taking sides in conflicts, which asserts that strategies of in/exclusion are carried out in close interaction with the corresponding strategies of the neighbouring groups. He thus proposed the region as the appropriate unit of reference and not the group (Schlee 2004: 142).

22. See Hilgers (2011) for a discussion of autochthony as social capital.

23. This study connects to debates that challenge the dichotomy of civic/ethnic, often connected to ideas of West and East, and highlight civic and ethnic categories as ideal types, whereas in real situations variant civic and ethnic elements can be found (Zenker 2011: 67, Smith 1991, Brubaker 2004). Zenker makes an important point by highlighting the similarities of ethnic and civic forms by showing how both are ex/inclusionary notions based on collective and individual autochthony. However, I do not entirely follow Zenker, since he reduces differences between civic and ethnic (individualized and collective autochthony) to an inverted causal logic between shared descent/residence and shared culture, without paying attention to the disparate normative content of the invoked higher good. In my view ethnicity by prioritizing descent assigns each individual a position in a chain of dependencies that issues from an ancestor and thus constitutes a sort of hierarchical order, whereas the idea of citizenship is based on the fundamental equality of all citizens, precluding any hierarchies and priorities amongst the included citizenry – albeit both principles invoke notions of autochthony (cf. Boltanski & Thévenot 2006 on domestic and civic orders of worth).

9

Hausa and Fulbe on the Blue Nile: Land Conflicts between Farmers and Herders

ELHADI IBRAHIM OSMAN & GÜNTHER SCHLEE

Upon learning about a conflict between Hausa and Fulbe, the reader might feel transferred to the times of the 'Fulani jihad' in the early nineteenth century in what was later to become northern Nigeria. But indeed, we are talking about the Blue Nile area, more particularly the stretch of semi-arid land that the Blue Nile traverses after coming out of its gorge in the Ethiopian Highlands and pours into the Sudan. We and others have summarized how West Africans have come to the Sudan elsewhere (Abu-Manga & Miller 2005, Delmet 2000, Feyissa & Schlee 2009, Schlee 2000, 2009). Here it must suffice to say that many West African groups, often forming co-resident village communities or nomadic hamlets and preserving their different languages, are scattered all over Sudan. This corresponds to a general pattern: people tend to live within their ethnic groups, but increasingly often outside their home area (*dār* in Arabic). Also, people from Darfur (Fur, Zaghawa, Masalit[1]) can be found in largely ethnically homogeneous settlements in Eastern Sudan, and such examples could be multiplied.

This chapter focuses on the issue of farmer/herder conflicts about land use in the area adjacent to the reservoir of Roseires[2] dam south of Damazin. The Hausa farmers living in Rigeiba town and the group of ᶜAliwan Woyla[3] Fulbe – with a pastoral background – better known as Farig[4] Malakal constitute the focal point of this study. We thereby attempt to provide a chronological account of events to explain how a land conflict between the two groups started and developed through time. We venture from a situation in which the territory at first enabled various livelihoods and was open to in-migration, to one where new claims to land made access gradually become problematic. In doing so, we aim to relate the evolution of the conflict to socio-economic, environmental and territorial transformations at the local and national level, such as the impacts of sprawling mechanized farming schemes and the migratory movements of people displaced by the civil war. The study also seeks to elaborate how other groups are incorporated into the conflict. After discussing the context which contributed to a climate of violence, special attention will be paid to events in 2009, a year of scarce forage and water due to poor rainfall, in which the conflict between the two groups escalated, becoming entirely violent. Our genealogy of the conflict raises the question why rapid increases of the conflict did not take place, but rather were restricted to two groups to whom a West-African origin is attributed, farming Hausa and nomadic Fulbe.

The researchers' contact with the region goes back to 1996. In April 2005, Elhadi spent four days in Farig Malakal and visited Madyam market twice. Madyam is just west of Rigeiba and is one of the markets frequented by all ethnic groups in the area. At the same time Madyam is the alternative market to which the Fulbe resort when they refrain from going to Rigeiba and Sinja-Nabag where the majority of merchants are Hausa. During that period, he learned that relations between the Hausa of Rigeiba and Farig Malakal have long been hostile and that there is high competition between the two groups over land use on the periodically flooded land on the dam reservoir shore. This competition had led to many clashes between the two groups. The Hausa complained of frequent crop damage by Woyla, while the Fulbe lamented suffering from the Hausa's farming expansion at the expense of pasture and water points. In April 2009, Elhadi was informed that youths of the Hausa and of the Fulbe had fought in Rigeiba market. Since then Hausa motorcyclists have become the target of young Fulbe herders who have attacked them while crossing Khor Bobok, a sandy riverbed which forces them to slow down, south of Rigeiba. To stop this and to prevent clashes between the two groups, the police of Rigeiba pitched a shelter on the bed of the Khor and used that as a control point. At the beginning of May 2009, Elhadi received a phone call from his field assistant telling him that the Hausa of Rigeiba had attacked Farig Malakal and many people of both groups had died and more were wounded. On May 7, 2009, Elhadi went to Farig Malakal for survey work and he found camp members anxiously holding their bows and arrows expecting an attack by the Hausa. On June 20, 2009, the researcher witnessed part of a peace ceremony in Rigeiba, where the representatives of the Hausa and the Fulbe undertook to stop hostilities and during which they signed a peace agreement.

The above scenario provides a broad outline of the nature of the conflict between the Hausa of Rigeiba and Farig Malakal. Both authors had the opportunity to visit the area from November 20 to 24, 2009. After discussing and evaluating the data collected, Elhadi returned to the field in December (23–26) to fill information gaps. During these field work periods we visited Farig Malakal (the Woyla Fulbe hamlet), Maganza (populated by Gumuz[5] who hold land rights both the Hausa and the Fulbe wish to acquire) and Madyam (a settlement comprising Masalit and Ingessana[6]) and Ufut at-Tum (a Berta village which also comprises Ingessana) and conducted interviews with many of the sheikhs of the different groups, heads and members of both the Pastoralists Association (PA) and the Farmers Association (FA), and village popular committee heads. The data collection focused on the social history of the region and the emergence of the Hausa-Fulbe conflict and its development. The researchers listened to diverse narrations from different ethnic groups, each presenting the case from its own perspective. In the following we shall try to make clear what is common between the different narrations.

In some cases we will be able to distinguish between factual and false elements of the accounts, while in others we will have to restrict ourselves to just stating the different points of view as mentioned by our interlocutors. This chapter starts with a brief note on the history of the research area: the population, economic activities, land ownership and land use. The second section is the core of the study and it tackles the issue of Hausa–Fulbe conflicts on land use, explaining how the conflict emerged and developed. Our theoretical aims are modest. But in the concluding remarks we shall try to identify some patterns of conflict at work here and even make some very general policy recommendations.

RESEARCH AREA

The research area includes four villages in the area adjacent to the reservoir of Roseires dam south of Damazin: Rigeiba, Maganza, Ufut at-Tum and Madyam.

The research area is populated by various ethnic groups representing different categories of the population. We here take up local categories, 'emic' ones, as they are used by the actors themselves, and these are often highly politicized. The main categories are: (1) Indigenous (Gumuz, Ingessana, Dauwala[7], Berta[8] and Funj[9]), (2) Gharaba (westerners[10]) (the Hausa, Fulbe and the Masalit[11]) and (3) Northern Sudanese Arabs (Gawasma and Rufaᶜa al-Hoi: Wad Hawati and Sibeihab). The total population in the resea rch area is about 18,000 people. The Hausa constitute about 70 per cent of the population.[12] They live in Rigeiba. Rigeiba is the largest centre in the area with a total population above 12,000. The Gumuz form the majority of the population in Maganza which is located south of Rigeiba. Some of the Hausa live with the Gumuz in Maganza. To the south of Maganza live the Berta in Ufut at-Tum. With the Berta live some of the Ingessana who migrated from the Ingessana hills during war time in 1997. The Ingessana also live in Madyam but many detached Ingessana homesteads are scattered in the vicinity of Madyam and Gangar and from there all the way to Tireik in the Ingessana hills. In Madyam one finds also Masalit who came from Darfur in 1966. The village, in fact, has become known to most people as Madyam Masalit. The Masalit are economically more active than the Ingessana and outnumber them. More important is that, unlike the Ingessana, they live in compact settlements.

Different languages are spoken in the research area. Arabic, as the lingua franca, is spoken by all groups. Other languages include Berta, Gam – the language of the Ingessana, Gumuz, Masalit, Hausa and Fulfulde the language of the Fulbe. But generally the community in the Blue Nile State (BNS), to some extent, has become multilingual. For instance, the Gumuz of Maganza speak Gumuz and when children go to school they learn Arabic. The sheikh of Maganza, besides Gumuz, speaks Arabic, Hausa and Berta.

With the exception of Madyam, all the villages in the research area had earlier been located by the riverside and were transferred west to

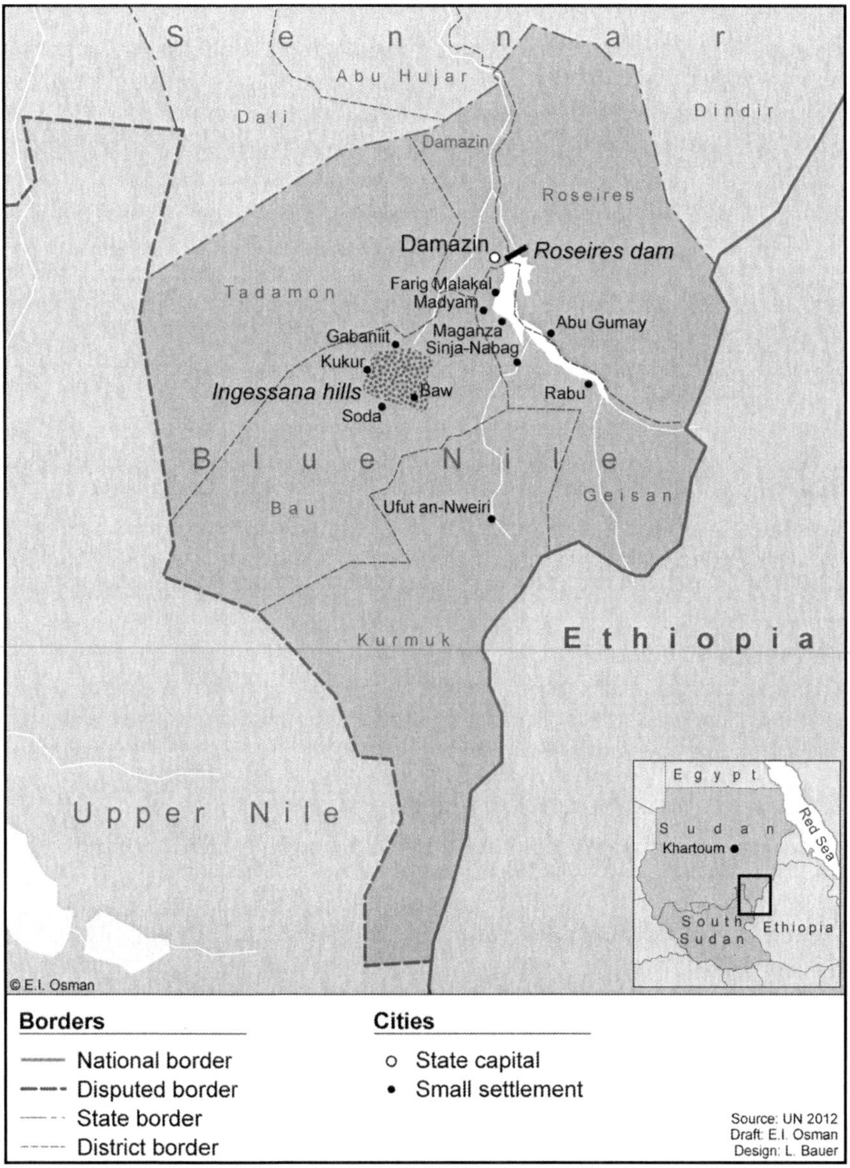

Map 9.1 Research Area in Blue Nile State

their present locations in response to flooding. The research area experienced three remarkable floods in 1916, 1943 and 1948. The fourth flood occurred in 1966 after the construction of the dam, which led to a rise of the water level as the reservoir filled up to reach its present size. The area will also be affected by the ongoing heightening of the dam. Gumuz elders noted that in 1966 the authorized engineer told their grandfathers that the dam will be heightened by ten metres and the site they chose for their village will be below the new water level. They refused to move to another place, saying they would do so when the heightening has actually been done. Retrospectively, one must say that this was a wise response, because since then they have benefited from cultivating their coastal land for over half a century and it is only now that the work of heightening the dam is under way.

Agriculture is the main economic activity in the research area. All groups practise rain-fed farming. They produce sorghum and sesame but the introduction of mechanized farming in a grand capitalist way in the area has reduced the space available for this activity. For instance, Dali and Mazmuum Company appropriated part of the Masalit farm land (Ar. *bildāt*). The Masalit complained to the local government. The local government then demarcated the village *ḥaram* (limited, forbidden to outsiders).

In addition to rain-fed cultivation, the population practises *ḥauḍ,* flood recession cultivation in the dam reservoir. The dam was constructed in 1966 to provide water for irrigation in the Gezira Scheme (Ministry of Irrigation and Hydro Power 1966). After the construction of the dam, flood water covered an area of 61,190 feddans.[13] This area is considered as *ǧirūf,* flood irrigated land. The state distributed 60 per cent of the *ǧirūf* land to villagers on the banks of the river. The rest of the land, as will be explained below is, either uncultivable or difficult to cultivate with the prevailing low technology available. The land was distributed by the survey authority in coordination with Roseires agricultural authority and village sheikhs. Limits between villages were demarcated and many water points were created to mitigate herder/farmer conflicts. The agricultural authority collects taxes from the farmers and passes them to the administrative councils (Ishaag 2007). But in 1987, the supervision of *ǧirūf* and the collection of taxes became the responsibility of the administrative councils (BNS 2005). The use of pumps and ploughs or any similar equipment is prohibited in the *ḥauḍ* area. Only recently have some of the farmers resorted to well digging and the use of pumps to irrigate plots outside the *ǧirūf* land. This extension of farming comes at the expense of the pasture, but is also regarded as harmful to the structure of the dam itself.

The total cultivated area of the *ḥauḍ* is about 15,000 feddans (6,300 hectares, 15,570 acres) (BNS 2005). The production season in the *ḥaud* depends on the water level behind the dam and flood retreat. The *ḥauḍ* has a very long season starting in January or February and ending in September. Cultivation in the *ḥauḍ* depends on the rate of soil moisture. The shores of the reservoir from which water retreats first (in November or December) will not sustain the moisture rate required for cultivation. To make use of these fertile margins the farmers usually cultivate it after April, depending on early rainfall. Rainfall thus supplements the moisture usually left from flooding and extends the overall length of the growing season (Ishaag 2007).

The *ḥauḍ* constitutes an important source of fish with total annual production of about 1,700 tons. All the fishermen had been Hausa, but some Gumuz and Berta who learned the tradition from them have started fishing in pools and ditches. The fishing camps are mostly found near ponds (*mayaᶜa*) or temporary water courses. In addition to farming and fishing, the moisture ratio in the *ḥauḍ* and the *mayaᶜa* supports growing rich forage that attracts many pastoralists during the dry season (Ishaag 2007).

The research area is characterized by uneven distribution of land ownership. (1) The indigenous groups Gumuz, Berta and Dauwala own most of the *ḥauḍ* land. (2) The Hausa of Rigeiba complain that, despite their large population, they only own 5 per cent of the *ḥauḍ* land, while the Gumuz own 95 per cent of the *ḥauḍ* land. The Hausa attribute this injustice to ethnic discrimination. They explain that at the time of *ǧirūf* distribution many Hausa were excluded because they did not provide nationality certificates, while the Dauwala and the Berta were allotted land without being asked to provide them. The Hausa depend wholly on renting land from the Gumuz and the Dauwala but they complain that, sometimes, the Gumuz refuse to rent land to them. The Gumuz, owning most of the *ḥauḍ* land, cultivate only a small portion of it and rent the larger portion to the Hausa. The Gumuz also maintain a claim on the *mayaᶜa* (ponds) of Maganza and receive regular payments from Woyla, who graze on them.

The Masalit rent land from the Gumuz and have practised *ǧirūf* cultivation since 1994, but most of them ceased cultivation because flood water often swept across their crops before reaching harvest time. This land that the Masalit abandoned has become part of the land the Gumuz allow Woyla to graze on.

The Berta report that the *ǧirūf* boundaries between them and the Gumuz of Maganza were demarcated for the first time in 1920. Now most of the Berta own small plots in the *ǧirūf* land while some of them own more than one plot. However they cultivate all the land they own and, unlike the Gumuz, do not rent it to others.

The Ingessana of Madyam own some *ǧirūf* land facing Gangar, a small hill located just west of Rigeiba, neighbouring the *ǧirūf* of the Gumuz, but flood water used to sweep across their crops frequently and most of them have ceased cultivation. These abandoned *ǧirūf* are now under the control of the Gumuz, which they rent to others. In fact, the Gumuz, living next to the reservoir, claim any unused land of the coastal strip and commercialize its use.

With regard to rain-fed farming, there is no detailed information on the pattern of land ownership, but the appropriation of land by mechanized farmers seems to be the sole problem. Most, if not all, villagers in the research area own farming land. Some own more land than they can cultivate and allow others to farm it free of charge.[14]

The relations between the different ethnic groups in the research area have been characterized by reciprocal exchanges, intermarriage and peaceful contact. According to the Gumuz of Maganza problems occur when outsiders, such as Woyla, come into contact with them. The Berta of Ufut welcomed Woyla and other Fulbe groups and had good relations with them when they met in the market place, and their women come to grind grain in their houses. The Berta commented that those Fulbe, unlike the Woyla of Farig Malakal, were peaceful.

LAND USE CONFLICTS

Within the context described in the previous section, the Hausa of Rigeiba and the Fulbe of Farig Malakal, with their different economic specializations, have interacted and engaged in economic exchanges. But also forms of competition have developed. The interplay of many factors, prominent among them competition for land, has changed their formerly peaceful relationship to conflict-ridden and intermittently violent. The rest of this chapter will be devoted to this issue.

During the 1920s a group of Dauwala migrated from Ethiopia and lived on the bank of the river in a place which later came to be known as Rigeiba. Later in 1949 different Hausa groups came there from different places.[15] Like other migrants, they were attracted by the rich and unused fertile land in the Blue Nile Province (BNP). The Dauwala welcomed the Hausa and aided them in settling. The Hausa intermarried[16] with the Dauwala and introduced the cultivation of new crops. The Hausa contributed to a flourishing local economy and Rigeiba became a centre with a total population of more than 12,000. The increase is due to the enterprising spirit the Hausa exhibit. Their diverse economic activities made the place a market that attracts people from surrounding areas. As well as in-migration, natural increase also explains the growth of Rigeiba. The polygynous marriages of many Hausa and the larger size of their families contributed to population increase.

Some sedentarized Fulbe, distinguished from the pastoral Fulbe, generally known as Mbororo, have settled amongst the Hausa.[17] The term Mbororo refers to the relatively recently arrived pastoral Fulbe; the owners of the large West African red and long horned cattle (*kūrī 'aḥmar*), a high-performance breed of the zebus (*bos indicus*) (Feyissa & Schlee 2009). Mbororo were first seen in the BNP in the 1940s, with numerous arrivals in 1948. In 1954, they were expelled to Kordofan and Darfur but they returned after a few years and were seen again in the area in the beginning of the 1960s (Ahmed 1973). The Woyla Fulbe are part of these pastoral people. Their coming to the area is dated differently. The Hausa of Rigeiba spoke of 1970, while the Gumuz of Maganza related their arrival to the time of the invasion of Kurmuk by the Sudan People's Liberation Army/Movement (SPLM/A) in 1986. The Ingessana of Madyam noted that they saw Woyla wandering in the area before the construction of the dam. The Woyla themselves claim that they have spent the dry season in Gangar for 27 years and had buried 65 of their kinsmen in the place. It is evident that for more than 20 years, they have paid the Gumuz of Maganza a nominal sum for grazing on the *mayaᶜa* near Khor Maganza (Osman 2008).

During the 1980s and 1990s, some Mbororo and Uuda Fulbe nomads settled in Rigeiba, escaping the hell of the civil war in the south. During that period, many people fled from the war into the area south of Damazin. These migrations have led to huge expansion of agriculture on the flood irrigated land and increased competition between farmers and herders. However there were no violent conflicts because pastures were good. The nomads were not concentrated in one place as the rich summer grazing land in the Kurmuk district, further south, attracted many pastoral groups. The Hausa welcomed the Fulbe and assisted them in settling so that they could stand together against the Dauwala, who as indigenous or long-standing residents dominate the Native Administration.

In Rigeiba district, the Hausa and the Fulbe used to have peaceful and cooperative relations though, from time to time, minor disputes occurred between the young men. In 1990, the elders of the two groups agreed that all involved in a dispute should be taken to task. In 1992, some Woyla young men involved in a dispute were sent to prison even before court trial and that was appreciated by both parties. These local regulations proved fruitful as the different groups lived in peace for a long period with no need for the police station in Rigeiba until 2001.

Many factors have contributed to the decline of peace in Rigeiba. By the early 2000s, the huge expansion of agriculture had created high competition over limited land resources between different users, mainly between Hausa cultivators and Fulbe cattle owners. Due to population growth and the resulting scarcity of land, farmers have begun to cultivate in new places outside the coastal belt of *ǧirūf* land. This expansion has made watering animals from the river or floodwater very difficult and sometimes impossible without crop damage (Osman 2008).

From a Hausa perspective, Woyla cattle have been causing crop damage for more than 20 years at a level they regard as normal. These issues were solved by mediation. But from the 1990s onwards incidents of crop damage rapidly increased. The Farmers' Association (FA) formed a crop-damage committee, with the Fulbe and the Dauwala being represented. The Fulbe always complain that the estimates for crop damage are high, and they pay unwillingly. In fact, they accused the committee of favouring the farmers. So the FA and the PA formed a joint crop-damage committee. This worked well for a while, but recently problems of crop damage have proliferated due to the increased number of cattle in the district as many nomads have come from the south. Some of these nomads have changed their dry season grazing lands. Others were blocked during the civil war and returned to the area after the signing of the CPA.[18] At the same time, the Hausa complain that the Fulbe attitude has drastically changed and become violent. In the case of crop damage, the Fulbe, instead of initiating negotiation, respond with violence which aggravates the problem.

The year 2000 represents a remarkable turning point in Fulbe-Hausa relations. The Gumuz had rented the *maya^c^a* of Maganza, which they previously rented to the Fulbe, to the Hausa of Rigeiba. The Hausa cultivated crops in it. This new cultivation reduced the grazing area and blocked the corridor to the watering point. When the Fulbe came, much crop damage occurred. The Hausa held a meeting in Rigeiba to discuss the problem and resorted to the police. The police visited the location and called representatives of the Hausa, the Fulbe and the Gumuz for a meeting in Damazin. At the meeting, the pastoral Fulbe requested that the Hausa let them continue their old contract with the Gumuz but the Hausa refused. The Gumuz likewise preferred to rent land to the Hausa. The Fulbe thus lost their access to a valuable resource that they had used for a long period. This specific event ignited the conflict between the two groups (Osman 2008).

In fact, what the Fulbe had given the Gumuz in return for the use of the resources was very nominal and had become insignificant because of increased monetization of the regional economy and the relative rise in the standard of living in recent years. The Fulbe, as nomads, are unwilling to pay more while the Hausa, as capitalist farmers, can and do pay more. The Fulbe complain that the Hausa sell farm residues to Arabs but refuse to sell the residues to them. The Hausa claim in defence that the Fulbe offer lower prices and they may try to graze farm residues without paying.

The year 2004 witnessed a further deterioration in Hausa-Fulbe relations in the Blue Nile region. Political rivalry between the two groups in the Omdurman Falata of Lakandi locality in Sennar State resulted in bloodshed in February 2004. This reverberated in Hausa-Fulbe relations in Rigeiba which became very reserved (Osman 2008). Leaders of the two groups barely managed to mitigate tensions. In March/April 2004, a dispute took place between the two groups, a third party mediated, and for the first time the Hausa demanded the expulsion of the Fulbe from the area. The Woyla claimed they purchased the land they live on from the sheikh of Gumuz. The omda of the Hamaj[19] intervened and the case was taken to the paramount chief of the Funj region tribes at Roseires. There the Fulbe failed to provide any documentation to support their claims.

According to the people of Farig Malakal, in June 2004 a police force from Rigeiba tried to disarm them. They refused to hand over their arms and were about to fire at the police. The case was taken to Damazin and was resolved in favour of the camp members, who possessed firearms in line with the Popular Defence Forces' (PDF's) law. The Hausa mentioned a similar case in 2005 where, when one of the Hausa quarrelled with a Woyla herder who brought his animals to graze near his farm, the herder fired a shot in order to threaten him. The police of Rigeiba heard the noise of the gun and, as it is generally known that the Woyla – who have to move far south seasonally with their cattle – own arms, the police went to their camp to investigate the matter. The Woyla regarded this as an attempt to disarm them.

Farig Malakal members were convinced that the Hausa were behind the police attempt to disarm them and retaliated by organizing a boycott of Hausa traders in Rigeiba in collaboration with other Fulbe. This affected the Hausa severely and they sought mediation from a third party, namely the Sultan of Maiurno. In the negotiation process, the Fulbe demanded the opening of a corridor to the river in Rigeiba. The Hausa promised to open that corridor. The Fulbe in turn lifted their boycott (Osman 2008) but as of September 2010 no corridor had been opened.

In 2005 one household from Farig Malakal lived in an Ingessana hamlet near to the camp to the west of Ganger. Soon other households joined the settlement. In 2006, new huts were built beyond Khor Maganza. The Gumuz overtly opposed this new trend of building huts in 'their' land without permission, but the Woyla claimed that they had the permission of the omda of the Hamaj, under whose authority the Gumuz of Maganza fall. The omda, however, denied having given permission to Woyla and ordered them to remove the huts, which they did.

From 2007/8 Woyla changed their pastoral strategy and started to separate between herds and households. The Hausa complain that the Woyla did not move their tents for two years from their rainy season location and so the Hausa could not cultivate their farms. It has been a long standing arrangement that the Woyla pitch their camps in Hausa farms after the harvest has finished. The Hausa, in turn, wait until the Woyla had moved to their wet season grazing lands before beginning cultivation.

By 2009, the conflict between the Hausa and the Fulbe had entered a stage of violent interaction and bloodshed. In January 2009, a young man from Farig Malakal went to Rigeiba market to buy sorghum. His bargaining with one of the Hausa traders developed into a heated discussion that ended with a fight between the groups of young men. The conflict next escalated when the Fulbe ceased attending Rigeiba market and young Fulbe began beating up passing Hausa motorcyclists. In April 2009, a police point was located on the bed of Khor Bobok, south of Rigeiba – which, as explained above, was where the motorcyclists were being intercepted – to prevent clashes between the two groups. In mid-April, the Hausa of Rigeiba launched a campaign, mobilizing their kinsmen from many local villages, and attacked Farig Malakal. Two security members hurried to stop the fight but the angry Hausa beat them up, set their motorbikes on fire and headed towards the camp. They killed one of the Fulbe and wounded five others. Continuous arrow shooting by the Woyla also caused many deaths and wounded many Hausa.

Ever since, tension has continued to simmer between the two groups, but they have been cautious. Rumour spread that the Hausa were mobilizing for revenge. On 7 May, Farig Malakal members spent the whole day with their bows and arrows at the ready, expecting a Hausa attack. The Hausa motorcyclists began moving only in groups. The Fulbe reported that these bands of motorcyclists were several times seen close to the camp. On one occasion they claimed that they were there to protect one of their tribal chiefs on his return from Geisan, fearing that the Fulbe would harm him. The Fulbe, on the other hand, hold their bows and arrows at the ready wherever they go, and in the camp they are very busy making more.

The authorities in Damazin and the leaders of the Hausa and the Fulbe have engaged in a long process to settle the conflict. In Rigeiba on 20 June 2009, representatives from both groups participated in a peace ceremony to end hostilities. They also suggested forming a neutral mechanism for crop damage estimates and forming a joint council to serve the interests of both groups.

But relations between the two groups did not improve after signing the agreement. According to the Fulbe, the Hausa signed the agreement tactically because they want to cultivate their *bildāt* (rain-fed fields) which they could not do if their relations with the Fulbe remained hostile. Despite the agreement, the Hausa continued to try and expel the Fulbe, while the nomadic Fulbe continued building huts.

The Hausa complained that the site on which the Fulbe are intending to settle is not suitable as it is located in agricultural land at the junction of four villages: Rigeiba, Maganza, Madyam and Ufut. The Hausa resorted to demanding the intervention of the amir of the Fulbe in the Blue Nile State to convince Farig Malakal members to spend the wet season (*ḫarīf*) away to allow them to cultivate their farms. The amir tried to persuade the leaders of the Fulbe to move but they refused and stressed that they had decided to settle permanently. Later, the representatives of the Fulbe and the Hausa met again in the PA headquarters in Damazin and the two parties were insistent on their standpoints. The Fulbe claimed that they had registered the land with the commissioner of Baw. They added that the Hausa had tried many times to expel them from the site by force and when this failed have resorted to tricks and bribed the Hamaj, Gumuz and Berta to do so.

To claim legality according to Baw authorities does not solve the matter, as there is conflict over boundaries between Baw and Geisan localities. The area of Ganagar, Madyam and other places in the area are contested between Geisan and Baw localities. This conflict is ongoing. The Masalit of Madyam noted that when they first arrived, they found all the Ingessana of Madyam were attached to the omda of the Hamaj in Abu Gumay (Geisan locality), though the Ingessana deny this. They explain that they once asked the chief of the Gumuz of Maganza to settle a crop damage dispute with the Arabs, and that this had been mistakenly understood as an indication of their attachment to the Hamaj authority. At that time, they had no sheikh in Madyam,[20] they added.

From 1995 onward, the Ingessana turned to the Baw locality instead of Geisan. Despite the existence of a primary school attended by Masalit and Ingessana boys, the Baw authority established another primary school in Madyam for Ingessana boys in 1997. Moreover, the Baw local authority established a police station in Madyam. But some of the Ingessana sheikhs in Madyam have listed their people as belonging to the Geisan locality. Other Ingessana consider these sheikhs as allies to the Masalit.

The Fulbe have good relations with both the Masalit and the Ingessana of Madyam but their boys go to the latter's school. The Geisan commissioner formed a committee to look from Rigeiba up to Geisan for an alternative site suitable for the Fulbe to settle, away from the villagers' farms. The committee was headed by a *pullo*[21] police officer called Lutfi. The Gumuz accused Lutfi of favouring the Fulbe, saying that in August they went to their farms but the Fulbe prevented them from beginning cultivation. They appealed to Lutfi and he replied that it was 'too late for cultivation anyhow'. They added that Lutfi allowed the Fulbe to settle even after the site had been ploughed. The Gumuz also complained that the committee did not perform its work. To bypass the committee, ten of the village sheikhs went to the police director of Geisan locality for an immediate solution to the problem. The outcome of this step will be seen below.

In August 2009, Farig Malakal members moved their camp one kilometre south to a relatively higher location to escape the biting insects that proliferate with the advance of the rainy season. The Hausa used this opportunity to call for a collective labour party (*nafīr*) and cultivated sunflower in the camp area. Seven tractors ploughed the site; dozens of people sowed while dozens more stood guard. There were about 50 motorcycles on the farm. The Hausa explained that, as the land belonged to individual farmers who would not be able to stand against Woyla by themselves, it was pooled into a cooperative with returns going to the village fund. The Fulbe noted that the Hausa called this farm 'the evil farm' and also complained that the Hausa set fire to a shelter and damaged the school located in the middle of the field. When the Fulbe saw the tractors ploughing, they wanted to fight the Hausa, but their tribal section omda prevented them, instead complaining to the authorities in Damazin.

The same collective labour and guarding scenario was repeated for weeding. The Fulbe claimed that the Hausa decided not to harvest the crop so they could fine any herder whose flock damaged it and thus deprive the Fulbe of any chance of returning. They also bemoaned that the Hausa motorcyclists had run over some Fulbe and that they often heard provocative shouts of *Allāhu 'akbar* from within the sunflower field – a cry that embodies victory and/or threat. The Fulbe also asserted that the Hausa added poison to surface water in the *ğirūf* and some Fulbe calves died after drinking it. According to the Fulbe this was intentional, but it may also have been accidental since the inappropriate use of pesticides is widespread in rural Sudan.

In September, the Uuda Fulbe living in Rigeiba quarrelled with the Hausa and from then the Hausa refrained from buying Fulbe milk and cattle and when one of them bought an ox from Farig Malakal, they fined him and refused to eat the beef fearing Fulbe magic. In the last week of October or the first week of November 2009, one of the Fulbe was moving his sheep to Geisan district. One of the Gumuz or Gawasma of Maganza accused him of damaging crops and tried to capture him. The herder shot the farmer with an arrow, wounding him in his leg and then escaped without being recognized. The Gumuz of Maganza directed their accusation at Farig Malakal, insisting on capturing the offender, but were prevented by the Ufat police. The police, some of the Gumuz and the wounded went to the camp three times to look for the offender but they did not find him.

Clashes between the two groups continued throughout November 2009. The Fulbe reported that the Hausa accused one of their sheep herders of damaging Hausa crops. In response 400 Hausa mobilized to seek revenge for the incident and attack Farig Malakal. The herders in Ufut lamented that farmers began to light the standing hay in order to push them out of the area. They also complained that one of themselves was fined 1,000 Sudanese Pounds for damaging crops of much lower worth.

Soon the sheikhs of Maganza and Ufut appealed to the Geisan locality commissioner and demanded the expulsion of the Fulbe from Gangar. The commissioner called for a meeting with the Fulbe amir, the head of the PA, the head of the FA and others. At the meeting, the commissioner suggested looking for a suitable place for the Fulbe to settle. The representatives of the Fulbe accepted the proposal. An appointment was made for another meeting in Ufut. The meeting was held in the Ufut administrative unit (UAU) at the village administration building on November 14, 2009. It was attended by the head of the PA, the head of the FA, the omda of the Hamaj, the police director of Geisan locality and the representatives of the Hausa, Dauwala, Gumuz, Berta and Woyla. At the meeting, the representatives of each group demanded the expulsion of the Fulbe and transfer of the Rigeiba police director out of the area. They stressed that the site, being adjacent to villagers' farms, was not suitable for settlement. At the end of the meeting the commissioner issued a decree that the Fulbe must settle in another location, away from villagers' farms, and formed a committee to determine a site. The committee, headed by the police director, selected a site between Maganza and Ufut. The commissioner, the sheikh of Maganza and Fulbe representatives went to see the site.

From the beginning, the Fulbe representatives declared the place unsuitable and suggested looking for another. The Fulbe's rejection of the site was based on the fact that it is very narrow, surrounded by water on all sides and has only one route leading to Ufut. While they were examining the site, a group of enraged people from Maganza advanced towards them, with fresh memories of recent crop damage, holding their traditional weapons (spears and sticks); the Fulbe representatives barely managed to escape. But the angry crowd, followed by ululating women, continued their march and attacked the head office of UAU. They wounded one of the policemen, set a hut on fire and beat the sheikh of Maganza accusing him of trying to settle the enemy in the village's vicinity. They also targeted the police director Lutfi by twice hurling a spear at him, but failed to harm him. A police force from Damazin was sent. Some of the Gumuz were arrested and the judicial process was still ongoing at the time of writing (2010).

The different parties to the conflict, of course, have different perceptions of the problem. The Fulbe are convinced that the Hausa are behind all these events. They explained that when the Hausa failed to expel them by force, they bribed the Gumuz to expel them by other means and so they will fight to stay. On the other hand, the angry people of Maganza believe that the Fulbe bribed Lutfi and the Geisan locality commissioner and they accuse the two of politicizing the problem, which aggravated them to react violently. The sheikh of Maganza Gumuz noted that one of the SPLM affiliates in Maganza mobilized the people and led the demonstration but in the end was against settling the Fulbe in the district. The head of the FA accused the leadership of SPLM in the BNS of supporting these events.[22] Immediately after these events, some of the Gumuz and the Hausa in Maganza shifted from the NCP (the ruling National Congress Party of northern Sudan) and joined the SPLM,[23] the head of FA added. The Masalit criticized the way the government tried to solve the problem. The Masalit wanted to persuade the Hausa to give part of their land to the Woyla and they have already offered part of their land for this but the Woyla did not settle there. In fact, the Masalit have good relations with the Fulbe and they benefit economically from their presence in the area. However, after all this, everyone seemed convinced that finding a suitable place for Woyla in the area from Rigeiba up to Geisan is impossible.

At this critical junction, about 43 Woyla households under the leadership of Omar Mohammed Harun came from Gedaref and pitched their camps in the harvested Hausa farms in Gangar in mid-December 2009.[24] After spending 32 years in Gedaref, they came to live permanently in the Blue Nile State, pushed by drought and poor rainfall in 2009 as well as the accelerated privatization of pastoral resources. Their plan was to acquire land for settlement and concomitantly to continue moving with the herds. After their arrival, they started to go to Rigeiba for shopping and had no dispute with the Hausa until then.

Listening to advice from Farig Malakal, they decided to cease attending Rigeiba market. On December 24, a motorcycle ran over one of their old men and this strengthened their decision. About 13 households moved to Sinja-Nabag because they did not want to live in the Hausa neighbourhood. Burning hay and farm residues continued during December 2009. This adversely affected the pastoral economy of Farig Malakal, because the plan of the Omar Mohammed Harun group was to stay. They did not want to move to the south because their cattle were not adapted to the southern ecology. Rather than moving south, the pastoral strategy of the Mohammed Harun group for the rest of the dry season was to stay in the vicinity of Rigeiba and to make the maximum use of the available poor pasture. Only when they felt that the cattle were about to become weak would they go to Raaba where they paid the Dauwala for grazing the rich *birdī* grass in the *ḥauḍ*.

The strategy of the above group would be adopted by many pastoral groups. The range management officer in the Blue Nile State, Ab Sas, explained that because of the fodder gap, herders are concentrating near seasonal streams and the *ḥauḍ* and this leads to clashes. To solve this problem, he suggested that grazing in *ḥauḍ* should be regulated and the watering points specifically recognized. He also suggested forming a committee[25] to determine the price for *birdī* and to sell it to the herders on behalf of the villagers, and then the revenue would be divided between the villagers and the locality.

The matter is not helped by the fact that the *ḥauḍ* comprises land of different quality, suitable for different kinds of use, which are claimed by various categories of people. About 25 per cent of the *ḥauḍ* land (15,000 feddans – 6,300 hectares, 15,570 acres) cannot be cultivated. It is located on relatively high land and is covered by flood water only for a short period. The moisture rate in this land is lower than the level which supports farming but is suitable for the growth of good forage used by the pastoralists. In addition to this, there are some patches of poor soil remaining between the villages called *karab,* which are not included in the *ǧirūf* land. Some villagers used to rent this land to the nomads. The area from Rigeiba up to Maganza provides a good example of this type of land. Another type of land results from the accumulation of silt where the thickness of the silt layer does not reach the level required for *ǧirūf* cultivation. This type of land attracts migrant farmers, who rent the land from villagers and use pumps to produce crops. Needless to say that this new cultivation occurs at the expense of pasture.

The events outlined above clearly show that there is a conflict of interests, which from time to time takes a violent form, between different social entities at the local level around questions of resource allocation and resource management. This local conflict resonates with conflicts at higher levels, like the regional state (province) and the nation state. We are dealing with a web of mutual influences.

At the level of the Blue Nile State, the forage and range management authority is marginalized and subordinated to the forest authority. This results in a total disregard of pastoralists' interests and an increased expansion of agriculture at the expense of pasture. Stakeholders' organizations (PA and FA), as well as the many recently emerging native leaders, are not autonomous and are bound by the political agendas and the interests of the ruling party. This situation is aggravated by disputes over locality boundaries and complicated by the fluidity of groups and by ill-defined administrative responsibilities.

National policies add to the problem rather than solving it. The national government began implementing an agricultural revival project to modernize agriculture (the Sudanese Agricultural Revival Programme). Lip service is paid to the integration of crop and livestock production but, overall, state agencies often support large-scale mechanized agriculture and the privatization of pastoral resources. Mechanized agriculture produces plenty of crop residues and, in this area which is marginal to rain-fed agriculture, frequently also failed crops – stalks without mature grain. Pastoralists were allowed traditionally to use these resources for free, but now they have to pay for grazing the stubble or failed crops. Land rights have become more exclusive, being extended from leaseholders' normal crop rights to a right to everything that grows on the land, thereby aggravating land conflicts. It can therefore be concluded that the proclaimed policy of integrating pastoralism and agriculture has failed. This failure has become an additional factor in igniting local conflicts.

CONCLUSION

To draw some general conclusions from this complex case history, we move from partly theoretical perspectives to more practical and administrative considerations. On the level of general social theory one can read this case history as an example of the breakdown of complementary relationships. Farmers and herders all over the arid belt of the Old World for thousands of years have mostly managed to avoid competition by using a variety of different resources and by exchanging their products. The different ethnic groups of the Blue Nile State were no exception to this. This chapter has described how avoidance of competition by using different resources has failed because the resources claimed by the parties to the conflict have come to be the same. Even the access rights of the herds to the river became controversial because land needed for a corridor was cultivated by the villagers.

Resource scarcity is a frequent argument used to explain conflict. One may therefore consider demographic and ecological changes to see whether the contested resource – in this case pasture land, which is also marginally suitable for rain-fed agriculture – has become more scarce. There is some evidence for this. This chapter reports an influx of pastoralists from the neighbouring Gedaref State which was badly affected by a lack of rain in 2009, and other cases of immigration. Figures of population growth are not given, but we can assume that an excess of births over deaths adds to the rise in population density. The relationship between resource scarcity and the occurrence of conflict, however, cannot be assumed to be linear. Absolutely destitute people affected by food scarcity are not able to engage in conflict. On the other side we find wealthy and powerful actors far above the level of mere subsistence who engage in games of economic maximization. The Hausa traders in this case history, for example, can hardly be said to be defending a shrinking resource base or to be in one or the other form of economic or environmental distress.

State agencies do not enjoy the reputation of being neutral. Both conflicting parties in this case study accuse each other of colluding with the police or other state agencies. While the general trend is towards privatization of pastoral resources, and the State and its agencies often support this trend, in individual cases shared ethnicity means the police are not above suspicion of favouring the pastoralists.

An overall policy to combine different group interests and maintain or increase productivity of different forms of resource utilization is not in place. Such a policy would have to address an optimization problem in meeting different targets. Reserving some agricultural land for livestock corridors in order to give pastoralists' herds access to water or to connect different pasture areas with each other, would have to be part of such a policy. A limited area with agricultural potential would have to be taken out of the reserve of agricultural land and be integrated into the pastoralist system, in order to enable pastoralists to utilize vast areas without agricultural potential that can only be used by extensive forms of livestock husbandry. There are livestock corridors existing in the Sudan, but their exclusive use for herd movements is insufficiently enforced and agriculture is encroaching on them. In one case a conflict about a livestock corridor to the river was not resolved peacefully and led to bloodshed. The state needs to develop a policy of combined land use taking into account pastoral and agricultural interests and the productivity of the overall system, and it needs to build up its own credibility in enforcing such a policy.

REFERENCES

Abbute Deboch, W.-S. 2004. *Gumuz and Highland Resettlers: Differing Strategies of Livelihood and Ethnic Relations in Metekel, Northwestern Ethiopia.* Münster: Lit.

Abbute Deboch, W.-S. 2009. 'Identity, Encroachment and Ethnic Relations: The Gumuz and their Neighbours in North-Western Ethiopia'. In Schlee, G., Watson E. E. (eds), *Changing Identifications and Alliances in North-East Africa. Vol. I: Ethiopia and Kenya.* Oxford: Berghahn, 155–172.

Abu-Manga, A., Miller, C. 2005. 'The West African (Fallata) Communities in Gedaref State: Process of Settlement and Local Integration'. In Miller, C. (ed.), *Land, Ethnicity and Political Legitimacy in Eastern Sudan: Kassala and Gedaref States.* Cairo: CEDEJ, 375–423.

Ahmed, A. G. M. 1973. 'Nomadic Competition in the Funj Area'. *Sudan Notes and Records* 54, 43–56.

Bender, M. L. 1975. *The Ethiopian Nilo-Saharans.* Addis Ababa.

Blue Nile State (BNS) 2005. *Annual Report. The Agricultural Sector.* Khartoum: Sudan Ministry of Agriculture and Animal Resources.

Delmet, C. 2000. 'Les peules nomades au Soudan'. In Diallo, Y., Schlee, G. (eds), *L'ethnicité peule dans des contextes nouveaux.* Paris: Karthala, 191–206.

Feyissa, D., Schlee, G. 2009. 'Mbororo (FulBe) Migrations from Sudan into Ethiopia'. In Schlee, G., Watson, E. E. (eds), *Changing Identifications and Alliances in North-East Africa. Vol. II: Sudan, Uganda and the Ethiopia-Sudan Borderlands.* Oxford: Berghahn, 157–178.

Gadrimaari, B. H. 2003. 'At-tarkīb al-qabālī li-s-sukān wilāyat an-nīl al-'azraq wa qadīyat al-'intimāᶜ' [The Ethnic Composition of the Blue Nile State Population and the Question of Identity]. Paper presented at the Institute of African Research and Studies Forum, the International University of Africa, Khartoum.

Ishaag, S. I. 2007. ''Aṯār ḫazān ar-roseiris ᶜala at-tanmīya ar-rīfīya fī al-manṭiqa haula l-ḫazān'. [The effect of Roseires Dam on Rural Development in the Surrounding Area]. M.Sc. Thesis. University of Khartoum, Faculty of Agriculture, Khartoum.

Jedrej, C. 1995. *Ingessana: The Religious Institutions of a People of the Sudan-Ethiopia Borderland.* Leiden: Brill.

Jedrej, C. 2000. 'Ingessana and the Legacy of the Funj Sultanate: The Consequences of Turkish Conquest on the Blue Nile'. *Africa* 70 (2), 278–297.

Ministry of Irrigation and Hydro Power. 1966. *Annual Report*. Khartoum: Ministry of Irrigation and Hydro Power, Annual Report.

Osman, E. I. 2008. 'The Pastoral Fulbe in the Sudan Funj Region: A Study of the Interaction of State and Society'. Unpublished Ph.D. Thesis. University of Khartoum, Department of Sociology and Social Anthropology.

Schlee, G. 2000. 'Les Peuls du Nil'. In Diallo, Y., Schlee, G. (eds), *L'ethnicité peule dans des contextes nouveaux*. Paris: Karthala, 207–223.

Schlee, G. 2009. 'Descent and Descent Ideologies: The Blue Nile Area (Sudan) and Northern Kenya Compared'. In Schlee, G., Watson, E. E. (eds), *Changing Identifications and Alliances in North-East Africa. Vol. II: Sudan, Uganda and the Ethiopia-Sudan Borderlands*. Oxford: Berghahn, 117–135.

Triulzi, A., Dafallah, A. A., Bender, M. L. 1976. 'Berta'. In Bender, M. L. (ed.), *The Non-Semitic Languages of Ethiopia*. East Lansing MI: Michigan State University, 513–532.

United Nations (UN). 2012. Sudan and South Sudan. <www.un.org/depts/Cartographic/english/htmain.htm>, retrieved 25-06-2013.

United Nations Economic and Social Council. 2009, Government Agricultural Action Plan (2008–2011), Sudan. Online resources, <http://webpass01.un.org/nvp/frontend!policy.action?id=1658>, retrieved 26-09-2010.

ENDNOTES

1. Also spelled Massalit, Masalit. The Massaliit speak a Nilo-Saharan language.

2. When the dam was constructed, Damazin was a small village.

3. The Fulbe are one of those ethnic groups which have a level of sub-structuring below the overall ethnic category and above that of smaller named units, often called clans. We call these sub-ethnic groups and Woyla is one of them. Some Fulbe categories of self-classification refer to a special way of life (e.g. Huya (used in West Africa) for urban Fulbe or Fulbe ladde ('bush Fulbe') for pastoral Fulbe. The Woyla are pastoralists. Other Sudanese often refer to pastoral Fulbe in general as Mbororo, but the Fulbe themselves reserve the latter term for a specific group of Fulbe ladde.

4. Farig (Sudanese version of Ar. farīq), literally a segment or a section, is a residential unit of pastoral nomads, i.e. a group which camps and moves together. For lack of a better term in English, we translate it as 'hamlet'.

5. The majority of the Gumuz live in Ethiopia, on both sides of the Blue Nile, which is called Abbay there. Gumuz has been classified as belonging to the Koman branch of the Nilo-Saharan family, or forming a branch of its own. As it has many unique features, even the wider classification as Nilo-Saharan, however, is far from clear (Abbute Deboch 2004, 2009, Bender 1975: 61).

6. The Ingessana language or Gaam belongs to the Eastern Sudanic branch of the Nilo-Saharan languages. For an ethnographic and historical account see Jedrej (1995, 2000). Ingessana ethnicity has been associated with 'paganism', but in recent generations about half of the Ingessana have converted to Islam. They live in the Ingessana Hills south-west of Damazin. Gaam forms a continuum of dialects comprising Baw, Buk, Fadamiyya, Suuda, Kukur, Teigu, Bagis, Kamreik

and Gabanit (Gadrimaari 2003). The Ingessana are basically farmers but they have accumulated cattle and developed a system of short distance transhumance between the riverside and the hills (Ahmed 1973).

7. The Dauwala are a mixture of Berta and Arabs who migrated from Ethiopia to the east of Kurmuk. They speak Arabic and Berta. They are Muslims and relatively educated (Gadrimaari 2003).

8. The Berta live mainly on the Ethiopian side of the boundary, in Beni Shangul, but they are also numerous in the southern Funj region of the Sudan. Their main centres in the Sudan are Kurmuk, Keili, Ora, Yabus, Bakuuri, Geisaan, Damazin and Roseires. They were 'pagans' but converted to Islam under the influence of the early migrant Arabs. They speak Berta, a Nilo-Saharan language, and form a series of dialect groups, of which one or two may be different enough from the rest to be classified as separate languages (Ahmed 1973: 22–23; Gadrimaari 2003,Triulzi et al.1976).

9. The Funj are a Muslim Arabic-speaking indigenous group but there are different views on their origin. They claim to descend from the Umayyad dynasty. They allied with the Gawasma Arabs in the beginning of the sixteenth century and established the Funj Sultanate with its capital in Sennar. They live in Fazoghli, Roseires and Guli. Although not numerous, they are influential leaders. The Mak Yuusif Hassan Adlaan who descended from the ruling family of the Funj is now at the top of the Native Administration hierarchy as a paramount chief for all Funj region tribes (Gadrimaari 2003).

10. From western Sudan and West Africa.

11. This shows that the category 'Gharaba' combines people from West Africa, namely the Hausa (who speak an Afro-Asiatic language) and Fulbe (who speak a language of the west-Atlantic branch of Niger-Congo) and people from western Sudan. The Masaaliit, most of whom live in Darfur and extend into adjacent regions of Chad, speak a Nilo-Saharan language.

12. But this portion would decrease slightly if we include Ufut an-Niweiri, as this increases the portion of the Berta.

13. One feddan equals 0.42 hectare.

14. This practice is known as tā'kul gōm (lit: eat and move). The essence of it is a right to use land for a specific period of time free of charge and to hand it back to its owner at the end.

15. They came from local villages in the Blue Nile such as Badus and Shamaar and from the White Nile, Gezira, Kordofan and Darfur.

16. At first, only the Hausa married Dauwala women and not the other way round. The Hausa explained that when a Dauwala woman is married to one of the Hausa she enjoys a comfortable life because the Hausa, unlike the Dauwala, do not allow women to work outside the house or to fetch water and firewood. But now, as cars and donkeys have replaced women in water and firewood fetching, life has become easier also for the wives of Dauwala and a Hausa woman can be married to one of the Dauwala.

17. Non-Fulbe in the Sudan use the term Mbororo to refer to pastoral Fulbe or Fulbe ladde ('bush' Fulbe) in general. The latter comprise many groups, among them the Woyla, the Uuda and others, but the Fulbe do not use the term Mbororo in this general sense, but only for a specific subgroup, whom we might call the Mbororo in the narrow sense.

18. Comprehensive Peace Agreement, signed at Naivasha, Kenya, in 2005.

19. The Hamaj are indigenous Muslim farmers who are believed to have originated from intermarriage between the ᶜAwadiyya section of the Jacaliyin and the Nuba. They played an influential political role during the Funj Sultanate and consider themselves part of the Funj. The Hamaj have three chiefdoms (omodias), two in Roseires District and the third is in Abu-Gumay, headed by Omda al-Amiin al-Kurdi (Gadrimaari 2003). The area from Rigeiba to Abu-Gumay theoretically falls under the administrative authority of Omda al-Amin al-Kurdi.

20. This absence of sheikh is because the Ingessana live in dispersed settlements, considering the area from their hills to the river as one territory. They spend the rainy season in the hills and the dry season on the bank of the river.

21. Singular of Fulbe.

22. The Minister of Agriculture, Zayid cIsa Zayid, visited Maganza one day before these events and urged the people to demonstrate.

23. The SPLM are part of a power sharing arrangement in the Blue Nile State since the Naivasha peace agreement of 2005.

24. This newcomer group of Woyla is part of the Abdullah Musa Idris group. Other members of this group remain in Gedaref, where they have to pay for pasture. They cannot move on since water ponds en route to the Blue Nile have dried up. On January 20, 2010, Elhadi interviewed the head of this group in the vicinity of Ombaggara Dinder National Park.

25. This proposed committee would include the administrative officer, the head of the economic committee, and the heads of the PA and the FA.

10

A Central Marginality: The 'Invisibilization' of Urban Pastoralists in Khartoum State

BARBARA CASCIARRI

In Sudan, as well as in various African and Middle Eastern countries where nomadic groups are historically important, state officials and other actors tend to underestimate figures of nomads or populations with pastoral origin. For decades pastoralism[1] has been shown as in decline. However, there is still a need to reassert the persistence of nomadic pastoralism both at the socio-demographic and economic level (Casciarri & Ahmed 2009). The ecological features of the Sudan and its late and limited process of urbanization point to the viability and sustainability of pastoralism, despite strong pressures working against this complex socio-economic formation.

This chapter focuses on the process of 'invisibilization', which often is correlated by marginalization, affecting pastoral people in Sudan. Several factors account for such an invisibilization. First, the dominant vision enforced by the central state. In Sudan, unlike the Maghreb, nomadic peoples have never replaced sedentary peoples in the power hegemony. In the 'dynamic opposition' between nomad/sedentary, periphery/centre (or tribe/state), sedentary has been the victor since at least the Mahdist era (Grandin 1982: 33–34). This caused a shift from a threatening image of nomads, to denying the identity of the vanquished. While no longer seen as a danger, nomads have gradually become invisible in the dominant discourse. Second, post-colonial governments in Sudan have pursued the same deleterious tendency of the colonizer in addressing the 'nomadic problem' like most African and Middle East countries' (Bocco 1990). Conceiving of nomads as a hindrance to the process of nation building and modernization, the state has coupled material neglect of pastoralists with its social and economic policies (Mohamed Salih 1990), aiming at their ideological effacement as a fundamental component of the country.[2] Third, since the 1950s, international agencies for development also focused their interventions in Southern countries on the objective of sedentarizing nomads (Asad et al. 1965, Khogali 1983). It was only in recent years that a non-mainstream approach emerged, targeting pastoral elements in some projects. Yet, such a seemingly renewed interest does not blur the practical and ideological effects of the 'struggle' against nomadism and tribalism, which was supported by international agencies in the Third World after decolonization.

However, even if it has become more common to devote attention to pastoralists in regional (rural) contexts, a focus on pastoralists' presence and role in urban areas is still rare. Thus this chapter attempts to shed light on the situation of pastoral groups in the capital region (Khartoum State), where the recent and rapid expansion of the Three Towns (Khartoum, Omdurman, Bahri) produces new forms of urbanization and the urban element tends to 'swallow up' the rural element surrounding it. My aim is threefold: (1) to give an insight into the various configurations of 'pastoralists in town' through an ethnography of some pastoral nomad groups originating in Eastern Sudan who today live in Khartoum State (particularly in its eastern part) (Map 10.1); (2) to question the modes and reasons for the invisibilization affecting pastoralists and to detect the specificity of their situation in a context dominated by an urban dimension; (3) to apply the centre/periphery paradigm that, inspired by dependency theory for describing North/South relations, has often been successfully used to read Sudanese regional contexts (Harir & Tvedt 1994, Kevane & Stiansen 1998, Miller 2005, Battahani 2009). Focusing on the imbalance of political power, control of and access to economic resources, such a paradigm allows us to read the relations *within* the urban centre itself, considering urban pastoralists as the 'inner periphery'.

A PROBLEM OF APPROACH: ARE PASTORALISTS REALLY INVISIBLE IN TOWNS?

Since the great ecological crises and droughts of the 1970s and 1980s in Africa, more attention has been paid to the issue of 'pastoralists in town'. The massive arrival of pastoral populations in urban centres – often in very precarious conditions, searching for livelihoods after the loss of their herds – forced governments, relief organizations, and researchers as well, to take their presence into account. This was the case in the Maghreb, Sahel and the Horn of Africa, as well as in all places where pastoralism was persisting despite various attacks on its production and reproduction. From this turning point onwards, the image of pastoral nomads has been gradually dissociated from its stereotyped landscape, steppe or desert, and started to be associated with the town (URBAMA 1989, Piguet 1999, Puig 2003). In Sudan, this process has been striking. Yet, there is little work devoted to its analysis (see for example, El-Nagar 2001) since the pioneer text by Mohamed Salih (1985). One could say that pastoral nomads enter the urban space when their mobility becomes blurred, or animal wealth decreases and livelihood strategies change, then rapidly dissolve into other categories of population, disappearing and becoming invisible as 'nomads'. Due to this, I will underline some widespread biases about pastoralists in town, and the consequences of these images for the production of knowledge on the social dynamics of pastoralists and the groups who interact with them. These biases mainly affect interventions by the state or international actors in the political, social and economic domains, but are sometimes also reflected by scholarly approaches.

Overemphasizing Spatial Mobility

The relevance of spatial mobility in the definition of nomadic pastoralists as a pertinent category (distinguished from other ones) is undeniable. Nonetheless, anthropologists and social scientists, supported by in-depth fieldwork analysis and comparison, early highlighted that pastoral nomadism is much more than a by-product of physical mobility, where it is reduced to ecological constraints and economic productive systems. These scholars demonstrated that pastoralism would be properly conceived as an integrated economic, political and socio-cultural system, in which spatial mobility is only one of several parameters (Nelson 1973; Fabietti & Salzman 1996). As far as Sudan is concerned, such an holistic vision of pastoralism allows criticism of state policies that have shaped their interventions more in terms of 'livestock development' than in terms of 'pastoral development' (Mohamed Salih 1990). Even if we agree that other spheres of social action embedded in the pastoral complex undergo transformations due to changes in the degree of mobility, the pastoral system and community at large cannot be dissolved mechanically and rapidly into sedentariness. The political networks of solidarity and conflict management, labelled as 'tribal institutions', and their significance among settled pastoralists attest to this fact. Moreover, a kind of economy coexists that is not fully subordinated to capitalist market logics, which maintains its relevance even in the urban context and is also a legacy of nomadic pastoralism. The identity labels that townspeople or villagers continue to apply to former nomads – in Central and Northern Sudan the term *ᶜarab* is more often used as a synonym of 'pastoral nomad' (Grandin 1980, Casciarri 1999) – even when their presence in town and the abandonment of mobility are decades old, reveal that pastoralists are not merely defined by mobility, and the persistence of this category has roots going beyond cultural and symbolic parameters.

The Pastoralist – A 'New' Presence in Town?

Another trend linked to the invisibilization of pastoralists in town is the exaggeration of the new character of these actors in the urban space. Considering their presence as a striking novelty means forgetting that towns have always represented (also in phases of high mobility) an important nexus for the pastoral groups' socio-economic and political networks. Numerous studies emphasize that pastoralism cannot be understood apart from the 'ecological trilogy' steppe-village-town (Chatty 1990), or without taking into account the dialectic relation between nomads and settled peoples (Nelson 1973, Fabietti & Salzman 1996). Thus, recognizing that pastoralists have interacted (in various ways and times, and at various levels) with sedentary peoples and urbanites long before their more recent incorporation following the ecological crises, it is more surprising that their specificity within the urban space is barely recognized. Accordingly, pastoralists arriving in town are too hastily put into the category of 'rural migrants' (Mohamed Salih 1995). Consequently, the role of various forms of urban pastoralism is not analysed properly. Here geographical and economic approaches, which tend to classify every form of livestock-raising as a unique subcategory within 'agricultural production',[3] provide little help in understanding such complex dynamics. Thus pastoralists who enter towns are currently categorized, at best, as 'rural urbanized' people, or at worst, they dissolve into the huge misleading category of 'urban (poor) people'.

End of Mobility, End of Marginality?

Once the urgent situation that brought them there has passed, 'invisible' pastoralists living in town can also lose the right to be considered part of a 'marginal' group, which in their rural environment they were. The effacement of former nomad pastoralists' marginality in the urban context – where this label may give access to aid and advantages – often benefits other categories of 'first class' marginal people, like the internally displaced people (IDPs) in the capital and Khartoum State (Hamid 1996). Nonetheless, two significant elements have to be stressed. First of all, when compared to their neighbours, former (still pastoralist) nomads, especially if their urbanization is recent, often constitute pockets of real marginality within urban realities just like the groups that are considered to be the archetypal marginal (El-Nagar 2001). Second, a large proportion of the IDPs themselves are also pastoralists,[4] even if this particular status is neglected by the stress put on the category of internally displaced persons – and the same could be said for refugees from nomadic origins. This bias should raise questions. Surely, a tendency to choose labels (like 'IDPs') that are more visible, in sync with contemporary events of international interest, or adapted for political manipulation (by the state, by foreign agents, sometimes by the groups themselves) often prevails over a definition that allows for more nuances within recently urbanized peoples. After all, it should be asked whether the pastoralists, who are forced to move to the cities by droughts and by an aggressively capitalist economy that threatens their access to resources in their territories of origin, could not be classed as IDPs, if the category was not so rigidly defined and instrumental to relevant national and international issues.

Pastoralists go to Town, but the Town also goes to Pastoralists

More attention should also be paid to the temporal aspect in dynamics of change as well as to the modes of town expansion, in order to better understand who are and who became the urbanized pastoralists – and therefore to better define the features of urbanization. The Three Towns recently experienced a drastic demographic and spatial expansion (Denis 2005), in which pastoralists played a leading role – which has also been true in the more remote periods of the towns' history. Nonetheless, again, due to the invisibilization of pastoralists, it remains difficult to estimate the percentage of people from nomadic pastoral origin currently classified as 'townspeople' in Greater Khartoum. The history of their arrival and sedentarization (not only dates but also factors and modes) is also important in grasping the issues involved in the urban incorporation of certain groups, and, at the same time, in highlighting the role of pastoral backgrounds within general urban dynamics. So, although the usual scenario is that a pastoralist moves to town, the recent expansion of Khartoum begs an in-depth look into what is the opposite scenario. The town itself is extending its boundaries and entering pastoral territories as a physical, economic, political and identity space. This has been occurring since the early 2000s, as the rural region of Khartoum State has been rapidly and brutally incorporated into the capital's dynamics.

URBAN PASTORALISTS: THE VARIETY OF PRESENT CONFIGURATIONS

Without pretending to be exhaustive in such a complex, varied and pending situation as that of urban pastoralists in the capital region, I try here to illustrate some cases which portray the plurality of configurations emerging in this renewed centre/periphery relation, at the core of which pastoral societies are found. I take as examples three pastoral groups of central and eastern Sudan: the Ahamda, the Batahin, the Hassaniyya, and then add the case of early urbanized pastoralists of a popular quarter (Deim) in the centre of Khartoum.[5] I aim to show with the support of fieldwork data, some aspects of the insertion of pastoralists into urban dynamics. The four diverse cases, on the one hand, reveal the need to focus on their respective pastoral backgrounds, refusing assimilation and merger with sedentary/urban populations due to ideological invisibilization. On the other side, they illustrate the interaction between several aspects of pastoral societies and between these societies and their non-pastoral urban counterparts. The criterion of priority (and degree) of sedentarization is mentioned, but is not considered as the main parameter of the distinction between the four cases. I assert that a more complex set of factors interplay to define it. For each case I sketch a brief history of the group and the general framework of its present setting. Then I present its forms of production, livelihood strategies, and the relations with the town and the centre (mainly at an economic and political level). Finally, I give an insight into the perceptions *by* and *on* the group as far as local categories of nomad/pastoralist are concerned.

Case 1: Persistent Pastoralists within 'New' Urban Peripheries

Concerns groups that maintain a dominant orientation as pastoralists and are still surrounded by units of their own tribal group, although the town and its dynamics have drawn closer as Khartoum expands. This type of configuration has some basic features: the kind of habitat, the communal management of resources, the priority given to extensive livestock raising coupled with rain-fed agriculture (both subsistence-oriented), a minor engagement in wage labour, an organization of labour within the household, a limited access to services and, finally, a strong stress on values and practices of mutual aid and solidarity within the agnatic group. In the wider regional context, these cases stand as 'islets of resistance' against the centre's model, with their socio-economic and cultural patterns, which were previously shared by the whole tribal group.

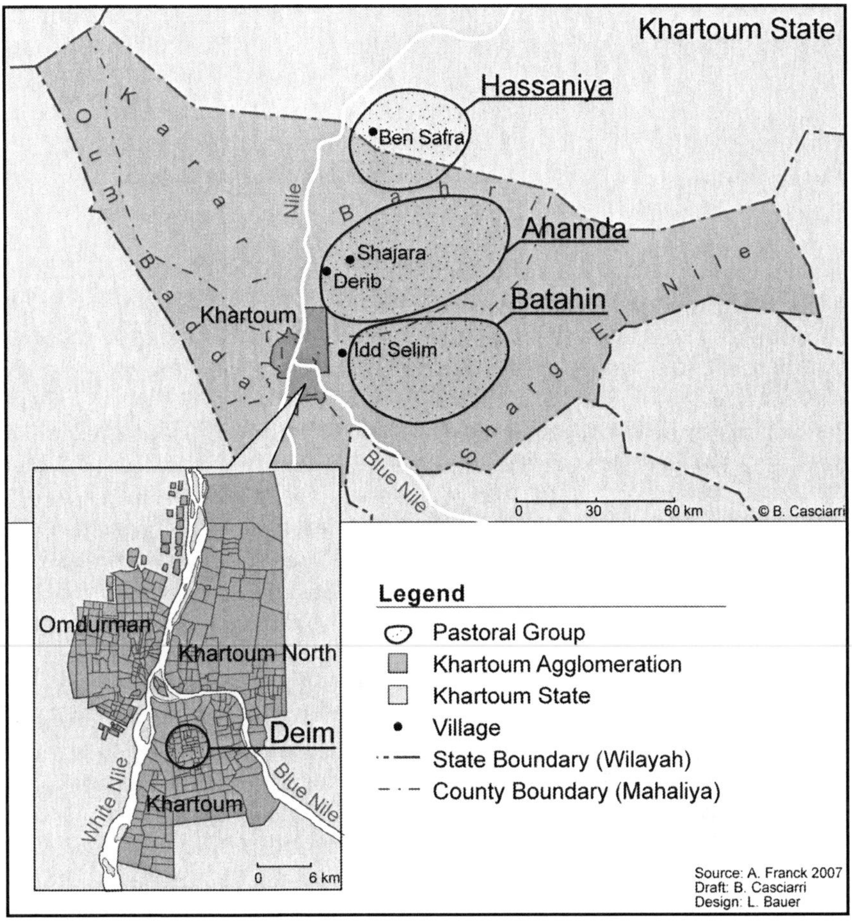

Map 10.1 The Three Pastoral Groups in Khartoum State and Deim Quarter in Khartoum

The case of the Ahamda *furqān* (camps) in Shajara[6] is a good example. The area is upstream from the Khor al-Asad, the main seasonal watercourse in the territory and approximately 50km north-east of Khartoum. It has been considered the tribal area of the *qabīla* Ahamda since at least the colonial period. When the Ahamda were still nomads in Butana, this area was occupied during the dry season, after the westward movement towards the Nile, by several households mainly belonging to two of their lineages.[7] Towards the end of the colonial phase, several Ahamda lineages (whose status as a unified and coherent *qabīla* was influenced by the appointment of an omda in the British Native Administration), built a deep well and, despite conflicts with neighbouring groups, they succeeded in formally registering it with the colonial administration. The Shajara well (Idd al-Shajara or Idd al-Ahamda par excellence) united the majority of the Ahamda lineages through its epic construction: by their spatial inscription into an articulated system of basins, thanks to the duties of common defence and maintenance of the well, the Ahamda turned it into a sort of pivot for their tribal unity (Casciarri 2011). According to oral witnesses, the main reason for digging the well was the encroachment of commercial irrigated agricultural schemes on the western part of their territory, which hindered their dry season access to the Nile waters and to the corridors established for the nomads by the British.[8] The presence of the well thus allowed an original form of sedentarization of the nomadic camps in the middle of a desert area, without obliging the Ahamda to settle precariously in the Nile villages or in town. The building of *ḥafīr*s (rainwater reservoirs) also contributed to maintaining the pastoral option and to matching it with sorghum rainfed agriculture in the wadis, hence abandoning the migratory 'long cycle' in the eastern Butana, yet not renouncing the reliance on herds as the main resource. Despite decreasing numbers during the last few years,[9] today 12 *furqān (*sg. *far q)* continue to live by exploiting Shajara's grazing lands, the water of 19 *ḥafīr*s and, in the dry season, the Shajara well. In recent years some important changes (apart from the indirect effects of Khartoum's expansion) have affected Shajara: the main transformations are the erection of a dam on the Khor al-Asad, the construction of an asphalt road connecting Khartoum Bahri to the Jeily refinery, and the spread of enterprises exploiting the soil for building materials. But, despite ongoing transformations, this group did not experience, as other households of their tribal group did, a total upsetting of its bases of production and reproduction. The town, by its actors and processes, has 'entered' into the Shajara space, but the people of Shajara created a relation with the urban context, which allows them to interact with it without assimilating into it.

The *farīq* of Ali Sirr Ali is a significant example. Its founder Sirr settled with his family soon after the Shajara well was dug and built his *ḥafīr* there, with the largest stocking capacity. Although until recently (1990s) the *farīq* lived in a nomadic camp pattern,[10] the group stopped engaging in nomadic migratory cycles, because it could maintain its pastoral economy with shorter movements to the surrounding grazing lands and produce grains on close rain-fed fields. Today the *farīq* is composed of 15 families (whose core are the sons and grandsons of Sirr), that is 58 people. Herd production remains the primary source of nutrition. A lesser part of the milk is sold by a transaction similar to barter: the herders give the milk to the *ᶜarabāt al-laban* (milk vehicles) to go daily to the Khartoum markets, and exchange them for other commodities (from animal fodder to drugs). As agro-pastoral activity requires significant manpower, few people can engage in wage labour. Most often young men work as occasional day labourers, without leaving the area, for instance, performing some of the arduous tasks for construction companies. Though animal property is individual or familial, various practices highlight the collective, non-market habits within the camp group (the exchange of water and services, the sharing of meals, the mutual aid work of *nafīr*, etc.). Marriages still follow their ideal pattern of (agnatic) proximity and frequently the bride-price is reduced,[11] unlike the inflationary trends affecting more urbanized Ahamda. Even if people of the *farīq* sometimes bemoan the lack of modern services (water, healthcare, schools), the presence of these services in other villages settled by Ahamda does not constitute a main driving force for change. As some informants said to me: 'why should we settle in the villages close to the Nile, if there you have to pay in cash for everything you get?' Neither unaware of ongoing global mutations nor totally isolated from the central economy, this group wishes to minimize its engagement in market relations and keep them to a low and thus manageable degree, aware of the dependencies linked to increased engagement. Classed as the most marginal within the *qabīla* Ahamda, people of the *farīq* Ali Sirr Ali seem to believe that 'anyway, the poor are not us' (Anderson & Broch-Due 1999) when they contemplate the situation of 'new' poverty experienced by their kin tribespeople after they settled and reduced (or abandoned) their pastoral way of life. As far as identity labels are concerned, Shajara people do not hesitate to define themselves (and are defined) as *ᶜarab* – meaning here pastoral nomads – even if they have long been settled in villages. This term differentiates them not only from the sedentary people of villages or towns, as it has always done, but today also sets them apart from their fellow Ahamda who choose to install themselves close to the Nile and adopt the dominant lifestyle patterns of the centre.

The situation of the *furqān* Hassaniyya in the area called Ben Safra is analogous. Unlike other Hassaniyya of the region north-east of Khartoum (some small villages near the railroad), their configuration is very close to the one described for Shajara as far as access to resources, priority of production for subsistence and the weak engagement in wage labour are concerned. Even though the capital is farther away than it is from Shajara (80km), here the proximity of the Jeily oil refinery and of the 'free market zone' developed between 2006 and 2009, marks another case of persistent pastoralists in an area where the dynamics of the centre and urban incorporation could have prevailed. Also, it is interesting to note the existence, at the core of the 13 *furqān* of Ben Safra, of nine shallow wells used for domestic and productive supply. Thus, compared with Shajara, one could argue for the fundamental role of tribal resources, especially water, and their communal management as a pivot for maintaining pastoralism as a viable option (Casciarri 2011). Finally, I note that, at the political level, in Ben Safra as well as in Shajara, there is still a strong recognition of the authority of ancient tribal chiefs (sheikhs). This is a further element of differentiation from their urbanized tribespeople who recently moved closer to the centre, and now follow the political authority of *lağna šaᶜbīya* (popular committees) or the new elites which were created after the revival of Native Administration by the present government (Casciarri 2006, 2009a).

Case 2: 'Post-Nomads' Entering the Centre from the Pastoral Periphery

The transformation affecting the region near Khartoum in the past decade has not been homogeneous, even within the same tribal group. Some Ahamda, who until recently (1990s) considered themselves to be, and behaved as, a coherent unit, have responded to the dynamics of expansion in a very different way from their kin in Shajara. This is well illustrated by groups who settle in villages spatially within the *ḫalā'* (desert)[12] but closer to the asphalt road and Nile villages.

An example of this configuration is the village of Derib (38km, 24 miles as the crow flies to the north-east of Khartoum). An ancient site of the dry season migration for some of the Ahamda, the first mud houses appeared by the late 1950s. The village rapidly became a place of temporary or definitive sedentarization for much of the group (mainly two of its lineages). Mobile houses were still widespread until the 1970s, however, and various households underwent a phase of 'renomadization' towards the east after a break for their herds to be refreshed. Particularly after the 1984 drought, some factors (the construction of a water tower, the establishment of a primary school, but mostly the attraction of wage labour due to the proximity of agricultural schemes, the Nile villages, the asphalt road and Khartoum) favoured the more definitive settlement of local households. This also contributed to the arrival of small pastoralist groups (of the same lineages, from distant kin, and also of non-Ahamda) for whom mobile life in distant camps strictly relying on subsistence agro-pastoral production had become too hard. Until the 1990s a fair number of these households still included pastoral production among their livelihood strategies and kept solid interactions with the 'tribal' (more clearly rural) socio-economic space. But in later years, following the profound transformations of the capital region, the village has become a larger agglomeration,[13] compared to the rather limited dimensions of settled pastoralists' ordinary camps, and the most important site of the *qabīla* Ahamda in this area. The influence of the expanding capital (with its flux of people, commodities, life patterns and ideas) here is fundamental to understanding the transformation of local configurations. Today, most of Derib's households have at least one or two members who provide for the household's needs through constant wage labour. Though often occasional and precarious, wage labour takes on a variety of forms: employment in the transport sector (by van or lorry, as owner of the vehicle or as worker), recruitment in the army, police or national intelligence services (a frequent option for the generation of young men lacking pastoral savoir-faire), small- or medium-sized commercial enterprises and finally, for the more destitute, various short-term jobs as unskilled workers. Yet one cannot say that their pastoral background does not play a relevant role. First, investment in animal wealth remains a very valuable option – even for those who generate their main income from other sectors. Second, the tribal political network is maintained to guarantee access to collective natural resources of the territory. Nonetheless, the peculiarities of this form of pastoralism have changed notably. Herders are now polarized between some entrepreneurs who assign pastoral tasks to subordinated wage workers – by a market exploitation of labour formerly conceived as unacceptable among tribespeople (Casciarri 2009b) – and impoverished households that must divide their time between pastoral production to care for the family's food needs and obtaining cash incomes that are so essential for life in this newly urbanized rural context. Moreover, urban consumption patterns have spread to the villages (Casciarri 2002) together with the cost of accessing local services (water, electricity, school, taxes), and market commodities replacing general-use goods. The payments of marriage transactions have risen to match town levels – with a parallel decline of 'cheaper' marriages to close agnatic kin.

The above phenomena are common processes of transformation affecting pastoral groups during their sedentarization or the encroachment of towns. Nonetheless, in the case of Derib, aspects of this evolution are best explained by considering some political phenomena. In fact, these dynamics took off with the government's revival of Native Administration in 1995 which favoured the formation of local elites. This group became economically and politically dominant due to its position between rural tribesmen and an urban middle class and its involvement in *al-lağna aš-šaᶜbīya* or in the 'new' sheikhships. This elite benefits from its role in supporting Khartoum's interests and that of the politically dominant classes of the centre, often at the expense of their fellow tribespeople, whom they should represent but often in fact turn into a tool for their control and subordination (Casciarri 2009a). Thus, faced with an eruption of 'modern' dynamics from urban expansion, these pastoralists have reacted differently from the first case study. They have opted to exploit the advantages of being incorporated by the centre, entering from the periphery, but without remaining completely marginal, and concomitantly without renouncing the benefits of their pastoral background. At the level of self-image, their wish for 'modernity' leads them to understate their pastoral nomadic past and to often reject their identity as *ᶜarab*, a label that they use now for their Ahamda 'cousins' who are surrounded by urban dynamics but remain quite resilient to them. But actually there is an ambiguity in their discourse that reveals the instrumental use and the transitory phase. Thus, the rhetoric of tribal collectivism can still be used economically, for the exploitation of territory (natural resources as well as labour force) and for its defence vis-à-vis foreigners, and politically, in alliance with the 'traditional' *qabīla* when they need to oppose external attacks,[14] or in alliance with the 'detribalized' Ahamda elite of Khartoum and other towns.

Case 3: Early Settled Pastoralists Feeding the Town and Themselves
In an area long since included in the urban space (Khartoum Bahri), there is a neighbourhood, Idd Selim, which is largely made up of settled pastoralists. Today Idd Selim refers to a cluster of about 20 villages, but originally it was the name of a deep well dug in the Turkish period in the tribal territory of the Batahin, one of the most important nomadic *qabīla* of the Butana. A site for the seasonal supply of various lineages of this tribe, it became the focus of the first wave of sedentarization that took place after the big drought of 1949. Most of the villages retained the shape of camps until the 1960s and 1970s. Later the main concentration of villages for this group was in this area and it continued to attract an increased number of new settlers in the aftermath of the 1984 drought. However, even if ecological crises were a main trigger for migration, in the social actors' discourse it is clear that the expansion of Khartoum functioned as a strong pole of attraction in a twofold sense: first, due to the job opportunities offered by the urban agglomeration, and second, due to the rich potential for daily marketing of milk and meat to urban customers. Largely due to the Batahin migration, the present composition of the Idd Selim villages, where the ancient well has been replaced by several water towers in recent years, has been simultaneously shaped by the urban evolution of the rest of the town. Since the 1970s the close quarter of Hajj Yusif developed, largely based on a migratory influx mainly from the Nuba Mountains, western and southern Sudan. This presence of people originally from other regions of the country is more and more visible today: new IDPs quarters have been 'established' by the government near Idd Selim, and some 'new' villages have been founded by migrants coming from the north.

The Batahin, the original core of Idd Selim dwellers, continue to claim if not their status as autochthonous – not usually evoked by nomad groups – at least their exclusivity of territorial possession that they try to claim by right of their early settlement. Thus newcomers are often designated as *'ağānib*, foreigners. The 'others' who have settled more recently within Batahin villages, close to them or even via the purchase of 'their' lands, continue to label them as *ᶜarab* (i.e. pastoral nomads) despite their early sedentarization. The persistence of this identification is linked to the fact that the pastoral background of the Idd Selim's Batahin has informed their urbanization and economic activities. For them, livestock-raising remains the main activity and most households derive their main incomes from the sale of milk and meat. Of course, this type of livestock production has been deeply transformed compared with nomadic practices. First, herd composition has altered, in that camels, sheep and goats have almost disappeared and have been replaced by cows. Second, the cattle are no longer a local indigenous stock that is adapted to the desert and tolerates little water, but a high productivity European breed. In the local discourse, the real breaking point between the ancient way of life and the new one is not associated with sedentarization but rather with the period when 'we exchanged camels and goats for cows', that is the moment when livestock raising changed its orientation from the supply of the domestic unit to commercial livestock production. Some Batahin in Idd Selim express pride and claim a crucial role: 'we feed the town, the town could not eat or live without us', they say. These practices of urban pastoralists also become visible by the choices they make as agriculturalists in the irrigated schemes of Khartoum Bahri, where most of the plots owned by Batahin are devoted to fodder cultivation. Moreover, even the settlement in the urban space – an urban character which is sometimes questionable as some quarters are very similar to pastoral rural villages – evinces the pastoral background of the Idd Selim's Batahin. It is also expressed in occasional economic strategies: for example, some of them still own plots of arable land in the eastern desert where they engage in rain-fed agriculture in good years.[15] Although the lack of official recognition of tribal chiefs that other pastoral groups obtained in the revival of Native Administration of the 1990s prevented them from a closer relationship with the power dynamics of the centre, the *qabīla* and its sheikhs nevertheless remain an important reference point for the political networks of the group. At the same time, they try to push their influence into *al-lağna aš-šaᶜbīya* of various villages. The Batahin in Idd Selim present another configuration of urban pastoralists that have not been 'transformed into sedentary' by their spatial incorporation into the town and the process of invisibilization despite early sedentarization and urbanization.

Case 4: Pastoralists Merging into the Centre due to the Early Formation of an Urban Working Class

The fourth case study focuses on people from nomadic pastoral origins in a popular quarter of Khartoum, known as Dyum Ash-Sharqyia,[16] or simply Deim, located between the residential bourgeois quarters of Khartoum 2 and Amarat. Despite its transformation of the past few decades, this quarter is still characterized by a 'popular' social composition. It was created in the 1950s, when the British wanted to eradicate the shanty towns (known as 'Dyūm'), hosting a huge ethnically heterogeneous population, that were located in the centre of the colonial town since the Mahdist period, in order to build 'clean' residential quarters (today Khartoum 2 and 3). The inhabitants of the Dyūm, originally grouped according to ethnic and tribal categories, were displaced in several waves and resettled in what is today the Deim quarter (Sikainga 1996). At first composed of mostly emancipated (military) slaves, Deim increased in size due to further rural immigration. Since the beginning of the twentieth century it contributed to the formation of the bulk of an urban working class originally developed in the colonial era, and continued later to host other national and foreign migrants. The former are mainly from the Nuba Mountains and Western Sudan, the latter are Ethiopians and Eritrean refugees that still privilege Deim as a site for settlement. As people say 'one can find the whole of Sudan in Deim'. This gives an idea of the multi-ethnic, multi-tribal and multi-religious nature of this popular quarter which has become central as Khartoum has expanded. I analyse two aspects: first, the presence of pastoral nomads in the quarter, and second, the status of Deim dwellers from pastoral origins.

Concerning the first aspect, due to the central and urban character of the quarter (coupled with its spatial and socio-professional connotation), there are no nomads among the settled inhabitants of Deim that are still significantly linked to pastoral activities and to their wider (tribal) group. Nevertheless, nomads 'pass' through Deim and enter into a network of relations with Deim dwellers. These are especially people (not families) belonging to pastoral groups, either settled in the fringes of Greater Khartoum or living in rural areas surrounding the capital, who come regularly to Deim to sell their products and offer their services to the quarter's inhabitants. The commonest case is vendors of fresh milk (or of such minor products as the *nabag* or *laloba* fruits) coming to sell their goods, riding camels, donkeys or most frequently vans, and others, usually from impoverished groups of the Khartoum periphery, selling their work undertaking services considered derogatory by urban dwellers, like the cleaning of siphons and septic tanks of houses.[17] Although the term *ᶜarab* is used by people in Deim when talking about those in this social category that interact with them without living in their quarter, the label is here quite ambiguous compared to other contexts. In fact, most of the inhabitants of Deim, linguistically and culturally Arabized and Islamized since early times, still show an awareness of their non-Arab origin (from Nuba Mountains, Western and South Sudan and even from Chadian or Central Africa tribes). Thus the term *ᶜarab* can be pertinently used by them to denote their Arab neighbours (Jaᶜaliyin, Shaiqiyya or others) when the discursive context leads them to differentiate themselves from the latter. However, the presence of widespread stereotypes and a certain disregard of people defined as *ᶜarab* (in the sense of pastoral nomad) is noticeable, following a very urban image of the nomad, as one living in a desolate and depressed rural space, poor and ignorant, not to say bellicose, aggressive and thievish.[18]

The second aspect concerns some individuals or families of pastoral nomadic origin who constitute part of the ancient Deim inhabitants. Statistically a minority, they come from various groups from Western Sudan labelled generally as Baggara (Hawazma, Missiriyya, Rizaiqat, Ta'hisa), and more rarely from eastern nomadic groups (Hassaniyya, Shukriyya) or Kordofan camel herders (Kababish, Kawahla). In this case, the current inhabitants are the children or grandchildren of pastoral nomads who settled in Deim in the colonial period. This means that, even if they can maintain an awareness of their ethno-tribal origin and its implications as far as economic specialization and tribal extra-urban political relations are concerned, the specific marks of the category (in terms of dwelling patterns, professional activities, marriage strategies and the like) within the group of Deim dwellers are much weaker. Thus, quite ambiguously a speaker may evoke the persistence of relations with the original tribal group in its rural territory (uncommon for the 'Dayama'[19] of western and southern non-Arab groups) and even vaguely evoke a fluid label like 'nomad' (using the term *ruḥḥal* to avoid *ᶜarab* which in the urban context may be pejorative and misleading), or can also indicate the maintenance of a certain respect vis-à-vis their group's tribal chiefs (sheikhs and omdas) living in the rural territory of their tribe. Nevertheless, this group has been firmly assimilated into other groups in Deim whose origins differ in ethnic, tribal or productive terms. This should lead us to question whether the merging of urbanized pastoral nomads with the urban dimension at large (in this case, far from the invisibilization imposed by the state power on nomads in town) is merely the product of an early sedentarization and the abandonment of livestock raising, or rather a phenomenon of the construction of a 'Sudanese' national identity achieved in the multi-ethnic and multi-tribal Deim by means of a non-marginal working class identity.

CONCLUSION

The cases illustrated offer only a partial insight into the broad variety of configurations of 'urban pastoralists' in Sudan. Despite their limitations, these insights help to answer questions which are often neglected: what do pastoral nomads become once they are incorporated in an urban context? How do they relate to the centre? What are the dynamics that lead to their transformation, at various degrees and speeds? Which 'new' settings are thus produced? The fieldwork suggests that the assimilation of such groups to urban peoples is not an automatic result emerging simply from the abandonment of nomadic pastoralism (or of mobility when livestock-raising persists as an economic base), but rather it is a matter of the invisibilization produced by a dominant vision and supported by some lasting prejudices about what a pastoral nomad is or should be. Beyond this biased vision, pastoralists reveal some specificity in their way of 'producing' politics, economy and society that, even when they settle in towns, is somewhat different from the 'real' urban people or urbanized rural people, due to their links with a more or less distant pastoral global background.

The expression 'central marginality', apparently paradoxical, can thus be read in a double sense. In a first sense, the incorporation by the centre – be it the pastoralist who goes towards it or the centre which extends into the periphery – often results in ignoring or underestimating the fact that processes of incorporation do not remove the economic, political and ideological marginality of the pastoralist, who is no longer located in the spatial periphery. The case of the persistent pastoralists, the Shajara's Ahamda and the Ben Safra's Hassaniyya, indicates that even when the centre expands dynamically and suddenly includes an ancient periphery and disrupts its territory, a 'way out' from marginality is not offered to pastoralists, even if their persistence on the margins (of an invading capitalist system or of a state political model) may partially be an active choice. At a different level, the persistence of some marginalization within the centre may be confirmed by the case of the Idd Selim's Batahin. Here, even though their migration to and settlement in town is of ancient origin, they have not yet been transformed into 'pure' urban people as far as the political recognition and socio-economic development is concerned. One could add to these cases a number of groups of pastoral origin living in the interstices of the town that governmental and external interventions, as well as sometimes scholars, persist in 'not seeing'.

In the second sense of central marginality, former nomadic pastoralists (at least some of them) who are incorporated into the centre by restructuring of its boundaries, may succeed in finding their place without completely denying their background as groups historically labelled as peripheral and marginal. They deploy strategies that allow them to take advantage of the new situation and to become a subject that the centre must take into account either for its own stability and political consensus or for economic exchange and urban supply. This is true in the case of the Derib's Ahamda and the network of tribal elites they gathered. Due to the favourable combination of the revival of the Native Administration and the ruralization of *al-lağna aš-šaᶜbīya*, the encroachment *to* and *of* the centre allowed them to insert themselves into the political arena of the centre. Simultaneously, conversion to a market economy provided material advantages after they had accepted the stronger socio-economic stratification within the *qabīla*. Finally, the case of Deim and its inhabitants from pastoral origins serves to reveal what pastoralists can become in the long run when they find themselves inside the centre. By matching an historical perspective with a contemporary anthropological view, this last case seems to suggest that it is not simply when the state erases, materially and symbolically, the pastoral/marginal element in favour of the sedentary/central one that pastoralists dissolve totally and merge with the urban category. This process is more likely to develop when there is a wider dynamic 'from below' that couples the replacement of pastoral activities with other viable forms of subsistence, political relations and sociability. In this case the prominent and interconnected elements of the pastoralist configuration (tribal solidarity, endogamy, identity as nomads) can fade and gradually 'disappear' because another basis for livelihood (a working class one), linked to identity and political forms that are not marginal, consolidates and becomes relevant. This brief and limited review of urban pastoralists in the capital region makes a case for more in-depth fieldwork in order to revisit related categories such as 'nomad', 'pastoralist', 'sedentary', 'urban' and 'rural', 'centre' and 'periphery'. The pastoralists' exit from their invisibilization, at the practical level and as a scientific object, may contribute to understanding not only their societies and the ongoing changes, but also the other (non-pastoral) societies that have interacted with them in complex ways (since early times) and continue to do so more and more in the present context of globalization in Sudan.

REFERENCES

Anderson, D. M., Broch-Due, V. (eds) 1999. *The Poor are not Us: Poverty and Pastoralism in Eastern Africa*. Oxford and Athens OH: James Currey.

Asad, T., Cunnison, I., Hill, L. G. 1965. 'The Settlement of Nomads in the Sudan: A Critique of Present Plans'. In Ahmed, A. M. (ed.) *Some Aspects of Pastoral Nomadism in the Sudan*. Khartoum: Khartoum University Press, 174–192.

Battahani, A. 2009. *Nationalism and Peasant Politics in the Nuba Mountains Region of Sudan, 1924–1966*. Khartoum: University of Khartoum Press.

Bocco, R. 1990. 'La sédentarisation des pasteurs nomades: les experts internationaux face à la question bédouine dans le Moyen-Orient arabe (1950–1970)'. Sociétés pastorales et développement. *Cahiers des Sciences Humaines* 26 (1–2), 97–117.

Casciarri, B. 1997. 'Les Pasteurs Ahamda du Soudan Central. Usages de la parenté arabe dans l'histoire d'une recomposition territoriale, politique et identitaire'. Unpublished Ph.D. Thesis, Paris, EHESS.

Casciarri, B. 1999. 'Essere '*arab* tra gli Ahamda del Sudan centrale. Riflessioni sull'identità nomade tra Africa e Medio-Oriente'. In Arioti, M., Casciarri, B. (eds), 'Società pastorali d'Africa e d'Asia'. *La Ricerca Folklorica* 40, 117–134.

Casciarri, B. 2002. 'Local Trends and Perceptions of Processes of Commoditisation in Central Sudan: the Response of Ahâmda Pastoral System to State Pressures and Capitalist Dynamics'. *Nomadic Peoples* 6 (2), 32–50.

Casciarri, B. 2006. 'Readapting the Gabila: The Ahamda Pastoralists of Central Sudan and the State 'Tribal Federalism' Politics in the Mid-1990s'. In Chatty, D. (ed.), *Nomadic Societies in the Middle East and North Africa: Entering the 21st Century*. Leiden: Brill, 204–238.

Casciarri, B. 2009a. 'Hommes, troupeaux et capitaux: Notes sur le phénomène tribal au Soudan de la globalisation'. In Bonte, P., Ben-Hounet, Y. (eds), 'La tribu à l'heure de la globalisation'. Special issue of *Etudes Rurales* 184, 47–64.

Casciarri, B. 2009b. 'Between Market Logic and Communal Practices: Pastoral Nomad Groups and Globalization in Contemporary Sudan'. *Nomadic Peoples* 13 (1), 60–82.

Casciarri, B. 2011. 'La desocialización del agua en las comunidades del Sur en tiempos de globalización capitalista: del sureste de Marueccos al Sudán central'. In Ayeb, H. (ed), E*l agua en el mundo árabe: percepciones globales y realidades locales*. Madrid, Casa Árabe, 107–139.

Casciarri, B., Ahmed, A. G. M. (eds) 2009. 'Pastoralists under Pressure in Present-Day Sudan'. Special issue of *Nomadic Peoples* 13 (1).

Chatty, D. 1990. 'The Current Situation of Bedouin in Syria, Jordan and Saudi Arabia and Their Prospects for the Future'. In Galaty, J., Salzman, C. (eds), *Nomads in a Changing World*. Naples: Istituto Universitario Orientale, 123–137.

Denis, E. 2005. 'De quelques dimensions de Khartoum et de l'urbanisation au Soudan'. *Lettre de l'OUCC* 6–7, 19–29.

El-Nagar, S. E. 2001. 'Changing Gender Roles and Pastoral Adaptation in Omdurman, Sudan'. In Mohamed Salih, M., Dietz, T., Ahmed, A. G. M. (eds), *African Pastoralism: Conflict, Institutions and Government*. London and Sterling VA: Pluto Press, 247–277.

Fabietti, U., Salzman, P. C. (eds) 1996. *The Anthropology of Tribal and Peasant*

Pastoral Societies: The Dialectics of Social Cohesion and Fragmentation. Pavia (Italy): Ibis.

Franck, A. 2007. 'Produire pour la ville, produire la ville. Etude de l'intégration des activités agricoles et des agriculteurs dans l'agglomération du Grand Khartoum (Soudan)'. Unpublished Ph.D. Thesis, Paris, University Paris X Nanterre.

Grandin, N. 1980. 'Note bibliographique sur les pasteurs nomades au Nord Soudan'. *Production Pastorale et Société* 7, 98–118.

Grandin, N. 1982. *Le Soudan nilotique et l'administration britannique (1898–1956)*. Leiden: Brill.

Hamid, G. M. 1996. *Population Displacement in the Sudan: Patterns, Responses, Coping Strategies*. New York: Center for Migration Studies.

Harir, S., Tvedt, T. (eds) 1994. *Short-cut to Decay: The Case of the Sudan*. Uppsala: Nordisaka Afrikaninstitutet.

Kevane, E., Stiansen, M. (eds) 1998. *Kordofan Invaded: Peripheral Incorporation and Social Transformation in Islamic Africa*. Leiden: Brill.

Khogali, M. M. 1983. 'Sédentarisation des pasteurs nomades au Soudan'. In Galaty, J. G., Aronson, D., Salzman, P. C., Chouinard, A. (eds), *L'avenir des peuples pasteurs: compte rendu de la conférence tenue à Nairobi (Kenya)*. Ottawa: Centre de Recherches pour le Développement International, 333–350.

Miller, C. (ed). 2005. *Land, Ethnicity and Political Legitimacy in Eastern Sudan*. Cairo: CEDEJ.

Mohamed Salih, M. 1985. 'Pastoralists in Town. Some Recent Trends in Pastoralism in the North West of Omdurman District'. Pastoral Development Network Paper 20b, London: Overseas Development Institute.

Mohamed Salih, M. 1990. 'Government Policy and Pastoral Development in the Sudan'. *Nomadic Peoples* 25/26, 65–78.

Mohamed Salih, M. 1995. 'Pastoralists Migration to Small Towns in Africa'. In Baker, J., Aina, T. A. (eds), *The Migration Experience in Africa*. Uppsala: Nordiska Afrikainstitutet, 181–195.

Nelson, C. (ed.) 1973. *The Desert and the Sown: Nomads and the Wider Society*. Berkeley CA: University of California.

Piguet, F. 1999. *Des nomades entre la ville et les sables: sédentarisation dans la Corne de l'Afrique*. Paris: Karthala.

Puig, N. 2003. *Bédouins sédentarisés et société citadine à Tozeur (Sud-ouest Tunisien)*. Paris: Karthala.

Sikainga, A. A. 1996. *Slaves into Workers: Emancipation and Labor in Colonial Sudan*. Austin TX: University of Texas Press.

URBAMA (Urbanisation du Monde Arabe) 1989. 'Le nomade, l'oasis et la ville'. *Fascicule de Recherche* 20. Tours.

ENDNOTES

1. In most cases I prefer to use the term 'pastoralists' to define such populations. Indeed, the term 'nomad' has multiple typologies which lack consensus among social scientists, and entails a double bias. First, it includes mobile populations who do not rely on livestock-raising for subsistence. Second, its implicit focus on physical mobility denies the particularity of interlinked political, economic and socio-cultural settings and thus transforms into 'sedentary' every pastoral nomad who temporarily or permanently abandons seasonal movements.

2. The ambiguity of classification criteria and their aim of minimizing the presence of nomads are manifest in all the population censuses since the first held by an independent Sudan (1955/56).

3. An example of this trend in recent studies on Sudan is the work of Franck (2007): focusing on the modes and strategies of animal and milk production in Greater Khartoum, other than offering some generalities on ethnic origin of the 'producers', this rich work does not take into account the urban pastoral dimension and all its implications.

4. This aspect is stressed by Mohamed Salih evoking the case of Nuer and Dinka, a major part of Khartoum and Sudanese IDPs, whose pastoral background is entirely neglected (1995).

5. My fieldwork among the Ahamda was carried out between 1989 and 1995 for my Ph.D. thesis (Casciarri 1997). I returned for another study between 2006 and 2009. In this last period I carried out shorter researches among the three other groups. Due to the continuous and rapid transformations that affected this region, the situation has further changed in recent times: the dynamics I examine in this chapter thus refer to the period between 2006 and 2009. The use of the present tense also corresponds to this historical span.

6. I preferred to omit the real names of persons, local groups and specific places to avoid an identification which could lead to disadvantages for people concerned. I have replaced their names by fictive ones or omitted them.

7. Praised in the Ahamda poetry and traditional songs, the Khor al-Asad was highly appreciated for its water resources and the rich vegetation, constituting one of the grazing land paths of the whole tribal group.

8. The last builder of the well, who lived until 2008, explained: 'The agricultural projects jailed us, thus we were forced to dig the well in order to feed our people and their animals'.

9. Sometimes, upon the death of the father and head of the camp, his sons may choose to settle in villages near the Nile, or, as the Ahamda say, 'to go down (*nazal*) towards the river', a verb that in its absolute form is a synonymous of 'to settle, to leave (pastoral) life in the desert'.

10. This means the presence of huts (*bait ša*ᶜ*ar*), collective spaces for herds, common *diwān* for guests and communal meals for the camp's men, dispersion of family dwellings and the spatial proximity of close agnatic kin.

11. In 2006–09 the average bride-wealth in Shajara was 250 SDG (c. GBP £66, US $117), while at the same time marriages of the Ahamda in Derib or other villages raised up to ten times this amount, very near to urban levels. The various expenses for the ceremony and other goods are also insignificant compared to 'urbanized' villages. (Exchange rates taken from the average rates during the period 2007 to 2009 – 1 SDG: £0.2621, $0.4696 – according to <www.oanda.com/currency/historical-rates> retrieved 19-11-2013.)

12. The translation of the term as 'desert' – literally 'emptiness' – is approximate. In fact even if the ecological aspect of the term prevails, the way it is used gives the notion of *balā*' social dimensions. In this region the balā' area, conventionally defined as the territory east of the Khartoum-Atbara railway track, is considered as the space inhabited by nomads, where modern services are lacking, irrigated agricultural schemes stop, and where land relies on collective exploitation by 'tribal' pastoralists who live and govern themselves according to socio-economic forms different from the Nile villages.

13. The figure of 275 households for Derib has been personally provided by the clerks who counted the population in May 2008.

14. An example of this was the conflict between the Ahamda and one of the neighbouring tribes, who claimed land that became valuable after the construction of the asphalt road. Although the Ahamda had previously refused to protest against territorial intrusions by the state or the private sector (the building of dams, roads, oil refineries), the Ahamda elite exploited the discourse of 'tribal unity' and the defence of territorial integrity to obtain the support of the 'desert' Ahamda, usually left on the margin of local political action.

15. Harvests from rain-fed agriculture sometimes provide the poorest families with an independent source of sorghum for their diet.

16. The data for this case study did not come from research focused on pastoral populations. My fieldwork in Deim (2007–09) focused on oral history of the quarter (namely Deim Abu Rish, Deim Kara, Deim Berti and Deim Benda) and identity-building processes. During this inquiry, I collected data about the life trajectories of people belonging to pastoral nomadic groups and on the views of the presence of nomads in the quarter.

17. As far as this activity is concerned, the oral memory of Deim people recalls that the *ᶜarab*, nomads have been known for their professional specialization of digging wells and pits since colonial times.

18. Sometimes, as for some Fur inhabitants of Deim (a majority in some sub-quarters such as Deim Ibrish), the recent war in the Darfur has added to this connotation the assimilation of 'nomad' with the 'Arab' militias ranging in the region.

19. 'Dayāma' is the term used to define the inhabitants of Deim: the term, used both by the inhabitants themselves and the others, stresses awareness of this group's peculiarity as they do not assimilate to merely become 'Khartoum dwellers' and underlines a common denominator beyond their tribal and ethnic heterogeneity.

INDEX

EASTERN AFRICAN STUDIES

These titles published in the United States and Canada by Ohio University Press

Revealing Prophets
Edited by DAVID M. ANDERSON & DOUGLAS H. JOHNSON

East African Expressions of Chistianity
Edited by THOMAS SPEAR & ISARIA N. KIMAMBO

The Poor Are Not Us
Edited by DAVID M. ANDERSON & VIGDIS BROCH-DUE

Potent Brews
JUSTIN WILLIS

Swahili Origins
JAMES DE VERE ALLEN

Being Maasai
Edited by THOMAS SPEAR & RICHARD WALLER

Jua Kali Kerya
KENNETH KING

Control & Crisis in Colonial Kenya
BRUCE BERMAN

Unhappy Valley
Book One: State & Class
Book Two: Violence & Ethnicity
BRUCE BERMAN & JOHN LONSDALE

Mau Mau from Below
GREET KERSHAW

The Mau Mau War in Perspective
FRANK FUREDI

Squatters & the Roots of Mau Mau 1905-63
TABITHA KANOGO

Economic & Social Origins of Mau Mau 1945-53
DAVID W. THROUP

Multi-Party Politics in Kenya
DAVID W. THROUP & CHARLES HORNSBY

Empire State-Building
JOANNA LEWIS

Decolonization & Independence in Kenya 1940-93
Edited by B.A. OGOT & WILLIAM R. OCHIENG'

Eroding the Commons
DAVID ANDERSON

Penetration & Protest in Tanzania
ISARIA N. KIMAMBO

Custodians of the Land
Edited by GREGORY MADDOX, JAMES L. GIBLIN & ISARIA N. KIMAMBO

Education in the Development of Tanzania 1919-1990
LENE BUCHERT

The Second Economy in Tanzania
T.L. MALIYAMKONO & M.S.D. BAGACHWA

Ecology Control & Economic Development in East African History
HELGE KJEKSHUS

Siaya
DAVID WILLIAM COHEN & E.S. ATIENO ODHIAMBO

Uganda Now • Changing Uganda Developing Uganda • From Chaos to Order • Religion & Politics in East Africa
Edited by HOLGER BERNT HANSEN & MICHAEL TWADDLE

Kakungulu & the Creation of Uganda 1868-1928
MICHAEL TWADDLE

Controlling Anger
SUZETTE HEALD

Kampala Women Getting By
SANDRA WALLMAN

Political Power in Pre-Colonial Buganda
RICHARD J. REID

Alice Lakwena & the Holy Spirits
HEIKE BEHREND

Slaves, Spices & Ivory in Zanzibar
ABDUL SHERIFF

Zanzibar Under Colonial Rule
Edited by ABDUL SHERIFF & ED FERGUSON

The History & Conservation of Zanzibar Stone Town
Edited by ABDUL SHERIFF

Pastimes & Politics
LAURA FAIR

Ethnicity & Conflict in the Horn of Africa
Edited by KATSUYOSHI FUKUI & JOHN MARKAKIS

Conflict, Age & Power in North East Africa
Edited by EISEI KURIMOTO & SIMON SIMONSE

Propery Rights & Political Development in Ethiopia & Eritrea
SANDRA FULLERTON JOIREMAN

Revolution & Religion in Ethiopia
ØYVIND M. EIDE

Brothers at War
TEKESTE NEGASH & KJETIL TRONVOLL

From Guerrillas to Government
DAVID POOL

Mau Mau & Nationhood
Edited by E.S. ATIENO ODHIAMBO & JOHN LONSDALE

A History of Modern Ethiopia, 1855-1991(2nd edn)
BAHRU ZEWDE

Pioneers of Change in Ethiopia
BAHRU ZEWDE

Remapping Ethiopia
Edited by W. JAMES, D. DONHAM, E. KURIMOTO & A. TRIULZI

Southern Marches of Imperial Ethiopia
Edited by DONALD L. DONHAM & WENDY JAMES

A Modern History of the Somali (4th edn)
I.M. LEWIS

Islands of Intensive Agriculture in East Africa
Edited by MATS WIDGREN & JOHN E.G. SUTTON

Leaf of Allah
EZEKIEL GEBISSA

Dhows & the Colonial Economy of Zanzibar 1860-1970
ERIK GILBERT

African Womanhood in Colonial Kerya
TABITHA KANOGO

African Underclass
ANDREW BURTON

In Search of a Nation
Edited by GREGORY H. MADDOX & JAMES L. GIBLIN

A History of the Excluded
JAMES L. GIBLIN

Black Poachers, White Hunters
EDWARD I. STEINHART

Ethnic Federalism
DAVID TURTON

Crisis & Decline in Bunyoro
SHANE DOYLE

Emancipation without Abolition in German East Africa
JAN-GEORG DEUTSCH

Women, Work & Domestic Virtue in Uganda 1900-2003
GRACE BANTEBYA KYOMUHENDO & MARJORIE KENISTON McINTOSH

Cultivating Success in Uganda
GRACE CARSWELL

War in Pre-Colonial Eastern Africa
RICHARD REID

Slavery in the Great Lakes Region of East Africa
Edited by HENRI MÉDARD & SHANE DOYLE

The Benefits of Famine
DAVID KEEN